READING
KARL BARTH
FOR THE
CHURCH

READING KARL BARTH FOR THE CHURCH

A GUIDE AND COMPANION

KIMLYN J. BENDER

Baker Academic

a division of Baker Publishing Group
Grand Rapids, Michigan

Published by Baker Academic
a division of Baker Publishing Group
PO Box 6287, Grand Rapids, MI 49516-6287
www.bakeracademic.com

Printed in the United States of America

Library of Congress Cataloging-in-Publication Data
Names: Bender, Kimlyn J., 1969– author.
Title: Reading Karl Barth for the Church : a guide and companion / Kimlyn J. Bender.
Description: Grand Rapids : Baker Publishing Group, 2019. | Includes index.
Identifiers: LCCN 2018043171 | ISBN 9780801097584 (pbk. : alk. paper)
Subjects: LCSH: Barth, Karl, 1886–1968. Kirchliche Dogmatik. | Theology, Doctrinal.
Classification: LCC BT75.B286 B46 2019 | DDC 230/.044092—dc23
LC record available at https://lccn.loc.gov/2018043171

ISBN 978-1-5409-6209-6 (casebound)

19 20 21 22 23 24 25   7 6 5 4 3 2 1

For Kerry Bender, my brother,
and Ryan Balsan, my friend,
Pastors who serve the gospel and the church

The community in and for which I have written it [*CD* I/1] is that of the Church and not a community of theological endeavor.

CD I/1, xv

It is certainly as well to reflect that at any moment it is possible that the question of dogma may be put and answered much more seriously and fruitfully in the unassuming Bible class of an unknown country parson than in the most exact academic discussion imaginable. School dogmatics should not try to regard itself as better dogmatics, only as a necessary second form of dogmatics.

CD I/1, 279

Not all human talk is talk about God. It could be and should be.

CD I/1, 47

Now revelation is no more and no less than the life of God Himself turned to us, the Word of God coming to us by the Holy Spirit, Jesus Christ.

CD I/2, 483

For it is an honour and a joy, an inner necessity and a gracious privilege to serve and therefore to teach the Word of God. Indeed, it is the whole meaning of the church's existence.

CD I/2, 852–53

Contents

Detailed Contents

Abbreviations

CD   Barth, Karl. *Church Dogmatics*. Edited by G. W. Bromiley and T. F. Torrance. Translated by G. W. Bromiley, G. T. Thomson, et al. Four volumes in 13 parts. Edinburgh: T&T Clark, 1936–77.

KD   Barth, Karl. *Kirchliche Dogmatik*. Four volumes in 13 parts. Munich: Kaiser, 1932; Zürich: Evangelischer Verlag, 1938–65.

NT   New Testament

OT   Old Testament

WGT   Barth, Karl. *The Word of God and Theology*. Translated by Amy Marga. New York: T&T Clark, 2011.

Preface

This book is perhaps best described by stating what it is not. It is not a general introduction to the theology of Karl Barth. It is not a biography of his person (as interesting as his life may have been). It is also not a historical account tracing the development of his thought, convictions, and theological positions. Nor is this a constructive work, an attempt to draw upon Barth either for a new presentation of theological material or to argue where the trajectories of his thought should lead us. There are many excellent books that provide such an overview of his life, that track the development of his thought, or that excavate the sources from which he drew for his own work of theological description. Moreover, there are other fine books that provide exciting avenues for thinking not only with but also beyond him into new territories. Yet there is always a danger that examinations of his theology begin to gravitate predominantly to the far margins—on one side, to increasingly fine-grained historical studies in which his timeline of life and thought becomes ever more subdivided, and on the other constructive side, to explorations into areas that are ever more technical, ethereal, and inaccessible to any but those who are deeply steeped not only in the theology of Barth himself but also in an ever-expanding and nearly inexhaustible wealth of secondary literature.

Barth's theology is, of course, fertile and complex, as is that of any great theologian worthy of preservation and abiding study. For this reason, such historical and constructive examinations of his theology are appropriate and helpful to mine the riches of his achievement. I not only am greatly indebted to such studies but also have added to the mound of secondary literature mentioned above. Yet even as I have labored in the field of Barth studies and recognize its necessary and beneficial academic program, I have become concerned that a theologian whose magnum opus is titled *Church Dogmatics* (hereafter *CD*) is read more and more in the academy by specialists and less and less in the church itself by pastors and other Christian disciples. As one friend of mine once said, what is so often forgotten is that the *CD* includes a "register," or index, volume, which contains not only general indexes of Scripture passages, persons, and theological subjects but also exegetical and theological excerpts from the *CD* organized to serve as aids to preachers and correspondingly arranged following the Christian year as to be beneficial for the church's rhythms of worship and life. And this was done, as stated by the editors in the preface to that Index volume, because it was recognized that from the appearance of the very first volume of the *CD* "many pastors and church workers have consulted the *Church Dogmatics* as an exegetical, theological and practical aid in the preparation of sermons and other forms of Gospel proclamation."[1] I wonder how much of this is still done today, and moreover whether Barth is still read as a theological teacher by and for those in pastoral ministry and in the pews.[2]

The reasons why I believe that he can be read as such a teacher with great benefit I will briefly state here but ultimately leave to the reader's self-discovery. The *CD* was written for the church, and it can be read for not only instruction but also even, dare I say, edification. Furthermore, Barth asks questions so incisively and with such depth and insight that reading him is of benefit for all students of Scripture, even for those who do not or will not accept all or even the majority of his answers, or those who have reservations about his personal failings or his theological program. Barth is, quite frankly, a theologian of unquestionable stature if for no other reason than the scope and gravity of his theological achievement. Most importantly, however, he is a theologian steeped in Scripture who drives us back to it. The *CD* contains more than fifteen thousand biblical references and two thousand exegetical investigations of specific biblical passages.[3] Barth's singular attention to Christ as the center of Scripture and of all of the ways and means of God is unparalleled in the modern period and, arguably, in all periods before it.

This book attempts to fulfill a modest purpose. It is a guide to assist in reading what is, without question, a daunting piece of theology, yet one of

1. Karl Barth, *Church Dogmatics: Index Volume with Aids for the Preacher*, ed. G. W. Bromiley and T. F. Torrance (Edinburgh: T&T Clark, 1977), vii.

2. One of the first persons in the English-speaking world to take this question with real seriousness was Arnold Come—see *An Introduction to Barth's "Dogmatics" for Preachers* (Philadelphia: Westminster, 1963). Though dated, this work can still be read with benefit.

3. Richard Burnett, *Karl Barth's Theological Exegesis: The Hermeneutical Principles of the "Römerbrief" Period* (Grand Rapids: Eerdmans, 2004), 9.

the most significant theological achievements in the history of the church. It is a companion to the first volume of Barth's *CD* that attempts to provide straightforward help for reading and understanding that work and gaining skills necessary to navigate its depth and breadth. It also provides commentary on some significant themes and arguments found there with a special eye toward the contemporary church and its life, as well as questions for further reflection. An appendix provides schedules that may help in reading the first volume of the *CD* or the entire work. This book can be read from cover to cover, or, in light of the detailed table of contents, it may serve as a reference work that can be consulted for assistance in regard to specific passages of the *CD*.

A few years ago, my family toured the National Cathedral in Washington, DC. The highlight of that day was not only the cathedral itself but also the very helpful guide who took us through that overwhelming structure, orienting us as to its geography as well as pointing out to my wife, my children, and me what would no doubt have escaped our notice—or, more likely, have been briefly passed over with little understanding as to its detail and meaning. This wonderful guide helped make that rich structure intelligible and meaningful for us as she directed and instructed us to gain a provisional understanding of its architecture, art, and furnishings. This book serves a similar purpose. It is not in any way meant to be exhaustive. It cannot hope or aspire to examine every architectural detail in the magnificent theological cathedral that is the *CD*.[4] But it is a guide to highlight what I believe is still the most logical place to begin in reading the *CD*—the first volume. Barth had intended to write five volumes of the *CD*—the first on the Word of God, the second on the doctrine of God, the third on creation, the fourth on reconciliation, and the fifth on redemption. That was his original intention, but he never wrote the fifth and did not finish the fourth. Yet we are left with over nine thousand pages of material, and it must be admitted that few will read the whole from cover to cover. The book in your hands is a guide and commentary to the first of the volumes, and reading through that volume is a very doable endeavor, though it will take some dedication and work, as all good things do. As I will address further in the introduction below, it is also an implicit argument that, if you can read the first volume, you are well prepared to read the others.

4. Here I not only draw upon my own experience of the National Cathedral but also openly borrow from George Hunsinger's comparison of the *CD* to the cathedral in Chartres in *How to Read Karl Barth: The Shape of His Theology* (Oxford: Oxford University Press, 1991), 27–28. Cathedrals are, of course, the products of time and took generations to complete. We should not be surprised to find remarkable consistency, yet also innovation and development, in evidence in the final product. The same is true of Barth's *CD*.

The first volume of the *CD* will be the focus here, furthermore, because its themes of the Trinity, Christology, Scripture, proclamation, and theological reflection have immediate contact with the life of the church and its ministry. This companion examines these themes for the purpose of illuminating Barth's ongoing relevance for assisting the faith and life of the church today, and it further attempts to provide insight into certain recurring and regulative patterns of thought that shape Barth's particular forms of description and argumentation. This book serves this purpose with the hope that the reader will then be equipped and even inspired to keep reading and to see that these topics themselves not only are of immediate relevance to the life of the church and the Christian but also are in fact connected to others both in the first and in the later volumes of the *CD* whose importance and significance are perhaps less apparent. Yet it points beyond the first number of themes toward the second in order to commend to the reader that all are needed not only to form the entire structure but also to witness to the One who is the Way, the Truth, and the Life. If the *CD* does anything, it attests God's great act of grace and giving that is revealed, enacted, completed, and consummated in the life and work of Jesus Christ and given to us by his Spirit.

Some of the architecture and furnishings of Barth's theological edifice are easily discerned as bearing on the church's day-to-day life and the life and ministry of its servants and members, and these provide the primary focus of the commentary at the end of each chapter. Others stretch higher into the air and seem distant, and perhaps even esoteric, to our nearsighted eyes. This guide will attend to things lower to the ground and give itself to the sight we have of more accessible things, but it will not remain only there. For it also encourages an upward gaze, not in order to take our eyes off the immediate beauty and gifts of the near and present, but to see that these things are complemented and not compromised by those lofty things that are perhaps less immediately accessible but nonetheless no less important to the entire structure of the Christian faith.

As this book differs from some in its purpose, so, too, does it differ in its audience. It is written not for specialists in Barth studies but for those pastors, students, and other Christian persons who are beginning to approach his *CD* or who are relatively early in their journey with him, looking either to understand this daunting figure or simply to see if there is anything of value for their own Christian life and ministry that can be offered by his theology. Perceptive scholars will note, however, a number of important moves that run against the grain of some dominant paradigms of reading Barth, so there may be some things here for them as well. Yet this companion remains primarily an introductory manual, not a critical commentary of sources.

In writing this guide, I am simply attempting to assist others in discovering a theology that was intended for them all along. As Barth said in a radio interview late in his life, "My whole theology, you see, is fundamentally a theology for pastors."[5] It was in fact a theology that was born out of his pastoral experience and the struggle to move from Scripture to sermon, and Barth took great joy in his later years in hearing reports of its help for ministers.[6] And I found, during my own years as a young pastor, that Barth was of great benefit to me as I thought about preaching in particular and theological reflection more generally. I found this to be the case for a number of reasons, though none more important than that his theology filled me simultaneously with such a sense of humility and of hope, both reverence before "so great a salvation" and courage to proclaim it and to live in its light. Reading Barth allowed me to see the scope and wonder of the gospel from a vista that was startling in its range and expansiveness yet ever concentrated on a single point at the center. It reminded me that Scripture from first to last is about the gospel of Jesus Christ, that this gospel is truly good news, and that it can and should be proclaimed with a proper confidence to those who come each Sunday, persons who come to hear not simply the profound or clever reflections of a pastor, but a Word from God. Furthermore, it reminded me that God is not only free to convict his assailants as well as his defenders but also faithful to show mercy upon both, and therein to uphold his promise to speak to his people and to show his love to the world.

It is thus fitting that this book is dedicated to two pastors, to my brother who is also a dear friend, and to my friend who is close to me like a brother. It is also written with fond memories of the Sioux Falls Karl Barth Reading Group and its members and with gratitude to the students at Truett Seminary who have participated in my seminars on Barth's theology. It is my hope that this book will help others in the church discover the riches that Barth offers, riches not best appreciated by simple agreement with him (and there has been little danger of that in America or elsewhere), but found in considering the great cathedral he constructed and, more important still, contemplating and reflecting *within* that cathedral the things to which it gestures, things far beyond and grander than its lofty spires. For the cathedral itself is but a testimony to riches that far exceed its ability to contain them. In their light, Barth was keenly enough aware of the structure's own deep inadequacy. Moreover,

---

5. Karl Barth, *Final Testimonies*, ed. Eberhard Busch, trans. Geoffrey Bromiley (Grand Rapids: Eerdmans, 1977; Eugene, OR: Wipf & Stock, 2003), 23.

6. See Come, *Barth's "Dogmatics" for Preachers*, 14–22; and Karl Barth, "Recapitulation Number Three," *The Christian Century* 77, no. 3 (January 20, 1960): 74.

he also knew that, like Ludwig Wittgenstein's city[7] and many great cathedrals themselves, a cathedral of speech about God is never really finished, nor can it ever be. Indeed, he was convinced that the structure needed to be rebuilt again and again in light of a new and better understanding of the blazing and transformative light of the gospel. Yet the final structure that he did build, the *CD*, is an enduring and noteworthy testimony, though, like the great cathedral of Aachen, Germany, with its Byzantine, Romanesque, and Gothic elements, it, too, bears the marks of having been built over a significant period of time. It is, nonetheless, a structure of remarkable consistency that is worthy of entrance and reflection, if only for the way it points so well to things far beyond its ability to describe and to paths that lead out of its doors.[8]

Finally, a few brief words of further thanks are in order. First and ever, to my family for the patience, support, understanding, and grace they show me daily. Second, to my fellow colleagues in the theological task: those near, at Truett Theological Seminary and Baylor University; those past, at the University of Sioux Falls; and those far, the many friends and colleagues who toil in the field of theology and the gospel. Special thanks are extended to the administration of Truett Seminary and Baylor University for granting me a research leave during which this volume was written. Finally, I thank Dave Nelson, my editor at Baker, for his wise and patient counsel and warm camaraderie, and Sam Davidson and Jake Raabe for their indefatigable and sterling work as my graduate assistants and on the reading schedules.

7. See Ludwig Wittgenstein, *Philosophical Investigations*, 3rd ed., trans. G. E. M. Anscombe (Englewood Cliffs, NJ: Prentice Hall, 1958), 8 (§18).

8. The limitations of architectural imagery for describing Barth's *CD* must also be appreciated. As Eberhard Busch has noted, "Whoever engages Barth's theology does not enter a building of ideas but embarks upon a path." Eberhard Busch, *The Great Passion: An Introduction to Karl Barth's Theology*, ed. Darrell Guder and Judith Guder, trans. Geoffrey Bromiley (Grand Rapids: Eerdmans, 2004), 16.

⊹ 1 ⊹

Introduction

Karl Barth was one of the most significant theologians of the twentieth century, arguably its most significant, and a reasonable if not unquestionable case could be made that he is one of the most important in the history of the church. Yet, for a number of reasons, his work is difficult to approach. First, there is the scope as well as the range of his work in general. Barth wrote many, many things—sermons, lectures, essays, theological treatises, and other pieces large and small, not even considering his extensive correspondence. Perhaps one profitable way to begin reading him is with his lectures given in the United States in 1962, titled *Evangelical Theology*, and to move from there to his short theology lecture cycle, titled *Dogmatics in Outline*. These are wonderful pieces in their own right and may be the most accessible works to read first to get a feel for both the content and some of the significant themes of his mature thought. Yet to truly appreciate Barth and his gravity, and to truly glean from his bounty, there is no more important work to read than that to which he dedicated most of his adult life, his massive yet unfinished *CD*. While there are many other treasures to be found in his writings, this is his quintessential achievement and the most mature and developed expression of his theology. It is this work that will be the focus of this companion, and specifically, its first volume, titled *The Doctrine of the Word of God*.

Approaching the *CD* is daunting. It sits like an encyclopedia upon a shelf, and its very mass and length are intimidating. The longer a work, the more likely it is never finished by the reader (and Barth did not even complete writing it). And this is true not only because its length hinders many from reaching the end but also because it keeps more from even making a start. How many persons have abandoned reading Tolstoy's *War and Peace* having begun with the best of intentions? And how many more were deterred from even picking it up simply by looking at the space between its front and back covers? Barth referred to the ivory-covered volumes of his original *Kirchliche Dogmatik* as his "white whale," and it is true that many have not read it for the same reason they have not read Melville's *Moby-Dick*—namely, the energy, time, concentration, and dedication it takes to read such a significant work. And if that is true for Melville's work that in one edition approaches nine hundred pages, how much more true it is for Barth's work that exceeds nine *thousand* when its prefaces and indexes are included. So a first and sensible goal might be to read the first volume, comprising, in English, a much more manageable, if still sobering, total of approximately fourteen hundred pages.

This companion will focus upon this goal. While it is hoped that readers continue to read the CD beyond the first volume, my experience of teaching Barth in the classroom and leading reading groups over the years has taught me that for many, this first goal is a realistic and reasonable one. I still think that most readers will begin reading the CD at the beginning, and Sister Maria's advice, that the beginning is "a very good place to start,"[1] seems to me after numerous years of teaching the CD to remain sound, even if many may consider Barth's greatest achievements to lie in the second and fourth volumes of the CD. Though many other riches lie in these later volumes, it is nonetheless true that if someone learns to read the first volume well and with some facility, that person will be readily equipped to continue on to read the rest of the CD, for it is the first volume that introduces the themes and questions that provide the context, tone, and structure for the later ones. Indeed, two things may strike the reader who goes on to read those volumes: first, almost all of the major patterns of Barth's ways of thinking witnessed throughout the CD are present in its very first volume; and second, despite real discoveries and significant developments along the way that mark his theology, he is nevertheless remarkably consistent throughout the CD in his overarching theological convictions. The remaining volumes of the CD in turn uphold and develop these larger themes witnessed in volume 1, even if they display real growth, development, and even innovation.

While many introductions to Barth provide an overview of his theological works as a whole, or over the entire range of the doctrinal topics present in the CD, this companion serves as an introductory guide that spans less material but treats it in much more detail. It sacrifices breadth for depth, again in the

---

1. *The Sound of Music* (1965).

interest of facilitating the development of the skills needed to become a reader of all of the volumes of the *CD* by concentrating on a detailed reading of the first. While not comprehensive in attempting to outline the content of the entire *CD*, it is intensive in its detailed attention to a more circumscribed range of material. It takes this particular approach for the purpose of providing the reader with a firm comprehension and understanding of a part with a view toward a facility to read the whole. For this reason, more attention will be paid to gaining a foothold at the very beginning of the first volume of the *CD*, and thus the difficult initial themes will receive more extensive exposition than some of the later ones that are more accessible once one has found a bit of traction. For the reality is that for good or ill, Barth does not provide his readers with a gentle introduction that draws them in by reference to some point of general and common experience, but rather dives right into the depth of dogmatic thought and some quite difficult questions of theology and its practice.

Each chapter below will begin with summary and explanation that attempt to illumine the meaning of the content in each section, or what are called *paragraphs* (marked by a § symbol), of the *CD*. The chapters will normally follow Barth's structure of paragraphs and subdivisions (e.g., §5; §5.1) but may at times provide more in-depth discussions of specific themes within them (designated as an "excursus"). As stated earlier, not all sections will receive equal treatment. Each chapter will conclude with a commentary section that attempts to highlight and raise questions regarding how the material that Barth discusses might bear upon the life and ministry of the church for today. This commentary and the ensuing questions will thereby attempt to provoke further thought and theological reflection regarding perennial and relevant questions for the church's witness.

Getting Oriented

The *CD* is composed of four volumes, themselves broken into smaller "part volumes." The following is a general sketch of its contents:

Volume 1: The Doctrine of the Word of God
    Part 1 (*CD* I/1)
    Part 2 (*CD* I/2)

Volume 2: The Doctrine of God
    Part 1 (*CD* II/1)
    Part 2 (*CD* II/2)

Volume 3: The Doctrine of Creation
  Part 1 (*CD* III/1)
  Part 2 (*CD* III/2)
  Part 3 (*CD* III/3)
  Part 4 (*CD* III/4)

Volume 4: The Doctrine of Reconciliation
  Part 1 (*CD* IV/1)
  Part 2 (*CD* IV/2)
  Part 3, First Half (*CD* IV/3.1)
  Part 3, Second Half (*CD* IV/3.2)
  Part 4, Unfinished Fragment (*CD* IV/4)
  Note: In addition to the volumes above is Part 4, Lecture Fragments (published in English under the title *The Christian Life*)

Volume 5: The Doctrine of Redemption
  Note: This volume was envisioned but was never written by Barth.

These volumes exist in an English translation referenced on the abbreviations page. Since the appearance of that English work, a study edition of the *CD* has been published by T&T Clark. While more expensive than the original edition, it provides translations of the French, Greek, and Latin words and passages found in the original *CD*. Although the pagination of the study edition is different from the earlier English one, it helpfully provides the original page numbers in the margins. For this reason, and because of the standard edition's general use in all secondary literature and its more ready availability, the page numbers provided in this guide will refer to those of the standard English edition mentioned on the abbreviations page.

As a matter of style, while this book will incorporate inclusive language for humanity, it will follow the language of the English translation of the *CD* in direct quotation that itself does not provide such inclusive usage. Moreover, and also in line with the English *CD*, it will utilize masculine personal pronouns for God rather than the awkward "Godself" construction. The Christian faith has, of course, always affirmed that God is beyond sex or gender, and correspondingly, this use of language in no way implies that God is male (nor, of course, is God female). Finally, all biblical quotations, unless otherwise noted, are from the New Revised Standard Version of the Bible.

Addendum

Not all of Karl Barth's extant works have been translated from German into English, nor have all of his writings even been published. The massive task of bringing all of Barth's collected works into print is under way, and the definitive edition of his writings is a work titled *Karl Barth—Gesamtausgabe* ("Complete Edition"), published by TVZ (Theologischer Verlag Zürich). Since 1971, volumes have continued to appear, now numbering beyond fifty and counting. This collection of Barth's writings is broken into five sections or series of volumes, the first containing his sermons, the second comprising academic works, the third containing his lectures and shorter essays and articles, the fourth presenting transcripts of conversations he had with others, and the fifth containing his letters. Quite a number of these sermons, academic works, lectures, essays, articles, and letters have been translated into English in various collections.

Getting Started

A further difficulty with reading Barth's *CD* is not only its length but also a quality related to its length—namely, his wordy and expansive style. Perhaps no one has expressed this challenge of reading Barth better than John Webster:

> Reading Barth is no easy task. Because the corpus of his writing is so massive and complex, what he has to say cannot be neatly summarized. Moreover, his preferred method of exposition, especially in the *Church Dogmatics*, is frustrating for readers looking to follow a linear thread of argument. Commentators often note the musical structure of Barth's major writings: the announcement of a theme, and its further extension in a long series of developments and recapitulations, through which the reader is invited to consider the theme from a number of different angles and in a number of different relations. No one stage of the argument is definitive; rather, it is the whole that conveys the substance of what he has to say. As a result, Barth's views on any given topic cannot be comprehended in a single statement (even if the statement be one of his own), but only in the interplay of a range of articulations of a theme.[2]

Everything that Webster has said here merits careful consideration. Barth's exposition can be brilliant but also maddening at times due to its prolixity and, dare we say, convolutedness, marked by what one astute American

---

2. John Webster, "Introducing Barth," in *The Cambridge Companion to Karl Barth*, ed. John Webster (Cambridge: Cambridge University Press, 2000), 9.

commentator has called the *CD*'s "endless repetition of themes and its stylistic heaviness."[3] It is always helpful to remember that some of this is due to the simple fact that the content of the *CD* began as lectures Barth presented in his teaching over a period of three decades. This partly explains his verbosity and occasional repetitiveness. But just as important to ponder is that he was attempting to renarrate the teaching of the church in a way that recovered the insights of the early church and the Reformation after what he considered problematic developments in theology that betrayed those insights in subsequent centuries. In this, he was re-creating a "universe of discourse," and creating such a world is an extensive undertaking—one need only think of J. R. R. Tolkien's volumes creating Middle Earth in his *The Lord of the Rings* trilogy.[4] Finally, and perhaps most of all, the very inexhaustible richness of God's revelation in Christ as attested in Holy Scripture was something that led Barth to ever-new and ever-expanding description. In this regard, the very content of theology's reflection necessitated an expansive and contrapuntal treatment of its theme.

The following factors make reading the *CD* no small challenge (not to mention that it is read in English translation from Barth's German original): (1) Barth's unique style of writing that relies on extended description and repetition; (2) the source of the contents of the *CD* in the perennial but also hurried task of delivering lectures perhaps only lightly edited; (3) his ambitious goal to recover the past and correct the present in a way that rendered Christian theology in its full range and in a comprehensive account for his day; and (4) the unfathomable and overflowing richness of theology's own subject matter of God's revelation that led Barth to expansive explication. Yet there are some ways to approach the task of reading Barth that can be of significant help as one enters upon its path.

First, it is always a good thing to know where you are. When reading, note, of course, the volume and chapter but also the specific paragraph and its topic within the chapters (marked, again, by a § symbol). The bold-print thesis statement at the beginning of each paragraph should be read carefully and kept in view, for it provides both the content that will be elucidated and

---

3. Hans Frei, *Types of Christian Theology* (New Haven: Yale University Press, 1992), 157.

4. In commenting on Barth's verbosity, Frei states that its ultimate reason is that Barth "was restating or re-using a language that had once been accustomed talk, both in first-order use in ordinary or real life, and in second-order technical theological reflection, but had now for a long time, perhaps more than 250 years, been receding from natural familiarity, certainly in theological discourse. So Barth had as it were to recreate a universe of discourse, and he had to put the reader in the middle of that world, instructing him in the use of that language by showing him how—extensively, and not only by stating the rules or principles of the discourse." Frei, *Types of Christian Theology*, 159.

the general structure for the following exposition in the paragraph. This thesis statement is therefore a good thing to reread when one is lost in the forest of Barth's exposition in a particular section. It is also very helpful to pay particular attention to the first paragraph in Barth's chapters and especially careful attention to the opening discussion of that paragraph. The first paragraph of a chapter most often sets the agenda and provides an introduction for the following ones, and the opening discussion of that first paragraph introduces its theme and often the themes for those paragraphs that follow in the chapter. It should not be surprising, therefore, that we will often spend more time below discussing these first paragraphs of Barth's chapters than the later ones.

Second, do not ignore, but also do not get bogged down in, the small-print sections. These sections do not provide the flow of Barth's argument that can be discerned in the main body (i.e., larger print) of the text. The small-print sections are best thought of as extended footnotes, or as expanded treatments of themes that either directly or indirectly provide explanation of, illumination upon, or argument, support, and warrant for Barth's larger constructive claims. They can be of various types, though these types can be combined in a single small-print section: (1) they can be exegetical investigations of scriptural terms or passages; (2) they can be historical accounts of the development of a doctrine or a specific theological question or controversy, often examining a theme by comparing its presence in different historical theologians or church traditions or in Western culture at large; (3) they can be polemical engagements with past or contemporary theological, philosophical, or cultural figures or positions in which Barth provides not only argumentation for a constructive position but also reasons why other alternatives must be rejected. This list is not meant to be exhaustive, but it certainly is representative—most of the small-print sections are concerned with such exegetical, historical, or polemical matters. Knowing the nature of the small-print section that one is reading, and answering the question of how it serves Barth's larger exposition or argument at the time, will go a long way in helping to read and appreciate it. And again, when all else fails, such small-print sections can be skipped in order to find the flow of the larger constructive argument in the main body of the text. This is particularly true when such sections are filled with untranslated Hebrew, Greek, Latin, and French terms and phrases (which, again, the study edition helpfully translates in footnotes).

Correspondingly, I often tell students that there are at least three ways of reading Barth. The first is simply to gain an understanding of Barth's own theological position on a given question. This is to learn Barth's own theology. The second is to gain an understanding of the history of exegesis and of doctrine as he presents these in various sections throughout the *CD*. And the third is to read him as a teacher for how to think theologically and how to become a theologian, reading him not only for his content or historical understanding but also for a critical appreciation of his patterns of thought, his astute ability to frame a question or get at the heart of an issue, and thus to understand his characteristic ways of theological description, engagement, and argumentation. Our primary goal is simply to learn the first way of reading, but our ultimate goal is to introduce the third, as well as to perceive how the theological themes he addresses continue to speak to and impact the church of today. The small-print sections are most concerned with the second way of reading Barth, and while important, they are not crucial for a first reading and should not hinder one from pressing on with his larger argument. Nevertheless—and this needs to be stated clearly—some of the most pointed and eye-opening assertions and incisive arguments of the *CD* are actually found in these small-print sections, and they therefore add to the first and third types of reading and not only the second. Moreover, I might add at this point that understanding Barth is greatly helped by appreciating his historiography—that is, his underlying construal of how theology developed (and devolved) over time. This historiography illuminates his concepts and arguments, and perhaps especially assists in grasping his suspicion of any theological system predicated upon the human subject and experience. The extensive discussions of this historiography are found in the small-print sections of the *CD*.

Third, observe that within the main body of the text itself Barth often provides points and sections that are numerically ordered. Paying attention to this ordering and being cognizant of where one is reading within the sequence can be quite helpful in tracing his argument and keeping the vast range of material organized. There are a few things that should be noted in this regard. First, the material covered in each subsection can be vast, and it is very helpful to underline or highlight the numeric terms in the text (whether words ["First," "Second"] or Arabic numerals ["1.," "2."]). Even better, in my opinion, is to write the numbers in the margin where they occur so that one can find them readily. The *CD* will be best used over time if it is personalized and inscribed in this and other ways so that future reference is easier and more efficient. Second, Barth at times includes a numerical list of subpoints within a discussion of a numbered point in an already occurring sequence, and this can at times be confusing. This practice makes noting location and order all the more important. The reader can signal subpoints in the margins with a switch to either letters ("a.," "b.") or numbering them in a decimal system where the larger point is followed by a subpoint (e.g., "3.1," "3.2"—here signifying the third element in a sequence and its subpoints). Please notice that this manner of points and subpoints is occurring *in this very paragraph I am now writing*, for I am now making a second subpoint under the larger third point in a series of points on how to read Barth! Lastly, it should also be noted that on very rare occasions numbers apparently are dropped for inexplicable reasons in a sequence of points in Barth's own text. This, understandably, can lead to confusion.

Fourth, begin early to notice images that Barth uses frequently and that may serve various purposes. Many of these are geometric images—such as a vertical line intersecting a horizontal one (often representing God's eschatological incursion into human history, or the intersection of divine and human agency or action). Particularly important and prevalent is Barth's penchant for concentric circles and the language of a center and its periphery, where the center gives the larger meaning and purpose to those areas that extend from that center. Examples of this can include Barth's understanding of Christ (center) and the church and then world or state (respective concentric circles), or his understanding of covenant (center) and creation (periphery). These two geometric images of intersecting vertical and horizontal lines and nestled concentric circles with a center and a periphery run throughout the *CD* (and precede it) and can be used in various ways in discussing a number of doctrinal themes. Beginning to notice how such concrete images function within his discussion allows in turn for a recognition of more nuanced and more abstract (rather than pictorial) forms of thought. One can therefore in time move on from noting these concrete and visual images to discovering and appreciating more conceptual recurring patterns and themes as well.[5] Not to be overlooked are the larger trinitarian shape and patterns of Barth's entire structure, both within and across the volumes of the *CD*. None of this should be taken to imply that these patterns exist apart from the material doctrinal content he is addressing. Such patterns are not superimposed upon that content, but they can be discerned in reading across the *CD*, for in his discussion of specific theological and doctrinal topics certain recurring patterns of thought are readily discerned. They arise from, rather than are superimposed on, the content itself. But they are there.

Fifth, a reader must not only make peace with the fact but also learn to appreciate that Barth's thought is often expressed in a dialectical way, which here means that he attempts to present the truth of a theological reality by

5. One of the most astute and well-known studies of such themes is that of George Hunsinger, *How to Read Karl Barth: The Shape of His Theology* (Oxford: Oxford University Press, 1991).

placing and holding in tension two things that on the surface appear to be in conflict or even contradictory but that must both be stated in order to give proper witness to the reality itself. Such dialectical descriptions can range from (1) the full affirmation of God as one and as irreducibly three as the Father, Son, and Holy Spirit to (2) the confession of both the full divinity and the full humanity of Jesus Christ to (3) a correspondent confession of Scripture as the Word of God and as a human witness to that Word to (4) the simultaneous avowal of the agency of God the Holy Spirit as well as the agency of the church or the human person, where divine sovereign freedom does not undermine but paradoxically establishes human freedom. This is not an exhaustive list. Yet in all such things Barth finds that the truth of the mystery under review is best attested not by resolving these polarities into a higher synthesis where the tension is diffused but in holding each constituent aspect of the professed truth in an ordered and asymmetrical juxtaposition. In such juxtaposition the truth of each element is maintained and affirmed even if together they appear on the surface to be in seeming conflict with their alternate. Such a relation is also construed in such a way that the divine side of the polarity (in those that relate God to the world) always maintains an irreversible preeminence, prerogative, and determination in the relation. Such dialectical ways of thought permeate Barth's theology, and learning to appreciate and navigate and indeed comprehend them is crucial for understanding how he thinks theologically and constructs his positions. Highlighting them in the actual content of the *CD* will be an important part of our work below.

Sixth and finally, it is always important to remember that Barth wrote his dogmatics as a *church* dogmatics. No matter how esoteric or eccentric a given topic may appear on the surface or in the course of his description, his theology was never intended to be in the service of idle speculation on divine things or an exercise in academic arcana, though it always exhibits a deep respect for divine mystery. It was, in the end, to be a description of the theology of the church, and for Barth, this entailed especially that it be a description of the theology of the Evangelical (i.e., Protestant) and specifically the Reformed churches, though he saw his presentation as not parochial but catholic in intent. The *CD* is put forward to be an articulation of the theology of the entire church, so that while Barth wrote from within a particular tradition, he took his project to be an exercise in articulating the faith confessed by the church universal. In writing for the church, he did not confuse theology and preaching, but he did think that theology serves preaching and instruction and the practical life of the church in an indispensable if humble way. That conviction guides this companion as well. To honor Barth's own intention, his ultimate home as a theologian cannot be set within the academy but rather must find its place in the church and its life of proclamation, confession, and witness. In the end, if his theology is to thrive, it will do so as it is embodied in and serves the Christian community, rather than simply being carried on as an argument in the academy.[6]

These ways of reading Barth do not all come naturally, perhaps, but this companion will attempt to assist with each of the above. It serves its purpose best if it points beyond itself, assisting readers and reading groups to take up the CD, even as the CD itself is best read as an exposition of the revelation of God that is confessed by the church in its proclamation and normatively attested in Holy Scripture. It is Scripture that witnesses to God's personal revelation in Jesus Christ and that is best read first, and best read last. If Barth's theology can have any enduring value, it can only be as it assists us as readers of Scripture itself.

Reading Further On and Further In

Of the writing of books there is no end—and this is as true of books about Barth as of others. The following books are particularly recommended to readers who would like to know more about his life and the content of his thought in the CD and elsewhere.

Introductory Works

Busch, Eberhard. *Barth*. Translated by Richard Burnett and Martha Burnett. Abingdon Pillars of Theology. Nashville: Abingdon, 2008.

Guretzki, David. *An Explorer's Guide to Karl Barth*. Downers Grove, IL: IVP Academic, 2016.

Morgan, D. Densil. *The SPCK Introduction to Karl Barth*. London: SPCK, 2010.

Intermediate Works

Mangina, Joseph. *Karl Barth: Theologian of Christian Witness*. Louisville: Westminster John Knox, 2004.

Nimmo, Paul. *Barth: A Guide for the Perplexed*. New York: Bloomsbury T&T Clark, 2017.

Webster, John. *Karl Barth*. 2nd ed. New York: Continuum, 2004.

6. This matter is discussed incisively yet critically by D. Stephen Long in *Saving Karl Barth: Hans Urs von Balthasar's Preoccupation* (Minneapolis: Fortress, 2014), 12–13. While sympathetic to Long's larger point, I perhaps have more hope and conviction than he that the evangelical vision that Barth espoused is in fact embodied in various ways in various churches.

Advanced Works

Busch, Eberhard. *The Great Passion: An Introduction to Karl Barth's Theology*. Translated by Geoffrey Bromiley. Grand Rapids: Eerdmans, 2004.

———. *Karl Barth: His Life from Letters and Autobiographical Texts*. Translated by John Bowden. Grand Rapids: Eerdmans, 1994.

Dorrien, Gary. *The Barthian Revolt in Modern Theology: Theology without Weapons*. Louisville: Westminster John Knox, 2000.

⊹ 2 ⊹

Dogmatics as a Theological Discipline of the Church

CD §§1–2

The introduction to the *CD* is composed of two brief introductory paragraphs (§1–2). Here Barth provides a prologue to his work that takes up questions pertaining to the nature and task of theological inquiry. Because these paragraphs set the table for all that will follow in volume 1 of the *CD* and for all of the subsequent volumes, and because they contain some particularly challenging material and concepts at the very outset of reading the *CD*, they here receive detailed attention. Because of the brevity of these first two paragraphs, the themes of the subsections will be treated together in one discussion.

The Task of Dogmatics (§1)

In the opening two paragraphs of the *CD* Barth sets forth what might be called matters of prolegomena—that is, introductory matters that introduce the subject matter to be examined, the nature of the discipline that examines them, and the methods that will be followed in this discipline. In the first paragraph he focuses upon the task of dogmatics as "the scientific self-examination of the Christian Church with respect to the content of its distinctive talk about God" (3).

The Church, Theology, Science (§1.1); Dogmatics as an Enquiry (§1.2); Dogmatics as an Act of Faith (§1.3)

The *CD* begins with a discussion of the theme named in its very title: dogmatics. "Dogmatics" is a word that has almost disappeared from common Christian discourse, and certainly is unknown beyond it, though the word "dogmatic" remains. Any time the word "dogmatic" is used, however, it rarely, if ever, refers to something good.[1] When we say that someone is dogmatic, we usually refer to a person who is unbending in thought and overbearing in argument, tone, and demeanor. Barth does not, of course, have any of this in mind when he begins by talking about dogmatics and its task. Dogmatics is, rather, the examination of "dogma," also a word with few positive connotations today, but which in the past has simply denoted a specific doctrine or the body of doctrine held and taught by a church or the church universal. When Barth uses the word "dogma" in the singular rather than in the plural, however, he usually does not use it to refer to a singular teaching of the church or a body of teaching. It points, rather, to the truth and content *behind* the various teachings and doctrines (dogmas) themselves. More pointedly, "dogma" in the singular refers to God's revelation in Christ himself, God's own self-revelation that lies behind all church dogmas and to which they refer. Dogmatics is, then, the church's examination of its own dogmas and, more inclusively, all of the church's speech and action, in light of its dogma—that is, the truth of God's revelation that all dogmas intend to expound and elucidate.

As such, dogmatics is a theological discipline required by the church as a test of its own faithfulness in speech to what has been spoken to it by God's Word in Christ and heard in Holy Scripture. As Barth succinctly writes, "Dogmatics is the self-examination of the Christian Church in respect of the content of its distinctive talk about God" (*CD* I/1, 11 [all following in-text citations are from this volume until otherwise noted]). Dogmatics is the science of dogma, of the content of the church's proclamation, confession, and teaching. Contemporary readers might think of dogmatics more broadly under the familiar name of "theology," though the latter is a broader term that Barth uses to include the disciplines of biblical theology (i.e., biblical studies) and practical theology as well as dogmatics (though he can also use "theology" as a way to refer to dogmatics specifically). We might think of dogmatics roughly along the lines of what today is commonly called systematic or constructive theology. Barth's preference for the designation "dogmatics" arises from his

---

1. One could do the same type of comparison with the word "rhetoric," which also did not originally have the nearly universal negative implications it has today.

suspicion of "systems" imposed upon the teaching of the church's doctrine that can force-fit its content into foreign categories and organizational patterns that in turn distort it. Moreover, he favors this term because dogmatics historically describes not the system of an individual theologian so much as the teaching of a confessional community of faith. Dogmatics thus deals with the teachings of the church as found in its creeds and confessions or any commonly held statements of faith. It has, in turn, a number of qualities and characteristics.

First, dogmatics is a theological discipline the primary task of which is to examine the content of the church's "distinctive talk about God." This examination, we might say, is its primary *purpose*. Dogmatics is a discipline that examines things, and specifically, examines the church's speech of God. Dogmatics is for this reason a critical discipline insofar as it is a detailed and intensive examination of the church's speech. This speech is wide-ranging and can broadly include all of the church's words and activity, as we will see in a moment, though Barth has something more specific in mind—namely, the church's proclamation and confession. Dogmatics is a testing of such speech, and this testing is necessary because the witness and the confession of the church are never in perfect conformity to God's own will, truth, and revelation. This is so not only because of the church's creaturely nature but also, more importantly, because the church exists with its members in a fallen and sinful state and therefore can live only by God's grace. Dogmatics undertakes the necessary task of the church to test its speech about God in regard to the question of its truthfulness and faithfulness to God and God's revelation. It must do this in the face of temptation, and as it does so the church recognizes its need to "give an account to God for the way in which it speaks" (3). Dogmatics is an act of obedience to God even as it can exist only because of the prior grace of God that has been shown to the church and that has called it into existence and sustains its life.

Because there is a distinction and indeed division between God's revelation and our appropriation of and speech about revelation due both to human finitude and to sin, the church's teaching, and thus dogmatics, must always be open to further reflection and correction and take a stance of humility even as it speaks with confidence.[2] Dogmatics, as a human discipline dependent upon God's prior action and activity, can never make a claim to be a perfect articulation of truth. It lives, as does the Christian and the church, in every

2. Drawing on Luther, Barth states that dogmatics is possible "only as a *theologia crucis*," or theology of the cross (*CD* I/1, 14). This might be placed in contrast to a triumphalist theology of glory, where truth is comprehensively, completely, and perfectly known.

moment by faith in the One who justifies its existence and makes its task possible. There can be, therefore, no final dogmatics—in this time of the church's existence here on earth, dogmatics must always be done anew in each age and in light of a constant and ever-new listening to God's revelation as witnessed in Scripture (14).

Moreover, the task of dogmatics is not simply the repetition of past doctrinal statements but rather is the testing of such statements in light of the truth of God's revelation in Christ as witnessed in Scripture.[3] To see the dogmas of the past as infallible, Barth asserts, is to attribute divine status to human descriptions. It is to fail to understand "the divine-human character of the being of the Church" (15). This dialectic of humility and fallibilism (an admission that one may be wrong) on one side and confidence and certainty on the other is a necessary tension for all human creatures who would speak of divine things. If these are not easily reconciled, that is for Barth the point, and this relation of humility and confidence in the dogmatic task is one of the first dialectical tensions we encounter in reading the *CD*, and it corresponds to the dialectic between divine speech and human speech.[4] Dogmatics deals with human speech about *God*, and it must confidently proclaim what it has heard. But dogmatics deals with *human* speech about God, and therefore it must always be open to testing and even, at times, correction. There can be no room for presumption in dogmatics: "We always seem to be handling an intractable object with inadequate means" (23). The church lives between judgment and promise, and therefore with both chastened humility and confident hope, and both of these dialectical realities are equally present in the opening volumes of the *CD*.

The second quality of dogmatics is that it is undertaken within and by the church. The church is the *context* in which it is practiced as well as the *agent* of its practice. Barth does not think of dogmatics primarily as an academic or university exercise, but an ecclesial one—that is, one undertaken in and by and for the church. Because it is the church that has been addressed by

3. Barth also does not think that the task of dogmatics is simply to collect the various statements of Scripture. He writes, "Exegetical theology investigates biblical teaching as the basis of our talk about God. Dogmatics, too, must constantly keep it in view. But only in God and not for us is the true basis of Christian utterance identical with its true content. Hence dogmatics as such does not ask what the apostles and prophets said but what we must say on the basis of the apostles and prophets. This task is not taken from us because it is first necessary that we should know the biblical basis" (*CD* I/1, 16).

4. Barth put this dilemma famously in a lecture of 1922 titled "The Word of God as the Task of Theology": "*As theologians, we ought to speak of God. But we are humans and as such cannot speak of God. We ought to do both, to know the 'ought' and the 'not able to,' and precisely in this way give God the glory*" (*WGT*, 177).

God and commissioned with the gospel, and because the church itself has been commanded to proclaim the revelation of God in Christ to the world, dogmatics is intrinsically a task that the church takes up for testing and determining whether its own speech and action are faithful or unfaithful to God's revelation in Christ attested in Scripture. Because faith is central to theology's task, Barth starkly asserts that there is "no possibility of dogmatics at all outside the Church" (17).

Third, dogmatics as a theological discipline has a specific object of study. This is the *content* that it investigates. It is for this reason scientific in nature, not in the sense that it pertains to the natural sciences, but scientific in the sense that dogmatics is a systematic examination of the church's speech about God, and thus an examination of God's revelation, which such speech is to serve and to which it is to testify. Dogmatics is scientific simply because, like any science, it has a specific subject matter that it examines in a disciplined and intentional way (see 7–8). The distinctive subject matter of dogmatics is the revelation of God in Christ as attested in Holy Scripture and proclaimed in the church.[5]

While God's revelation in Christ is the subject matter of theology, it is also important to appreciate Barth's singular conviction that God remains ever free and is never an object that we can know or grasp by our own efforts or manipulate for our own ends. God is the Lord, an inalienable Subject and the enactor of his own action and revelation. This is a consistent and important conviction that shapes all of Barth's theology. He opposes any description in which God is objectified and in turn domesticated as a mascot for our own cultural, political, social, or personal ends. It is also important to note that in his time he claimed that such objectification could be found on both the theological right and the left, among both "conservative" and "liberal" theological

---

5. To state that theology is a science is, for Barth, not akin to stating that, like the natural or perhaps even social sciences, we have a command of our subject matter and manipulate it in order to gain mastery over it. It certainly does not mean that theology must follow some sort of universal "scientific method" akin to the natural sciences. Indeed, he will spend some time arguing against those who would state that for theology to be a science it must conform to the methods and means of the natural or social sciences. In short, he will argue not for the superiority of theology over all other sciences but for the integrity and necessity of its practice (*CD* I/1, 8). The background of the arguments that he conducts here need not unduly detain us for the purposes of our own investigation of theology as an exercise of the church's life. They were arguments perhaps for a time when the natural sciences were seen as bound by a single method that was considered as superior to that of all other disciplines. Few people take this as a given today. For an examination of Barth's understanding of theology as a science and his refusal to concede that theology must meet external criteria from other sciences to be called such, see Kimlyn J. Bender, *Confessing Christ for Church and World: Studies in Modern Theology* (Downers Grove, IL: InterVarsity, 2014), chap. 11.

and political programs. Against any such triumphalist claims to have "God on our side," Barth stresses that the ultimate subject matter of dogmatics is never at our disposal. It is revealed by divine grace for our salvation, demanding the church's reverent reflection and providing the content of its confession.

Finally, dogmatics is a work of faith, for the relation of the church to its Lord is one of faith, an obedient attendance of the church to Christ as it listens for his voice in Holy Scripture. This has great implications for theology's *method*. The knowledge that dogmatics gives is knowledge that comes by God's initiative and comes by faith, not by the exercise of autonomous human reason (17–18). Faith itself is "the gracious address of God to man, the free personal presence of Jesus Christ in his activity" (18). This does not mean that Barth places knowledge of God and faith in God in opposition, however—that is a false dichotomy that he actively rejected.[6] But the knowledge that we receive comes to us through an act of faith and faithful reception, though Barth's position prioritizes an election that makes human reception itself a divinely determined fact: "It always rests with God and not with us whether our hearing is real hearing and our obedience real obedience, whether our dogmatics is blessed and sanctified as knowledge of the true content of Christian utterance or whether it is idle speculation" (18; cf. 21). Dogmatics must trust in God's revelation, which is both the content of its knowledge (the "ontic basis") and the means by which it is known (the "noetic basis") (22). This entails that God is both the One who is revealed and the One who reveals—a truth that we will explore further below. If, then, revelation can occur only by God's action, then the first and proper act of dogmatics is prayer, for only by entreating God for illumination and revelation can dogmatics be undertaken by the church and a knowledge of God be received (23–24). As Barth writes, prayer is "the attitude without which there can be no dogmatic work" (23). Faith and prayer, along with the exegesis of Scripture, thus exist at the beginning and at the heart of theology's method and Barth's understanding of it.

Before moving on from this discussion of the *purpose, context, content,* and *method* of dogmatics, let us return briefly to the third of these, the question of the content and subject matter of dogmatics. One of the ways to misread the *CD* from the very beginning is to overlook the fact that the examination that dogmatics undertakes really has two things in view, rather than one, though they are intricately related: the church's speech about God,

---

6. Barth's refusal to set these in opposition marks one of numerous ways that he differed from his teacher, Wilhelm Herrmann, and Herrmann's other famous student, and Barth's contemporary, Rudolf Bultmann.

and the divine Word that stands behind and gives rise to this speech. Barth is at times not altogether clear as to which is in view when he discusses the object of dogmatics, even though he carefully distinguishes these in relation to each other.

In the foreground, dogmatics takes as its subject matter the church's speech about God (3–5). This speech can be found in the life of the individual believer, or in the speech and action of a particular Christian fellowship or community (3). Theology is not, however, solely or even primarily concerned with the day-to-day speech and action of the Christian or of the congregation. It is, rather, in its proper sense a principled and systematic examination of the church's speech in its proclamation and its confessional/doctrinal teaching for the purpose of determining whether this speech is faithful to God's revelation to the church.

As noted above, because such preaching and teaching are human speech, it is always open to divine judgment. Yet because the church has also received a divine promise, it can boldly speak what it has heard (4), and as it hears it speaks (12). The perfection of this divine revelation is nevertheless only appropriated and perceived by a very imperfect human act, and therefore the church's speech is not only fallible but also "stands in need of criticism, of correction, of critical amendment and repetition" (14). It is not surprising that Barth therefore quotes (in Greek) two fundamental biblical verses (1 Cor. 13:12 and 2 Cor. 4:7) that reference the limitations of human perception of divine revelation. This relationship between judgment and promise, and in turn that between God and the creature with the truth and perfection of divine revelation on one side and the fallibility and partiality of its human perception and articulation on the other, displays a kind of dialectical thinking that will be frequently seen in the CD. This dialectical thought attempts to speak Christian truth by holding in tension two seemingly irreconcilable things that are inseparably united yet irreducibly distinct, things such as divine judgment and mercy, or eternity and time, or divine and human action simultaneously present in the incarnation, in the production and reception of Scripture, and in the church's proclamation. The attempt to express the truth of the gospel by maintaining this tension is a significant part of what it means to say that Barth is a dialectical theologian. We will see other examples of dialectical thinking in later chapters as well, and any reader of the CD would be well served to be sensitive to such patterns of thought and argumentation.[7] As

---

7. For a very accessible description of various aspects of dialectic in Barth's theology, see David Guretzki, *An Explorer's Guide to Karl Barth* (Downers Grove, IL: IVP Academic, 2016), 64–72.

one interpreter of Barth has rightly said, "Nothing is more likely to lead the reader of the *Church Dogmatics* astray than a nondialectical imagination."[8]

This brings us to the subject matter that stands in the background of the church's examination in dogmatics. Theology is not only an examination of the church's speech, the subject matter of theology in the foreground; it also is an examination of that speech as this speech is itself a reflection upon and confession of the church's true subject matter, which is the revelation of God in Jesus Christ through the Holy Spirit. Dogmatics is therefore reflection upon the revelatory and salvific act of God in Jesus Christ and the Holy Spirit as this is attested in Scripture. For Barth, to appreciate and grasp theology's task as the twofold examination of its immediate subject matter of the church's speech and its ultimate subject matter of God's revelation is to understand the heart of dogmatics. In short, the relation between God's revelation in Jesus Christ through the Spirit and the church's own existence expressed in its speech and action is fundamental to all that he addresses in the first volume of the *CD*. Everything that follows is in one way or another an elaboration of this theme and its manifold implications. We can begin to explore this theme by considering a very important phrase in Barth's exposition.

EXCURSUS: "The Being of the Church"

The Church produces theology in this special and peculiar sense by subjecting itself to self-examination. It puts to itself the question of truth, i.e., it measures its action, its talk about God, against its being as the Church. Thus theology exists in this special and peculiar sense because before it and apart from it there is in the Church talk about God. Theology follows the talk of the Church to the extent that in its question as to the correctness of its utterance it does not measure it by an alien standard but by its own source and object. (4)

One of the most curious statements that Barth makes in the first volume of the *CD* is that dogmatics is the church's self-examination of its own speech and action against the standard of "its being as the Church." This cryptic phrase, which occurs numerous times throughout the first volume of the *CD*, is frequently overlooked, and because of this, the first volume of the *CD* is often thought to be predominantly about epistemology (i.e., how we know God), when in fact this question of knowledge is itself set within a larger framework of the relation of Jesus Christ and the church and how Christ's lordship over

8. George Hunsinger, *How to Read Karl Barth: The Shape of His Theology* (Oxford: Oxford University Press, 1991), ix.

the church is established, exercised, and maintained. Pointedly stated: everything Barth says about theological epistemology that will follow in *CD* volume 1 is already set within the context of ecclesiology, which itself is set within the larger frame of God's activity of revelation and salvation in Jesus Christ and thus within a specific Christology. In brief, theological epistemology as Barth sets it forth is not an abstract philosophical discussion of divine knowledge. Rather, it is simply asking how the church, which exists, already knows God and speaks of God because of what God has done in Jesus Christ and through the Spirit in calling it into existence. In this sense, both epistemology and ecclesiology are derivative and mutually involved doctrines predicated upon and subsumed within a larger Christology and indeed a trinitarian understanding of God that frame the relation of Jesus Christ to the church.

It must, of course, be admitted that there is some circularity here: the question of the knowledge of God takes place within the church, and the church exists because God has made himself known to the world and in so doing called the church into existence. Barth therefore begins not with the question about whether it might be *possible* to know God, but rather with the reality that the church does know God and speaks of God and can do both because it finds that it already exists by divine grace. Therefore, he insists, when reflecting upon its speech and life and its very existence, the church "does not have to begin by finding or inventing the standard by which it measures. It sees and recognizes that this is given with the Church. . . . Dogmatics presupposes that, as God in Jesus Christ is the essence [i.e., the being] of the Church, having promised Himself to it, so He is the truth, not merely in Himself, but also for us as we know Him solely by faith in Jesus Christ" (12; cf. 14).[9] Dogmatics does not argue for, but presupposes, "that the true content of Christian talk about God must be known by men" (13). This content as "the being of the Church" is the "source and object" and "basis, goal, and content" as well as the standard of the church's speech and the criterion against which it is tested (4, 6; see also, e.g., 10, 12). So Barth states that the church's speech about God "has true content when it conforms to the being of the Church, i.e., when it conforms to Jesus Christ" (12).

Yet without further elaboration or qualification, this phrase remains open to misinterpretation. For Barth, the church is not itself Christ. It might reasonably be asked: Why not speak simply of Jesus Christ and speak of the church? Why speak of "the being of the Church," which is then defined as Jesus Christ? Here we are confronted with the fact that Barth puzzlingly seems to define the church's own "being" or "essence" with that which is not itself the church, for as will become evident as we delve deeper into his *CD*, he does not simply equate Jesus Christ and the church or see the church as

---

9. The German word that Barth uses here, *Sein*, translated as "essence" (of the church), is the same as for "being" (of the church) used earlier—that is, "*das Sein der Kirche*" ("the being of the Church").

an extension of his incarnation, life, and ministry (see, as but one significant example, *CD* IV/2, 59–60).

What in fact Barth intends to designate with this phrase is a specific *relationship*, that of Christ to the church, and it is this relationship that dominates and lies in the background of the entire first volume of the *CD* (and beyond). To properly set forth the nature of this relationship is central to his task, for to understand it rightly is to understand both members in the relationship—both Jesus Christ, the Lord, and the church, his servant. The church's own existence and being are rooted in this relationship, and the church receives its own existence and essence, its very life, from its Lord, Jesus Christ, who stands not only in faithfulness with and within the church but also in freedom over, and over against, it.

This dialectical relationship between Christ and the church is itself grounded in an understanding of the relation of how the divine and the human are related in the person of Christ, and it is expressed and mirrored in various other subsidiary relationships, such as the authority of Christ expressed in Scripture set over that of the church expressed in its tradition and confessions, as well as the relationship between the hidden activity of the Holy Spirit and the activity of the Christian community (or the individual Christian) expressed in traditional sacramental or ethical categories. These themes will appear throughout the *CD*. For Barth, nearly all theological errors can be traced back either directly or indirectly to a mistaken understanding of this primary relationship of Christ to the church (itself a reflection of the logic of the incarnation and its mystery and in turn of the relation of the Creator to the creature). This will become more concretely evident when Barth speaks of Protestant liberalism and Roman Catholicism, as will be examined in the next chapter.

A further aspect of "the being of the Church" is that this phrase includes within it Barth's attempt to set forth both the means by which Jesus Christ is the source of the church's knowledge of God as well as the source of the church's salvation. As he notes, the being of the church is Jesus Christ, "God in His gracious revealing and reconciling address to man" (4; see also, e.g., 6, 12). Notice that this is a relation that is both *revelatory* and *reconciling*. As the *CD* attests throughout, revelation and reconciliation are for him two sides of one reality. For God to reveal himself to us is for God to act for our reconciliation. Barth does not separate but rather unites revelation and reconciliation, or divine disclosure and salvation, into one act of God.

To understand this indirect identification of revelation and salvation is to understand why Barth rejected natural theology—a knowledge of God apart from God's revelation in Christ—one of the most contentious and controversial elements of his theology. Put simply: just as we are saved by Christ alone and thereby grace alone through faith alone (reconciliation), so also do we know God by Christ alone and thereby grace alone through faith alone (revelation). Barth has in effect translated the Reformation commitments of Christ alone, by grace alone, through faith alone, from the sphere of salvation to that of revelation, from soteriology to theological epistemology. In this, he saw himself as bringing the Reformation insights into consistent application in a way that the Reformers themselves and their heirs should have done but did not.[10]

Revelation and salvation are therefore two sides of one act of God, for in making himself known to us in Christ, God acts to save us through Christ, and in saving us, we have come to know the true God. Christ is both the revelation and the salvation of God—the one who reveals the love of God and the one through whom the power of God is manifested and directed for our salvation. All is a work of divine grace. Jesus Christ is the name that belongs to this divine revelatory and salvific work accomplished "for us and for our salvation," in the words of the Nicene Creed. In this way, too, Jesus Christ is "the being of the Church."

At the very beginning of Barth's dogmatics we are therefore confronted with one of its most important traits: its singular, sustained, and unbroken focus upon Jesus Christ as the center of God's revelation to and reconciliation of the world. This is in no small part what it means to say that Barth is a christocentric theologian. For him, we are saved by Christ alone and we know God by Christ alone, and in his thought, these questions of reconciliation and revelation are very closely related. To understand this focus upon Jesus Christ will help us to understand not only why Barth opposes all forms of "works righteousness" or human cooperation in salvation but also why he will oppose all forms of natural theology that are set over against Christ as another, independent way of knowing God. Because the knowledge of God and the salvation of God are for him two sides of one reality, and because humanity is fallen not only in its moral capacities but also in its intellectual ones (consistent with the doctrine of total depravity), both reconciliation and revelation must be seen as coming to us by God's work in Christ by grace alone. These matters of salvation and knowledge of God are, of course, contested and difficult topics, but the reason for Barth's positions on them can be grasped here at the outset and set under the banner of the Evangelical principles of Christ alone (*solus Christus*), grace alone (*sola gratia*), and faith alone (*sola fide*). Both knowing God and receiving his salvation are gifts of God's grace. To say that Barth is a christocentric theologian also in turn entails that every doctrine of which the church speaks and that it teaches as knowledge of God must be derived from the revelation of God in Jesus Christ.

The *CD* therefore begins with the reality of God's revelation in Christ. It does not begin with the question "How might we know God?" To do so would be to begin with an inquiry shaped overmuch by general and abstract philosophical concerns as to the coherence and possibility of knowledge of the divine. Rather, Barth begins with the fact

10. Barth is not so much concerned about solving a modern problem of epistemology as he is dedicated to bringing a Reformation tradition to its logical and complete end. It was a failure of the latter, he held, that opened the door to the former problems in modernity and gave rise in time to a full flowering of natural theology and all of its problems.

that the church already exists and speaks of God and therefore knows God. Dogmatics is the examination of whether this speech is true to the revelation and salvation of God that has already been accomplished and revealed in Christ, "the being of the Church" who has called it into existence, and the one who is the standard and criterion against which the church's own speech is tested.

This recognition and appreciation of the being of the church lead naturally to the questions that dogmatics asks of the church's speech in relation to Christ: "Does Christian utterance derive from Him? Does it lead to Him? Is it conformable to Him?" (4). The theological task is carried out by three theological subdisciplines that in turn answer these respective questions. Biblical theology, which asks as to the "basis" of the church's speech, and which is understood specifically as addressing the task of exegesis, is the discipline particularly focused on the question of the derivation or source of the church's speech from Christ as attested in Holy Scripture. Practical theology asks as to the "goal" and application of the church's speech, and so whether the church's speech leads to Christ. Between them exists dogmatic theology that inquires as to the "content" and truth of the church's speech and to the question of conformity of the church's speech to Christ.[11] None of these questions, however, are absolutely restricted to a specific field—certainly dogmatics always presupposes the exegetical task. Moreover, these are the questions that lie behind any theological task.[12]

Nevertheless, Barth's *CD* is an exercise in dogmatic (rather than specifically in exegetical or practical) theology. It is not solely exegetical because it is not a commentary seeking to elucidate a specific book of Scripture in its historical context (though it does have large sections devoted to biblical exegesis and draws liberally upon its findings). Nor is it a work in pastoral or practical theology, asking how the church is to preach, or give pastoral care, or counsel its members, though it can at times address such questions. It seeks, rather, to give an account of what the church should teach and confess in its own speech based upon the findings of the exegesis of Scripture and with an eye toward how such truth is to find its concrete application in the church (5). Insofar as it stays true to its task of examining the church's teaching in light of the revelation and reconciliation that have come in Jesus Christ, dogmatics fulfills its modest but necessary purpose for the church. In light of the fact that the other sciences as avenues of human exploration do not take up this investigation of God's revelation, a critical theology is indispensable: "Its task, not in fact discharged by other sciences, is

---

11. Today dogmatic theology is known more widely as constructive theology or systematic theology, though Barth did not know of the first and was suspicious of the second for, in his thinking, it could imply the imposition of a system upon the witness to God's revelation and thus distort it rather than make it known. At any rate, dogmatics, as the thinking of the church rather than an academic discipline, cannot be fully captured by the terms "constructive theology" or "systematic theology."

12. Interestingly, church history is not an independent area of theological study for Barth but is "an auxiliary science indispensable to exegetical, dogmatic, and practical theology" (*CD* I/1, 5).

that of the criticism and correction of talk about God according to the criterion of the Church's own principle" (6).[13]

In the end, it must be said that the church speaks of God only because God has first spoken to it in the Word of God, Jesus Christ, and in the witness to Christ in Holy Scripture. Insofar as the church receives this Word and hears this Word, it does so by faith, for the Word never comes under human control or subjection. As Barth writes, again exhibiting both humility and confidence, "The intractability of faith and its object guarantees that divine certainty cannot become human security. But it is this intractable faith and its intractable object which make possible the certain divine knowledge which is at issue in dogmatics" (12–13). This is unquestionably paradoxical. Barth maintains both the divine promise that God gives to the church and the divine freedom such that God is not placed under the church's control or manipulation. This, too, is an expression of the fundamental relationship between Christ and the church and its dialectical expression. This relationship will lie at the heart of his criticisms of two confessional traditions against which he opposes the Evangelical ones—criticisms that we will witness below.

The Task of Prolegomena to Dogmatics (§2)

In the second paragraph, Barth addresses the topic of theological prolegomena explicitly. He identifies it as the determination and articulation of "the particular way of knowledge," or path, that dogmatics follows in order to understand its theme. This paragraph therefore concerns itself with both the subject matter and the method of dogmatics.

The Necessity of Dogmatic Prolegomena (§2.1); The Possibility of Dogmatic Prolegomena (§2.2)

The word "prolegomena" (like "dogmatics") is a term that is not familiar to many. Barth states that "prolegomena" is simply the preface to any science in which the means and methods by which it gains knowledge of its subject matter are set forth and explained (25). In this, he sees himself as providing something of the same thing—an initial presentation of the manner in which the knowledge of God is received by the church. As he writes, "By prolegomena to dogmatics . . . , we understand the attempt to give an explicit account

---

13. Once again, Barth will not allow any secular science, whether natural or social, to dictate to theology how it is to fulfill its obligation to the church and how it is to conduct its business—nor should theology be overly concerned with its claim upon the word "science" at all, though he retains it for a number of specified reasons (CD I/1, 7–9).

of the particular way of knowledge taken in dogmatics, . . . of the particular point from which we are to look, think and judge in dogmatics" (25). He is not entirely invested in providing a detailed description of this kind, and he does not think that it is intrinsically necessary for doing dogmatics. He does acknowledge, however, that in light of a rise in "paganism" (secularization?) and "the radicalism of rational thought" (post-Enlightenment rationalism), the question of knowledge and the problem of its justification seem to be necessary (26). This is perhaps his most ready and explicit acknowledgment of the significance of modernity upon his method and execution of dogmatics.

It should be noted that while Barth takes account of these changes of modernity, they are not overly decisive for him and should not be overestimated. He does not think that the modern world requires a turn from dogmatics to apologetics as a necessary second task, a task that seeks to demonstrate a knowledge of God based simply on an innate capacity of humanity (like reason or the moral conscience) or on the universe (whether its existence, order, or design) that is separate from the knowledge we have of Christ. Nor does he think that the task of theology requires or should attempt a demonstration of a point of contact between natural reason and God's revelation.

For Barth, dogmatics attends to God's revelation and is not to be a kind of justification of Christianity before the tribunal of an "objective" reason. To be smitten with modernity as necessitating a new plan for theology (which he sees in Emil Brunner) is precisely to concede the proper task of the church to pronounce its message and replace it with a kind of philosophical apologetics that seeks not to articulate the church's distinctive gospel but instead to find a neutral common ground with other forms of thought or belief. Besides, he does not think that the present age actually differs as much from those before it as other persons seem to suppose—this age, like those prior ones, is marked by "unbelief" in God's revelation (27–31). And this unbelief is the same today as it was in Paul's day, and has been ever since. The ancient world with its spiritualism was no easier than the secular realm of today for Christianity. Barth's judgment is uncompromising on this point: "Knowledge of the revelation believed in the Church does not stand or fall with the general religious possibility that is made easier by the ancient view of things and more difficult by the modern" (28). In this section, his clear preference for dogmatics rather than for apologetics is on full display, and he is always concerned that when driven by apologetic aims, faith takes the unbelief of the world more seriously than it takes itself (30). His response is shaped by the conviction that knowledge of God is a matter of a divine act of self-giving received in faith rather than the result of conclusions drawn from arguments of a dispassionate reason.

This section and its questions need not overly detain us, but what should be noted is that Barth here sets forth a very important understanding of the "Evangelical" (i.e., Protestant) dogmatics that he espouses over against two other forms of dogmatics and confessional traditions that he places as alternatives to his own. What must not be overlooked is that he does not think that dogmatics is to be primarily concerned with addressing, opposing, and providing answers for modernity, secularization, rationalism, or even paganism. Dogmatics is, in truth, primarily set not against an external opposition to the church but against other forms of Christian faith that it judges to be deficient, against "a form or forms of faith in which it recognises itself in respect of form but not of content" (31). These are types of Christian faith in name that share a similar form but with a different view of truth (31). He designates such forms of Christianity that possess a differing content "heresies." However polemical and perhaps even harsh his point might be to modern ears, the first volume of the *CD* will not be rightly understood unless one sees it not only as a constructive dogmatics but also as one directed against two Christian traditions that he judges not only to be deficient but also to be, ultimately, heretical. These are traditions over against which he formulates his own answer as Evangelical Christian faith. Here, too, failure to understand his dogmatic presentation over against these two alternatives will result in a failure to understand his theological program in the first volume of the *CD*.

EXCURSUS: Evangelical Dogmatics in Opposition to Two Rival Traditions

Barth's theological project was set firmly within the modern period, but it would be a mistake in reading the *CD* to see it as a work addressing the challenges of modernity as its sole or primary focus. Rather, his concerns with modernity were always subjected to a larger question and set against the relief of a much broader historical framework. It is noteworthy that he rarely mentions significant figures who shaped the modern theological project, such as Descartes, Kant, or Hegel, in the first volume of the *CD*. In striking contrast, he quotes Luther extensively, indeed, more than any other single figure, and this holds true not only for the first volume but also for the *CD* as a whole. This is in no small part due to the fact that he writes the *CD* as an answer to the question of what the Reformation was truly about in its protest against the medieval church, and how its decisive insights were lost even to those who carried on the Reformation tradition in name up to and into the modern period. The *CD* is in fact a dogmatic work with an intrinsic polemical agenda that accompanies its constructive project.

Barth sets his Reformed Evangelical dogmatics in contrast and conversation with two primary dialogue partners: Roman Catholicism on one side, and the Protestant liberal tradition on the other. The means by which the distinction is made between the Evangelical church (which he takes to be the Protestant church comprising its Lutheran and Reformed branches) and these other church traditions are based upon their respective understandings of "the being of the Church" and Jesus Christ as the "norm of Church action" (31–32). It is, once again, precisely the relation between Jesus Christ and the church that is at issue—the ultimate question is how the lordship of Christ is exercised, acknowledged, and understood in each of the three traditions. He understands these rival traditions to the Evangelical one not as plural and complementary ways of thinking of the same faith, but rather esteems each "only as a possibility which is hostile to faith, and therefore as unbelief, even though it must still be understood as a possibility of faith in virtue of its formal presuppositions" (32). In other words, these other traditions share with the Evangelical faith the same Christian form, for they, too, are concerned with "the being of the Church" and the relation of Christ to his church, but in reality they possess a different understanding of this relation that betrays the content and proper ordering of the relation itself. They thereby sacrifice Christ's singular and unique lordship. This distinction between formal similarity (a similarity in appearance and structure) and material difference (a difference of actual content) is what defines the notion of heresy for Barth, and, in contrast to our own age's more irenic and ecumenical proclivities, he defines Evangelical dogmatics and theology explicitly against two such heresies: liberal Protestantism and Roman Catholicism.

It should be mentioned that in later years Barth could be much more irenic in tone toward both, though more so toward Catholicism than nineteenth-century liberalism. Indeed, he believed Roman Catholicism was the more weighty and respectable opponent. He took it with more seriousness as time went on while becoming less preoccupied with Protestant liberalism, even though, or perhaps precisely because, liberalism was the very tradition in which he began but from which he sharply and famously turned in the years during and following the First World War. It certainly is the case that his tone toward Catholicism softened, particularly in light of the Second Vatican Council, even while his protests against it remained resolute. Before examining his stance toward Catholicism in more detail, we can consider his understanding of Protestant liberalism.

It should be noted at the outset that the Protestant liberalism that Barth was opposing is a very specific tradition traced from the theologian Friedrich Schleiermacher up to Barth's day, exemplified and embodied in his own revered teacher Wilhelm Herrmann and characterized by other significant figures such as Albrecht Ritschl, Adolf von Harnack, and later and in a different way, Ernst Troeltsch. In truth, however, his opposition to the liberal tradition was based upon a critical judgment upon not only Schleiermacher and his successors but also a broad development in post-Reformation Protestant theology. Barth was suspicious and critical of a broad theological trajectory that focused upon the faith and religious experience of the human subject rather than upon the objective reality of God's revelation in its particularity in Jesus Christ and Scripture. He saw precedents to the subjectivism of Protestant liberalism in seventeenth-century pietism and eighteenth-century Enlightenment rationalism (32–33). He even elsewhere cautiously proffered that the problem of subjectivism was already troublingly present in some of Luther's thought that focused on the justification of the individual believer and the believer's experience of condemnation and grace. In truth, for Barth, the heresy at the root of Protestant liberalism, or what he could call "Protestant Modernism," did not begin with Schleiermacher but found its full culmination in him and continued on in the Protestant liberal tradition that succeeded him (36; cf. 62–64).

This did not mean, however, that Barth did not place a particular emphasis upon Schleiermacher as the root of the problems of Protestant liberalism. Put succinctly: he held that what made Schleiermacher uniquely significant is that he replaced Jesus Christ with Christian piety as "the being of the Church," and this replacement was in fact the "formal foundation" of the heresy of modern Protestantism. Such modernism substituted the particular revelation of God in Jesus Christ with a human religious capacity found in all persons and a general "self-understanding of human existence" (36–39; cf. 61–64). The basis of the church for Protestant liberalism thus became human religiosity or piety. It is not a tradition, as Barth later wrote, that hears a voice from outside itself, but rather one in which humanity simply listens to its own inner voice: "Modernist dogmatics hears man answer when no one has called him" (61–62; cf. 61–64). The appearance of Jesus in history was correspondingly understood by liberalism as the actualization of a general religious "existential potentiality" that in fact exists in all persons (38–39). Jesus was therefore more quantitatively rather than qualitatively different from other human persons.

The Protestant liberal tradition that Barth inherited from his teachers like Adolf von Harnack and Wilhelm Herrmann and later famously abandoned was for him a betrayal of the Reformation and its central insights. His *CD*, as an Evangelical dogmatics, is an attempt to outline the convictions and doctrinal commitments of a church faithful to the Reformation that rejects these later errors. He finds examples of such errors not only in Schleiermacher but also (whether fairly or not) in the existentialism of Søren Kierkegaard and in the theology of Barth's contemporaries Rudolf Bultmann and Paul Tillich. This entire tradition of "Modernist" dogmatics is one that he sets over against a true Reformation and Evangelical dogmatics, and it is the first tradition that serves as his foil in the *CD*.

Roman Catholicism is the second tradition that Barth engages, though his opposition to it is different from that against Protestant modernism. Catholicism is in his estimation less openly heretical in that it has not substituted a general human religious capacity for

Jesus Christ, or in other words, an anthropology for Christology. The problem is rather more subtle, if no less problematic. Catholicism has confused the relationship between Jesus Christ and the church such that in the end the voice of the first and the voice of the second, and in turn their realities, are indistinguishable (40–41). The voice of Christ is subsumed into the teaching office of the Catholic Church such that the voice of the church is directly equated with the voice of Christ himself. For the Catholic Church, Barth contends, its "presupposition is that the being of the Church, Jesus Christ, is no longer the free Lord of its existence, but that He is incorporated into the existence of the Church, and is thus ultimately restricted and conditioned by certain concrete forms of the human understanding of His revelation and of the faith which grasps it" (40). The free and authoritative voice of Christ is now identified directly with the dogmas and pronouncements of the church. Divine revelation and the church's dogmas are now esteemed identical. In effect, God's being and activity are merged and confused with creaturely reality and activity: "Grace here becomes nature, the action of God immediately disappears and is taken up into the action of the recipient of grace, that which is beyond all human possibilities changes at once into that which is enclosed within the reality of the Church, and the personal act of divine address becomes a constantly available relationship" (41).[14] In short, revelation is no longer a divinely enacted event but instead a permanent possession of the church.

In response, and in the same way that Barth set the tradition of Luther and Calvin over against the later Neo-Protestant or "Modernist" tradition, he now upholds the Reformation objections that had been raised against medieval Catholicism. He asserts that this protest of the Evangelical church is still necessary and meaningful in the face of uncorrected Roman Catholic positions. Once again, it must be remembered that he is writing about a Catholicism that is very different from that presented years later in the Second Vatican Council, though it would be an overstatement and irresponsible to say that he would have no objections to that later form.

Evangelical dogmatics therefore stands against Roman Catholicism on one side and "pietistic and rationalistic Modernism as rooted in mediaeval mysticism and the humanistic Renaissance" on the other (34). The task of Evangelical dogmatics is "to explain to itself why it thinks it should go its own distinctive way and what this way is" in contrast to Protestant liberalism and Roman Catholicism (287). Again, Barth's judgment upon these confessions may seem harsh to modern ears: "And as we listen to them, not evading the formal justice of their claim [as possibilities and forms of Christian faith], we are forced to say that in them we do not recognize faith and the Church" (34). Yet regardless of how such questions might be answered today, it is impossible fully to

14. Barth's rejection of the *analogia entis*, or analogy of being, is a subsidiary problem to this larger christological and ecclesiological one. It is a general problem made known through the particular one.

appreciate what he is attempting in the *CD* unless one sees it as a dogmatics written directly to present the Evangelical (i.e., Reformation, Protestant) faith in contrast to these two rejected positions.

Failure to appreciate this reality is a failure to understand what the *CD* is truly about in its opening volume. It is not at its core an attempt to provide an answer to the challenges of modernity, though Barth will address such challenges throughout the *CD* in various passages and is not unaware of them. It is, rather, an attempt to present a viable Evangelical theology, and specifically, a Reformed one, in light of Protestantism's own failures in the post-Reformation period culminating in Protestant liberalism, and in light of its ongoing disagreements with its weighty Roman Catholic alternative. To note this confessional and indeed polemical theme in the *CD* is not, however, to imply that Barth was attempting to present a sectarian faith in his dogmatics. Quite the opposite. He writes and intends the *CD* to be a truly catholic and even ecumenical dogmatics—a work that takes the entire history of theology into account (and not solely theology in the Protestant tradition since the Reformation), a work that attempts in scope and ambition to present a full and comprehensive account of the Christian faith, and a work that is written for the universal church and presented to all of the churches for consideration as giving voice to the true Christian faith for all. In this, he commends it to all Christian readers, even to those in traditions that are set in opposition to his own.

This catholic project of dogmatics is thus undertaken by means of serious, and at times polemical, dialogue with these rival traditions. The differences between the Evangelical faith that Barth puts forward in the first volume of the *CD* and its rivals in Protestant liberalism and Roman Catholicism are at their root differences in how each understands and construes the relationship between Christ and the church and defines "the being of the church." These differences in turn have ramifications for how the church understands "the way of knowledge" (35). The task of dogmatic prolegomena is to articulate how dogmatics goes about its task, and the specific task of Evangelical dogmatics is to articulate its own convictions over against the other forms of faith that appear to be similar but in reality are different from it in this understanding of "the being of the Church" and "the way of knowledge" (35).

It was in the Reformation that these divergences appeared with striking force. Barth contends that the central formal principle (or principle of authority from which doctrine is derived) of the Reformers that guided them and marked them off from their opponents was their commitment to the Scripture principle—that Scripture was the norm and judge standing above and over against all other doctrinal teaching in the church (35–36).[15]

---

15. A formal principle refers to that source of authority from which doctrine is derived and which in turn judges and tests all doctrine. A material principle is the primary doctrine around which other doctrines revolve. As these terms developed, the formal principle of the Lutheran Reformation was designated to be the Scripture principle (*sola Scriptura*), whereas the material principle was stated to be the doctrine of justification by faith alone (*sola fide*).

Notice, however, that this principle was not simply about the Bible. At its heart, it was a conviction about how Jesus Christ was known, and where he spoke, and how he exercised authority not only within but also over the church. It was a conviction about how the distinction of Christ and church was maintained (35). The Scripture principle was not only a new formal principle of determining the truth of doctrine and recognizing the sole normativity of Holy Scripture for the teaching of the church; it was also first a "new material knowledge of Jesus Christ" himself (35). It was the recognition that Christ's voice had been heard in Scripture anew and that this voice could not be subsumed into the teaching office of the church, or, later, into the piety of the individual Christian. For Barth, the question of Scripture is thus ultimately a christological one.

Here again, a careful reading of the *CD* reveals that from the start it is not simply concerned with answering epistemological questions, but rather sets these questions themselves within the framework of how "the being of the Church" is to be understood—how Jesus Christ's relationship to the church is to be properly defined and articulated, and how the distinction between them is to be maintained such that Christ remains the Lord in relation to the church as his servant. At its heart, Barth's rejection of both Protestant liberalism and Roman Catholicism is predicated upon their failure to maintain this distinction and thus recognize and acknowledge Christ's unique and singular lordship. He rejects these two positions: the first substitutes human religious experience for God's unique revelation that comes to us in Jesus Christ, and the second retains Jesus Christ's centrality but sacrifices his lordship as his agency and voice are assumed by and subsumed into the teaching office, dogma, and tradition of the church. This move is mirrored in subjecting Scripture to present religious experience (in liberalism) or subsuming Scripture into the church's own tradition (in Catholicism), thereby relativizing it. The tragedy, for Barth, is that in both errors humanity no longer hears the Word of God but instead is left alone conversing with itself: in the first case, the individual religious personality turns within to hear its own voice in reason, conscience, or feeling; and in the second, the Catholic Church's magisterium and its membership are engaged in a mutual though self-contained discussion (62, 103–4; cf. *CD* I/2, 584).

Against both must be placed the firm statement that Jesus Christ speaks a word that comes to us from outside our own subjectivity and outside the community of the church itself. The being of the church must be understood in such a way that the relation between Christ and the church, and therefore that between God and humanity, is one that is only enacted freely from the divine side and is never construed as a permanent condition of human existence per se or as a possession of the church. It is and remains always an address from God to us that is graciously given, not a material condition transferred from Christ to the church such that the latter takes over his role and authority in the world (see 41–42). Dogmatics can take its rise only from "the present moment of the speaking and hearing of Jesus Christ Himself, the divine creating of light in our hearts" (41). The "proper way of knowledge" in dogmatics is thus dictated by the reality of this relation

(42). Dogmatics cannot be a general science of "being" (ontology) or human existence or religiosity. The way of knowledge that it takes must be defined within dogmatics itself, which is the examination of this relation of Christ and the church, and thus of the revelation of God in Christ through the Spirit that establishes this relation and the very existence of the church. It is God in his Word who calls the church and individual Christians into being by a free and gracious act comparable to the free and gracious act that spoke the world itself into being in creation. The church can speak of God only because God has first spoken to it, and indeed to the world, in Jesus Christ (43).

Dogmatics is in turn the attempt by the church to criticize and correct its own speech about God in light of this revelation. To do so, it requires a norm and criterion by which its speech is measured. This norm and criterion is the Word of God: the Word incarnate and present to the world in Jesus Christ, the Word written and recorded in Holy Scripture, and the Word proclaimed by the church. The means by which Christ the Word governs and guides not only dogmatics but also the church is Holy Scripture. This is but another way of expressing the Scripture principle, and it is this principle (and its surrounding convictions pertaining to "the being of the Church") that distinguishes Evangelical dogmatics from the ways taken by Protestant liberalism and Roman Catholicism. So Barth concludes, "We shall see that the cardinal statement of the doctrine of the Word of God which we shall try to develop in what follows is indeed materially the same as the assertion of the authority and normativeness of Holy Scripture as the witness to divine revelation and the presupposition of Church proclamation" (43).

Barth notes, however, that Scripture, which stands over the church, itself must be set within a larger context for its significance and meaning to be understood. In effect, what he will elucidate and elaborate are the underlying convictions regarding Scripture as the Word of God such that its relations to God's revelation in Jesus Christ, which precedes Scripture, and to the proclamation of the church, which follows from it, are all put in plain view. Therefore, what he sets out to provide is not simply a doctrine of Scripture, but a doctrine of the Word of God, one that incorporates Scripture within it and sets all of this within an elaboration of God's triune identity (43–44). Another way perhaps to put this is that his discussion of the formal criterion of all doctrine already presupposes that it includes all the material doctrines within it, and therefore presupposes them. In Barth's judgment, to speak of this formal dogma (of the Word of God and thus of Scripture) as the source and criterion of all material dogmas requires that we anticipate and speak of those doctrines themselves (43–44). This formal doctrine of the Word of God, which is a doctrine of revelation, stands at the head of his entire *CD* and is presupposed throughout all that he will later say with regard to the material content of doctrines. It is to this doctrine of the Word of God that we turn in the next chapter.

COMMENTARY

The Nature and Task of Theological Reflection and Dogmatics

We began this chapter by noting that the word "dogmatics" has fallen almost completely out of use within the church. Yet Barth's chapter raises important questions for the church when we focus on the meaning and significance of the term rather than the word itself. He construes dogmatics as the discipline that undertakes critical reflection on the church's speech and provides constructive articulation of the church's doctrinal convictions. When this is remembered, we might appreciate the practice and consider dogmatics necessary and inevitable, even if we might call it by another name.

That the church is called to proclaim the gospel as well as live in its light requires that its talk about God and its life before God be examined in view of God's revelation in Christ and Holy Scripture. That the church's speech and life can betray, rather than portray, the gospel was no idle danger for Barth. In the year after the first part of volume 1 was published, Adolf Hitler was appointed chancellor of Germany, and ensuing events would throw the German churches into turmoil. One year after this election, Barth would play the primary role in drafting the Barmen Declaration, a confession that opposed encroaching state control of the churches, and which stated, "Jesus Christ, as he is attested for us in Holy Scripture, is the one Word of God which we have to hear and which we have to trust and obey in life and in death. We reject the false doctrine, as though the church could and would have to acknowledge as a source of its proclamation, apart from and besides this one Word of God, still other events and powers, figures and truths, as God's revelation."[16]

Not all "events and powers" that stand before the church's life may have such stark and dramatic repercussions as those of Barth's day in Germany. Yet the temptation for the church to confuse the gospel with social customs, cultural norms, and political platforms of both right and left remains an ever-recurrent danger for it in whatever time or place it exists. Perhaps even less perceptible is the more mundane danger of allowing its talk of God to fall into easy platitudes that betray the miraculous and revolutionary character of the message it proclaims and domesticate its radical truth and power. God then is spoken of in ways that, when stripped of their liturgical elegance or homespun piety, reveal at their heart a picture of an absentee landlord. This is, as Barth stated much later in life, a kind of low-grade Christian atheism that for all practical purposes thinks and behaves as if there were no God:

16. See "The Barmen Declaration," in *Karl Barth: Theologian of Freedom*, ed. Clifford Green (Minneapolis: Fortress, 1991), 149.

It professes its belief in him, lauds and praises him, while in practice he is the last of the things it thinks about, takes seriously, fears or loves. God is thus turned into an item in the inventory of the contents of an old-fashioned or partially modernized house, a piece of furniture the owner would refuse to part with in any circumstances, but for which he has nevertheless ceased to have any real use; or rather, which he has very good reasons for taking care not to use, for it might be uncomfortable or dangerous. God is spoken of, but what is meant is an idol that one treats as one sees fit.[17]

For these and all such reasons, dogmatics as critical reflection on the church's speech and life is a crucial element of the church's obedience and faithfulness, a caution against heresy and idolatry. In short, dogmatics is the intentional and formal task in which the church renders faithful obedience to the biblical command that it give careful thought to its ways and pay close attention to its speech (Hag. 1:7; 1 Tim. 4:16).

In addition to this critical task of theology is a constructive and positive one. The church must confess its faith and give voice to its convictions. What the church has heard in Holy Scripture must be set forth before the world but first must be set forth before the church itself. Even for churches for which the word "dogmatics" may seem strange and perhaps even pretentious, the theological task that this word describes regularly surfaces in ordinary and perhaps very informal practices. It goes on in the Sunday school classes of children who are taught not only the narratives of Scripture but also the (theological!) truths that God alone is God yet this God is known as Father, Son, and Spirit, and it is in this threefold name that we are baptized (Matt. 28:19); that Jesus Christ was a man who lived a long time ago but is also one with his Father in eternal power, authority, and wisdom, and therefore like his Father he is present with us now "wherever two or three are gathered" in his name (Matt. 18:20); and that the Spirit of God is nearer to us than we are to ourselves yet remains a Spirit who is holy in a way that is entirely different from any holiness we might see even in the best Christian we know, yet who with grace founds the church and fills our lives (Acts 2:4, 38). In other words, there is perhaps no more formative theological training conducted anywhere in the world than that which takes place in homes and church classrooms with children in their first decade of life, and this instruction is nothing if not both (gently) critical and (lovingly) constructive. Yet the convictions taught around those small tables belong to the church as a whole, from its oldest to its youngest members, and such convictions require reflection, articulation,

17. Karl Barth, *Fragments Grave and Gay*, ed. Martin Rumscheidt, trans. Eric Mosbacher (London: Collins, 1971), 46–47.

and even refinement. They are the stuff that forms the church's confession, life, and service—and its children. It might be helpful to remember that Barth himself decided to become a theologian not during the time he was a student in the exhilarating university classrooms of famous scholars like Adolf von Harnack or Wilhelm Herrmann but as a teenager in the inauspicious catechism class of his own pastor. In this regard, his most important theology teacher could rightfully be said to be his first.

Yet academic "school dogmatics" need not be seen in competition with this regular theological instruction in the church but may rightly be understood to complement and serve this church teaching (see 279). Dogmatics is simply the formal and systematic discipline that tests, examines, and in turn expounds upon these church convictions regarding the revelation of God in Christ through the Spirit. Whether or not this is carried out in such an intentional and systematic way, the practice of theological reflection itself will be done regardless, for it lies at the heart of what happens each week in the classes of the young and in the pastor's study as sermons take shape in the light of Scripture and with an eye toward the congregation. It also, Barth states, takes place in the discipline of dogmatics that is practiced by and within the church and in turn serves it. It is this discipline that he is describing here.

The Relation of Christ and the Church

A central theme that runs through these opening paragraphs and beyond is the relation of Christ and the church. A pressing question for Barth was how this relation is best understood and described, and his entire historiography and understanding of Roman Catholicism and modern Protestantism were shaped by the way he understood this relationship. These questions remain to this day insofar as the differing churches, whether Roman Catholic, Eastern Orthodox, or Protestant (with its own constituent confessional and evangelical traditions), continue to differ on the answers they give. His own dogmatics reflects his commitment to the Reformation and its abiding convictions, and perhaps its most central one regarding the distinction between Christ and his church. As we have seen, for Barth, a primary task of the church in its confession and in turn its dogmatics is to articulate the proper understanding of this relationship and to denounce false (heretical) alternatives. Even if one were to opt for a more ecumenical rather than polemical approach to such questions, and even if one gave a very different answer than Barth provides, it nevertheless remains true that every church and every Christian embraces a particular way of understanding this relation of Christ and Christ's church, whether implicitly or explicitly. A central task of the church's confession is to set forth this relationship such that Christ remains the Lord and the church remains his servant.

Perhaps another way to approach this relation of Christ and church is to ask, Where is the living voice of Jesus Christ heard with authority and power in the present? To place the question this way raises questions of Scripture, of a singular teaching office within the church (for instance, questions of a magisterium and papacy), and of various conceptions of plural teaching offices (for instance, of bishops and an episcopal structure, or of teaching elders and the role of synods or presbyteries). It also introduces the question of whether Christ is heard in the corporate body of the church as a whole (as in some forms of congregationalism).

If nothing else, Barth's theology serves as a warning beacon against a church that would confuse or straightforwardly identify its own voice with that of its Lord. His theology is worthy of reflection for many reasons, but perhaps it would be so if only because of its unparalleled and constant warning against the danger of self-deception and the never-ending temptation to confuse the voice of Christ with our own and to cast him into our own image, or to melt him into the church. When this confusion occurs, the church is left having a conversation with itself.

QUESTIONS FOR REFLECTION

- Are theological reflection and self-examination necessary in the life of the church? What are the advantages of such reflection? What are the inherent dangers? Who is responsible for its practice? How might such self-examination protect the church from both heresy within and capitulation to "other events and powers, figures and truths" without?

- How should the testing of preaching and the church's speech take place? How might sermons be tested? Church confessions? Who is responsible for the dogmatic (i.e., theological) task, in both its critical and constructive aspects? How does Barth differentiate these formal and material tasks, as well as the norm and the content of dogmatics?

- Must the church have a dedicated academic discipline of dogmatics (or constructive theology) to undertake this practice? What role does formal theology play in helping the church test and articulate its convictions and speech? What role does it play in relation to the church's reflection upon its surrounding society and culture?

- How can the *purpose*, *context*, *content*, and *method* of dogmatics be articulated?
- Why does Barth favor dogmatics over apologetics? What are the particular dangers that he sees in apologetic programs? Why does he feel that the questions of culture cannot receive the same weight as the gospel itself?
- What does it mean when Barth speaks of the church being left alone in conversation with itself? Why and where does he think this is a particular danger? Is it a perennial one?
- What does Barth mean when he states that "dogmatics is possible only as an act of faith" and that prayer is "the attitude without which there can be no dogmatic work" (23)? What is the relationship between the *mystery* of theology, the *faith* required for its practice, and the necessity of *prayer* for its understanding?

3

Church Proclamation and Dogmatics

CD §3

After examining the task of dogmatics and dogmatic prolegomena in the introduction to volume 1 of the *CD*, Barth turns in chapter 1 (titled "The Word of God as the Criterion of Dogmatics") to discuss the norm by which it tests the church's speech about God. These topics are taken up in §§3–7.

In §3 Barth begins by looking at the speech of God in the church's proclamation. The content of dogmatics is the church's own speech about God, and here he focuses on the relationship between that speech about God in the church through which God himself speaks to reveal himself (proclamation) and the speech of the church that is a reflection upon what it has heard in proclamation and that attempts to declare its content (dogmas, or doctrine).

Church Proclamation as the Material of Dogmatics (§3)

In §3 Barth designates the church's proclamation as the subject matter to be examined by dogmatics and distinguishes proclamation from other forms of church discourse, practice, and activity. Key for understanding this discussion is the distinction he makes between the church's speech to God and that speech of the church which is "directed to men with the definitive claim and expectation that it has to declare the Word of God to them," the act of the church's proclamation in worship through which God himself speaks (51).

It may be helpful when beginning this difficult section to note that church proclamation stands between God and the human person similarly to how the church stands between Jesus Christ and the individual Christian. When Barth examines talk within the church about God that seeks to be proclamation, he is taking up the highly dialectical and paradoxical reality that when the church speaks and acts in the proclamation of the gospel in preaching and in the enactment of the sacraments of baptism and the Lord's Supper, this speech and action of the church are not only a human activity but also, when God so chooses, a divinely spoken and enacted Word of God. When the church proclaims the gospel of Christ, God himself speaks. It is not, however, the first that guarantees the second, but rather the second that grounds the efficacy and reality of the first. God speaks, and so the church speaks. And as the church speaks, God himself may speak, though the church has no intrinsic power to make this so. Barth always emphasizes, again, that God remains the Subject who is free to speak and act—it is not the human activity of proclamation that makes this so. Nevertheless, the church stands between God and the world as the place where God's Word is spoken, and therefore where God is revealed.

This does not mean that the proclamation of the church can be *directly* equated with God's Word, however—it cannot, because the church is not God, and the words it speaks are human words. Yet church proclamation is nevertheless the place where God is revealed in the present. It addresses the human person not only as the words of the church but also as the Word of God, God's own revelation through the voice of Christ made effective and received by the power of the Holy Spirit. In brief, the proclamation of the church in its preaching and sacraments is the location where God chooses to take up human words and acts to speak his own Word so that he might be revealed to the church, and the church might be renewed. To understand this, one has to always keep in view that, for Barth, revelation is not properly thought of as information *about* God, but rather as God's own act of speaking in proclamation and self-revelation to the hearer. Think, for instance, of the difference between reading about a person and hearing the person speak directly to you. This is an analogy, of course, but it does illumine what Barth means by divine revelation as God's own act of speaking his Word.

Dogmatics is in this light the testing of the church's own proclamation (as human speech) by its subject matter, which is also its criterion and norm, the Word of God. This could, and may to some, appear hopelessly circular—and perhaps it would be, if the Word of God were nothing other than the church's own proclamation. For how can the church's speech be tested by itself? Yet a vicious circularity is in fact avoided because the subject matter of dogmatics is not only the church's own speech, which is in the foreground, but also the rich conception of the Word of God that stands in the background. In truth, the Word of God not only comes through the church's proclamation, but it is also first God's revelation in Christ and then the witness to this event in Holy Scripture. God's revelation in Christ as attested in Holy Scripture is thus the basis, source, and standard of the church's proclamation. For the church after Christ's ascension, Scripture is the place where Christ's voice is heard, and it serves as the origin from which the church's proclamation takes its rise and as the criterion and standard by which it is tested. And as the church proclaims the Word it has heard in Scripture, God himself speaks.

At this point it is important to note, however, that this relationship between God and the church is always predicated on grace. It is one that God freely establishes, not one necessary for God such that he is dependent upon it for his own life or the efficacy of his action. One of Barth's more controversial statements (and there are many) is his assertion that "God is not bound to the historical Church" (45). On the surface, such might seem to be making light of the importance of the church, but in fact this is a statement not of divine caprice but of divine freedom, and this freedom can only be understood as underwriting the fact that God's relation to the church is one of grace, not of necessity. Moreover, this freedom must be balanced by and juxtaposed with an account of divine faithfulness to the church that cannot be questioned. It is this faithfulness that entails that the visible church itself is the place where persons are "visibly awakened, separated and gathered by God" to faith and obedience in this new calling (48). The church is composed of those who are awakened and called by God so that they might proclaim the good news of God to the world. This is the peculiarity and particularity of the church's existence and of its speech. As Barth writes, "If the being of the Church, Jesus Christ as the acting person of God, sanctifies the being of man in the visible sphere of human occurrence as being in the Church, then He also sanctifies its talk as talk about God taking place in the Church" (49).

Proclamation as this paradoxical unity of God's revelation in his Word and the church's speech is the theme that Barth focuses upon in this paragraph. Yet not all speech in the church is proclamation, for the church's prayers and hymns and confessions and even its theology (which, he says, is really nothing other than "Church instruction of youth on a higher grade") are responses from humans to God (49–51).[1] Proclamation, rather, is God's

---

1. As Barth says in the original, "Sie ist kirchlicher Jugendunterricht auf höherer Stufe" ("It is youth instruction on a higher level") (*KD* I/1, 51).

Word addressed to the church in the present in the special acts of the church's preaching and sacraments. Talk in the church is proclamation when "it is directed to men with the definitive claim and expectation that it has to declare the Word of God to them" (51).[2] Barth defines proclamation as "human speech in and by which God Himself speaks like a king through the mouth of his herald, and which is meant to be heard and accepted as speech in and by which God Himself speaks, and therefore heard and accepted in faith as divine decision concerning life and death, as divine judgment and pardon, eternal Law and eternal Gospel both together" (52). Here again we see a twofold dialectical way of thinking and speaking: first, God's Word comes to the church through human words, and second, God's Word to humanity is one of both condemnation and justification, both held together in a necessary tension.

As already noted, proclamation comprises both preaching and sacrament, for these are the divinely appointed means by which God addresses the church (56). Proclamation is the taking up of human words and signs by God to be the medium for the communication of his Word. This is not guaranteed simply by their human enactment, as if these words or signs had an intrinsic, inalienable power. They are, rather, the site of human expectation—that God, here in their occurrence, will once again graciously address humanity. The church's performance of them is a "service of grace or means of grace," not grace itself (52). Human talk serves the Word of God, but real proclamation is brought about not by our intention or even by the perfection of preaching's form or content but rather by God's own action (53). Proclamation is an address of God to humanity and is the event in which God encounters us.

Once again, throughout this section Barth sets this emphasis upon proclamation over against what he sees as the mistaken conceptions of Protestant modernism on one hand and Roman Catholicism on the other. While he can be read simply for his constructive explanation of proclamation, this polemical context is, as noted above, unavoidable in order to understand his argument fully. He is perpetually setting forth his description of the Evangelical viewpoint over against these other two positions. In liberal Protestantism, proclamation is replaced by a kind of introspection, or, if the practice of preaching is maintained, by an understanding of preaching as the communication of the inner life of piety of the person preaching set forth in speech (60). In Roman Catholicism, proclamation is replaced by a sacramental system for the distribution of grace by the church at its own will and discretion and as a

---

2. Barth buttresses this point with appeals to 1 Thess. 2:13; 2 Cor. 2:17; and 1 Pet. 4:11. See *CD* I/1, 52.

permanent possession. If preaching is maintained, it is primarily "apologetic instruction and moral exhortation" (67).

For Barth, this Catholic tradition understands grace not as the relationship between the Word proclaimed and received in faith, but as the relationship between a divine being as cause and a creaturely being as effect (68–70). He writes, "It sees the presence of Jesus Christ in His Church, the mystical unity of the Head with the whole body, in the fact that under certain conditions there flows forth from Jesus Christ a steady and unbroken stream or influence of divine-human being on His people" (68). In this, he sees a connection between Protestant modernism and Roman Catholicism in that both presuppose a relation of God and humanity that is intrinsic and unbroken by sin, and thus a permanent possession and one not predicated on a special act of grace (68). He consistently opposes any such conception. Proclamation of the gospel of grace is, for him, as for the Reformers, "not a material connexion but a personal encounter" (70).

Talk about God and Church Proclamation (§3.1)

In confronting Barth's understanding of proclamation, we are left with a fundamental question that has plagued all who have wrestled with his thought: How are we to understand this highly dialectical relationship between God's Word, which is God's own divine self-communication, and the church's words and signs of proclamation in preaching and sacrament? How can this "human utterance" be said to be God's Word, so that Barth can say that as this utterance serves God's Word, "it is itself God's own Word," even as he refuses to straightforwardly collapse them (52)?[3] He provides an answer in a very short small-print section that simply states that the "is" in this statement must be understood along the lines of "the Christological doctrine of the two natures" (52).

This answer, often overlooked, is in fact a decisive and crucial move that will have long-standing repercussions throughout the CD. What Barth is stating is that the relationship between the Word that God speaks in the church's proclamation and the proclaimed words of the church must be understood along the lines of the relationship between the divine and the human natures of Christ (and, it seems, as these have been understood particularly in the patristic Chalcedonian definition that emphasized that these natures are

---

3. Of course, one way to resolve this tension *is* simply to collapse them. Yet Barth did not, and he did not precisely because he refused to collapse God into creation, or God's Word into human words, in a direct way. This dialectical tension of divine Word and human words will be a topic addressed further in later chapters.

"without division and separation" but also "without confusion or change"). It should be added and not missed that he sees this relation of the divine and human natures in the incarnation as a singular and unique reality that has no real analogy in the world. The hypostatic union in Jesus Christ is without parallel or rival. Yet, this union of the divine and the human in the hypostatic union also paradoxically and simultaneously serves as the singular and unique pattern by which the relationship between Christ and the church can be understood, as well as the pattern that Barth here evinces for understanding the relation of the divine Word and human words in proclamation.

It must be stated without equivocation at the outset that Barth in no way intends to say by this that the church's proclamation (or the church itself) is a kind of second incarnation. The incarnation is, in itself, without analogy (see *CD* IV/2, 59–60; cf. *CD* IV/1, 210). Nor is he in any way minimizing or relativizing the fact that the uniqueness of the union of the natures of Christ in the incarnation entails that this union cannot be compared to or itself grounded in any other more general relationship of God and world. The incarnation is not a member of a larger class of relations between God and humanity (including sacramental ones—as if the incarnation was simply the pinnacle, but still a member, of a larger class of "sacrament"). No, as he will consistently maintain throughout the *CD*, the incarnation stands without analogy to any other relationship between the Creator and the creature. There is no other union of God and humanity comparable to the hypostatic union, the singular and personal union of God and humanity in Jesus Christ.

Yet it must also be said that already here, in the first volume of the *CD*, Barth sets forth the incarnation as the ground, basis, and pattern for every other relationship between God and the world. In its incomparable uniqueness, it casts light on the formal arrangements of all other divine and human relations. What that means here is that God's Word that God himself speaks, and the human words of the church in its proclamation, are inextricably joined together, yet inalienably distinct, and with God's Word giving meaning and effectiveness to the human words in an irreversible relation. They are, in one sense, joined such that they are identical. Yet, in another sense, they can never be simplistically identified such that the church's speech can be straightforwardly equated with God's own, any more than Christ can be simplistically identified with the church such that the distinction between them is eradicated. God's speech and the church's speech in proclamation are *indirectly identical* (a phrase that will be of some great importance later in discussing related matters in the *CD*). In other words, and to follow the language of Chalcedon, God's Word and human words are in proclamation inseparably united and yet irrevocably distinct and not collapsed into each other, as well as irreversible in their meaning, effectiveness, and importance, with the divine Word establishing, calling forth, and making effective the human words spoken. This pattern is one that we will see often in Barth's thought, and it appears here for the first time in the CD and is set forth along these christological lines.[4]

It is important, once again, to notice that this pattern is first introduced to designate the relationship between God's speech and human speaking in proclamation, specifically, and the relationship between Christ and the church more generally. It is, moreover, not a foreign pattern that is superimposed upon Barth's thought; rather, he provides it as the means by which to understand this dialectical reality of divine and human speech that he sets forth. It arises from his material description of how God's Word and human words are related. So he can write, "If, then, human talk about God aims to be proclamation, this can only mean that it wills to serve the Word of God and thus to point to its prior utterance by God Himself" (52). The description for this human word and task, then, is that of witness, and this will remain his favored description for the assigned commission of the church in relation to God and to Christ.

Because proclamation as God's revelation is something that God, rather than the human speaker, brings about, the church cannot make the mistake of insisting that the only place that God is able to speak is within its walls. The church with its proclamation cannot be "master of the Word, nor try to regard the Word as confined within its own borders" (54). Yet this, too, does not point to a divine capriciousness or undercut the particularity of God's revelation and the unique witness of the church itself. Even though God is free to speak outside the walls of the church, Christians are nevertheless bound to attend where God has chosen to speak and continues to speak, which is within the proclamation of the church in its preaching and sacraments.

Barth therefore rejects two mistaken positions. The first would maintain that God is bound to the church such that he is not free to speak and act elsewhere (Barth makes his point against this position by reminding his readers that God can speak and work through such irregular and non-Israelite figures as Melchizedek, Balaam, and Cyrus) (54). The second would interpret this divine freedom to mean that God has not in fact freely committed himself to specific places for his communication and commanded the church to attend

---

4. For a developed account of the logic of these relations between Christ and the church in the CD, see Kimlyn J. Bender, *Karl Barth's Christological Ecclesiology* (Burlington, VT: Ashgate, 2005). George Hunsinger has designated the relation between God and humanity in the form here witnessed as a "Chalcedonian pattern." See Hunsinger, *How to Read Karl Barth: The Shape of His Theology* (Oxford: Oxford University Press, 1991), 85–86, 185–88, 201–18.

to them. With an eye on both of these mistaken positions, Barth writes, "If the question what God can do forces theology to be humble, the question what is commanded of us forces it to concrete obedience" (55). He then continues on with what may be one of the most famous passages in all of the *CD*: "God may speak to us through Russian Communism, a flute concerto, a blossoming shrub, or a dead dog. We do well to listen to Him if He really does. But, unless we regard ourselves as the prophets and founders of a new Church, we cannot say that we are commissioned to pass on what we have heard as independent proclamation" (55).

The church therefore must attend to its "specially commissioned proclamation." Once again, this exists in the two forms of preaching and sacrament, and we learn from Scripture that these are the forms of proclamation that Christ has commanded and entrusted to his Church (57). It should be evident that Barth, following the Reformers, places singular importance upon the preaching of the Word of God. It is the locus of God's address to his people, and the sacrament as a sign must follow and be interpreted by preaching. It is preaching accompanied by the sacrament, and not the sacrament of the altar itself, that stands at the center of the church's worship (70).[5] Moreover, preaching is not only the locus of the divine address in the present but also the means by which all other hearing of the Word in other places might be recognized (58; see also 217). Barth is often misunderstood to say that God is heard only in the church. But it is perhaps more accurate to say that one can identify God's voice outside of the church only if one has truly heard him within it, for it is the church's proclamation wherein God is known, and it is the standard for all other hearing, for proclamation arises from hearing the Word of God in Holy Scripture as the testimony to the Word of God that has appeared to us in Jesus Christ (see 58). It is in Jesus Christ that God is present and revealed to us. He alone is the Word of God; all other truths are true only insofar as they reflect the truth he is and reveals.

Once we understand Barth's position here on the question of proclamation, we can understand a whole range of his thought. What he now says of proclamation he will reiterate in his reflection upon Scripture—namely, that Scripture is not the only good book but is the standard by which all good books are judged.[6] And he will later in time extend this judgment to

5. "Hence not the sacrament alone nor preaching alone, nor yet, to speak meticulously, preaching and the sacrament in double track, but preaching with the sacrament, with the visible act that confirms human speech as God's act, is the constitutive element, the perspicuous centre of the Church's life" (*CD* I/1, 70).

6. Barth made this point already in *The Göttingen Dogmatics: Instruction in the Christian Religion*, vol. 1, ed. Hannelotte Reiffen, trans. Geoffrey Bromiley (Grand Rapids: Eerdmans, 1991), 213.

understand divine disclosures in the larger world. He does not outright deny that such may exist, but he insists that such are true only if they truly reveal Jesus Christ, who is God's revelation in history (see *CD* IV/3.2, 38–165). The church's proclamation is therefore at the center of a circle of human speech, and at the center of this center is the Word of God, the "Lord of the Church" (57). In order to understand Barth's thought, one has to grasp his concept of this Word of God that comes to us in this threefold way—that is, as Jesus Christ as attested in Scripture and as announced in the church's proclamation. This will be the topic of our next chapter.

Dogmatics and Church Proclamation (§3.2)

We can now turn to consider what preaching truly is. Preaching cannot simply be the reading of Scripture or even a summary of its contents. Rather, the preacher "must be ready to make the promise given to the Church intelligible" in his or her own words to people in their own time (59). Insofar as this is so, the human words of the preacher are taken up by God to speak his own Word in the present (72–73). And because proclamation is an exercise in faithfulness to God, the manner of its practice must center on this fact. Barth is adamant in his insistence that proclamation neither fall prey to nor serve any form of ethnic, national, political, scientific, aesthetic, social, or economic program or ideology (72). The church's primary task is not to be relevant but to be faithful: "The Church should fear God and not fear the world" (73). Relevance to culture can never be the defining mark of the church's proclamation. If it is, the church cannot help but sacrifice its own particular commission to proclaim the gospel. This truth stands behind the fact that Barth values dogmatics more highly than apologetics, for the first attends to the Word of God as attested in Scripture and seeks to understand it, whereas the second takes the questions of the world and the contemporary context as its starting point and moves from there to find pertinent answers in the Christian message. For Barth, this entails that the church takes the questions of the world more seriously than it takes the gospel. For those with some knowledge of the theological programs of this period, it should not be surprising that he singles out Emil Brunner and Paul Tillich in these opening paragraphs as those who approach the theological task in a way that contrasts to his own and make apologetics central to the theological task.

Barth turns the discussion at the end once more to the need for a healthy dogmatics to serve the church in testing the truth and faithfulness of its speech and action in light of the revelation it has received. To focus on other things— "liturgical reform or social work or Christian education or the ordering of its relation to state and society or ecumenical understanding"—without focusing upon this theological responsibility that is the "obvious centre of its life" can only mean that the church will not truly be reformed (76). To ignore dogmatics for these seemingly more practical tasks would in fact reveal a preoccupation with things at the periphery instead of at the center of the church's existence and would betray in effect a false center. In contrast, attention to the church's proclamation of the gospel is a task dedicated to the center of the church's existence rather than to things along the periphery of its life. By this point, it should be appreciated how dominant Barth's imagery of center and periphery, accompanied by that of nestled concentric circles, truly is. This imagery will be found throughout the CD to articulate a variety of relationships, though the inner and absolute center of God's revelation in Christ will remain consistent throughout. The ability to navigate this language of center and periphery, along with the imagery of concentric circles, is a necessary skill in order to come to grips with Barth's theology. In every case, it is the center that gives meaning and significance to the periphery, rather than the reverse.

Barth's argument for the necessary role of theology for the health and vitality of the church is striking, particularly for its contrast to our age's constant emphasis upon immediate practical application and effectiveness. He will have none of this, but neither will he settle for theology as a task for academic or spiritual elites. Indeed, theology can never be practiced just by professional theologians nor exchanged for more practical concerns, and he rejects the pragmatism of those who reject the need for theological reflection: "As though these practical men were not continually preaching and speaking and writing, and were not genuinely questioned as to the rightness of their activity in this regard!" (76). He reminds those who think that the crises of our time require a special turn to practical affairs that the church is and has always been engaged in an emergency situation simply because of the nature of its proclamation. The pressing nature of the situation does not, however, excuse a neglect of self-examination. Theological work must be done, or the church will suffer for it. In the end, however, only the church can take responsibility for its practice and insist that it occur: "The whole Church must seriously want a serious theology if it is to have a serious theology" (77).

In closing, proclamation and dogmatics are related though distinct. Each is needed, though proclamation gives meaning to dogmatics and not the other way around: "Proclamation is required as the execution of God's command to the Church. Dogmatics is required because proclamation is a fallible human work" (82). Proclamation is primary, dogmatics secondary. Dogmatics serves the task of proclamation; it does not have an intrinsic value apart from this prior one. Likewise, theologians do not enjoy some kind of privileged position within the church with regard to faith or knowledge (83–86). The task of dogmatics as theological reflection is a necessary one, and while there is an appropriate and even necessary place for school (academic) dogmatics and vocational theologians, the dogmatic task is one that every church, and indeed every church member, is called to take up with quiet determination.

COMMENTARY

Preaching and Proclamation in the Life of the Church

Barth wrote an essay in 1922 titled "The Need and Promise of Christian Proclamation," in which he asked why persons go to church. The answer, he concluded, was that the great anticipation of people who come to church is not first and foremost to be instructed, entertained, or even edified. They come, rather, in great anticipation of an event. This anticipation is of nothing less than that God himself will speak to his people in the address of the preacher. Barth concludes, "They passionately desire to have *the* Word spoken to them, *the* Word, which promises grace in *judgment*, life in *death*, the beyond in the *here and now*."[7]

Preaching, for Barth, thus takes a central place in the church's worship. If worship must entail more than our speech and songs and prayers to God but must be marked by God's own address to us, and if the sermon is finally about God speaking rather than solely the speech of a preacher, it should not be surprising that for Barth the invocation of God's presence and power before preaching is no longer a liturgical placeholder but a matter of spiritual life and death. If God himself does not speak, Barth insists, all is lost. Preaching may continue, but proclamation, true proclamation, will not. That God is *free* in this event to speak (or not to speak) should lead to a preacher's deep humility, knowing that, while our effort and work are called for, the ultimate effectiveness of a sermon is out of our hands, a matter purely dependent in the end upon God's grace. That God is *faithful* to his church in keeping his promise to speak should lead to a preacher's deep confidence that overcomes all personal inadequacies, exhaustion, and even the personal despair that questions whether what is proclaimed might reach not only the stiff-necked and stubborn people sitting in the pews but also the preacher's own stiff and numb heart. It is the dialectical relation of God's freedom and faithfulness that underwrites, calls forth, and requires both the humility and the confidence of the preacher, and, in turn, of every Christian.

7. *WGT,* 111; see 101–29.

To regain such humility and such confidence is required of the church in every age. If Barth is to be believed, there is no activity from our side by which we can proceed on such a path but that of prayer that God might send his Spirit and speak to us again. The hope of preaching lies in God, not in method (and certainly not in clever irony), though our human efforts do have their place, as we are invited and indeed commanded to speak, and to speak as well as we might. Yet such efforts, while required, cannot be the focus of our hope, for our hope can rest solely in God. Believing that this is so, however, is a challenge for churches shaped by pragmatism, practicality, and the belief that there is no problem that a new method or turn of phrase cannot solve. Yet such things do not bring dead bones to life again (Ezek. 37). Only God's Spirit can do this. It is this reality and conviction, not any particular skill or talent, that stands at the beginning of true Christian proclamation.

Preaching and the Question of Human Religiosity

Barth's emphasis that God's free and faithful presence and address to the church occur in preaching is a challenge to an age that seeks to find the divine voice increasingly in the depths of the self. That God's Word comes to us from outside ourselves, as the Reformation firmly held, and that it comes to us in the Word incarnate in Christ, written in Scripture, and proclaimed in the preaching of the church is a perspective that stands increasingly in conflict with an age in which not only those outside the church but also those within it think of God's voice as preeminently found within the deep recesses of the conscience, of feeling, and of emotion—in short, of "the heart."

Apart from the fact that the discernment of God's voice from our own is quite difficult when we think we hear God's voice in our own heart's timbre, it should be apparent with but a little introspection that the danger of self-deception is enormous. Barth was educated in theologies of feeling and conscience as the seat of divine revelation. He renounced them when he witnessed such self-deception on scales large and small, not least in the support of his former teachers for the German declaration of war on England that commenced the First World War. These theologies also, in the end, failed him as a preacher.

Here in the CD we see his emphasis upon the Word of God as God's revelation, and in this chapter the particular emphasis is upon the proclamation of the gospel as the means by which it comes to us in the present. It is in this external divine address that we might be convicted as well as comforted and confronted with a Word that we ourselves know we did not conjure from the deep recesses of our inner souls. Yet ours is an age in which the scandal of the gospel and its radical particularity truly is a scandal. Barth, like Paul, would not find this at all surprising. He stands in a long line, going to back to Paul and Jeremiah before him, that had a clear-headed appreciation for our human proclivities for self-deception, proclivities rightfully revealed and challenged by a gospel that comes to us from outside ourselves: "The heart is deceitful above all things, and desperately wicked: who can know it?" (Jer. 17:9 KJV). Such words run against the grain of this age and the ages.

Dogmatic Theology and the Ministry of the Church

We have already examined dogmatic reflection upon the speech of the church as a form of testing required for the church's faithfulness, but it is useful to see how Barth believes that such reflection is both intrinsically necessary and also of great practical import. He refuses to cordon off the everyday and practical areas of the church from such inspection. As but one example, he believes that dogmatic theology should be a resource not only for the instruction of the church and the question of its doctrine but also for the worship of the church and the question of its liturgy. As he notes, "It is a strange thing that when there are revisions of books of order and hymn-books in the Evangelical churches every possible authority is usually consulted as a standard but not dogmatic science. The results naturally correspond" (81).

Barth's dry comment may seem unduly harsh, but he does raise the matter of whether those involved in writing the church's music, which is perhaps more formative than any instructional curriculum for the faith and convictions of both young and old, should be theologically trained themselves. It is therefore a real question in turn whether the liturgical and worship arts should include more intentional, disciplined, and extensive instruction in dogmatics. As he writes, such dogmatic questions must be pressed with necessity upon those who plan the church's worship: "Again, the dogmatic question has to be put to the practical theologian too, because even the most external question regarding the conduct of worship to-day can be given very different answers according to the insight into what is proper proclamation and what is not" (81).

This could perhaps be extended to the practical field of social action and social work as well. Significant terms such as "inclusivity," "justice," and "freedom" become platitudes that are often appropriated by the church without careful attention to how they require redefinition in light of the gospel when taken over from culture. For example, cultural conceptions of freedom are quite different from those presented in Scripture, where the world's freedom is a form of slavery, and slavery to Christ is true freedom (Rom. 6:15–23). Simple appeals to "inclusion" need to wrestle with Jesus's frequent warnings of tragic exclusion where there will be "weeping and gnashing of teeth" (Matt. 8:12; 13:42, 50; 22:13; 24:51; 25:30; Luke 13:28). An equally serious consideration is whether some concepts are concordant with the gospel at all. For instance, it might be helpful to consider how our quick appeals to justice might be chastened in light of such careful theological reflection. Diogenes Allen provides one such example of a chastened view:

> Our demand that social and personal wrongs be put right requires those of us who are guilty of wrongdoing to suffer for our misdeeds. Today many of us claim to be victims because we are dissatisfied with our social status, our income, or our lot in life, but even if we are victims of serious injustice, we probably are guilty of committing injustice as well. If we are genuinely committed to justice, we ought to wish that the consequences of all the wrong we have done should fall solely on ourselves, not on others. That would be just. It does not take much reflection for us to realize that we do not really want true justice, and indeed we fear it.[8]

Such is not, of course, a renunciation of a search for justice, nor should it undercut its true importance and the church's commitment to it. This is, however, a reminder that for the church such terms cannot be separated from the questions of Christ's atonement, reconciliation, and redemption, and that the church may have to take the depth of human tragedy with much more seriousness. In the end, theological reflection must always stand vigilant against those who might claim that the daily bread that persons require is of no ultimate importance (1 John 3:17; cf. James 2:14–16), but also remind others that "one does not live by bread alone" (Matt. 4:4). It may also need to remind us that we cannot, in the end, save ourselves.

QUESTIONS FOR REFLECTION

- How are we to think of the church's proclamation and preaching? What particular challenges and questions does Barth's description of proclamation raise for the understanding and practice of preaching?
- What should be the relationship between the church's doctrinal instruction and its worship? Between dogmatics and worship arts? How might they inform each other? Should theology intentionally inform

8. Diogenes Allen, *Spiritual Theology: The Theology of Yesterday for Spiritual Help Today* (Lanham, MD: Cowley Publications, 1997), 45.

the worship of the church, including the composition of its hymnody, worship music, and prayers? If so, how might this be done?

- What might Barth mean when he states, "If the social work of the Church as such were to try to be proclamation, it could only become propaganda, and not very worthy propaganda at that" (50)?

- What can be made of Barth's quotation of August Vilmar of Marburg: "According as dogmatics removes itself from the sphere of the Church, it no longer serves salvation but panders to the intellectual vanity of the individual" (80)?

- Barth states that "the normal and central *factum* on which dogmatics focuses will always be quite simply the Church's Sunday sermon of yesterday and to-morrow" (81). Do you agree? If dogmatics is to be concerned with the Sunday sermon, what will this reflection look like in practice?

- How might thinking of dogmatics as "Church instruction of youth on a higher grade" (51) change one's perception of what it is and why it is necessary? How might it change our conceptions of youth ministry?

✝ 4 ✝

The Threefold Form
of the Word of God

CD §4

Barth moves from the question of the church's practice of proclamation to a paragraph that addresses the basis and content of that proclamation, "the presupposition which makes proclamation proclamation and therewith makes the Church the Church" (88). Here he puts forth his famous conception of the Word of God in threefold form. While this conception of the Word is not entirely new and unique to Barth, he develops it in a way that marks a new achievement in theology.

The Word of God in Its Threefold Form (§4)

When Christians hear the phrase "The Word of God," they most often think of the Bible. While Barth does not reject such thinking, his conception of the Word of God is both more complex and richer. First, the Word of God exists as the Word who is God himself, the One who has taken up flesh in Jesus Christ. This is what Barth refers to as the Word of God revealed. We can think here of the famous prologue of the Gospel of John, where the Word is with God, and is God, and takes up flesh to dwell among us (John 1:1, 14).

In the first and proper sense, then, the Word of God is God present with us in Jesus Christ.

Yet the Word also exists in written and spoken forms. Holy Scripture as the canon, the collected witness of the prophets and apostles, is the written Word of God, the prophetic and apostolic testimony to Jesus Christ, God's personal revelation. Lastly, as discussed in the previous chapter, the church's proclamation of the gospel in preaching accompanied by the sacraments is the third form of God's Word. As the church proclaims what it has heard in Holy Scripture, the Word of God is spoken when God takes up the human words of the preacher to proclaim God's own Word of revelation. The Word of God exists in the unity of this threefold form of the one Word—revealed, written, and proclaimed. When Barth addresses these three realities, he takes them up in the opposite order that I have given, moving from the outer circle of preaching to Holy Scripture as its basis, and from Scripture to its center found in the revelation of God in Jesus Christ to which it attests. We can examine these in turn.

The Word of God Preached (§4.1)

Barth begins by taking up the Word of God preached and extends the theme of the prior paragraph (§3). Proclamation is the center of the church's life and is the locus of the event in which the church encounters God and ever again becomes the church (88). Here we come upon the event character of the church and what some have called Barth's *actualism*. This idea is another of the more difficult and controversial in his thought. In short, he presents the church in the first volume of the *CD* not primarily as a static institution that exists through time but as a reality that comes into existence ever anew as it hears the Word of God in proclamation: "Thus the Church is not constantly or continuously the Church of Jesus Christ. It is this in the event of the Word of God being spoken to it and believed by it" (261). Both revelation and the church in his thought here have the character of a divinely actualized happening, an event without historical duration. The church exists by means of a fresh encounter of God and his people that in fact constitutes them as such. In this way, Barth thinks of both revelation and the church not as static entities (as dogmas, in the first, or as an institution, in the case of the second), but as dynamic events that occur anew as God speaks and in turn calls the church ever again into reality.

How the church is both an event and a historical reality that endures through time has been a question that many have posed regarding Barth's ecclesiology. At this point, he is emphasizing the freedom of God and the event character of the church; later he will place more emphasis upon God's faithfulness and the historical duration of the church. Yet while he would find more sophisticated and balanced ways of addressing this issue as the *CD* progressed, he never abandoned his conviction that the church was the product of an event of divine grace before it was a historical entity enduring through time. Indeed, it was divine event that gave reality to its historical existence.[1]

Turning again to the theme of proclamation as God's dynamic and gracious speech to humanity, Barth outlines four aspects of proclamation, setting forth the Word of God as the commission, theme, judgment, and event of proclamation (see 89–95). As noted earlier, he holds the relation between the divine act of proclamation and the human act as one characterized by a unity-in-distinction. In no way is the human act of proclamation set aside in real proclamation. He is, however, quite uninterested in spelling out the manner of their interaction and rather straightforwardly juxtaposes them, describing each in turn. God's act of proclamation and the human act of preaching are not competitive but neither are they best thought of as cooperative, as if each stood on the same plane, equally and similarly efficacious and necessary for revelation to occur. In contrast, human proclamation serves the divine Word as its creature and annexed servant, but one with its own integrity and proper agency. The word that Barth prefers for this human action over those of replacement or cooperation is in fact the language of service (94–95). God takes up the creaturely work in service to his own "without depriving the human element of its freedom, its earthly substance, its humanity, without obliterating the human subject, or making its activity a purely mechanical event" (94).

The following passage demonstrates and illustrates the consistent manner in which Barth thinks of all divine and human interaction, whether that between God's speech and that of the preacher, or God's Word that gives rise to and speaks through the humanly written words of Scripture, or God's action and human action enacted in all particular joined activities. Here he takes up the question of proclamation as both the event of God's self-revelation and the act of a human preacher. Having emphasized that human preaching remains a creaturely reality, he continues:

1. For related discussions of the event character of revelation and the church, see David Guretzki, *An Explorer's Guide to Karl Barth* (Downers Grove, IL: IVP Academic, 2016), 74–76. For a more technical and developed discussion of Barth's actualism, see George Hunsinger, *How to Read Karl Barth: The Shape of His Theology* (Oxford: Oxford University Press, 1991), 30–32. For the tensions in Barth's understanding of the church as both event and historical reality, see Kimlyn J. Bender, *Karl Barth's Christological Ecclesiology* (Burlington, VT: Ashgate, 2005), 152–58, 168–74.

On the other hand, through the new robe of righteousness thrown over it [i.e., human proclamation], even in its earthly character it becomes a new event, the event of God's own speaking in the sphere of earthly events, the event of the authoritative vicariate of Jesus Christ. Real proclamation as this new event, in which the event of human talk is not set aside by God but exalted, is the Word of God. Again, then, real proclamation means the Word of God preached. Only now is it clear that "preached" belongs to the predicate, and to what degree. The Word of God preached means in this fourth and innermost circle man's talk about God in which and through which God speaks about Himself. (95)

In this section again we see the highly dialectical way in which God's Word, God's own speaking, and the words of the church in proclamation are related. If there is an inspiration and predecessor that stands behind Barth's discussion of divine and human speech, it is Luther. Luther's fingerprints (and references to his works) are everywhere in this section (and particularly in the small-print discussions). It would be difficult to overestimate Luther's influence here. In fact, Barth sets the Evangelical dialectical position of divine and human action in which each is preserved but not directly equated over against a Roman Catholic position that he believes has not maintained this strict demarcation and irreversibility. In contrast, its position is one in which the rule of Christ simply comes to be "equated with that of the Church" (97–99).

Here we come across, in a small-print section, a central concern for Barth: How can the lordship of Christ not only within his church but also over and against it be maintained if his authority is subsumed into a historical succession of bishops, into the office of the priest himself by virtue of his ordination, or into the irreformable dogmas of the church that claim to bear the authority of revelation themselves? While these realities might be seen as a sacralization and thus elevation of the creature, Barth contends that these lose the distinction between divinity and humanity and more specifically sacrifice the demarcation between Christ as Lord and the church as his servant. In so doing, they do not in fact exalt humanity but instead extinguish and dehumanize the creature and render the church's human activity not only impersonal but also no longer a *human* action of service (97–98). As he writes, "According to the Evangelical view one can no longer speak of an action of Christ's person in and over the Church when human authorities in the Church are deprived of their humanity in the way described and when Christ's own decisions are swallowed up in the decisions of these authorities" (98). He therefore goes on to reject the Catholic doctrines of apostolic succession, of an indelible character imposed upon a priest in ordination, and of irreformable dogmas. Christ is not bound to the church, but the church is bound to him (following the logic discussed in our prior chapter). To think otherwise is to sacrifice divine freedom, and to sacrifice freedom is ultimately to sacrifice grace. Just as stunning is Barth's contention that this leads to a sacrifice of the integrity of the creature as creature and a loss of the full humanity of Christ's servants.

The Word of God Written (§4.2)

Barth turns next to the Word of God in its written form, Holy Scripture. Here again he rejects a permanent relation to God grounded in the self or even in the church such that this relation can be taken for granted and only needs to be brought again to mind. He argues against any kind of immanent awareness of God discovered through self-reflection and introspection, and he can even be quite critical of Augustine on this front (99–101). Instead, Barth understands God's relation to us as based on his free action of grace in a revelation that comes to us from outside ourselves, found and heard in Scripture. This insistence that God's Word to us comes not from inside ourselves or from the voice of the church's teaching office is at the heart, he contends, of the Evangelical and Reformation tradition. The church cannot turn to itself for revelation, but must return to its

> self-transcendent being, to Jesus Christ as the heavenly Head to whom it, the earthly body, is attached as such, but in relation to whom it is also distinct as such, who has the Church within Himself but whom the Church does not have within itself, between whom and it there is no reversible or alternating relation, just as the relation between master and servant is not reversible. He is immanent in it only as He is transcendent to it. This is the fact which makes the recollection of God's past revelation different from reflection on its own timeless ground of being. It has pleased God to be its God in another way than that of pure immanence. (100–101)

Akin to those passages given attention in our previous chapter, this is one of singular importance for understanding Barth's project. At the heart of his concern is the relation of God to the world, but more specifically, the relation of Christ and the church, and he will remain consistently faithful to the understanding given here in the first volume of the CD (see, e.g., CD IV/2, 59–60). Here again he outlines the grammar and logic of that relationship: it is one in which Christ is united to his church, but one in which this unity is grounded in and qualified by an inalienable distinction between Christ and the church, where Christ remains the head and the church his body. It is, as he states, "no reversible or alternating relation," and the church remains ever dependent upon its Lord, who provides its existence and being.

The key question becomes, then: How is the lordship of Christ over his church exercised, enacted, and expressed in the present, in this time of Christ's ascension and apparent absence? Barth's answer is not that the authority of Christ has now been passed on to the church as one might think of a baton handed off in a relay race. He does not think of the church as the replacement, or even the extension, of Christ's ministry on earth, but rather as a particular witness to Christ's unique and perfect ministry. Moreover, he does not think that Christ is now absent from the world with the church as his successor. Christ remains present to the church, and the place where his unique voice is heard is in Holy Scripture. The church does not look within itself (either individually or corporately) for Christ's voice but rather looks to Scripture as a witness from the past that stands not only within but also over and even against it, and thus serves as the criterion of its proclamation in the present. It is the "bolt" that shuts the door on any kind of understanding of revelation as immanent within the individual person or the church itself.

Jesus Christ therefore enacts his lordship over the church as he continues to speak through the testimonies of the prophets and the apostles now in written form in Holy Scripture. Scripture in turn stands over against the proclamation of the church as its norm and therefore as the guarantor that Christ's voice and that of the church cannot be confused or equated. In short, Scripture is that which prevents Christ from being understood as subsumed into the church, for it is the witness and testimony of Jesus Christ himself, the means of his own self-announcement. Scripture and proclamation are thus united as the Word of God "under a single genus, Scripture as the commencement and present-day preaching as the continuation of one and the same event" (102). The contemporary preacher therefore stands in a long line stretching back through Paul to Jeremiah. Nevertheless, in this relation Scripture takes supremacy over later proclamation, for the latter finds its content and basis only as it is grounded upon and takes its rise from the former, even as it is tested against it (102). For Barth, this lies at the root of the unparalleled and unique authority that Scripture takes in the life of the church.

In this section of the CD under review, the centrality of Scripture for Barth becomes abundantly clear. Scripture is the basis for the church's teaching precisely because Scripture stands not only within the church but also over it as the voice of the first divinely appointed witnesses. It shares the authority of the prophets and apostles, and moreover, as the written witness of these witnesses, it serves as the voice of Christ for the church in the present. Functioning in this way, its written character is not incidental but indeed necessary to the nature of its witness, for as a written text it cannot simply be dissolved into later oral tradition but instead retains its integrity against the changes that are unavoidable for unwritten sources over time (105–7). This is what it means to say that Scripture is the canon of the church. Canon means "rule" or "standard," and Scripture serves as such a rule and standard for the church's own proclamation and teaching because in Scripture the church hears the voice of Christ today. Scripture is, moreover, the canon as it retains its own integrity and independence over against later traditions simply due to its written character, though it is the Spirit who speaks uniquely through it that is its ultimate source of power and conviction. Historical apostolic succession thus means for Barth, as it did for the Reformers, not a line of persons installed in an office but the line of those who proclaim the gospel as attested in Holy Scripture through time (see 100–111).

This unique role of Scripture as source of revelation and norm for the church's life and teaching is what is called the *Scripture principle*. Throughout this section Barth once again sets this Evangelical understanding over against the modern turn toward finding truth within the self—whether in reason (as in the philosopher Descartes), or in feeling (as in Schleiermacher and the romantic tradition), or in the moral conscience (as in Barth's teacher Wilhelm Herrmann, drawing upon the legacy of Immanuel Kant). He also sets this Evangelical understanding against the Roman Catholic conception that the voice of revelation is found within the church's own voice in the church's magisterium (i.e., the teaching office of the pope with the bishops), or in the infallible dogmas that it propounds. He consistently opposes mechanical and depersonalized understandings of apostolic succession, just as he opposes depersonalized understandings of revelation that see it only in terms of dogmatic propositions (see 270). His opposition to such conceptions stems not only from his fear that in them the Lord of the church becomes confused with and subsumed into the church; he is also keenly aware that, as earlier noted, such conceptions in the end leave the church alone with itself (104, 105; cf., e.g., 147).

This theme of the church "being left alone with itself" is an important one and runs throughout the first volume of the *CD*. It is, for Barth, the unavoidable result of misconstruing the proper relation between Christ and the church. The immediate danger is that the church no longer hears the voice of Christ but simply, in Barth's frequently used phrase, is left having a conversation with itself. The even more insidious danger is that the church no longer hears the voice of its Shepherd but begins to listen, even if at first innocently, to the voice of a stranger—and such can lead to particularly troubling things. It should never be forgotten that Barth writes *CD* I/1 (= *KD* I/1, 1932) and *CD* I/2 (= *KD* I/2, 1938) in the period in which National Socialism was on the rise and putting pressure upon the churches in Germany (Hitler was appointed chancellor in 1933). So when he speaks against natural theology and insists that we know God and understand ourselves as sinners only in the light of God's revelation, and that this revelation comes only through God's Word, this context was ever in view. In listening only to their own voice, he notes, humans never came to this realization of their own depravity, not "on the Nile or the Euphrates or amid the forests of Germany," but such only occurs when God's Word confronts humanity and reveals its sinfulness (*CD* I/2, 92). This reference to Germany should not be overlooked.

Scripture thus serves as the locus of both Christ's conviction and comfort of his church, the place where both God's judgment and God's mercy are revealed and proclaimed. Yet Barth is not so naïve as to think that Scripture cannot be misread, misinterpreted, and misused. The solution to this problem, however, is not to subsume its interpretation under a single infallible teaching office or a scientific academic discipline of historical criticism. These moves would simply cover the problem with another, setting up "a norm over the norm" whereby Scripture's authority was domesticated by an official interpretation either of a church or of an academic guild (106). In contrast to these solutions, he argues that the "exegesis of the Bible should rather be left open on all sides, not for the sake of free thought, as Liberalism would demand, but for the sake of a free Bible. Here as everywhere the defense against possible violence to the text must be left to the text itself" (106). Scripture therefore must not only be its own best interpreter but also its own best defender.

Scripture, then, serves in its freedom as the voice of Christ in the present to the church, and as a written text stands over against the church as an external Word. It serves not only as the criterion by which all church proclamation and teaching are tested but also as the source from which all such proclamation arises and from which it draws. As Barth writes, "The prophetic and apostolic word is the word, witness, proclamation and preaching of Jesus Christ" (107). This is, in the end, what makes the canon the canon: "Thus Scripture imposes itself in virtue of this its content" (108). Even Scripture, however, points beyond itself to that which it attests, the revelation of God given to us in Jesus Christ. This distinction between God's Word as revelation and the words of the writers of Holy Scripture that attest to that Word lies at the heart of one of the most contentious aspects of Barth's thought. So this question merits some calm attention here, though an extensive discussion will be reserved for the chapter on Scripture below.

There are two mistakes that can be made as one begins to consider Barth's understanding of Scripture. One is to think that he simply relativizes the Bible and separates God's Word from the words of the Bible. He does not. Not only does he hold these closely together; he also states that Scripture is itself a form of the Word of God. Yet it is nevertheless true that Barth does not *directly* identify God's Word with the words on the page. That God speaks and that Paul speaks cannot simply be collapsed into one thing (113). Yet it is nevertheless true that God speaks through these words of Paul. Scripture must therefore be seen both as God's Word and as the words of Paul and the other witnesses, but Barth refuses a flat identification of the two.

What we have here, then, is a view of revelation in which the act of God speaking to us cannot be separated from, but also cannot simply be collapsed into, the witnesses who testify to God's Word. Once again we are confronted with a highly dialectical understanding of God's Word and its relation to the Bible. For some, Barth's view may be forever considered deficient. His view of the Bible as God's Word may not please those in the liberal tradition who see Scripture as solely a book recording past religious experiences or providing broad moral guidance but who do not think of it as possessing absolute divine authority for the church and its life. Nor may it placate those in more conservative circles who equate Scripture and revelation without remainder and see the Bible itself as simply a book of God's own words with little or no room for recognizing its human component and little patience for Barth's dialectical distinctions. Barth does not fit into either of these camps.

In contrast to them, Barth sets the Bible within a larger field of divine activity, an activity in which God calls forth witnesses that in turn serve God's own purposes of self-communication. In other words, he sees Scripture within the entire scope of God's revelatory and redemptive history for the sake of humanity, and in this way Scripture is neither neglected nor relativized but contextualized. God's personal revelation in Jesus Christ becomes the primary focus of God's activity, with Scripture serving this larger purpose. As such, revelation "engenders the Bible that attests it," just as "Jesus Christ has called the Old and New Testaments into existence" (115). But Jesus Christ and the Bible are not simply the same thing, and while both are God's Word, they are distinguished. Jesus Christ does not exist for the sake of Scripture, but Scripture exists as a witness and testimony to Jesus Christ. Scripture serves the Word that took on flesh. This is at the center of what Barth means when he refers to prophets and apostles of Scripture as *witnesses*—a witness points beyond himself to one to whom he attests. The authority of the biblical witnesses resides not within an intrinsic genius or brilliance that they possess, nor even in the quality of "inspiredness" of the texts that they produce, but rather in the authority of the One who has called them and commissioned them to speak (112–13). This stands behind Barth's refusal to see a "direct identification" between revelation and the Bible (113). The Bible is not an end in itself—it serves God's revelation in Jesus Christ in both OT and NT testimonies.

As with proclamation earlier discussed, so here also with Barth's understanding of Scripture we are confronted with the event character of God's revelation. Just as proclamation must ever and again become God's Word, so also must Scripture: "The Bible is God's Word to the extent that God causes it to be His Word, to the extent that He speaks through it" (109). Yet this must be carefully understood, for even though Barth can speak of Scripture becoming God's Word, he can also later in the *CD* state that the Bible can become the Word of God because it *is* the Word of God, a fact often overlooked (*CD* I/2, 537; cf. 498). Moreover, the confession that the Bible is the Word of God is an act of faith, but it is not faith that makes Scripture what it is—Scripture is the Word apart from our faith in it or recognition of its truth. To say that the Bible becomes the Word of God is not a description "of our experience of the Bible" (110). All criticisms of Barth that state that for him the reader decides if the Bible is the Word of God get him exactly wrong here. What he has in mind is certainly not a view of Scripture in which it is the Word because the reader makes it so. Rather, the opposite is true. Scripture reveals God to the reader precisely because God takes up the words on the page to be the means by which God addresses the reader. This act of revelation is an act of "divine decision"—it is not a human one (117). As he will later write, "The conclusion that because I believe, and because for me as a believer the Bible is the Word of God, therefore and thus far it is God's Word, destroys the divinity of the Word of God, since it is no longer understood as the Word that stands over the Church and is directed to it" (262). To say the Bible "is" God's Word "refers to its being in this becoming" (110).

Barth's conception of revelation is on this account highly dynamic. The revelation of God that comes to us in proclamation and Scripture is not a static state of affairs or simply the passing on of information about God or other things. Rather, revelation is the personal encounter with God that takes place according to the "freedom of God's grace," which is "the basis and boundary, the presupposition and proviso, of the statements according to which the Bible and proclamation are the Word of God" (117). To understand Barth correctly is to appreciate that God's freedom from his witnesses must be seen over against God's faithfulness to them. This faithfulness is demonstrated in his binding himself freely to the testimony of these witnesses such that their testimony serves as the place where he might be sought and where he gives himself to be found. In short: "Revelation is itself the divine decision which is taken in the Bible and proclamation, which makes use of them, which thus confirms, ratifies and fulfills them. It is itself the Word of God which the

Bible and proclamation are as they become it" (118).[2] And they become such because in their relation to revelation they are such.

The Word of God Revealed (§4.3)

In order to understand revelation in this section, one must think of "the "being of the church," Jesus Christ, not only as God's revelation in past history but also as the living Christ who continues to speak through his Spirit to the church as it hears Scripture anew in its reading and who addresses the church in its preaching. As Barth can write, "Revelation in fact does not differ from the person of Jesus Christ nor from the reconciliation accomplished in Him. To say revelation is to say 'The Word became flesh'" (119). Notice that revelation can be spoken of in terms of both Christ's person and his work.

Barth's understanding of the threefold form of the one Word of God is nothing if not dynamic and seeks to portray the disruptive and revolutionary event of God's revelation in Jesus Christ. This revelation is not only a past event but also a present and ever-new one as the church is confronted with Christ in Scripture and proclamation. Scripture and proclamation thus bear witness to past revelation and promise a future revelation to be given again (see 111, 117). This revelation of God in Christ, the object of the church's remembrance and hope, provides the crux of Scripture's purpose and meaning: "To understand the Bible from beginning to end, from verse to verse, is to understand how everything in it relates to this as its invisible-visible centre" (116). Scripture stands both as a witness to this past revelation and as a promise of future revelation.

While all three elements of the threefold Word of God are God's Word, Barth nevertheless places God's personal revelation in Christ in a superior position because it undergirds and underwrites the others that arise from it. Scripture and the proclamation of the church point beyond themselves to God's revelation, and as they do so, they become God's Word, God's personal address. But God's revelation in Christ *is* God's Word present in human form, Jesus Christ, whereas Scripture and proclamation attest him. For this reason, revelation is "originally and directly what the Bible and Church proclamation are derivatively and indirectly, i.e., God's Word" (117).

2. For the event character of Scripture in which it both *becomes* the Word of God and *is* the Word of God, see Bruce McCormack, "The Being of Holy Scripture Is in Becoming: Karl Barth in Conversation with American Evangelical Criticism," in *Evangelicals and Scripture: Tradition, Authority and Hermeneutics*, ed. Vincent Bacote, Laura C. Miguélez, and Dennis L. Okholm (Downers Grove, IL: InterVarsity, 2004), 55–75.

The Unity of the Word of God (§4.4)

The one Word of God thus exists in this threefold form, and as such, it is, Barth avers, the only true analogy to the triunity of God (121). We will have to examine his doctrine of the Trinity below, but it should be noted that the doctrine of the Trinity runs through the doctrine of revelation here given as the answer to the question of the identity of the God that is revealed through this threefold Word. The doctrines of revelation and of the Trinity are the spelling out and elucidation of convictions that the church holds in its relationship to Christ as the being of the church, and thus to God. They are the presuppositions that lie behind the reality and thus possibility of the existence of this relationship and of the church's very being.

We might turn to look at one more aspect of revelation a bit more closely. Just as with proclamation and Scripture, Barth thinks of the action of God in the action of this man Jesus in highly dialectical terms. In one regard, the revelation of God and the person of Jesus are the same event. Yet here, too, Barth does not simply collapse the Creator into the creature, or directly identify the revelation of God in Christ with the humanity of Jesus. To put this in more traditional terms: he does not forgo the distinction of the divine and human natures of Christ. Each retains its integrity and distinction in the unity of God and humanity, of Word and flesh, in Jesus Christ.

Barth's way of relating revelation and the person of Jesus along these lines has strong echoes of Luther and Kierkegaard, as well as of earlier patristic authors. In the act of self-giving, God reveals himself precisely by taking on a creaturely form and reveals himself in and through the concealment of this form. Revelation therefore takes place, paradoxically, in this very act of hiddenness. As Barth states, revelation is "the unveiling of what is veiled" (118). This dialectic of *unveiling and veiling* in which God is revealed by taking up a created medium and is thus both hidden and revealed through this form (human flesh, in the case of Christ, or the words of the text or the preacher, in the case of Scripture and of proclamation) is central to Barth's understanding of revelation and has direct import upon his doctrine of the Trinity. This conception of veiling and unveiling will be further examined in the next chapter.

Barth ends this paragraph by summing up the unity of these three forms of the Word of God. Jesus Christ, as he is attested in Holy Scripture and proclaimed in the preaching of the church, is the Word of God, and as the latter two serve in this attestation and proclamation, they, too, can rightly be called the Word of God. We have no access to the first apart from the mediation of the second and the third—in other words, we know Christ only through Scripture and the proclamation of the church (120–21). This is an important aspect of what Barth means when he states that we know revelation indirectly, and this is his very circumscribed and idiosyncratic understanding of mediation—revelation comes to us firstly through the witness of Scripture and secondly through the church, just as the divine and eternal Word is known only as mediated by the flesh taken up by the Word in the incarnation.

Again, Barth's conception here, though original and unique in its vigorous articulation, is in fact not new.[3] What is presented is, in Barth's view, the developed dogmatic articulation of the convictions of the Reformation and the following Evangelical tradition in its Reformed and Lutheran tributaries. Indeed, if there is a preeminent figure who stands behind Barth's thought throughout his elucidation of the doctrine of the Word of God, it is Luther. What Luther and the Reformers had that the later Protestant orthodox did not have, Barth maintained, was a deep understanding of the "mutual relationships of the three forms" of God's Word in which they were not simply collapsed into the others even in their unity (124). Following the Reformation, the richness of this understanding of the Word of God eventually collapsed into a doctrine of Scripture divorced from these rich trinitarian and christological connections such that the intimate relation of Christ and Scripture and proclamation was lost. In time, more and more focus came to be placed upon the text of Scripture alone as the Word of God. For Barth, to become a Reformation theologian was to recover this rich and multifaceted conception of the Word of God as Jesus Christ attested in Scripture and proclaimed by the church.

COMMENTARY

The Word of God, Christology, Scripture, and Proclamation

Barth's explication of the Word of God recovers its basis in Christology and sets it within God's grand revelatory action from the calling of Abraham, to the Word of God that came to the prophets of old, to the Word that became incarnate in the person of Jesus of Nazareth, to the Word that comes through

---

3. It must also be admitted that Barth would later question whether he would present this threefold form of God's Word in the same way (see CD IV/3.1, 114). For an insightful discussion of the development of Barth's thought in this regard, as well as an engagement with critics of Barth's conception of the Word of God, see Thomas C. Currie, *The Only Sacrament Left to Us: The Threefold Word of God in the Theology and Ecclesiology of Karl Barth* (Eugene, OR: Pickwick, 2015).

the written words of Scripture, to today, when the proclaimed words of the preacher and of the church at large pronounce the Word of the gospel to the world. This view of the Word of God reminds the church that it is not first a religion of a book but rather the fellowship of a person, Jesus Christ, the Son of God, the Word who reveals the Father through the power of the Spirit.

It was a loss of this truth that marked, for Barth, a turn from the vibrancy of the Reformers and their view of the Word of God and Scripture to that of their immediate progeny. The problem of later Protestant orthodoxy (i.e., scholasticism) was, he asserted, that it depersonalized revelation in relation to Scripture such that the texts themselves and the information they provided were directly identified with revelation. Insofar as this occurred, they ceased to serve as witnesses to something (Someone) beyond themselves. The Bible was then most often described and characterized in terms of an impersonal spiritual quality ("inspired-ness") rather than explicated in terms of its role as personal witness to the person of God in Christ. It may be too simple to say that the supremacy of Christ was replaced by a focus upon the supremacy of a text, and yet this seems to be the trajectory of Barth's argument in which revelation became depersonalized and the inner testimony of the Holy Spirit as the basis for Scripture's efficacy and truth (so central to Calvin) gave way to an emphasis upon the qualities of the text itself as the foundation of its authority.

Barth is therefore quite ambivalent about the resulting Protestant orthodox theory of inspiration, which for him "implies a freezing, as it were, of the relation between Scripture and revelation" (124). Correspondingly, he bemoans the growing neglect of the third form of the Word of God—proclamation—in Protestant orthodoxy. When it was addressed, it turned away from the objectivity of God's work in the Word of proclamation and focused more and more upon the "knowledge, faith, sanctification and blessedness of the individual" (124). In this sense, Barth traces modern individualism not only back to pietism but behind it, finding its origin ironically in Protestant orthodoxy with its subsumption of revelation into the Bible and its emphasis upon subjectivity in proclamation. In effect, the three-part dynamic and dialectical form of the Word of God now collapsed into the text of Scripture itself. It is not surprising, then, that the doctrine of Scripture began exclusively to take on the role of prolegomena in theology, and Scripture became separated and abstracted from the entire range of God's revelation and salvific activity in Israel, the incarnation, the witness of the apostles, and the proclamation of the church today. This was, no doubt, meant to heighten Scripture's stature, but Barth considers it as a hidden if unintended demotion, a freezing and depersonalizing of revelation, an exchange of a dynamic divine address that occurs through Scripture for an inspired yet static biblical text (see 121–24).

This is Barth's estimation of why Protestant orthodoxy itself, in the end, failed. It was predicated on a human discernment of qualities of a text, and in time, such qualities could be questioned and argued, leading to the secularization of the text in modernity. The irony is that it was the elevation of these qualities in orthodoxy that led to the secularization of the Bible and its loss of stature. As Barth writes,

> Responsibility for the disaster must be borne, not by the philosophy of the world, which had become critical, but by the theology of the Church which had become too uncritical, which no longer understood itself at the centre. For all our great respect for the work done by orthodoxy, and for all our understanding of the ultimate intentions of this work, our task to-day must be the different one of re-adopting Luther's concepts and taking proclamation seriously again as the work of the Church in and through which God is to be served, and not man, and God is to speak. On that basis we must then try to understand once again in what sense first the Bible, and even before that revelation, is really the Word of God. (124)

Barth's account of this history and its significance will perhaps remain contested. Yet what cannot be questioned is that, at least in North America, the first response almost universally given to the question "What is the first thing you think of when you hear the phrase 'Word of God'?" is "The Bible." This answer, while understandable, perhaps merits some reflection in light of Barth's discussion of God's Word as God's revelation to us. That "the Word was with God" (John 1:1–2; cf. 1:14) before a single word was written on a page or spoken by human breath should lead us to question how the Bible has become so isolated from the entire field of God's revelatory and reconciliatory activity. It has led to understandings of the Bible that have very little to do with God's personal revelation in Christ and that have separated Scripture from its active proclamation by the church. In short, it has led to a privatization of the Bible and the exaltation of personal reflection that may take its rise from, but in truth stands over, the Bible.

There are other results of this view of Scripture as well. It has led to a focus upon the Bible as a talisman superficially revered but often left unread. It has also led to battles for the Bible that have little to do with the Bible's own understanding of itself and certainly of its authors' own explicit concerns (for instance, see John 20:30–31). A healthy rediscovery of the Bible might begin not by esteeming it in its splendid isolation or attempting to elaborate the superiority of its intrinsic qualities (factual, moral, literary, or aesthetic), but by rightly honoring it by appreciating it in its residence within the entire range of God's act of revelation that was spoken long ago "at sundry times and in divers manners" through prophets but found its final and perfect fulfillment in the appearance of the Son, Jesus of Nazareth, who is the very Word of God (Heb. 1:1–2 KJV). Scripture is, in both its Old and New Covenants, a testimony to him. And its authority is not lessened, but is grounded, in this fact.

To come at this distinction of Christ and Scripture perhaps more bluntly, we might ask why the church worships Jesus Christ but does not worship the Bible if both are (rightly) called the Word of God. That is perhaps another starting point to consider Barth's distinction of revelation and the Bible, and it may cause those more critical of his dialectical views to at least ponder the real issues lying behind his dialectical distinctions and doctrine of Scripture.

The Divine Word of God and the Human Words of Scripture

One of the abiding difficulties of Barth's understanding of Scripture is the strong distinction he draws between the Word of God and the words of the prophets and apostles that are recorded in the Bible. Certainly with it he displays an intention to take both divine and human origins of the Bible with seriousness, but it must also be appreciated that this distinction rests not simply upon a commitment to give the human authorship of the Bible its due but to respect the more fundamental distinction between the Creator and the creature such that the divine Word of God is not collapsed into the human words of the biblical authors. He sees this not as a denigration of Scripture but as a necessary mark of its proper esteem. Just as it is a misunderstanding to consider Peter as a religious genius rather than a witness to something beyond himself (a distinction that Barth owes to Kierkegaard [see 112]), so it is a misunderstanding to attribute divinity to the biblical text itself rather than to the Lord who speaks through the words of these very human witnesses.

To collapse the Word and the words is, then, not to honor Scripture but rather to dishonor both the Lord of Scripture and the human authors of its constituent books. That God uses human persons as his heralds retains both God's freedom and singular holiness, and the faithfulness he exhibits in deigning to honor human persons with a sanctified yet still very human task. To exalt the authors of Scripture as somehow more than human is in effect to undercut the assurance that God can use us, in all of our frailty, fickleness, imperfection, and even fallenness, for his purposes in our time. That Peter is more like than unlike me in his person is the assurance that I, too, can be used by God as an "earthen vessel" (2 Cor. 4:7). Alternatively, that he is unlike me in his unique calling as an apostolic witness to Christ and to his resurrection is the ground for why Scripture stands not beside my own subjective deliberations (or the deliberations of the church) but presides over them (1 Cor. 12:28; Eph. 2:20).

In short, both "conservative" and "liberal" conceptions of Scripture (and these labels are used with great reluctance) will not serve us well if they either dehumanize the Bible or fail to recognize and confess its singular divine authority. These matters will be visited again in chapter 9 below. At any rate, Barth's careful distinction of the Word and the words has left those who follow him with the difficult task of understanding his alternate confession of their unity, as well as of conceiving how the words on the page not only are the site of an ongoing event of God's speech and personal address that miraculously occurs ever anew but also serve as ongoing, binding instructions for the church in their stability and constant availability as a written text enduring through time.[4] The question of the event character of revelation and the historical duration of its medium is thus seen in the question of Scripture as the divine Word that comes through human words, just as it is also reflected in the question of the church as an event occurring ever anew by a miraculous work of the Spirit, and as a historical institution existing through time.

Finally, the way to get at the real tensions in Barth's doctrine of Scripture is not to judge whether his view adequately accounts for the Bible's divine or human origin and nature, or to endlessly debate whether he thinks that Scripture is the Word of God or only "contains" the Word of God as a witness to it, but rather to understand his position as one that comes down on one side of a tension between seeing Scripture as the locus of God's free personal address and seeing the Bible as an enduring text that itself is the product and result of the will and work of God. Perhaps one way to get at this way of thinking is to say that Barth prioritizes divine illumination over divine inspiration, but that is not truly accurate, for he does have a doctrine of inspiration, though not a "mechanical" one focused on the resultant qualities of the text. Another way to approach this issue may be to say that he prioritizes God's use of the text to address the hearer in the present over the production of the text itself in the past, but this, too, does not get to the essence of his argument. Closer to the truth is to say that Barth is more concerned with elaborating the freedom of God and the miraculous character of revelation as an event as it comes to us through Scripture than he is with elaborating the character of the Bible itself as the result of a past divine work.

4. For a recent significant explication of Scripture sympathetic to Barth's account yet attempting to further answer such questions, see John Webster, *Holy Scripture: A Dogmatic Sketch* (Cambridge: Cambridge University Press, 2003).

Perhaps a charitable reading of both Barth and some of his evangelical crit-ics is to say that he presents a biblical actualism that stresses divine freedom and the *event* of illumination and revelation, Scripture *becoming* the Word of God, whereas many evangelicals emphasize that Scripture *is and remains* the Word of God, a view that stresses the inspiration of Scripture with regard to the *enduring result* of the Spirit's work, though both at their best include the other view as well. In brief, Scripture is understood as a being in *becoming*, and a *being* in becoming, respectively.[5] At least, such questions may be worth exploring from such a perspective. They certainly point more closely to what is truly at stake in Barth's doctrine of Scripture, rather than simply dismiss-ing him as thinking of Scripture as becoming the Word of God through our subjectivity and faith. Such a view is best laid to rest.[6]

QUESTIONS FOR REFLECTION

- How might the nature and relationship of the revealed, written, and proclaimed Word of God be understood, articulated, and in turn taught to a group of church members?
- Why do Christians worship Jesus Christ but not the Bible if both are "the Word of God"?
- Why does Barth think that the uniqueness of Scripture (as ensconced in the Scripture principle and in the Reformation conviction of *sola Scriptura*) is necessary for preserving a proper distinction of Jesus Christ

5. Again, this phrase is borrowed from McCormack, "The Being of Holy Scripture," 55.

6. For important recent discussions of Barth and Scripture with an eye toward evangelical concerns, see McCormack, "The Being of Holy Scripture"; Kevin Vanhoozer, "A Person of the Book? Barth on Biblical Authority and Interpretation," in *Karl Barth and Evangelical Theology: Convergences and Divergences*, ed. Sung Wook Chung (Grand Rapids: Baker Academic; Milton Keynes: Paternoster, 2006), 26–59; and John D. Morrison, "Barth, Barthians, and Evangelicals: Reassessing the Question of the Relation of Holy Scripture and the Word of God," *Trinity Journal* 25 (2004): 187–213. The most insightful and balanced critical evaluation of Barth's doctrine of Scripture from the evangelical side in recent years is that of Mark D. Thompson, "Witness to the Word: On Barth's Doctrine of Scripture," in *Engaging with Barth: Contem-porary Evangelical Critiques*, ed. David Gibson and Daniel Strange (New York: T&T Clark, 2008), 168–97; see also Mark Galli, *Karl Barth: An Introductory Biography for Evangelicals* (Grand Rapids: Eerdmans, 2017), 108–16. Barth's own thought on Scripture was in fact not static and underwent development. For a rich though dense account of his development as the *CD* progressed, see Katherine Sonderegger, "The Doctrine of Inspiration and the Reliability of Scripture," in *Thy Word Is Truth: Barth on Scripture*, ed. George Hunsinger (Grand Rapids: Eerdmans: 2012), 20–28.

and the church? How does his conception of the threefold form of the Word of God correspond to how this relation of Christ and church is to be understood?

- Why does Barth oppose both a single authoritative teaching office in the church with an infallible interpretation of Scripture and a single interpretation of Scripture as ascertained by historical-critical science? What does he mean when he speaks of the "freedom" of the Bible with regard to both? What is his response to the obvious question that Scripture might be misread without such authoritative interpretations?

- Why is the fact that Scripture is a *written* witness so central to Barth's understanding of its role as canon and norm for the church? Why could the apostolic witness not simply be an oral tradition (rather than a written one)? How might his answer be related and illustrated by a discussion of the unique characteristics of the "telephone game," where persons seated in a circle whisper the same information from one to the other around the circle and in the end compare the original information as again articulated out loud by the first person in the circle with that recounted out loud by the last recipient of it?

- Without attempting to cover over remaining differences between Catholic and Protestant traditions, is there a possibility for constructive ecumenical and not only polemical conversation when one compares the following two statements, the first Protestant, the second Roman Catholic?

  "The preaching of the Word of God is the Word of God." (*The Second Helvetic Confession*, chap. 1)

  "When the sacred scriptures are read in the church, God himself speaks to his people, and Christ, present in his word, proclaims the gospel." (*General Instruction of the Roman Missal*, no. 29)

- What does it mean to say that Christ is present to the church through his Word?

- Why is Barth so concerned about the depersonalization of revelation and the dehumanization of the creature in some conceptions of apostolic succession and ministry as he understands them?

- What does Barth mean when he speaks of the church being "left alone with itself" or "alone in conversation with itself"? Is this a danger for the church today?

✝ 5 ✝

The Nature and Knowability of the Word of God

CD §§5–7

This chapter will examine the final three paragraphs of chapter 1 of the *CD*. In §5 Barth addresses the nature of the Word of God as God's speech, action, and mystery. In §6 he takes up the question of how the Word of God comes to be known by human persons, as well as the matter of the personal appropriation of revelation in the faith and experience of the Christian. He frames this reception in terms of the divine activity that makes this faith and experience possible, addressing the human act of reception only within this larger context, and always emphasizing the reality of revelation over the question of its possibility. In the final paragraph (§7) he revisits and recapitulates themes regarding the nature and task of dogmatics presented in the first two paragraphs of the introduction and brings the first chapter on the Word of God to a close.

The Nature of the Word of God (§5)

In §5, "The Nature of the Word of God," Barth continues his discussion of the previous section and maintains that all true knowledge of God comes to us by means of the Word of God in revelation, Scripture, and proclamation.

That God is revealed in this particular way precludes arguments for a natural theology founded on a general revelation that exists apart from God's special revelation in Jesus Christ.

The Question of the Nature of the Word of God (§5.1)

Barth begins with a quite technical historical discussion in small print that need not overly detain us, but it reveals that he consistently rejects any attempt to base theology upon human experience or an intrinsic capacity or element of human nature. In brief, he opposes any theological program that begins with humanity abstracted from God's revelation and as an independent avenue of theological exploration. The first to carry out such a program systematically, in his estimation, was Schleiermacher. The next, with "malicious intent," was Ludwig Feuerbach (128). Schleiermacher made the religious person and "feeling" the theme of theology's task, whereas Feuerbach argued that God was simply a projection of human experience. Barth sees these, regardless of their intentions, as linked, the first leading inevitably to the claims of the second, theology giving way entirely in time to anthropology. When we begin to think about God by thinking about humanity, he contends, we end up simply with humanity and God as a projection of it.

Barth therefore sees Schleiermacher's turn to the human subject in theology as insidious. Schleiermacher attempted to begin with human experience for apologetic reasons (in his *Speeches on Religion*), trying to find a universal basis for human religion in human self-awareness and feeling. Barth finds successors to this way of thinking in figures as diverse as Kierkegaard, his own teacher Herrmann, and his contemporaries Friedrich Gogarten and Rudolf Bultmann. He thinks that this road can only lead in the end to atheism, for God is portrayed as a postulate of human existence and therefore can only finally be seen as an invention of humanity. Whether Barth is or is not entirely fair to each of the figures he references, certainly he is on to something here with his criticisms of grounding theology in anthropology, particularly when one realizes that not only Feuerbach but also Karl Marx and Sigmund Freud would later say in essence the same thing: religion is a human phenomenon that when stripped of its veneer of transcendence reveals that God is an invention of humanity.

In his rejection of the move from anthropology to theology, from human experience of any kind to a knowledge of God, we see a very important conviction and pattern of Barth's thought: knowledge of God can only come from God to humanity and cannot begin with reflection upon human nature, life, experience, or culture. As he bluntly states, "Knowledge in this circle is irreversible" (131). He concludes, "Thus to understand God from man is either an impossibility or something one can do only in the form of Christology and not of anthropology (not even a Christology translated into anthropology). There is a way from Christology to anthropology, but there is no way from anthropology to Christology" (131). He would never abandon this conviction in its pure form, regardless of his later theological developments resulting from his growing appreciation of the incarnation as revealing "the humanity of God."[1]

Another way to approach this theme is to recognize that Barth prioritizes the reality of the Word of God over the possibility of knowing the Word, or, stated differently, he prioritizes divine ontology (God's being) over human epistemology (human knowing). Just as God is sovereign and supreme over humanity in his existence, so also is he supreme and sovereign over humanity in the knowledge that he grants humanity of himself. It is the reality of God that provides the means by which God is known. God is only known, Barth contends, by God and God's action alone. This is what makes knowledge of God an act of God's grace. It can never be the result of a human (epistemological) achievement.

The Word of God as the Speech of God (§5.2)

In the second subsection of this paragraph Barth takes up the fact that God's Word is his speech, and he addresses three themes under this heading. It may be helpful to discuss these briefly in turn. First, this speech of God is to be characterized as *spiritual*, even as it takes place as God takes up physical things as the means of his revelation (i.e., the voice of a preacher, the words written in the biblical texts, the flesh of Christ). Moreover, God addresses us as persons of reason, and addresses us in a rational way (133–36). Contrary to some mischaracterizations of Barth's thought, he construes the Word not as an irrational mystery but as a mystery that nevertheless transcends our reason. It is a Word that addresses us and engages our intellect, calling for an understanding that comes by faith as well as for obedience.

Second, the Word is also *personal*, for it is the revelation of God himself, and not the revelation simply of information, concepts, or ideas about God. The Word of God is God himself: "God's revelation is Jesus Christ, the Son of God" (137; cf. 119, 153). Revelation therefore cannot be identified, as it often is in both Roman Catholic conceptions of dogma and in Protestant orthodox understandings of the Bible, as "a fixed sum of revealed propositions

---

1. See Karl Barth, "The Humanity of God," in *The Humanity of God*, trans. John N. Thomas (Richmond: John Knox, 1960), 37–68.

which can be systematized like the sections of a corpus of law" (137). Barth refuses, however, to play this personal character over against its verbal, or cognitive, character. The person of Jesus Christ is revealed to us through the verbal witness of Scripture and the proclamation of the church (138). This conviction is central to Barth's conception that God's revelation comes to us in an indirect (i.e., mediated) way. He is adamant that revelation can never simply be equated with a system of doctrine that, once we have mastered it, makes the act of God's speaking to us superfluous or unnecessary, even if it is the doctrine found in the biblical text. He opposes all attempts to think of revelation as something we can gain control over or possess in some way (139). It is, rather, the event of God's pronouncement that both judges and reconciles us and that is nothing less than God's promise to be with the human person (136–39; see also 141–43).

Finally, the Word of God is *purposive*, directed toward us and toward our salvation. God's revelation therefore has a goal that is nothing less than the world's redemption. Even though God's act of revelation thereby includes us, this does not imply, Barth contends, that we or the world are necessary for God to be God. God is God apart from the existence of the world, and Barth adamantly affirms God's freedom in this subsection (139–40). Nor is God's address simply a general one; rather, "God always has something specific to say to each man, something that applies to him and to him alone" (140). Here the particularity and the event character of Barth's understanding of revelation are in full view. Indeed, revelation is an event just because it is a particular address, and it is a particular address just as it is an event. This is a form of his particularism and actualism.[2]

The Speech of God as the Act of God (§5.3)

Barth next turns to discuss the speech of God as God's act, for in God's speaking God is also acting for our salvation such that these two cannot be separated. Here again we see how revelation and salvation are inextricably joined and united in Barth's theology. For God to speak and for God to act are the same thing: "The Word of God is itself the act of God" (143). He addresses the fact that God's act occurs differently in different times: first, as the time of "the direct, original speech of God Himself in His revelation"— that is, in the time of Jesus Christ in his earthly ministry; then in the time of the prophets and apostles whose witness takes written form in the canon of Scripture; and finally in the time of the church with its proclamation of what

---

2. See George Hunsinger, *How to Read Karl Barth: The Shape of His Theology* (Oxford: Oxford University Press, 1991), 30–35.

it has heard in Scripture. It is clear that the threefold form of God's Word determines Barth's understanding of the speech and act of God in these times.

This is a particularly difficult subsection, examining the theme of the Word of God's contemporaneity (i.e., Christ's living presence to us by means of Scripture and proclamation such that he is not simply a figure of the past but is present to us as a living Lord, even as we are now made present to him) as well as the other related and no less complex themes of the Word's sovereignty and character as a divine decision (149–56 and 157–62, respectively). This subsection is, moreover, a very important one. In this segment the irreversible and qualitative distinction between Christ and the church is mirrored now in the irreversible and qualitative distinction between revelation and Scripture on one side and history and the church's tradition on the other. Whereas Barth had earlier distinguished revelation and Scripture, he now treats them as a unity set over against the history and tradition of the church, which are themselves united as a second term in an equation. In short, he sets Scripture over against tradition in an irreversible relation.

Barth holds that should Scripture instead be seen as the earliest form of the church's testimony, yet of the same type as all later testimony, then the distinction between Scripture and later church tradition would be a quantitative, rather than qualitative, one. This view would, in effect, entail "incorporating Scripture and revelation into the life of humanity" as Scripture would be subsumed under the larger category of tradition (147). Contrary to such a conception, he insists that the testimony of the prophets and apostles found in Scripture is not simply the first in time but is the first in status, and is in fact unique and unrivaled. The difference between the testimony of the original prophets and apostles as God's chosen witnesses to revelation, and the later testimony of the church in its tradition, is a qualitative, and not solely temporal, difference. Scripture, as the authoritative testimony of the prophets and apostles, is thus on an entirely different plane from all later church tradition. Scripture is not merely the first testimony of the church but is the standard of all later testimony. It does not so much stand within a line of tradition as it stands over it, not only coming first in time but also existing without peer in the order of authority, for it shares in the very authority of God.

In addition to this point about the nature of Scripture, Barth also makes a hermeneutical one. He argues that God's Word comes to us not solely by means of historical study or our interpretive efforts but rather is dependent upon God's own act. He makes this point in the most striking way: "When God's Word is heard and proclaimed, something takes place that for all our hermeneutical skill cannot be brought about by hermeneutical skill" (148). This means that we do not come to know revelation as an object of historical investigation or interpretation, but rather Christ himself speaks to us as Lord through Scripture by the Spirit. Christ establishes our relation to him; it is not our historical study that establishes his relation to us (148). This rightful understanding of Christ and Scripture is thus crucial for Barth, for it grounds, qualifies, and is tied up with Christ's relation to his church. As he writes, "The Word of Scripture in its very different time and with its very different temporal content as compared with the Word of revelation is now put in its proper position. It is called the Word of the prophets and apostles, and as such, as witness of Christ and in subordination to the Word of Christ, it also speaks the Word of Christ" (148).

In brief, Barth here is addressing the question of how Christ is present to the church in this time of his ascended lordship rather than that of his earthly ministry with the disciples, and how this lordship is in fact exercised, a further unfolding of implications from earlier discussions of the Word of God and Scripture. It is in this time of the ascension that the canon, composed of the testimony of the prophets and apostles who serve as the unique witnesses to Jesus Christ, takes on particular significance. Here again we see a unity and yet differentiation between the three forms of the Word, and also a direction of revelation and authority flowing from one to the other: "Three times there is a saying of the Word of God through human lips. But only twice, in the biblical witnesses and us, is there first a letting of it be said to us, and only once, in our case, an indirect letting of it be said to us mediated through the Bible" (145). As he eloquently states in a later section, "Jesus Christ Himself lives in the message of His witnesses, lives in the proclamation of His Church on the basis of this message, strides forward as the Lord of grace and judgment to meet the existence of the hearer of the Word" (206).

Once again we see that the primary relationship in question is that between Christ and the church, the Lord with his earthly body. That Christ is active and present in his revelation through Scripture and the church's proclamation is a mark of "the sovereignty of God's Word in the Church," and the rightful understanding of this sovereignty is what characterizes "the Reformation view of God and the Church" (150–51).

The Speech of God as the Mystery of God (§5.4)

The last subsection addresses the speech of God as the mystery of God under the themes of its secularity (165–74), one-sidedness (174–81), and spirituality (182–86). Here Barth reiterates that in the end we can know and speak of God's Word only because God himself speaks (163). He is again adamant in warning of the danger of the Word's objectification—that is, the treating of the Word as if it were an object that we possessed and that was at our disposal and under our control (164). The sovereign, personal, active, and dynamic character of revelation is again front and center.

What Barth means by secularity perhaps needs some elaboration. To speak of the secularity of God's revelation has nothing to do with secularization as spoken of today. Instead, it signifies the manner in which God takes up a created medium as the means by which such revelation is accomplished. This created medium, however, hides God even as it serves the ultimate goal of revealing God. This is another way of speaking of the veiling and unveiling of God previously discussed. As he puts this paradoxical point in a small-print section, "Mystery is the concealment of God in which He meets us precisely when He unveils Himself to us, because He will not and cannot unveil Himself except by veiling Himself" (165).

This veil is a created reality that Barth refers to as revelation's "secularity" (165). Secularity entails that God's revelation comes to us in historical realities that, on their own and on the surface, appear simply to be events and facts of history—the church is a sociological and communal reality in time; preaching is a verbal human address; the Bible records the history of an ancient Near Eastern people; and Jesus Christ himself is a historical figure of the first century AD. God's revelation is hidden in and behind all of these historical realities, realities that are themselves participants not only in a created but also a fallen order that stands in contradiction to God (166; cf. 167). Barth writes, "The veil is thick. We do not have the Word of God otherwise than in the mystery of its secularity" (165). This is true even for the flesh of Christ, for Jesus appears in history as a poor Nazarene carpenter. Moreover, because it is God who veils himself, he alone can unveil (i.e., reveal) himself to us (168–69). The historical and created realities God takes up for his self-communication have no intrinsic ability to bring this about, nor can they as veils be pierced from our side to discern the divine behind them, either by reason or by any other intrinsic capacity or intuitive insight. Revelation would not be an act of divine grace if this were so (169). Revelation means incarnation, and incarnation means "entry into this secularity," which means hiddenness (168). Barth concludes,

> Thus in all applications of the proposition that proclamation, Scripture or revelation is God's Word we must have regard to the fact that this is true only in this twofold indirectness. In the speaking and receiving of God's Word what is involved is not just an act of God generally, and not just an act of God in creaturely reality as such, but an act of God in the reality which contradicts God, which conceals Him, and in which His revelation is not just

His act but His miraculous act, the tearing of an untearably thick veil, i.e., His mystery. (168)

This talk of veiling and unveiling is Barth at his most dialectical.[3] It constitutes what he calls the "one-sidedness" of the mystery of God's revelation (174–81). God's self-giving always occurs in and through secular, or created, realities—through spoken and written words, through church-enacted signs of baptism and the Lord's Supper, or through the human life of Jesus. But God cannot be simply equated with these created mediums. This distinction lies at the heart of Barth's dialectic between God the Creator and the creature, and specifically of that between the divine Son, who speaks to his church through the Spirit, and the human and created witnesses and words through which this is done. In revelation there must always be two things spoken, and not only one, for there is no synthesis of God and the creature, of the divine and the human: "Are we taking the secularity and hiddenness of God's Word seriously if we think we can say the one thing in one word instead of two?" (173).[4] Stated differently: the form of revelation (the created reality) and the content of revelation (God himself present in power to speak and thus to act) are united yet ever distinguished: "The secular form without the divine content is not the Word of God and the divine content without the secular form is also not the Word of God" (175). Barth draws on the language of "paradox" and of "indirect communication" in contrast to "direct communication" to speak of this, and in this sense he reveals his ongoing debt to Kierkegaard and, more distantly, to Luther (165–66, 167).

Indeed, behind the language of "veiling and unveiling" lies Luther's distinction between a theology of glory and a theology of the cross, a theme that runs throughout, and has great import within, this section. The first, a theology of glory, is a direct revelation of God directly perceived, a revelation devoid of paradox, tension, crisis, or embarrassment. The second, a theology of the cross, is indirect, wherein God is revealed precisely through the hiddenness and scandal of the cross and of suffering, God's mercy and grace revealed not in spite of but through his judgment. Luther, of course, stated that while our natural desire was for a theology of glory, in actuality God's chosen means of revelation was through a cross. Barth has applied this hiddenness of God in the suffering of Jesus on the cross to the incarnation in its entirety. In the appearance of Jesus of Nazareth, God is hidden in a veil of tears and suffering

---

3. For the various dialectical pairings summarized at the end of this section, see *CD* I/1, 179.

4. For an early argument along these lines that provides the very terms for the present discussion, see Karl Barth, "Church and Theology (1925)," in *Theology and Church: Shorter Writings 1920–1928*, trans. Louise Pettibone Smith (New York: Harper & Row, 1962), 286–306, esp. 301.

and human flesh, and it is only by God's work through the Spirit that the veil of suffering and humanity is made transparent to us through faith so that we can perceive and come to know the God who is hidden behind it. Barth brings all of these themes together when he states that "in the unveiling of God there is to be seen and acknowledged His veiling, i.e., the close relation between the content and the form, the glory and the humility, the goodness and the severity of the Word of God" (178; see also 179).

At the end of this section Barth concludes by examining the theme of the speech of God as the mystery of God in relation to the Holy Spirit (182–86). He here turns from objective revelation (God in his revelation through secularity that takes place outside of the human person) to subjective revelation (the work of God in the human person whereby God's objective revelation comes to be perceived, known, acknowledged, and confessed by faith). If God's revelation is objective in the action of Christ (and in turn in Scripture and the proclamation of the gospel), this work within the believer is the action of the Holy Spirit. In effect, both the act of revelation whereby God speaks, and the act whereby we hear God's Word and believe it, are actions of God himself: "The Lord of speech is also the Lord of our hearing. The Lord who gives the Word is also the Lord who gives faith" (182). Not only is it God who reveals himself, but also it is God who makes the perception of this revelation possible, allowing us to see beyond the form to the content of revelation, all the while "not giving Himself in either case into our hands but keeping us in His hands" (176). In keeping with his focus upon God's initiative and human receptivity, Barth focuses not on our act of faith but rather upon the work of the Holy Spirit that makes faith possible. Here too he turns faith from an act of the human subject who believes to one effected and made possible by the Holy Spirit, who acts to make this faith a reality (183). It is therefore not a refined exegetical practice or theological method but instead a miraculous work of the Holy Spirit we can only invoke in prayer that is the basis for hearing the Word of God (185).

As we leave this paragraph, it is worthwhile to emphasize that the secularity of the Word is a crucial aspect of Barth's thought, driven by the conception of God's veiling and unveiling, "the fact that it comes to us in a form which also means its concealment" (207). Revelation always comes about as God takes up a created reality for his own self-disclosure. This revelation is always "one-sided" in that what is perceived at any moment is either its divine content or its secular form, both held in tension in their unity and differentiation. It is the work of the Spirit within us that allows us to move from a perception of the creaturely form to a perception of its divine content, to hear God's Word behind the human words of Jesus, Scripture, and preaching by means of the Spirit (174–76). Here again we catch a glimpse of the deeply trinitarian underpinnings of Barth's understanding of revelation and of its actualization in the divine disclosure in veiling and unveiling. This trinitarian understanding of revelation will receive further attention in our next chapter.

The Knowability of the Word of God (§6)

In §6, "The Knowability of the Word of God," Barth takes up the presupposed conditions that make possible the knowledge of the Word of God already discussed. He does not, however, take up the question of knowledge of God (theological epistemology) in terms of its general possibility but instead begins with reflection upon the reality of this knowledge and then moves to consider the state of affairs that must be true for this knowledge to exist.

The Question of the Knowability of the Word of God (§6.1)

Dogmatics can begin as a discipline because the Word of God has been heard and is known. As Barth writes, "In the concept of the Church as a place where the truth is spoken and heard, and in the concept of Church proclamation and dogmatics as a meaningful activity, it is presupposed that there can be knowledge of the Word of God by men" (188). It is taken for granted that people do hear and speak, and thus know, the Word of God (188). The knowledge of the Word of God is therefore not an abstract possibility but a reality and a presupposition of the church's theological reflection. In brief, the conditions necessary for this knowledge to exist can be stipulated only because such knowledge is in fact a reality.

The place where this knowledge exists is in the church. As the context and subject of this knowledge, the church is, in this sense, the presupposition of this knowledge, even as the content of this knowledge is the presupposition of the church (188–89). There is therefore again an apparent circularity to this: dogmatics is the reflection by the church upon the Word of God, but it is the Word of God that brings the church itself into existence and continually calls it into existence. Here again, we should remember that the order and logic of this relationship is ultimately one where God's Word, as it exists as Jesus Christ, precedes and calls into existence the church in a relation that is ordered and irreversible.

This knowledge of the Word of God rests upon the church's recollection of the biblical promise and the expectation of its fulfillment in the future (197). God has spoken, and the church longs to hear God speak again. This dialectical relation of recollection and expectation lies at the heart of the church's knowledge of God and his revelation. In considering this particular knowledge, Barth is therefore concerned not with general questions (i.e., "How is God known by all people?" "Can God be known by anyone?"), but rather with the specific question of how God is in fact known in the church. This path of reality to possibility corresponds to the fact that the uniqueness of the subject matter under consideration (the revelation of God in his Word) requires a unique method by which dogmatics undertakes an examination of this knowledge. This knowledge is unique and not akin to the knowledge of other created realities (see 190).[5]

Barth's indifference to prolegomena, and certainly to certain modern forms of theological method consumed with specifying general conditions that must be true for the question of knowledge even to be intelligible, much less for such knowledge of God to be possible, is witnessed in this section and its placement after discussions of the reality of the Word of God. He was in truth not interested in developing a general philosophical or religious epistemology. Up to this point he has simply presupposed the knowledge of God for the task of dogmatics and the church's proclamation. Now he finally turns to address the question of how the Word itself is known, though of course this was already broached and implicated in his discussion of objective and subjective revelation in the previous paragraph. Yet the possibility of the knowledge of the Word of God is not in question. This knowledge exists, and all that remains for matters of epistemology is to reflect upon what must be true of God and humans for this to be the case.

The Word of God and Man (§6.2)

It should not surprise us at this point to find that Barth states that the Word can be known only through a divine act of revelation and not by an intrinsic potentiality or disposition within the human person to know God (193; cf. 209–10, 238). He rejects Protestant modernism's attempts to base religion upon an immanent awareness of the divine. For Barth, this was the tragic turn to anthropology and away from God's special revelation found in the modern period, a turn that was due to an "almost invincible development in the history of Protestant theology since the Reformation" (191). God's Word is known, rather, as it comes to us from outside of us. Knowledge of

5. Barth writes, "A result of the uniqueness of this object of knowledge might well be that the concept of its knowledge cannot be definitively measured by the concept of the knowledge of other objects or by a general concept of knowledge but that it can be defined at all only in terms of its own object" (CD I/1, 190).

God is miraculous in nature, for it comes to us apart from any faculty or skill that we might possess: "God's Word is no longer grace, and grace itself is no longer grace, if we ascribe to man a predisposition toward this Word, a possibility of knowledge regarding it that is intrinsically and independently native to him" (194).

The Word of God and Experience (§6.3)

Barth turns next to what is commonly referred to as religious experience. He does not intrinsically oppose this term, but he does qualify it greatly and is wary of a proclivity for its misuse (198–99). Experience of the Word of God is, again, not dependent upon an intrinsic capability or permanent possession of humanity simply as human. It comes about only from the divine side as an event of God's speech that is an activity and a mystery, as witnessed in the previous paragraph of the CD on the nature of the Word of God. Here Barth is trying to argue for God's sovereignty in the event of revelation while also upholding the agency of the human person who hears and experiences the Word. He continues to be frequently criticized for giving short shrift to the integrity, activity, and freedom of the human person, and this section on its own will perhaps do little to allay such charges. He is not unaware of this criticism or related ones that state that he focuses solely upon the content of the faith believed rather than the faith by which a person believes (209). Nevertheless, while upholding at least in intent and principle the self-determination and even freedom of the human creature, his emphasis here is upon the sovereign determination that God exercises over the human creature: "The possibility of knowledge of God's Word lies in God's Word and nowhere else" (222).

Nevertheless, that God's Word addresses, determines, judges, and impresses itself upon the human person should not be seen as denying the fact that the person is a self-determining agent (201). Barth does not want to undermine the integrity of the person as an agent of free action, but he is nevertheless wary of focusing upon the human response of faith, and in addressing it he constantly circles back to emphasize that this response is grounded in and framed by the prior divine revelation that addresses the person. The human act of acknowledgment of revelation must finally be understood as "the act of that self-determination of man whose meaning and basis, whose final seriousness and true content, whose truth and reality, cannot be ascribed to man himself but only to his determination by the Word of God" (208). Another way to say this is that Barth always sets the human act of faith within the larger framework of the divine activity of the Holy Spirit. He is always more interested in, and sets more faith by, the faithfulness of God than our own faith in God. One theme of dialectical tension in his work that will be frequently witnessed is precisely this relation of divine and human agency. It, too, is a theme that must be carefully navigated in order to read his theology with some facility.

When Barth does turn to the subjective reception of the Word, he moves against the grain of the modern period with its numerous gravitations to a single aspect of the human person as the locus of divine revelation and experience. He does not understand a person's relation to God as one mediated to or by a single faculty of his or her person. The confrontation of the Word of God that comes to humanity cannot be relegated to a single human capacity in this way—whether to the intellect and reason or to others such as will, conscience, or feeling (202). God's Word addresses, rather, the whole human person (202). None of these capacities should be marginalized or deprecated, though none are intrinsically capable of procuring a human experience of God's Word (202–4). God's Word is in reality a "determination of the whole self-determining man" (204).

Once again we return to the pressing question of the human reception of this Word. Put straightforwardly: How should the receptive action of the human person be described in response to the Word of God that confronts him or her? Barth's favored term for this response is "acknowledgment" (205). Yet even here the emphasis is upon God's action rather than that of the human person who acknowledges the Word and the act of acknowledgment itself. As he writes, "The final thing to be said is that while the attitude of acknowledgment *vis-à-vis* God's Word is really an attitude of man, an act of his self-determination, nevertheless it is the act of that self-determination of man whose meaning and basis, whose final seriousness and true content, whose truth and reality, cannot be ascribed to man himself but only to his determination by the Word of God" (208).

A constant refrain of the first volume of the *CD* is this singular focus on the content, rather than the reception, of revelation. Barth indeed seems to hold that the first explains the latter. This emphasis upon the objective rather than subjective elements of revelation is a central aspect of his theology, though he does not ignore the latter entirely. Yet he is ever wary of a turn toward subjectivity. He opposes any kind of religious knowledge that sees this knowledge as an intrinsic possibility of the human person so that "in it God hands something over to man in the sense that it really passes out of God's hand into the hands of man" (212). The human person, as a sinner, simply cannot reach or discover or bring about the Word of God (220–21).

In short, Barth is opposing the entire tradition of the eighteenth and nineteenth centuries that emphasized divine immanence and human autonomy, a tradition that maintained that humanity has an intrinsic capacity for and permanent relation with the divine. This tradition in his estimation began with medieval mysticism that emphasized an immediate—that is, unmediated—relation to God, flourished in Enlightenment rationalism and the moral rationality of Kant that turned away from the need for special revelation and the external authority of Scripture to autonomous reason, flowered in the romantic feeling of Schleiermacher that relativized external forms in favor of immediate "feeling" (at least in his *Speeches on Religion*), and continued on in the confluence of conscience and religious awareness in Herrmann and others in the liberalism of the time (see 212). Such theological projects were not usually an outright denial of God's revelation in Christ, but in most instances were a supplementation and perhaps even augmentation or grounding of this revelation in the intrinsic religiosity of the human person. With such moves, the knowledge of God as a circle with a single center became an ellipse with two independent foci of knowledge (213).

Barth's theology, in contrast, is a circle with a single center. The knowledge of God comes through the Word of God alone (and thus through Christ, Scripture, and the proclamation of the gospel). He sees the alternative—that is, arguments for a natural and immanent knowledge or awareness of God grounded in a natural and universal innate capacity of the human person—as logically ending in a replacement and at best overshadowing of the revelation of God in Christ. He finds such projects in the modern philosopher Descartes and in the earlier figures of Aristotle and Thomas Aquinas. He rejects them all.

For Barth, all such attempts that think of the knowledge of God as an ellipse with two focal points rather than one, no matter how well-intentioned, eventually marginalize God's revelation and, worse, see it as a human possession. They result in replacing God's special revelation with a permanent, ever-available relation of God and humanity grounded in a human capacity such as reason, will, conscience, or feeling. Against such construals, he consistently emphasizes the actuality, particularity, and uniqueness of God's revelation in Christ that comes in divine freedom. And it is this freedom of God that he maintains against all forms of domestication of divine revelation for our own personal ends. Such convictions can be sharply stated: "If a man, the Church, Church proclamation and dogmatics think they can handle the Word of faith like capital at their disposal, they simply prove thereby that they have neither the Word nor faith. When we have them, we do not regard them as a possession but strain after them, hungering and thirsting, and for that reason blessed" (225). He throws all hope for salvation and for the knowledge of God on God himself: "Because it is surrounded by this ultimate uncertainty, by the freedom of God, the assurance of our affirmation of the knowability of the Word of God cannot be great enough" (227). The attempt to answer where God is to be found is ultimately the same question as that which seeks to determine the criterion by which dogmatics does its work (214–15, 217). The source of the knowledge of dogmatics thus serves simultaneously as its norm. The Word of God is both.

The Word of God and Faith (§6.4)

Barth's final subsection of this paragraph addresses the question of faith. It is striking that even in a subsection explicitly dedicated to examining human faith, he still emphasizes the divine content rather than the human act of belief. Throughout this subsection he seems to be in a running debate with his contemporaries who emphasize this act of faith. Furthermore, this debate is in the end one over the meaning and legacy of the Reformation itself, and specifically, over how to understand and interpret Luther.[6] Was Luther closer to Barth, emphasizing the external Word of God that comes from outside of us in Christ and Scripture and the proclaimed gospel? Or was Luther primarily focused upon the faith of the human subject and the individual's experience of crisis and trust, and thus closer to Barth's Lutheran contemporaries such as Gogarten and Bultmann who emphasized human subjectivity? Much of this dispute is carried out in the small-print segments of this subsection, and this historical controversy, while crucial for Barth's larger purpose of providing an Evangelical dogmatics and identifying the Reformation's core convictions and its rightful legacy, need not detain us here.

For our present purposes, the more central question is not the historical but the constructive one: How are we to think of the relation between the Word of God as coming from outside of ourselves, and our reception of it in faith? Here again we are confronted with what we might call the relation between objective faith and its subjective appropriation.[7] And once again what we find is a relation that Barth construes along the lines of unity, differentiation, asymmetry, and irreversibility.

While both the Word of God and human faith are united in the revelatory and salvific event, Barth does not hold that the relation between the Word of God and human faith "is the symmetrical one of two partners, one superior

6. Barth seems particularly engaged with Bultmann, along with Albrecht Ritschl and Georg Wobbermin, over how to interpret Luther's own proclivity to emphasize faith as trust and human act. See the small-print section of *CD* I/1, 232–36.

7. For a further discussion of this theme of objectivism in Barth and its contrast to a focus upon subjectivity, see Hunsinger, *How to Read Karl Barth*, 35–39.

and the other subordinate but still two partners, and that this relation is just as basically grounded in faith as it is in the Word of God" (233). He sees this as a modern and very prevalent contemporary misreading of Luther. Rather, for Luther, "without the Word there can be no faith" (234). Certainly, Barth concedes, the Word does not exist without faith, though this requires careful articulation since God does not make the reality of the Word dependent upon the creature. While both are present in revelation, faith is present only by the Word and is not grounded in a human action or experience (233). He consistently emphasizes the divine act over the human one and yet strives and at times struggles to talk about the freedom of the human in a way that does not render the person entirely passive (see 246–47).

What is Barth's final conclusion about this relationship between the Word and faith? It is that for "the older Reformers and the whole of the older Protestant theology," faith as trust "has nothing whatever to do with a shifting of the reality of faith from its object to the believing subject" (234). He turns decisively away from a prior turn in the nineteenth century, one taken from faith as grounded in the objective Word and including knowledge, to a view in which faith was defined as a disposition and (noncognitive) experience of the human subject. His own turn is not simply a taking leave from thinking of faith as experience and trust to thinking of it solely in terms of knowledge. To force such an absolute choice would reveal a misunderstanding of what faith actually is. Faith has objective content but it is also self-involving. He refuses to see these as mutually exclusive. Faith is not, as we have seen, simply a collection of dogmas, but it is nevertheless a divine address that engages the entire human person, and this includes the intellect and the realm of knowledge. Faith is truly trust, but it can be rightly esteemed as trust only if it is also recognized as presupposing understanding and assent to the object, content, and ground of its trust, the "objective reference of faith" (235; cf. 270). In this respect, Barth seems to embrace earlier Protestant conceptions of faith as containing within itself knowledge, assent (or acknowledgment), and trust.

Faith, then, is not faith simply in reference to the act of trust in the human subject. Nor is faith what it is simply because it *has* a reference, an object, of any kind. It is the *particular* referent that calls forth faith and makes faith what it is: "It is faith by the fact that the Word of God is given to us as the object of this reference, as the object of acknowledgment, and therefore as the basis of real faith" (230). Barth is in the end much more interested in the faithfulness of God than in the faith of persons—it is the first that grounds and leads to the second and provides it with its significance. It is God's act that calls faith into existence, and there is nothing within the self that makes faith intrinsically possible, for it is not self-created (241, 244). In contrast to such a view, faith remains ever a gift granted from outside ourselves: "The Word of God becomes knowable by making itself known" (246).

The ultimate purpose of this revelation is moreover not to bring about the deification of the creature but to bring about in the creature "a conformity to God, i.e., an adapting of man to the Word of God" (238). This theme of conformity to God (*Gottförmigkeit*), elsewhere expressed in the language of correspondence (*Entsprechung*) to God's life and activity, is another significant theme that will be present and developed throughout the *CD*. It emphasizes that the human person, in his or her own way as a creature and without ceasing to be such, provides in his or her life of faith and obedience an analogical representation (*not* replication) of the life and activity of God.[8] In its concrete expression, such conformity of the believer entails that life is lived in conformity to Jesus Christ as Christ himself lived in conformity to his Father (see *CD* I/2, 277).

The Word of God, Dogma, and Dogmatics (§7)

This final paragraph can be more briefly examined, for Barth is in many ways bringing this first part of the *CD* to a close by summarizing much of what has already been addressed in §1 and §2 (reviewing those paragraphs before or even after reading this one is helpful and instructive).

The Problem of Dogmatics (§7.1)

Barth turns full circle back to the beginning by clarifying the task of dogmatics as "the critical question about dogma, i.e., about the Word of God in Church proclamation, or, concretely, about the agreement of the Church proclamation done and to be done by man with the revelation attested in Holy Scripture" (248; also 265, 283). Its task is fulfilled as it measures "Church

8. Again, there is no intrinsic ability on the part of the human person to bring about this life of obedience and correspondence. Barth sees no natural capacity within the sinful person for God, and none exists apart from faith, which itself is a miraculous work to bring the dead to life. Here he rejects Brunner's "point of contact" on one side, and the *analogia entis* of Catholicism on the other (*CD* I/1, 238–39). He rejects deification as well and argues that Augustine and Luther know nothing of this (240). For further discussions of correspondence in Barth's theology, see Kimlyn J. Bender, *Karl Barth's Christological Ecclesiology* (Burlington, VT: Ashgate, 2005), 5–7, 136–41; also John Webster, *Barth's Ethics of Reconciliation* (Cambridge: Cambridge University Press, 1995); Webster, *Barth's Moral Theology: Human Action in Barth's Thought* (Grand Rapids: Eerdmans, 1998); and Paul T. Nimmo, *Being in Action: The Theological Shape of Barth's Ethical Vision* (New York: T&T Clark, 2007).

proclamation as man's word by the second form of the Word of God, i.e., Holy Scripture, in so far as this itself is in turn witness to its third and original form, revelation" (265). Put more succinctly: "The task of dogmatics is the examination of Church proclamation in respect of its agreement with the Word of God, its congruity with what it is trying to proclaim" (250). The task of dogmatics is thus the testing of church proclamation against its criterion of the Word of God attested in Holy Scripture (250–52). This should by now be familiar.

Alongside this review of the task and criterion of dogmatics, Barth reintroduces the distinction of Evangelical dogmatics with its criterion over against Protestant modernism and Roman Catholicism as its rivals. He provides pointed criticisms of each, turning first to modern Protestantism. Acknowledging that it also had its own dogmatic task, he argues that its failure resides in the fact that "it had lost the proper criterion above and over against Church proclamation as the Reformation especially had put this in its hands" (251). Instead of the Word of God as attested in Holy Scripture, it replaced this criterion with "modern cultural awareness" as a surrogate in place of the Word of God (251–52; see also 256–59; cf. 283). For Protestant modernism, the internal religiosity or "Christian spirit" of the individual and the community became the norm and criterion not only of its own preaching and confession but also of the Bible. In doing so, the distinction of the Word of God and the church's own proclamation was lost. Once again, the end result of the church choosing its own criterion for its proclamation is that theology becomes "one of the many forms of dialogue that man has with himself about himself when what it ought to do is to serve the discourse that God directs to man" (256; cf. 257). The church is thus "left to itself and cast back on its own resources" (257).

Barth finds this same loss of distinction between the Word of God and the church in Roman Catholicism when it makes the official interpretation of Scripture in dogma the criterion of church proclamation and teaching (257–58). The ultimate criterion is therefore not Scripture but instead "the Bible as it is authoritatively interpreted by the Church itself or by its teaching office, which is the living voice of Christ" (257). Here the voice of Christ is ultimately located not in Scripture but rather in the teaching office of the church, which is taken to be the living Word of God for the church and the criterion of its proclamation. The teaching office thereby becomes the norm for the church and for dogmatics, and in this move it relativizes the distinction between its own voice and the voice of Scripture, effectively taking its place. The result of this substitution, as with that of Protestant liberalism, is a domestication of Scripture as the locus of the free and sovereign voice of Christ over, and not only within, his church.[9] The Bible no longer is an external Word over the church but is only one voice within it (258). This loss leaves the church alone to have a conversation with itself, such that in both Protestant modernism and Roman Catholicism "we ultimately find the Church dependent on itself and left to its own devices" and thus left "in splendid isolation" (257, 259; cf. 267). This isolation seems, in the end, to be Barth's understanding of how a heresy is divinely judged and punished—that is, not by active divine intervention but by a divine absence from a conversation where God is in truth ignored for an in-house conversation.

In the end, for both Protestant liberalism and Roman Catholicism, the relationship between Christ and the church is one in which the distinction between the Lord of the church and the church itself is not maintained but is sacrificed and Christ's voice is subsumed into another. It can be lost in the voice of the papacy or lost simply in the internal autonomous voice of the individual, "where every man is called upon to be his own pope in virtue of the spirit that is alive within him as a member of the Christian community" (258). In either case, the voice of Christ is replaced by a creaturely voice. Barth is not without hope, however, for either of these traditions, for as long as the Bible is read within the church, it is possible that it may also "find a voice *over against* the Church" (260). In the end, it is only the Bible that can answer this challenge for itself; it alone can call the church to this repentance and renewal.

As witnessed, Barth returns in this final paragraph to a reexamination of now familiar themes of prolegomena and polemics. He continues to engage this "twofold construct of Roman Catholicism and Protestant Modernism" in the rest of this section with what he can refer to as "just a little Protestantism" (261, 264). The irreversible distinction of Christ and the church, concretely expressed in the distinction between Scripture as the written testimony of Christ's authoritative witnesses on one side, and the church and its dogmas on the other, he contends, is the crux of such Protestantism.[10] Evangelical

9. For a contemporary articulation of this point in the sharpest of terms, see John Webster, who writes, "If the canon is a function of God's communicative fellowship with an unruly church, if it is part of the history of judgment and mercy, then it cannot simply be a stabilizing factor, a legitimating authority. Rather, as the place where divine speech may be heard, it is—or ought to be—a knife at the church's heart." John Webster, *Word and Church: Essays in Christian Dogmatics* (New York: T&T Clark, 2001), 46.

10. Barth's specific objections against Roman Catholicism here can be summarized as follows: Catholicism betrays a loss of distinction between revelation and the church's dogmas, an overrealized eschatology with regard to the church's claims to infallible doctrines, and a depersonalization of revelation such that the divine address of God is traded for the intellectual content of impersonal truth (see *CD* I/1, 270). Such truth is in turn abstracted from the God who

Protestantism lives by the recognition of this distinction and in opposition to positions—those of Roman Catholicism and Protestant modernism—in which this distinction is lost, where the Word of God is no longer "an entity distinct from Church proclamation" (265).

The confession of this distinction is once again concretely expressed in the Scripture principle, for it is in Scripture that this Word comes to us from outside ourselves, the Bible serving as a bridge between Christ and his church. As such, Scripture speaks with a divine voice and is moved by a divine power predicated on a divine decision. It is not in our control. What we are dealing with is (in the language of themes examined in §5) "God's Word in human words, the Word which God Himself speaks to man, the Word in which God acts on man, the Word in which God's mystery is manifest" (263). Dogmas are in turn not revelation but rather the church's response to revelation (268).[11] If dogma *did* perfectly correspond to God's Word, then dogmatics would come to an end, as would the church of God upon the earth, for the kingdom of God would have arrived (269).

Dogmatics as a Science (§7.2)

That Barth thinks about dogma along these lines demonstrates that he has what might be called an eschatological view of doctrine, and this characterizes his understanding of dogmatics as a distinct science. Human speech never reaches perfection and thus it requires constant testing and revision in light of the Word of God, and this testing will and must continue until the end of

---

reveals it and from the act of its revelation to the persons who receive it (270). Divine revelation thereby becomes equated with true propositional statements of doctrine that are possessed by and under the custody of the church, not the actual address of the church by God and the living encounter with God that must be sought ever anew. Dogmatics itself then is separated from its relation to church proclamation and becomes the cataloging of various dogmas.

11. "Dogmatic propositions, dogmas and dogma have this in common: They are not the truth of revelation" (*CD* I/1, 268). Shortly after this assertion, however, Barth can also say, "One may thus define dogma as Church proclamation to the degree that it really agrees with the Bible as the Word of God" (268). What can nonetheless be safely said is that he refuses to equate the Word of God with the church's own dogmas or teachings. The first comes from God; the second is the church's own word, its own attempt to articulate what it has heard from God. To fail to see how he distinguishes these leads to a failure to understand how he can see the dogmas of the church as both authoritative and yet not irreformable or irrevisable. In brief, for Barth, the dogmas of the church are the doctrinal attempts to put what it has heard in the Word of God as attested in Holy Scripture into contemporary human speech. But it is the church's speech, and therefore it is not itself revelation or the Word of God: "The Word of God is above dogma as the heavens are above the earth" (266). Here the distinction of Christ and his church is articulated in terms of the relation of the Word of God and the dogmas of the church. Barth will address this question of Scripture and confession in much more detail in his paragraphs on Holy Scripture that we will examine in chapter 9 below.

time. The necessary testing of the church's speech and doctrine must therefore take place as dogmatics focuses upon its proper theme, task, and criterion. It must apply itself to the theme of church proclamation and not to abstract metaphysical and philosophical questions (280); it must dedicate itself to the task of testing and correcting church proclamation and not simply to the repetition or cataloging of past doctrines (281); and it must subjugate itself to the criterion of the revelation of God in Christ as attested in Holy Scripture as its norm against which it tests church proclamation as to its agreement with this standard (283). And so, in conclusion: "Scripture should thus be and become and remain the master in theology's house" (285). For what is of final importance is "whether a dogmatics is scriptural" (287).

The Problem of Dogmatic Prolegomena (§7.3)

The final brief subsection of this paragraph requires no detailed attention here. It is a programmatic one in which Barth outlines the remaining topics that will be addressed in the first volume of the CD on the doctrine of the Word of God. These will include dedicated chapters on Holy Scripture, on proclamation, and on the revelation of God itself, including examinations of the triune nature of God, of the incarnation of Christ, and of the outpouring of the Holy Spirit. With this outline of what is ahead, he brings chapter 1 of the CD to a close.

COMMENTARY

The Word of God and Direct Appeals to the Holy Spirit

The emphasis that Barth places upon the fact that revelation comes from outside ourselves in the Word of God sets him at odds with forms of mysticism and spiritualism that claim a direct inner experience of God and deem all external means of revelation unnecessary (178–79). But that is not all. It also sets him against all appeals to the Holy Spirit as a foundation for knowledge of God that are established apart from or opposed to the Word of God in Holy Scripture. In contrast to such positions, Barth does not think that the Spirit should be seen as providing a revelation, or revelations, that are independent from the written Word of God if this means that such go against its teaching. Appeals to direct spiritual illumination apart from or even against the grain of Holy Scripture are seen by him as occasions not for churchly celebration but rather for dire warning and confession. Just as the Spirit is not independent of Christ, so the Spirit does not speak authoritatively for the church apart from or against Christ's witness in Holy Scripture or the signs of the gospel in preaching and sacraments or ordinances.

Long before Barth, Luther similarly engaged opponents who attempted to appeal directly to the Holy Spirit apart from Scripture. One of his famous retorts was to criticize such direct appeals to the Spirit by a reformer who, in Luther's words, "has devoured the Holy Spirit feathers and all."[12] Barth stands in this same Reformation tradition, and he emphasizes here and elsewhere that the Holy Spirit cannot be separated from Jesus Christ and that the Spirit's work is tied to "Scripture, preaching and the sacraments" (CD I/2, 251). Barth was preoccupied with how this Reformation legacy had been corrupted, and he believed that the unmooring of the Holy Spirit from Christ and Scripture by Neo-Protestantism had led to "all possible idols, including those with which we have to do to-day" (CD I/2, 252). If Luther stood against the appeals to the Spirit of persons recklessly pushing reform (Andreas Karlstadt) or violent insurrection (Thomas Müntzer), Barth in his time opposed not only the trajectories of the modern period and its turn to the self as the locus of revelation and authority but also the new rising spirit of German nationalism.

In light of these observations, it may be of interest to ask the following questions: Where are such appeals to immediate human experience as a new divine revelation being made today? Where do we see the clear teaching of Scripture (and perhaps also that of the historic church) quietly set aside or explicitly rejected for a "new light of the Spirit" that provides a new doctrinal or moral direction for the church? How can such appeals be shown to be grounded upon anything more firm than human subjectivity or cultural shifts?

Such questions may lead to some further uncomfortable ones, for such direct appeals to divine inspiration may not be reserved to peripheral "cultish" movements but may appear today at the heart of the mainstream Christian tradition. Such uncomfortable questions were, of course, not unknown to Luther and Barth and to the apostle Paul before them. Moreover, such spiritualist moves continue on long after them. The turn away from God's particular revelation in Christ and Scripture and its replacement with an appeal to an inner religious awareness or sensibility, grounded in reason, conscience, will, or feeling, is a turn with a long arc through history. In the modern period it runs from Schleiermacher's *Speeches on Religion* and the mysticism of romanticism and crosses to American shores, moving from the transcendentalism of Ralph Waldo Emerson and Henry David Thoreau to the poetry of

12. Martin Luther, *Luther's Works: Church and Ministry II*, vol. 40, ed. Conrad Bergendoff, gen. ed. Helmut T. Lehmann (Philadelphia: Fortress, 1958), 83. Luther could make a similar remark with regard to Thomas Müntzer; see the discussion in Roland H. Bainton, *Here I Stand: A Life of Martin Luther* (Nashville: Abingdon, 1950), 265.

Walt Whitman and continues on today in the popular amorphous spirituality that has left behind the "trappings" of organized Christianity. It is perfectly expressed in Emerson's religion of the self that renounces the "noxious exaggeration about the person of Jesus" in historic Christianity.[13] It is echoed in every theology where at the end of the day personal experience trumps all, and such theologies are found not only without but also within the churches. Yet it might at least be observed that such experience requires interpretation, and it may even require a norm, a confrontational Word, outside itself in order to check its unbridled authority (see 217). One of Barth's contributions is his insight that the road from the self to God arrives at its end with atheism, though it is perhaps more accurate to say that its final destination is the divinization of the self. This may in turn undergird the construction of Jesus in our own image, if he is retained at all.

For Barth, such spiritualities of "all thrills and no work" (to borrow a phrase from C. S. Lewis) were at their heart a rejection of the scandal of the gospel. Their rejection of the scandalous particularity of revelation that stood at its center was correspondingly always accompanied by a rejection of its particular and scandalous ethical demands.[14] In short, a rejection of the doctrinal center of the Christian faith always leads to a reorientation of the ethical compass. Yet what is perhaps less considered is that a recalibration of the moral compass and renunciation of the ethical implications of the gospel's christological and eschatological vision cannot be carried out without producing an effect upon the understanding of its doctrinal center. It is thus understandable that Barth was concerned that divine and human freedom and their relation be rightly understood. For if they are not, the first can only appear capricious rather than gracious, and the latter can become equated with license rather than a freely offered life of correspondence and conformity to the ways of God, a living and holy sacrifice offered "in view of God's mercies" (Rom. 12:1–2).

QUESTIONS FOR REFLECTION

- What does Barth mean when he says, "Theology has all too often tried to seek out and conquer the consciousness of an age on its own ground" (127)?

13. Ralph Waldo Emerson, "Divinity School Address," in *The Portable Emerson*, ed. Carl Bode, new ed. (New York: Penguin, 1981), 80.
14. C. S. Lewis, *Mere Christianity* (1952; repr. San Francisco: HarperCollins, 2001), 155.

- What might it mean to say that God's speech and God's act are the same? Or that revelation and reconciliation are two sides of one reality?
- How does Barth distinguish Scripture and revelation? How does he identify and relate them? In what way does Scripture stand on the human side over against revelation? In what way do revelation and Scripture stand on the same side over against the church and the individual Christian?
- What does Barth mean by the secularity of the speech of God?
- How is Barth's understanding of revelation distinguished from mysticism and spiritualism as he defines them? Where can such mysticism and spiritualism be witnessed today?

⊹ 6 ⊹

The Triune God

CD §§8–12

Chapter 2 of Barth's doctrine of the Word of God is titled "The Revelation of God" and consists of three parts. Part 1 is titled "The Triune God" and is composed of five paragraphs (§§8–12). Barth's understanding of the Trinity in these paragraphs will be the topic of our examination in this chapter, though most of our attention will be given to the first two of these paragraphs, while the final three will receive an abbreviated explication for reasons given below. Barth places the doctrine of the Trinity at the beginning of his dogmatics, demonstrating its prominence and its centrality for his theology.

God in His Revelation (§8)

Having addressed the criterion of dogmatics in chapter 1, Barth turns in chapter 2 to examine the content of revelation. This content is the God who reveals, and the identity of this God is set forth in the doctrine of the Trinity. His description here may be a bit confusing at first because he introduces the topic not by speaking of the familiar divine triune name of Father, Son, and Holy Spirit, but rather with the terms Revealer, Revelation, and Revealedness (295). Throughout this discussion he sets forth a doctrine of the Trinity that is closely related, though not identical, to the doctrine of revelation he has already introduced.

In accordance with all he has said earlier, Barth begins by stating that to speak of revelation, one must "keep to Holy Scripture as the witness of revelation" (295). The revelation we find in Scripture claims for itself an absolute uniqueness, which means that the revelation we find attested there "insists absolutely on being understood in terms of its object, God" (295). Barth commences his discussion of this God with three questions that introduce the topics of each of the three parts in chapter 2. First: What is the content of revelation? The answer given to this question is that the content of revelation is God himself in his revelation, the revelation of the one called Yahweh in the OT and the Lord in the NT. This question of the identity of God is set forth in part 1 (and is the subject of our current chapter). The second question is, How does it come about that God reveals himself? The answer given is that God reveals himself by means of the act of the incarnation of the Word, or Son, the Second Person of the Triune God, and this is the topic of part 2 (and the subject of our own chapter following this one). And the third question is, What is the result of this act of revelation? The answer given to this final question is the outpouring and work of the Holy Spirit to awaken persons to faith and obedience, which will in turn be the topic of part 3 (and the topic of our chapter following the next one).

In brief, these three questions introduce each of the three parts of chapter 2, and the answers to each question provide the theme of each corresponding part (295–96). Barth asserts that these questions can in no way be separated but are all part of the one revelation of God. As he summarizes this, "*God* reveals himself [part 1, the doctrine of the Trinity]. He reveals Himself *through Himself* [part 2, the doctrine of the incarnation of the Word]. He reveals *Himself* [part 3, the doctrine of the outpouring of the Holy Spirit]. If we really want to understand revelation in terms of its subject, i.e., God, then the first thing we have to realize is that this subject, God, the Revealer [part 1], is identical with His act in revelation [part 2] and also identical with its effect [part 3]" (296 [my additions in brackets]).

Put succinctly: God reveals himself through the Son by the Holy Spirit. Here Barth begins his reflection on the Trinity by attempting to discern and set forth the presuppositions that make the reality of revelation found in the biblical witness possible. In effect, the question he asks is, What must be true of God for this revelation to be a reality and thus possible? This approach does not mean that he simply derives the doctrine of the Trinity from an abstract conceptual doctrine of revelation in general (a mistake many readers have made in interpreting him). Rather, he sets forth the reality of the Trinity as that which both is presupposed by and gives meaning to the particular and unique revelation of God found in Scripture.[1] Before pressing on, we might also note that there is a rough correspondence between the parts of chapter 2 and prior paragraphs in chapter 1. Hence part 1 of chapter 2 on the Trinity corresponds to §4, "The Word of God in Its Threefold Form," in chapter 1; part 2 on the incarnation of the Word in the second chapter corresponds to §5, "The Nature of the Word of God," in the first chapter; and part 3 on the outpouring of the Holy Spirit corresponds to §6, "The Knowability of the Word of God."

To observe such correlations reminds us again that the CD is always read best when one appreciates that it is characterized by an ever-deepening development and circling repetition of themes that are introduced at one point in the exposition but may reappear in various forms and under differing doctrinal topics in later volumes. The movement from the first chapter to the second in the CD marks such development, and this form of description in which themes are introduced, highlighted, allowed to recede, and then reintroduced, often in new forms, will be present throughout the CD and is a central element of Barth's distinctive form of style and argument. It is a principal reason why his theology is often thought to have a kind of musical quality in which themes move in and out of the whole in contrapuntal fashion.[2]

We can now turn in full to Barth's understanding of the doctrine of the Trinity. What must first be appreciated is that he takes up the question of the Trinity by means of the question of revelation, just as he interprets revelation in a trinitarian manner. The Trinity is posited as the answer to the question of the content of revelation, which has been a driving theme of the first volume of the CD. As already noted, some have seen his attempt to explicate the doctrine of the Trinity from the doctrine of God's act of revelation as overly abstract. Yet whether one is fully satisfied with his doctrine of the Trinity here or not, what must be grasped is that he is in fact not deriving this doctrine from a general concept of revelation or of divine speech as a speculative or philosophical question, but is putting it forth as the proper description of the God who reveals himself through his own unique activity in Christ and through the Holy Spirit in history, as this activity is witnessed in Scripture and is thereby known by the church.

---

1. For an extended discussion of this somewhat technical point as well as of the relation of the doctrine of revelation to the doctrine of the Trinity in this section, see George Hunsinger, "Karl Barth on the Trinity," in *Evangelical, Catholic, and Reformed: Doctrinal Essays on Barth and Related Themes* (Grand Rapids: Eerdmans, 2015), 1–20, esp. 1–4. This essay is a very helpful discussion for the topics addressed here. It is also in *The Oxford Handbook of the Trinity*, ed. Gilles Emery and Matthew Levering (Oxford: Oxford University Press, 2011), 294–313.

2. See George Hunsinger, *How to Read Karl Barth: The Shape of His Theology* (Oxford: Oxford University Press, 1991), 29.

This undertaking is therefore not a project in apologetics (an attempt to prove the Trinity) but rather a project of description and explication (an attempt to set forth the inner logic and coherence of the doctrine of the Trinity, with the Triune God taken not as an object of argument but rather as a Subject acknowledged and worshiped). Barth looks to the manner in which God has been revealed to the world in Christ through the Spirit and inquires as to who God is in light of this revelation of God's own identity attested in Scripture. He summarizes this close relation, and indirect equation, of the doctrine of the Trinity and the doctrine of revelation in this way: "In practice the nature of the biblical answer to the question: Who is God in His revelation? is such as to answer at once the two other questions: What is He doing? and: What does He effect?" (297). Barth states that "in these three questions there is opened up a way, not to prove, but certainly to understand the doctrine of the Trinity" (297). One cannot answer one of these questions without addressing and answering the others. The answers to these questions that will occupy Barth in chapter 2 of the *CD* concern the Triune God, the incarnation, and the Holy Spirit, respectively.

The Place of the Doctrine of the Trinity in Dogmatics (§8.1)

After these introductory matters Barth turns in earnest to set forth the logic and rationale for the doctrine of the Trinity, which, as previously stated, is the answer to the question of the identity of the God who reveals himself. He states that the doctrine of the Trinity is the answer not only to revelation's objective (i.e., external and historical) content, which is the particular work of the Son in the incarnation, but also to its subjective (i.e., personal and effectual) appropriation, which is the particular work of the Holy Spirit in effecting revelation's reception in the life of the believer. As he summarizes this: "Thus it is God Himself, it is the same God in unimpaired unity, who according to the biblical understanding of revelation is *the revealing God* and *the event of revelation* and *its effect on man*" (299 [emphasis added]). Here again we see this threefold structure of revelation: this act of revelation is a single reality yet also exists in this irreducibly threefold form of the God who reveals, the act of revelation in history, and the impartation of the meaning and effect of this revelation within the human person (299).

Crucial for understanding Barth's thought here is to appreciate fully the conviction that the manner in which God is revealed in time is consistent with, and indeed in correspondence to, how God actually exists in eternity. There is no discrepancy between God as revealed in the world and God in himself transcendent to time and history. Because this is so, God in eternity exists in this irreducible threefold form as Father and Son (or Word) and Spirit in correspondence to God's revelation as the Father made known through the incarnation of Jesus Christ and through the outpouring of the Holy Spirit in time. The manner in which God reveals himself in history reflects who God truly is in eternity and requires that God be such a God: "Thus to the same God who in unimpaired unity is the Revealer, the revelation and the revealed-ness, there is also ascribed in unimpaired differentiation within Himself this threefold mode of being" (299). The doctrine of the Trinity is, for Barth, not only an interpretation of the understanding of God's revelation but also its presupposition and necessary prerequisite, and it is best thought of as an answer to the question of the identity of the God who is revealed. The God who is revealed in a threefold way in time is the God who exists in a triune way in eternity.

It is the unity of the one God who reveals himself in this irreducible dif-ferentiation as attested in Scripture that puts forth for us "the problem of the doctrine of the Trinity" (299). This problem arises from Scripture itself, where the singularity and one-ness of God are affirmed but where this ir-reducibly threefold act of revelation is also depicted. Against an immediate tradition in the nineteenth century that largely relegated the doctrine of the Trinity to the margins of theological discussion, Barth wants to bring it back front and center, and his purpose is not to retrieve patristic theology or the church's creedal tradition for its own sake but to take seriously once again the question that revelation itself puts inescapably before us (300). The doc-trine of the Trinity rightly takes its place at the beginning of dogmatics, he contends, for it is the identification of the distinct God of revelation and is "what basically distinguishes the Christian doctrine of God as Christian, and therefore what already distinguishes the Christian concept of revelation as Christian, in contrast to all other possible doctrines of God or concepts of revelation" (301).

It should not be overlooked how closely this doctrine of the Triune God is related to Scripture. As revelation and the Trinity are two sides of a single reality, so Scripture and the doctrine of the Trinity are intricately intertwined, closely related yet not directly identified such that the doctrine is thought to be explicitly found there. Scripture is unique and holy precisely because of the God it attests, a God who reveals himself in the history that Scripture records. Barth again states that it is the separation of the question of God from the question of Scripture that characterizes both Protestant liberal-ism, where the criterion of the content of faith is human religiosity, and Roman Catholicism, where the criterion is the teaching office. In both, the criterion of Holy Scripture (as earlier explicated in brief in chapter 1 of the

CD and later elucidated in full in chapter 3) is set aside, and for Barth, this has ramifications not only concerning the criterion of faith but also for the understanding of its content (300–301). This leads to another foundational insight: The question of God cannot be taken up or God known except in light of the revelation that is attested in the Bible. We might state that this is Barth's second great conviction regarding the doctrine of the Trinity, and it complements the first, in which the Triune God of eternity and the revealed God in time is the same God. God's identity cannot be known except in this singular and unique revelation. Any attempt to answer the question of God's identity that does not begin with this distinctive revelation witnessed in Holy Scripture is, he contends, speculation—and what can be safely said is that Barth, like Calvin before him, opposes speculation in any and all of its forms (301).

Theology must consequently advance from the question of God's identity as the very first question posed, not from questions about whether and how God may or may not be known or even exist (for reality precedes possibility). And the answer to the question of God's identity as this is provided in Holy Scripture is substantively given by the doctrine of the Trinity (301). Yet again we see that Barth's emphasis upon revelation and Scripture is now mirrored in the doctrine of the Trinity. Just as one cannot properly begin with a general notion of religion but must begin with the specific revelation of God in Christ through the Spirit, so one cannot begin with a general notion of God but must begin with the particular identity of the Triune God as this is attested in Holy Scripture. The particularity of revelation entails and indeed corresponds to the particular, singular, and incomparable identity of God as articulated in the doctrine of the Trinity.

In placing this doctrine at the head of dogmatics, Barth reveals its importance for understanding all of Christian theology. In this placement, he was breaking with an established Protestant tradition in modernity that saw the doctrine of the Trinity either as outdated metaphysics or as hopelessly incoherent. He was undeterred and in turn critiqued this tradition for its trinitarian failings. As he argued, the fact that Schleiermacher could relegate the doctrine of the Trinity to the end of his dogmatics shows that it did not have a "constitutive significance for him either" (303). This was not a passing observation; it was a larger judgment not only upon Schleiermacher but also upon the entire liberal tradition that followed him. Barth takes a different path. The answer to the question of the self-revealing God is given by Scripture in a triune portrayal of God and in the church's confession of the triunity of God (303). To fail to appreciate this is to fail all along the line in understanding God's identity and activity.

The Root of the Doctrine of the Trinity (§8.2)

The second subsection turns from the programmatic question of the doctrine of the Trinity's place in dogmatics to the matter of the grounding of the doctrine of the Trinity in revelation and Scripture. Here the crucial first conviction discussed earlier is rearticulated when Barth states that "here in God's revelation God's Word is identical with God Himself" (304). He commences by noting that in the revelation we find attested in Scripture we witness both the one-ness of God's Word in Christ with God the Father as well as the distinction between God's Word in Christ and God the Father. These two seemingly conflicting attestations cannot be synthesized and are not harmonized by Scripture, but are dialectically set forth as both true, and each confessed.

It should be noted that this dialectical identity and distinction of God and his Word can be said only of revelation proper—that is, of the Word that took on flesh in Jesus Christ—and cannot be attributed either to Scripture or to the proclamation of the church as these are corresponding forms of the Word of God. Scripture and proclamation cannot be directly or substantially equated with God as can Christ as the Word. They can be related to God only in a more distant, qualified, and indirect way, for the Word of God in Christ is mediated first through the words of the prophets and apostles in Scripture and in the second case through the contemporary expositors and preachers of the church (304). The divine Word of God comes to us through Scripture and proclamation, but these latter two are not themselves the eternal divine Word but rather are the human witnesses through which this Word continues to speak. As Barth writes, "If the Word of God is God Himself even in Holy Scripture and Church proclamation, it is because this is so in the revelation to which they bear witness" (304). This does not mean that Scripture and proclamation are any less the Word of God; however, they are not directly, but indirectly, God's revelation, just as they themselves are not the eternal Word that was with God before all time and who took on flesh. Here we might think again of the Word as expressed in the Gospel of John who was with God and indeed was God (John 1:1, 14). Christ can be identified as God in human form in a way that Scripture and proclamation cannot.

This careful delineation of the eternal unity of God with his Word, of the irrevocable distinction of God and his Word, and of the unity and distinction of the Word itself as revelation with and from its mediated forms in Scripture and proclamation, marks the beginning of trinitarian reflection for Barth and, he believes, stands at the beginning of such reflection's origin in the NT. This discussion also ties his doctrine of the Trinity back to his earlier discussion of the threefold form of the Word of God where he stated that this threefold form of the Word is the only true and proper analogy to God's own triune identity. These relations of unity and distinction are central to his understanding of both Trinity and revelation, each existing in a threefold manner. Another way to say this is that both the epistemological ground and the ontological ground of revelation are in fact the same: the God who is known in a triune way in revelation also exists in a triune way in his own eternal life (305).

This is not to say, however, that God's triune identity and God's activity in revelation can simply be equated such that they are collapsed one into the other. To do such would sacrifice God's freedom from the world in making its existence determinative for and necessarily constitutive of God's own being (332–33; cf. 364). In short, "revelation must indeed be understood as the root or ground of the doctrine of the Trinity," but these are not collapsed into one (332). God's triune existence is not comprised by revelation but transcends it, and revelation itself reveals this very transcendence. So while God truly is who he is in his revelation, God does not require revelation in the world to be who he is in eternity. Another way to state this is to say that God's act of revelation is an act of grace, not of necessity. Put even more succinctly: God does not require the existence of the world to be God. It should therefore be no surprise that Barth will oppose pantheism and process theism of any kind.

The doctrines of revelation and the Trinity are thus intricately interwoven for Barth, even as they cannot be identified or collapsed without remainder. The doctrine of the Trinity is the ontological basis of the doctrine of revelation (for the reality of the Triune God stands behind and effects revelation, making it possible), even as the doctrine of revelation is the epistemological basis for the doctrine of the Trinity (for we know the Triune God only by means of divine revelation), though it may be more accurate to state that Barth is simply positing that revelation has a trinitarian structure than that it is the Trinity's epistemological basis.[3] Regardless of how this is understood,

---

3. As Hunsinger notes, Barth's interests here in speaking of the root of the doctrine of the Trinity are more logical, conceptual, and analytical (explicating the inner logic and coherence of the doctrine of revelation and its implications for the doctrine of the Trinity) than epistemological (stating how the doctrine of the Trinity takes its rise and is known through revelation), though Hunsinger also rightly notes that such conceptual questions are not entirely isolated from epistemological ones and that Barth believed that "it is only through revelation that the dogma [of the Trinity] arises" (Hunsinger, "Karl Barth on the Trinity," 2, 3–4). He concludes, "Barth was offering a Trinitarian interpretation of revelation, not a revelational doctrine of the Trinity" (4). This may be true, but it is also true that the manner in which Barth describes these entails that each is mutually implicated in the other, such that they are not collapsed but dialectically and reciprocally involved even as the doctrine of the Trinity takes ontological

he is focused upon revelation, rather than the doctrine of the Trinity proper, in this second subsection of §8 in speaking of the root of the doctrine of the Trinity. In its briefest form, he can put forth the doctrine of revelation in this way: "God reveals Himself as the Lord" (306). This statement is in turn the root of the doctrine of the Trinity (307). It is also an analytical statement—its form reveals its content and is not distinguished from it. Put in other terms: we might say that the manner in which God reveals himself in Christ through the Spirit (which is the translation of this short, threefold statement) is the very way that God exists in himself. Or, put again as earlier addressed: the economic Trinity (i.e., God in the history of revelation in time) is the God who exists in eternity as the immanent Trinity (i.e., God in God's own eternal existence). Once again, there can be no difference, Barth insists, between the God who is revealed in time and history and the God who exists in eternity.

Later Barth interpreters will debate exactly how God's decision to be for us in history is related to God's being in eternity, but we can safely say that here Barth both equates the immanent and the economic Trinity (respectively, God in eternity, and God as revealed in history) with regard to God's identity, and also distinguishes them insofar as the world and God's revelation within it are not constitutive or necessary for God's being. Again, these relations will become, and are, matters of significant debate in Barth scholarship today.[4] Yet it is clear in the first volume of the CD that Barth is committed both to affirming the unity and identity of God as revealed in time with God in eternity and to maintaining God's freedom from the world such that God is not simply dissolved into history nor is history made a necessary constituent of God's being. This twofold conviction is clearly articulated in the following incisive passage:

> We are not saying, then, that revelation is the basis of the Trinity, as though God were the triune God only in His revelation and only for the sake of His revelation. What we are saying is that revelation is the basis of the doctrine of the Trinity; the doctrine of the Trinity has no other basis apart from this. We arrive at the doctrine of the Trinity by no other way than that of an analysis of the concept of revelation. Conversely, if revelation is to be interpreted aright,

---

precedence insofar as God exists as God apart from his revelation, even while we know him to be such only because of it (see CD I/1, 312). For another detailed examination of Barth's doctrine of the Trinity that addresses these questions, see Alan J. Torrance, *Persons in Communion: An Essay on Trinitarian Description and Human Participation, with Special Reference to Volume One of Karl Barth's "Church Dogmatics"* (Edinburgh: T&T Clark, 1996).

4. For an introduction to this debate, see the essays in Michael T. Dempsey, ed., *Trinity and Election in Contemporary Theology* (Grand Rapids: Eerdmans, 2011). This debate has continued beyond these essays and involves technical discussions of Barth's theology.

it must be interpreted as the basis of the doctrine of the Trinity. The crucial
question for the concept of revelation, that of the God who reveals Himself,
cannot be answered apart from the answer to this question given in the doctrine
of the Trinity. The doctrine of the Trinity is itself the answer that must be given
here. When we say, then, that the doctrine of the Trinity is the interpretation of
revelation or that revelation is the basis of the doctrine of the Trinity, we find
revelation itself attested in Holy Scripture in such a way that in relation to this
witness our understanding of revelation, or of the God who reveals Himself,
must be the doctrine of the Trinity. (312)

Barth is fully aware that the doctrine of the Trinity is not explicitly taught
in Scripture (indeed, the term "Trinity" cannot be found there). Nevertheless,
the doctrine is not a later addition to God's revelation that distorts or aug-
ments it but is instead an interpretation of what is already found in Scripture
regarding the unity and differentiation of the Father, the Son, and the Spirit.
The questions that this interpretation attempted to answer are thus "not alien
to the Bible but are at least prefigured in it" (314; cf. 332–33). In short, the
doctrine of the Trinity is the church's interpretation of Scripture by means
of which it attempts to set forth the identity of the God who reveals himself
as one Lord yet does so in an irreducibly threefold way as the Father and the
Son and the Holy Spirit:

> Generally and provisionally we mean by the doctrine of the Trinity the propo-
> sition that He whom the Christian Church calls God and proclaims as God,
> the God who has revealed Himself according to the witness of Scripture, is
> the same in unimpaired unity and yet also the same thrice in different ways in
> unimpaired distinction. Or, in the phraseology of the Church's dogma of the
> Trinity, the Father, the Son and the Holy Spirit in the biblical witness to reve-
> lation are the one God in the unity of their essence, and the one God in the
> biblical witness to revelation is the Father, the Son and the Holy Spirit in the
> distinction of His persons. (307–8)

This description should not be taken to mean that God's revelation and
the doctrine of the Trinity are the exact same thing or can be directly identified. God's revelation is the reality, while the doctrine of the Trinity is the
church's reflection upon that reality and the interpretation of its meaning.
Barth properly distinguishes between the revelation that is God's own act and
the doctrine that is the church's reflection upon that act. In effect, here again
we are confronted with his distinction between *dogma* and *dogmas*, between
the content of the church's teaching and the teaching itself, between God's
own reality and the church's reflection upon and articulation of that reality

(see 308). Moreover, the church's dogma of the Trinity is not Scripture, but is reflection upon Scripture.

In this sense, the church's doctrine of the Trinity is twice removed from revelation, for revelation is the reality that Scripture attests, and the church's doctrine is a reflection upon Scripture and the reality to which it points. The doctrine of the Trinity is neither revelation itself nor Scripture itself but, rather, an interpretation of Scripture, a translation and exegesis of the biblical text (308). Once again we have revelation and Scripture and church teaching in an ordered relation of unity but also inviolable and irreversible distinction. It cannot be emphasized too strongly that failure to comprehend such dialectical unity and ordered distinctions (and at times distinctions of subordination) leads to misinterpretations of Barth's theology all along the line. He can later conclude, "In calling revelation the root of the doctrine of the Trinity we are thus indicating that we do not confuse or equate the biblical witness to God in His revelation with the doctrine of the Trinity, but we do see an authentic and well-established connexion between the two" (310–11).

Trying to come to grips with such ordered relations that are without confusion or equation, yet also with real connection and coordination, is one of the challenges of Barth interpretation. It requires us to come to grips with his highly dialectical ways of thinking, which, contrary to some interpretations, are not grounded in modern philosophical conventions or commitments but instead arise from reflection upon the mysteries of God's revelation in Scripture in which God is both one and three, and in which the Christ who reveals God to us is both divine and human, and in which the Spirit who renews our own spirit acting upon us in the most intimate way is never confused with us. The first of these mysteries is the topic of Barth's current discussion, while the latter two take up the next two parts of Barth's discussion of "The Revelation of God" in chapter 2.

Having described the nature of the doctrine of the Trinity as an interpretation of Scripture, Barth next addresses the question of what purpose such an interpretation served and might continue to serve. In short, why did this interpretation arise, and why does it endure within the church? The answer Barth provides is that it was and continues to be the attempt of the church to interpret Scripture in light of contemporary challenges and for a new age, an attempt in turn to remain faithful to Scripture by providing a faithful interpretation of Scripture in the terminology of a later particular time and place. The doctrine of the Trinity was not simply an exercise in dogmatic description for catechetical purposes, but instead arose in a polemical contest: "Inaccurate explanation of the Bible, made in the speech of a later period, had to be countered in the speech of the same period. There thus arose in every age the task of dogma and dogmatics. This is what gives dogma and dogmatics their own special character as distinct from the Bible. But they are not necessarily on this account unbiblical or contrary to the Bible" (309).

If up to this point Barth has placed an emphasis upon the distinction between revelation and the doctrine of the Trinity, he now turns to emphasize their intimate relation. If the doctrine of the Trinity cannot be directly identified with revelation, it can be indirectly identified with it (309). The doctrine attempts to be a faithful articulation of God's identity and activity in self-revelation, and it has been held, and continues to be held, by the church as the correct and proper interpretation of revelation (310). So while the doctrine of the Trinity is not explicitly taught in the Bible, it is nonetheless a proper interpretation of what we do find in the Bible, the witness to God's revelation in Jesus Christ through the Spirit (310). Dogmas are thus judged only by the standard of whether they are or are not good and proper interpretations of the Bible (310). This testing of dogmas is the concern of the discipline of dogmatics. It is this testing that not only sets forth the truth that must be confessed in the light of revelation but also precludes certain (Roman Catholic and liberal Protestant) dogmas from being acceptable articulations of that truth (310).

EXCURSUS: The Christocentric Basis of the Doctrine of the Trinity

One very interesting fact of Barth's trinitarian thinking is that he does not think that the biblical witness places equal stress upon the questions and elements of "revealer, revelation, and being revealed" (314). The emphasis is in fact upon the second of these three concepts, and in its explication the answers to the first and the third questions as to the identity of revelation are provided. He therefore makes this astounding claim: "Similarly the doctrine of the Trinity, when considered historically in its origin and development, is not equally interested in the Father, the Son and the Holy Ghost. Here too the theme is primarily the second person of the Trinity, God the Son, the deity of Christ" (315).

A number of things should be noted regarding this quotation. First, Barth is, already here in the first volume of the CD, christological and indeed christocentric in his outlook and approach to dogmatics. The first and the third articles, those of the Father and the Spirit, are understood in light of the second, that of the Son. Those who may think that he became "christocentric" only with his revision of the doctrine of election in the second volume of the CD need to consider passages like this one. This is not in any way to downplay the remarkable achievement of his christological reorientation of the doctrine of election, nor to deny significant development in his theology. But his christological concentration is evident before that doctrine's appearance.

Second, this christocentric outlook is a foundational conviction for Barth that he will consistently hold throughout his theological maturity, evident here in the first volume of the *CD* and unflinchingly held ever after. This statement that he made in the early 1930s will simply be restated in his lectures in Bonn in 1946 after the war.[5] He never changes from this conviction that it is the second article of the creed (that dedicated to Christ) that illuminates the first (on the Father) and the third (on the Holy Spirit).

Third, all trinitarian reflection is on this account dependent for Barth upon a prior christological conviction. In other words, the doctrine of the Trinity begins with and is grounded in christological reflection. This is not to say that trinitarian reflection is of lesser importance. But the root of trinitarian reflection begins with a christological question—namely, the question of the unity, or one-ness, of Jesus Christ with the Father, and of the simultaneous inalienable distinction between them. This is the first and primary question that revelation presents to us as it is attested in the biblical witness. To say, as Barth does, that revelation is the root of the doctrine of the Trinity is simultaneously, and in the same way, to say that reflection upon Jesus Christ is the root of that doctrine (remembering that he can earlier equate revelation with Jesus Christ). The questions of the identity of the Father and of the Spirit thus follow upon that of the Son (see 315). Following this order of moving from Christ to his Father and then to the Spirit is, Barth contends, not only the historical one of doctrinal development but also the one that the logic of Scripture attests (315).

Two final elements round out this paragraph. First, having outlined the analytical nature of the doctrine of the Trinity, its biblical basis, and its christological foundation and form, Barth turns to a theme that has already been introduced and discussed in earlier sections—namely, the veiling of God in taking up a created, or secular, medium for the purpose of his self-revelation. Here again he carefully distinguishes between revelation and its medium, echoed in the distinction of revelation as an event and as a history (see 315–16). This distinction entails that "even in the form He assumes when He reveals Himself God is free to reveal Himself or not to reveal Himself" (321). That God exists as one God in an irreducible mode of threefold self-distinction is made manifest in God's revelatory act of veiling and unveiling. In turn, God's act of veiling and unveiling is itself predicated upon and made possible by the reality of God's own inalienable eternal distinctions as triune within the

5. See Karl Barth, *Dogmatics in Outline*, trans. G. T. Thomson (New York: Harper & Row, 1959), 52–53, 65–67.

Godhead. Trinitarian reflection thereby begins as the church contemplates this act whereby God "distinguishes Himself from Himself" and becomes God both in concealment and in manifestation, as both hidden and revealed, God "in the form of something He Himself is not" (316; cf. 319–20). What remains "beyond dispute is that the lordship of God discernible in the biblical revelation consists in this freedom of His, in His permanent freedom to unveil Himself or to veil Himself" (324; cf. 332–33).

Finally, this distinction of revelation from its historical medium and the freedom of God in revelation entails that revelation cannot simply be gleaned from our side through the historical study of the Bible, though Barth does think that history and historical study must be taken with seriousness because revelation entered history at a particular place and time (see 326–27). He therefore rejects thinking of Scripture in mythological terms even as he rejects historicism (329). Such matters pertaining to Scripture have already been addressed and will be addressed in more detail below, so we can now turn to the next subsection.

Vestigium Trinitatis (§8.3)

Before turning to examine the content of the doctrine of the Trinity, Barth provides a brief subsection on a particular question regarding the knowledge of the Trinity. He has argued and will consistently maintain that the only way by which God's triune nature is known is in and through God's own act of revelation in history as attested in the biblical witness. This, by now, should be quite clear and expected. He now turns to reject explicitly any position that states that God's triune identity can be known apart from God's special revelation in Christ and that argues that it can also be known in and through a general revelation of God reflected in created realities. The most famous such position, and the one that Barth engages, is Augustine's teaching on the *vestigia trinitatis* (i.e., vestiges of the Trinity), whereby the Trinity is seemingly perceptible in a threefold structure of the human person or the human soul (e.g., memory, understanding, and will).

In arguing against Augustine's notion of the vestiges of the Trinity within the human person, Barth, of course, does not deny that God is known through taking up created realities for the purpose of revelation. What he is arguing against, rather, is a kind of static, immanent, and enduring relationship between God and the world that makes possible a general knowledge of God grasped by reflecting upon a permanent element in the human person or world at large. In this case, the element is the human soul understood in a tripartite way and as providing a reflection of God's own tripartite nature (334–35). Should this sort of general knowledge of God's triunity be possible, there would be a second root for the doctrine of the Trinity, one not founded on God's special act of revelation in the incarnation of the Word within history and effected through the Spirit's work but rather grounded in a permanent relationship between God and the world.

Barth's arguments against such a position need not be given in great detail here. What is important to note is that, in brief, his rejection of *vestigia trinitatis* is simply an extension and particular example of his firm rejection of any form of natural theology that exists independently of God's special revelation. The rejection of the *vestigia trinitatis* is simply the other side of the coin of his rejection of the *analogia entis*, or analogy of being, which he so strongly opposed in this period.[6] Indeed, the former is a particular instance of the latter and rests upon it. To wit: his rejection of the ontological relation between God and the human person articulated in the *vestigia trinitatis* is a specific application of his rejection of a general permanent relation between God and the world (untouched by sin), one that can be discerned by considering both God and the world as sharing in being and in turn made the basis for an independent knowledge of God. As he will write later in the *CD*, "We possess no analogy on the basis of which the nature and being of God as the Lord can be accessible to us" (*CD* II/1, 75). He rebuffs any theology that does not begin and end with God's special revelation in the historical event of God's self-disclosure and that turns instead to a consideration of the world or of the human person as a microcosm within it. This includes Augustine's attempt to find the Trinity reflected and inscribed within the constituent elements of the human soul.

Barth's rejection of such conceptions rests on a number of theological convictions. First, if there are two bases, rather than one, for the doctrine of the Trinity, then the question becomes which one is primary, and this in turn raises the further question of whether God can be known just as well in creation as in biblical revelation. When this duality is accepted, he wonders if the doctrine of the Trinity will not in the end be seen simply as a projection by humanity to understand the world and humanity's place within it—in other words, the doctrine of the Trinity becomes a matter of speculation and in turn is seen as a myth to reify and magnify elements of human nature and culture or aspects of the cosmos (335). This undermines not only the doctrine of the Trinity but also the concept of revelation, leaving in its wake only "mere cosmology or anthropology" (335). When such tripartite metaphysical construals are then demystified, the end result is atheism, as theology again gives way to anthropology. He thus consistently rejects such approaches in

6. For Barth's comments on the *analogia entis*, see the preface in *CD* I/1, xiii.

every form, for the doctrine of the Trinity cannot be rooted in an extrapolation from created realities, whether these be nature, culture, history, religion, or, as for Augustine, the human soul (336–38). Rather, trinitarian doctrine is an explication of God's unique, contingent, and particular revelation in Christ within history that comes to us from outside ourselves. It is not an extrapolation from the self to a metaphysical reality.

This brings us to the second and equally significant reason Barth rejects such attempts to ground the knowledge of God in nature: in the end, we arrive at a different god, and not the Triune God of the biblical witness. We are left with "some principle of the world or of humanity, of some alien God" (344). He certainly is aware that this was not the intention of Christian theologians in the past (like Augustine) who spoke of the Trinity reflected in nature. Nor is he unaware that in speaking of the Triune God of the Bible theologians cannot help but draw upon language in our world in their explication of God as triune. Yet he makes a strong distinction between interpretation and illustration that some may find confusing, and others find not entirely convincing: "Interpretation means saying *the same thing* in other words. Illustration means saying the same thing *in other words*" (345).

Once again we are left with a deeply dialectical approach to theology. Barth concedes that in interpreting the singular and unique revelation of God, one can appropriate general language for this purpose. What he rejects, however, is beginning with a more general conception of revelation and then moving to see the particular simply as an illustration of this more general principle. *For Barth, the movement always must go from the particular to the general, and even then, with appropriate qualification and caution.* The uniqueness of the Triune God revealed in history cannot be subsumed under a general religious conception of nature, culture, or history, even as the language of these three may be taken up and reframed and indeed redefined in order to speak of the particular revelation of God in this threefold way. In the end, however, we know God as triune only because of God's particular revelation in Christ through the Spirit, not because we can discern in a threefold constitution of the human person (such as memory, understanding, and will, or any other kind of threefold construal of the soul) a weak or strong reflection of the Triune God.

The Triunity of God (§9)

We have given much attention to §8, understandably so in light of its placement and function as the introduction to the following paragraphs and its difficult subject matter. The following paragraphs that elucidate the doctrine of the

Trinity itself do not require such detailed consideration, for while Barth's exposition of the doctrine of the Trinity introduces a few unique elements, it is, for the most part, dominated by quite traditional and familiar conceptions.

In §9 Barth addresses the doctrine of the Trinity by examining in sequence four themes: (1) the unity of God in God's triune identity; (2) the triune existence of God in God's unity; (3) the matter of God's own unique triunity; and, finally, (4) the meaning of this doctrine of God's triune existence.

Unity in Trinity (§9.1)

The emphasis in this first subsection is upon the reality that God is one yet exists in three "modes of being" (348). Barth here sides with a tradition that begins with the unity of God and then moves to consider God's triunity, emphasizing the one-ness of God in a way that staves off all hints of tritheism. In light of the manner in which he does so, he has at times been criticized for modalism (i.e., a heresy where each of the three persons of the Trinity is thought to be only differing appearances at different times in history of a single God). This charge is given some traction by his preference for the term "modes of being" (*Seinweisen*) instead of the more traditional term "person" for the three members of the Trinity: Father, Son, Holy Spirit (348). Yet he explicitly rejects modalism and maintains that this triune identity of God is an eternal one such that God is one yet exists eternally as these three distinct modes of being. As he writes, "The name of Father, Son and Spirit means that God is the one God in threefold repetition, and this in such a way that the repetition itself is grounded in His Godhead, so that it implies no alteration in His Godhead, and yet in such a way also that He is the one God only in this repetition, so that His one Godhead stands or falls with the fact that He is God in this repetition, but for that very reason He is the one God in each repetition" (350).

The doctrine of the Trinity must therefore be understood as the interpretation or explication of the revelation of God in history attested in Scripture in a threefold way—that is, as Father, as Son, and as Holy Spirit. The threefold name of this God as Father, Son, and Holy Spirit should not be thought of, however, as three distinct names nor as specifying three separate objects or essences or "gods," and Barth is ever wary of the danger of tritheism as the most dangerous mistake threatening the doctrine of the Trinity (349–50).

Barth's reticence to employ the word "person" therefore becomes understandable when it is remembered that we now take "person" to imply an autonomous individual—that is, a unique agent and center of consciousness, intellect, and will, as well as a distinct "personality" (351; cf. 357). Should "person" be employed in this way in trinitarian thought, it indeed would be problematic. It is this understanding of person that Barth contends has no bearing or relation to what have historically been called the "persons" of the Trinity. Indeed, the doctrine of the Trinity was not intended to express a divine plurality, but rather had the express purpose of preserving the divine unity, as well as the unity between the confession of the singular and incomparable nature of Israel's God and the confession of the NT that this God exists as Father and Son and Spirit. Barth's entire focus in this first subsection is upon this nonnegotiable confession of God's unity and singularity expressed and preserved in the doctrine of the Trinity. All antitrinitarian thought denies either the revelation of God as threefold or the unity of God (352). Modalism and subordinationism, in which the Son and the Spirit are not seen as fully divine, fundamentally undermine the first, whereas tritheism betrays the second. Barth is adamant that God's revelation discloses that not only the Father but also Jesus Christ as the revelation of the Father and the Spirit as the witness to the Son are fully and equally divine: "Only the substantial equality of Christ and the Spirit with the Father is compatible with monotheism" (353; see also 381–83, 393). He therefore resolutely rejects modalism and subordinationism of any kind.

Trinity in Unity (§9.2)

In the next subsection Barth reverses this relationship of unity and plural-ity, now emphasizing that the unity of God cannot be understood as other than composed of this inalienable triune identity. God, as one, is nevertheless triune. It is indeed God's revelation that places before us the reality that God's unity is no simple unity or idealization of one-ness. It is this revelation that marks and lies behind the difference between the Christian doctrine of the Trinity and all philosophical commitments to a singular deity or principle, as well as those of other monotheistic faiths such as Judaism or Islam (353–54). As he writes, "The concept of the revealed unity of the revealed God, then, does not exclude but rather includes a distinction . . . or order . . . in the es-sence of God. This distinction or order is the distinction or order of the three 'persons,' or, as we prefer to say, the three 'modes (or ways) of being' in God" (355). God exists eternally, essentially, irreducibly, and ineffaceably in these three "modes of being" (360–68). Writing in summary, he states, "The state-ment that God is One in three ways of being, Father, Son and Holy Ghost, means, therefore, that the one God, i.e. the one Lord, the one personal God, is what He is not just in one mode but—we appeal in support simply to the result of our analysis of the biblical concept of revelation—in the mode of the Father, in the mode of the Son, and in the mode of the Holy Ghost" (359).

Once again, Barth explains why he is reticent to use the term "person" in relation to the *hypostases*, or members, of the Trinity, and he does so with extended investigations of the historical precedents of the term (355–58). He does not ban the use of the term outright, for it indeed has strong traditional pedigree, but neither does he see it as helpful. Yet even though it is problematic, he concedes that the uniqueness of the Triune God makes finding an entirely suitable term impossible. The preference for "mode of being" rather than "person" is thus a relative, not an absolute, improvement in the attempt to preserve the "unity in distinction" of God's being, yet a distinction that can be preserved and specified only by the modest means of stating that the origins of the modes differ (359, 362; cf. 367).

In all of this, Barth displays a reticence to specify the differences between Father and Son and Spirit other than, as the patristic fathers had done, by specifying their different origins and respective qualities: the Father is unbegotten and possesses the quality of fatherhood; the Son is begotten and possesses the quality of sonship; and the Holy Spirit proceeds and possesses the quality of spirit-hood. In all of these discussions, he refrains from the use of "person" as the preferred way to speak of these three trinitarian members. Instead, he returns to speaking of a revealer, a revelation, and a being revealed, though he also reiterates that the Trinity is derived not from a general conception of such a threefold revelation, but rather from the particular revelation of the God who exists as Father, Son, and Spirit (363–64).

All that need yet be said here is that his reasons for abstaining from adopting the term "person" have convinced some, but certainly not all (and certainly not most), of those who have followed him in this task of reflection upon God's identity. At any rate, he does not think that his preference allows for the overcoming of the deep mysteries, and indeed paradoxes, that have always marked trinitarian thought. His forthright admission of how little his own discussion has furthered that of his predecessors is striking. He attributes this lack of progress to the inability of any human and creaturely language to depict the absolutely unique and incomparable reality of God's singular yet triune being and existence. It is thus the subject matter that must chasten the language used, and not the language that limits the subject matter (367–68). In the end, the Trinity remains, and must remain, a mystery.

Triunity (§9.3)

In the next subsection Barth brings together the prior two with a discussion of the "triunity" of God. Here he again addresses the relationship between the revealing work of God in history and the identity of God in eternity.

While strongly asserting their identity such that the God revealed in time is none other than the God who exists in eternity, he also consistently contends that God's identity as triune is not dependent upon God's activity in history, such that God's essence and work must be distinguished in this way. As he writes, "God's work is, of course, the work of the whole essence of God. God gives Himself entirely to man in His revelation, but not in such a way as to make Himself man's prisoner. He remains free in His working, in giving Himself" (371).

This freedom of God is what protects the distinction between the immanent and the economic Trinity. The former grounds the latter but is not dependent upon the latter. Yet it is nevertheless God's revelation in history that allows us to know God as God truly is. And even though the works of God in history can be appropriated to distinct persons (for instance, it is the Son, and not the Father or Spirit, who dies on the cross in the person of Christ), all of the persons of the Trinity are involved in all of the divine works. Therefore, while specific works can be appropriated to each of the modes of being, such works are not absolutely separated from any of them (373–74; cf. 396–97).[7]

The Meaning of the Doctrine of the Trinity (§9.4)

Barth lastly takes up the theme of the meaning of the Trinity. While the doctrine itself is not present in the Old or New Testaments, it is an explication of the biblical reality that the God who is hidden has become known in the threefold movement of "veiling, unveiling and imparting" (375–76). That the doctrine of the Trinity draws on philosophical terminology that goes beyond that of Scripture in no way undermines its truth, for the church has always had to rely on borrowing from the wider world of language in addressing its truth to the world. To reject such borrowing in effect would be to "reject the confessions and theology of any age and school" (378).

When this is realized, there is no reason to distrust the intentions of the church of the fourth century and the great councils when they attempted to articulate the Christian understanding of God both in light of the questions that arose from Scripture and against challenges from those like Arius who questioned the eternal divinity of the Son. Their ancient decisions on the Trinity

7. That the works of the Trinity in the world are indivisible (even while they can be appropriated to certain members of the Trinity) is the meaning of the Latin phrase *opera trinitatis ad extra sunt indivisa*, a phrase Barth frequently references (e.g., *CD* I/1, 362, 375, 394, 397, 442). This doctrine is tied to the concept of *perichoresis*, in which the three persons of the Trinity coinhere in one another (see 370, 396, 397). It is also the doctrine that complements the doctrine of appropriations, which itself assigns specific works to specific members of the Trinity, even while recognizing that the divine work of God in the world is not ultimately divided (373–75).

hold sway not only for Roman Catholicism and Eastern Orthodoxy but also for all of the Evangelical (i.e., magisterial Protestant) churches. This is not to say, Barth declares, that these ancient decisions ensconced in the creeds are beyond question. Their only defense and enduring value rest in their faithful and accurate articulation of that which is the subject matter of Scripture—God's revelation of himself in Jesus Christ through the Holy Spirit (see 378–83). The doctrine of the Trinity serves no purpose other than to answer the question as to the identity of the God who reveals himself and is revealed (380).

In placing the doctrine of the Trinity as the complement to the doctrine of revelation, Barth is providing a description of the work and identity of God in one extended discussion in CD I/1. This God, even in his revelation, remains the Lord, giving himself freely, and is never made an object of human manipulation or control (381). That Barth places the Trinity at the very beginning of his dogmatics not only demonstrates the foundational and formative place of the doctrine in his entire theological project but also stands as a testament to his intention to correct the doctrine's neglect in the recent past of Protestant liberalism (see 379).

God the Father (§10)

The final three paragraphs of CD I/1 (§§10–12) respectively address each of the divine persons, or "modes of being," of the Trinity. In these paragraphs Barth follows along traditional paths with little that is novel or particularly difficult to follow. His expositions are heavily peppered with historical descriptions, and each of these sections can be taken up briefly in turn.

God as Creator (§10.1); The Eternal Father (§10.2)

In §10 Barth turns to address God as the Father and as the Creator. In God's revelation God is revealed as the Lord, as one who is superior to humanity and creation, and yet as one who claims humanity for a relationship with himself (384). To know this Lord, Scripture points us to a history, and at the center of this history, at its climax, is Jesus of Nazareth as the Lord (384). Yet Jesus's very identity as the Lord is framed by the reality that Scripture begins by speaking of a Lord who is other than Jesus (385). This Lord is Yahweh the God of Israel, whom the NT portrays as the God and Father of Jesus Christ (385–90).

The first impression that one takes from the biblical witness is therefore not the identity and unity of Jesus with his Father but rather their distinction.

And as Jesus reveals this God to us as his Father, he reveals God to be our Creator as well (389). This is not intrinsically self-apparent, Barth contends: "That God is our Creator is not a general truth that we can know in advance or acquire on our own; it is a truth of revelation" (389). Here, too, Barth's understanding of the knowledge of God as Creator is not predicated on a general observation of the world's order, design, or even existence but is the result of the particular revelation of the Father to us in Christ. Moreover, that God is Father is not simply the result of a role that God takes up in his relation to us as creatures; rather, God is eternally Father in himself (390). That God is eternally Father speaks not only to his eternal fellowship with the Son and the Spirit but also of the Father's eternal distinction from them (397).

Barth emphasizes that the revelation of the Father cannot be separated from the manifestation of the incarnate Son: "The form here is essential to the content, i.e., God is unknown as our Father, as the Creator, to the degree that He is not made known by Jesus" (390). This intricate relationship of Father and Son in revelation has implications for the doctrine of the Trinity, for while the Father and the Son might be distinguished, they cannot be placed in a ranking of subordination without losing the revelation altogether (393).[8] It also rules out any attempt to know the content of God's identity apart from the form that this has taken in the incarnation: "If this exclusiveness is accepted and taken seriously, if that abstraction between form and content is thus seen to be forbidden, this rules out the possibility of regarding the first article of the Christian faith as an article of natural theology" (391).

The repeated rejection of natural theology and of a knowledge of God apart from the revelation that comes to us in the incarnation entails that Barth's concerns seen earlier in his discussions of method are never far from his mind, and that the epistemological concerns are always related to ontological ones—that is, how God is known cannot be separated from questions of who God is, just as the content of revelation cannot be abstracted or separated from its form. He succinctly brings these points together when he states, "Jesus did not proclaim the familiar Creator God and interpret Him by the unfamiliar name of Father. He revealed the unknown Father, His Father, and in so doing, and only in so doing, He told us for the first time that the Creator is, what He is and that He is as such our Father" (391). Of course, here again we are faced with one of the most controversial aspects of Barth's

---

8. Rejecting subordination, Barth writes, "The divine essence would not be the divine essence if in it there were superiority and inferiority and also, then, various quanta of deity. The Son and the Spirit are of one essence with the Father" (CD I/1, 393).

thought, but one that is entirely consistent with his christological focus (his positive point) and his rejection of natural theology (his negative point).

God the Son (§11)

Barth will address Christology much more extensively in part 2 of chapter 2, "The Revelation of God," but here in §11 he provisionally examines the Son as the second member of the Trinity. As earlier discussed, he sees the second mode of divine being in Christ as the key for understanding the first and third modes of being.

God as Reconciler (§11.1); The Eternal Son (§11.2)

Barth begins with attention to the statement that Jesus of Nazareth is the Lord, the center of the witness of Scripture (399). If earlier in his paragraph on the Father he focused upon the identity of God the Father who is demarcated from Jesus, now in this paragraph on the Son he focuses upon the unity of the Father and the Son and provides a discussion of the divinity of the Son and the identity of the Son himself. It is impossible to read the NT attentively, Barth contends, and esteem Christ simply as a person who was "exalted as such to deity or appeared among us as the personification and symbol of a divine being" (402). This entire section argues against any position that would begin with Jesus as a historical man who later was conceived to be divine. Rather, from the very beginning, the NT presents Jesus as God in the flesh, the incarnation of God in our world.

In this respect, it may be a bit simplistic but not inaccurate to say that here, early in the CD, Barth presents a strong Christology "from above" (beginning with Jesus as God and then moving to understand his humanity) and rejects a Christology that begins "from below" (that begins its reflection from a consideration of Jesus as a historical and human figure and then moves to understand in what way he might be thought of as divine). It must immediately be said, however, that he rejects the conception of a heavenly figure who becomes human in the sense of an idea becoming particular (which he defines as the essence of myth) as much as he rejects the conception of Jesus as a distinctive and unique personality who later is exalted to the status of divinity (404; see 402–6). In truth, he rejects all Docetic Christologies (those that emphasize Christ's divine identity but reject his humanity and particular identity) as well as all Ebionitic Christologies (those that emphasize Christ's humanity and reject his divinity). These rejections are necessitated because of the witness of Scripture itself: "The material point in the New Testament texts is that *God* is found in Jesus because in fact Jesus Himself cannot be found as any other than God. And God is found in *Jesus* because in fact He is not found anywhere else but in Jesus, yet He is in fact found in Him" (405). In order to reveal the Father, to present to us God, Christ himself has to be God, for a creature could not reveal God to us, and therefore Christ must share in the divinity of the Father (406; cf. 410).

Another aspect of this christological fact is that, as spoken of in an earlier chapter, Barth thinks of revelation and reconciliation, God's act of self-disclosure to us and God's act of salvation for us, as two sides of one work of God (409). In this sense, as only God can reveal God, and therefore Jesus must be divine and share the same essence as the Father, so also only God can save us (as the patristic fathers also claimed), and therefore the Son must share in the divinity of the Father in order to bring about our salvation. Here arguments grounded in the doctrine of revelation are wedded to those of reconciliation and salvation, and all serve the trinitarian claim that the Son shares in the same divine essence as the Father (409). Only God can reveal God, and only God can save. Hence, as the agent of God's revelation and reconciliation, Jesus Christ must be divine.

Barth continues on with a consideration of the distinctive work of the Son. The divine lordship expressed in creation, and appropriated to the Father, finds its complement in reconciliation, the overcoming of sin on our behalf, and this is appropriated to the Son. As Barth expresses this, "For as we have to say that reconciliation or revelation is not creation or a continuation of creation but rather an inconceivably new work above and beyond creation, so we have also to say that the Son is not the Father but that here, in this work, the one God, though not without the Father, is the Son or Word of the Father" (410). The distinction of the work of God in the economy between creation and reconciliation is thus a reflection of God's own self-distinction as Father and Son in eternity. Again, contrary to the position of modalism, God is not Father and Son only in the economy. Rather, the revelation and reconciliation enacted in the world reflect God's nature as both Father and Son. The revelation of the Father is known in no other way than in Jesus, and Jesus is none other than the revelation of the Father (412). And so the revelation of God exists only in this twofold reality of Father and Son, of Creator and Revealer. Creation and reconciliation are thus known only together, just as the Creator and the Reconciler are known only together (412–13). The second mode of being of the Trinity is known as both the Word of God and the Son of God, and Barth posits that the first is perhaps most apt in speaking of the divine work of revelation, and the latter most apt in speaking of the divine work of reconciliation (434).

Along a similar line of thinking on the distinction of Creator and creation outlined in the last chapter, Barth maintains that even though the Son is known as Son through the act of reconciliation that he undertakes, he does not become the Son in or through or because of this action. The Son is the Son in eternity apart from his work in time. Here again, Barth preserves the freedom of God, now in the person of the Son, who is the Son apart from his manifestation and salvific activity in the world, and thus eternally and "antecedently in Himself," an important phrase in Barth's theology (e.g., 384, 399, 416, 422, 425, 428, 448, 466, 470, 471, 474, 484). As he puts this idea, "The deity of Christ is true, eternal deity. We see it in His work in revelation and reconciliation. But revelation and reconciliation do not create His deity. His deity creates revelation and reconciliation" (415; cf. 424). In brief: "He is the Son or Word of God for us because He is so antecedently in Himself" (416).

Similarly, Barth also rejects the absolute division drawn between God's works and the God who stands behind them that he finds in modern Protestant liberalism. That tradition for the most part considered the doctrine of the Trinity simply as a matter of metaphysical speculation that could be jettisoned in favor of an emphasis upon God's salvation in time. In contrast, Barth steadfastly insists that the doctrine of the Trinity is that which must stand behind and ground the doctrine of salvation, giving it its underlying ontological foundation, and he charges any reading of the Reformers as mistaken that disregards or misconstrues their trinitarian commitments. Indeed, as he argues, it is the separation of the doctrine of the eternal deity of the Son from his work of salvation that leads to all sorts of speculation regarding the latter and that in turn sacrifices the character of God's salvation for us as grace, for grace implies God's freedom to be God apart from us (see 416–23). It is this divine freedom that modern Protestantism has lost, and thus with it all attention to the doctrine of the Trinity. He goes so far as to say that this neglect of God's freedom has caused "the rift which divides the Evangelical Church" and adds that such a sacrifice of divine freedom can only be protested here "as we can only protest against the assertions of Roman Catholic theology in other contexts" (422–23).

In this paragraph, as in the last one on the Father, Barth carefully explicates a relation between God and the world in which God is known only through his revelation in the world in Christ but is not constituted by this revelation. God acts as the Creator and the Reconciler because God is in himself the Father and the Son. In making this argument, he sides with the ancient patristic writers and their conciliar decisions regularized in the creeds over against the critical, antitraditional, and even antitrinitarian arguments of modern

Protestantism. He sets forth the implications of these decisions in a section of extended commentary on the Nicene Creed (see 423–47).

God the Holy Spirit (§12)

In the two prior paragraphs Barth has outlined both the distinction and the unity of God the Father and Jesus Christ the Son. In §12 he takes up the person of the Holy Spirit as the one who reveals to us that Christ is indeed the revelation of God. That Christ is this revelation of God is neither self-evident nor an achievement of human perception but is known only by means of a further unique divine work, a third movement in God's act of revelation that points to a unique divine identity.

God as Redeemer (§12.1); The Eternal Spirit (§12.2)

In addressing the question of the identity of the Holy Spirit, Barth takes up what he designates as the "subjective side" in the event of revelation (448–49). This matter of subjectivity concerns how God's revelation in Christ comes to be recognized by persons and becomes a reality in their lives: "How does it happen that they believe the Father through the Son and the Son through the Father?" (448). This is the question of how persons come to faith, and it is one that he distinctly appropriates to the work of the Holy Spirit, who is the Redeemer, bringing the work of salvation to its proper completion and end. Indeed, to recognize that this man, Jesus Christ, is not simply a great teacher or holy person, but is God in the flesh, requires a divine work. This work is effected by the Spirit of God, apart from whom no one can confess that "Jesus is Lord" (460). The Spirit therefore reveals the true identity of the Son as the Son reveals the Father.

Barth begins here as in prior paragraphs by moving from the act of revelation to the question of God's triune identity. In the act of revelation, God the Father is revealed through the Revealer, the Son, who takes on flesh to reveal God to us. Yet in assuming human form, God is not only revealed but also hidden behind the veil of this human life. How, then, is God in Christ recognized, acknowledged, and indeed confessed? That persons do in fact come to this recognition, acknowledgment, and confession is nothing short of a miracle. This miracle is a work of the Holy Spirit as the Spirit awakens persons to faith and obedience and empowers them for witness, in turn taking up their own speech in order to awaken others to faith in turn (452–56). As Barth states, "The Holy Spirit is the authorization to speak about Christ;

He is the equipment of the prophet and apostle; He is the summons to the Church to minister the Word" (455).

This reality of faith awakened and of witness performed is the work of the third distinction in the divine identity, the special work of the Holy Spirit: "This special element in revelation is undoubtedly identical with what the New Testament usually calls the Holy Spirit as the subjective side in the event of revelation" (449). If the objective side of God's revelation is Jesus Christ, the Word who took on flesh, the Son who donned a creaturely form, then the subjective side of God's revelation—not that which stands apart from us and over against us, but the divine work that occurs within us, renewing, enlightening, and awakening us to faith and obedience—is the work of the Holy Spirit. Barth grounds this discussion of the Holy Spirit in God's act of revelation, driving home that the revelation of God can be achieved only by God, and thus the Spirit must be no less divine or different in divine essence and reality than the Father or the Son (459). As in the prior paragraphs, he examines this question by surveying a wide swath of scriptural passages and by revisiting the church's prior conciliar decisions in creeds and confessions.

Also as in previous paragraphs, God's freedom is given a prominent place. Barth writes, "The Spirit of God is God in His freedom to be present to the creature, and therefore to create this relation, and therefore to be the life of the creature. And God's Spirit, the Holy Spirit, especially in revelation, is God Himself to the extent that He can not only come to man but also be in man, and thus open up man and make him capable and ready for Himself, and thus achieve His revelation in him" (450). This relation of God and the human person is achieved not from the side of the creature but only from the side of the Creator. This, too, displays God's freedom, for it is a relationship freely established, and thus a relationship of pure grace. Moreover, the freedom of the Spirit also designates the distinction and irreversible relation between the Holy Spirit and the human spirit, a distinction that Barth believes was lost in modern Protestantism, and one that he wants to preserve at all costs, for its betrayal leads to both idolatry of the self and confusion of our own programs and desires with the will of God. As he insists, "the Spirit is not identical, and does not become identical, with ourselves" (454; cf. 462, 468).

It is important to note yet again that this freedom of the Spirit pertains not only to salvation but also to God's own being and identity. Indeed, salvation exists only because it is an expression of God's own character. If God were not God apart from the world (ontological freedom), then God could not establish this relation simply on the basis of mercy and grace (salvific freedom). Barth's emphasis that we know God only through God's activity of revelation and salvation in the world is not the same as saying that God's identity is nothing more than and exhausted by this activity. He consistently maintains, as in the prior two paragraphs on the Father and on the Son, that the Holy Spirit is the one who establishes this relationship between God and humanity, but the Spirit can do this because the Spirit already exists and lives eternally as the Triune God apart from this relationship:

> The Holy Spirit does not first become the Holy Spirit, the Spirit of God, in the event of revelation. The event of revelation has clarity and reality on its subjective side because the Holy Spirit, the subjective element in this event, is of the essence of God Himself. What He is in revelation He is antecedently in Himself. And what He is antecedently in Himself He is in revelation. Within the deepest depths of deity, as the final thing to be said about Him, God is God the Spirit as He is God the Father and God the Son. (466; cf. 467, 470–71)

This distinctive work of manifesting the revelation of God in Christ points to a distinct person, or mode of being, within the Godhead: "The Holy Spirit is not identical with Jesus Christ, with the Son or Word of God" (451). Neither is the Spirit identified with the Father. The Spirit exists in an irreducibly discrete yet united relation with both, as God with God (451, 459, 474).[9] Yet the revelation that the Spirit brings should not be seen in any way as a separate or different one from that brought by the Son, just as the Son is not a different revelation of the Father but is the Father's true revelation: "He is not to be regarded, then, as a revelation of independent content, as a new instruction, illumination and stimulation of man that goes beyond Christ, beyond the Word, but in every sense as the instruction, illumination and stimulation of man through the Word and for the Word" (452–53).

Barth concludes this section with a detailed examination of the Nicene Creed in similar fashion to that of the prior paragraph (see 468–89). As with his discussion of Christ, so here with the Spirit, he rejects all forms of modalism and subordinationism that would relativize and undermine the distinctive identity of the Spirit and the Spirit's status as a coequal member of the Triune God. Yet he also retains his reticence to designate the members of the Trinity as "persons," and he follows the Western (Augustinian) tradition of seeing the Spirit as the bond of fellowship between the Father and the Son and as proceeding from both the Father and the Son (rather than, as in the Eastern church, from the Father alone) (470, 473–87). No small reason is that the Spirit and the Word are not independent, but rather are intimately related,

---

9. Barth notes, interestingly, that the blasphemy against the Holy Spirit that renders a person guilty of an unforgivable sin (Matt. 12:31–32; Mark 3:28–29; Luke 12:10) could not be possible "if the Spirit were less or something other than God himself" (CD I/1, 460).

and this is true not only in the economy but also in God's eternal life. Thus the Spirit is the Spirit of Christ, proceeding from the Father and the Son.

COMMENTARY

The Doctrine of the Trinity as a Biblical Question

The doctrine of the Trinity is at the heart of historic Christianity in all of its major forms, yet admittedly it is one of the greatest sources of perplexity not only for those who stand outside the Christian faith and attempt to understand it but also for those within the church itself. In some traditions, Trinity Sunday brings with it a sense of anxiety for pastors who feel obligated to preach on a doctrine that they fear is beyond their own grasp, and certainly an enigma to those before them in the pews. Yet even Christians not bound by strict observance of the Christian year and its feast days subscribe to the doctrine of the Trinity, and even they must make sense of it not only for their own sake but also for that of the children they instruct in the faith and the converts who embrace it. Both this necessity and the perplexity should be appreciated. The Christian church must proclaim its allegiance to God, and to do so it must be able to state the identity of this God, yet this is no simple task. Indeed, the difficulty is an intrinsic element of the necessary task itself. The doctrine of the Trinity claims to speak of God, and God, Barth insists, is and remains a mystery even in his revelation to us.

It may be helpful to remember that the doctrine of the Trinity is in truth not a matter of ancient speculative metaphysics but of biblical exegesis and interpretation. In other words, the doctrine of the Trinity was intended to be not a philosophical puzzle but the answer given by the church to the question of the identity of the God it found in Holy Scripture and worshiped. This God was one God, a God revealed to Israel as unrivaled by other deities, a God whose reality showed all others to be false gods, shadows and powerless vestiges of human imagination. Yet the church's early confession was not only composed of declaring this one God but also included the radical conviction that Jesus is Lord. The full weight of such a pronouncement cannot be overestimated, especially when it is remembered that the Greek word for "Lord" (*kyrios*) was the word used in the Greek translation of the OT for the Hebrew name for God (YHWH, "Yahweh"). When Paul takes a passage of the OT with reference to the adoration and worship of God and then applies it to Jesus, so that it is now at *his* name that "every knee will bow . . . and every tongue confess, that Jesus Christ is Lord" (Phil. 2:9–11; cf. Isa. 45:23–24), this is an astonishing thing for a first-century Jewish writer to do. Moreover, Paul can also state that the Spirit is Lord, also with such weighty implications (2 Cor. 3:17). Such examples of divine transference and attribution to Jesus and the Spirit can be multiplied with any attentive reading of the NT.

Barth is, then, correct to emphasize that the question the doctrine of the Trinity attempts to answer is not a philosophical problem of the early church but arises from the pages of the NT itself. How can the one God of Israel in the OT be reconciled with the divine claims for Jesus in the NT, who, like God alone, can calm the sea, heal the sick, forgive sins, and even receive worship, create the world, and save it? And how can such claims for the Spirit also be so reconciled? In short, the doctrine of the Trinity, rather than an abandonment of Scripture's emphasis upon the unity and uniqueness of God, was in fact the church's means of preserving such claims in light of the equally striking divine claims made for Christ and the Spirit.

The doctrine of the Trinity is therefore an attempt by the church to articulate what must be said about the God of Israel in light of Jesus Christ's appearance in history and the Spirit's divine work in the church. When this is remembered, the doctrine of the Trinity can be seen for what it truly is: an articulation by the church of what it believes about the God who has been revealed as the Father through the Son, Jesus Christ, by means of the Spirit. This revelation is attested in Holy Scripture, and the doctrine of the Trinity is the attempt to read and understand Scripture rightly with regard to the identity of the God of whose revelation it tells. That the doctrine *itself* is not explicitly taught in Scripture does not undermine this fact, for the doctrine is an attempt to be faithful to Scripture by interpreting it rightly, not simply an attempt to mimic its language (hence the biblical truth of the doctrine is in no way undermined by the fact that the word "Trinity" itself is not found in the Bible's pages).

For this reason, the doctrine need not be treated as a philosophical problem, nor must the ancient church's language of "essence" and "person" be the first thing we say about it. We might rather say that the one God we worship comes to us as Father and Son and Spirit. The difficult questions about *how* this may be so are important, but they are not as important as the confession of this primary biblical truth. The doctrine of the Trinity attempts to articulate this truth and thus rightly shapes all of the church's life, from its prayer, to its worship and hymnody, to its witness to the world. It is foundational for how Christians attempt to speak of a loving and benevolent Father, a revealing Son who makes the Father known, and a life-giving and life-changing Spirit. It speaks of this one God who exists in this threefold way.

There have, of course, been those who have abandoned the doctrine of the Trinity, and Barth is well aware of such proclivities in the Protestant liberalism that he is polemically engaging. Yet the ramifications of the doctrine's abandonment are significant. To give up on the doctrine of the Trinity reduces Jesus from Lord to teacher, reduces the Spirit to an unknown or even nonexistent force, and leaves God, ultimately, unknowable. This agnosticism is yet one more reason to understand Barth's emphasis that God's revelation and God's triune identity are two sides of one coin, for God is nothing other than who he is in his revelation. Though some have judged Barth's reflections on the Trinity as somewhat circuitous, seeing the doctrine of the Trinity as both the ground and the result of revelation, we need not be overly bothered by such circular reasoning—God is known only in his revelation, but reflection upon this revelation reveals that it could not have occurred had God not been who he is in himself, preceding such revelation and making it possible. In this respect, it does seem that the doctrine of revelation is the epistemological basis for the doctrine of the Trinity, and the doctrine of the Trinity is the ontological basis for the doctrine of revelation. In older terms, the doctrine of revelation is first in the order of knowing, whereas the doctrine of the Trinity is first in the order of being. For Barth, these doctrines are necessarily distinguished, but they are also indissolubly united.

The Doctrine of the Trinity and the Particular Identity of God

In light of what has been said, a doctrine might be defined as a theological interpretation of the truth that is attested in Holy Scripture. Because of its dependence upon the exegesis of Scripture, a doctrine (as a result of doctrinal reflection itself) is therefore intrinsically set against all forms of speculation, philosophical or otherwise. The worship of God as one is a worship not of a philosophical principle of "One-ness" but of the singular, unrivaled, and holy God revealed to Israel and in Jesus Christ. In its trinitarian convictions that express a commitment to God as one and as three, Christian faith differs not only from all polytheistic religions but also from other Abrahamic faiths such as Judaism and Islam. Christian faith, too, claims to worship one God, but it does so in a way that also confesses that Jesus is Lord and that the Spirit is God's own presence in the church and is active in the world.

In the end, it is the uniqueness of the God revealed in Jesus Christ through the Spirit that requires that the doctrine of the Trinity follow the path of this divine revelation. Barth's rejection of natural theology, of the *analogia entis*, and of the *vestigium trinitatis*, are all, in the end, tied to a recognition that this Triune God cannot be known apart from this threefold revelation.

To take any other path to God is a matter of speculation, and for Barth, the road from such speculation leads in the end not to a confirmation of faith but to unbelief. Indeed, one could argue that the tendency in the modern (Enlightenment) period to rely on philosophical appeals to nature and the self in order to ground religious belief, coupled with a dismissal of Christology, was at the core of atheism's ascendency.[10] The doctrine of the Trinity hangs on Christology, and a low Christology leads to dissolution of the doctrine of the Trinity. Surrender the conviction of the divinity and distinctiveness of Jesus Christ, and the doctrine of the Trinity dissolves.

This observation perhaps adds weight to the question of whether theology has a necessary christocentric character. Barth can go so far as to claim that we know God the Creator only through the Son, not through general reflection upon the created order. Similarly, the Spirit, too, is known through this special revelation of the Son and not by means of the discernment of an immanent and universal divine religious experience. In both cases, the particularity of revelation in Jesus Christ protects the particularity of God the Father as Creator and of the Spirit as Redeemer. When this particularity is lost, we end up with vague and amorphous conceptions of a Creator and an immanent divine Spirit. The danger always exists that both can be defined as we want them to be. This explains Barth's reticence to have a general doctrine of a Creator God that was not understood through the revelation of the Son, or a general doctrine of a divine immanent Spirit that was also independent of the Word. His adoption of the *filioque* clause—that the Spirit proceeds from the Father and the Son—can be understood in light of the fact that the Spirit exists and acts only in accordance with the Son.

QUESTIONS FOR REFLECTION

- Why must the Christian doctrine of God begin with Scripture rather than with philosophical contemplation? How might remembering that the doctrine of the Trinity arises from and is rooted in biblical interpretation rather than philosophical speculation help the church in speaking about and teaching this doctrine? How might it help pastors as they prepare to preach about the Trinity on Trinity Sunday? How might it inform how the doctrine is to be taught to children and young adults within the church?

10. See Michael J. Buckley, *At the Origins of Modern Atheism* (New Haven: Yale University Press, 1987).

- Explain in your own words what Barth is saying in the following passage:

  > But we have consistently followed the rule, which we regard as basic, that
  > statements about the divine modes of being antecedently in themselves
  > cannot be different in content from those that are to be made about
  > their reality in revelation. All our statements concerning what is called
  > the immanent Trinity have been reached simply as confirmations or un-
  > derlinings or, materially, as the indispensable premises of the economic
  > Trinity. (CD I/1, 479)

  Why is Barth adamant that the God who is revealed in time is the God
  who exists in eternity?

- What are the problems with modalism? With tritheism? How does each
  distort the identity of God and in turn sacrifice the truth that the doctrine of the Trinity attempts to articulate and express?

- How does the doctrine of the Trinity differ from deism, where there is
  a God who stands transcendent from the world but does not interact
  within it? How does the doctrine of the Trinity differ from forms of
  pantheism and panentheism, where the Spirit is understood as a divine
  presence immanent in all things?

- How might greater attention to the doctrine of the Trinity change how
  we think about God and the world? About the Spirit's presence in the
  world? About the church's worship? About Christian life?

- Should theology be christocentric? Is there a danger that a focus on
  Christ will lead to a neglect of the Spirit? Why did Barth think that
  focusing upon the second article of the creed—that is, upon Christology—is the key for understanding the first and third articles (on the
  Father and the Spirit, respectively)? How might an emphasis upon them
  apart from Christology lead to a distortion of the Christian doctrine of
  God and of a Christian doctrine of the Holy Spirit? How are Barth's
  christocentric focus and rejection of natural theology two sides of one
  coin?

7

The Incarnation of the Word

CD §§13–15

The second part of chapter 2 is titled "The Incarnation of the Word." Here Barth makes his first extended foray into Christology on its own terms as a doctrine, having introduced this topic in the prior section on the Holy Trinity, and reserving his fullest description of Christology for the fourth volume of the CD on the doctrine of reconciliation. While the most developed discussion of Christology belongs there, its underlying convictions are already present here within the doctrine of the Word of God (CD I/2, 3).

This section on the incarnation is composed of §§13–15, which address the person of Jesus Christ as the objective revelation of God. It should be noted that we have now transitioned from CD I/1 to CD I/2, and therefore all page numbers included parenthetically in the text will from this point forward refer to this second part-volume (i.e., CD I/2) unless otherwise noted. This explains the fact that all page numbers now begin anew from page 1 onward.

God's Freedom for Man (§13)

In the first paragraph of part 2 Barth takes up the objective pole of revelation—the act whereby the Word takes up a human life such that Jesus Christ exists as God's presence in the world under the veil of created flesh. He orders his discussion such that it is the reality of this event that governs the reflection on the conditions for its possibility, rather than stipulating whether such an event is possible, and how Christ should be understood in light of such stipulations.

Jesus Christ the Objective Reality of Revelation (§13.1)

The objective reality of revelation is the incarnation of the Word in Jesus Christ, a free and sovereign work of God. In this work, God does not sacrifice his singular agency and lordship. In taking on a human life, in no way does God "become the predicate or object of our existence or action" (1). God is, and ever remains, the Subject of action and never the object of our action (objective revelation thus differs from *objectifying* revelation). As the Subject of this action of revelation is the divine Trinity, Barth now focuses upon the first movement of God to us, which is composed of God's taking up flesh for us in the incarnation of the Word, or Son (1). He designates this act as how God is *free for us* in Christ (the objective side of revelation, i.e., Christology), just as when he takes up the second movement of revelation he will designate it as how God is *free in us* through the Holy Spirit (the subjective side of revelation, i.e., pneumatology). The first describes the movement from God to us, whereas the second describes the movement from us to God (2).

Barth's focus is the miracle that makes revelation possible. This miracle is in fact constituted by two miracles: God's spontaneity to take on flesh in Christ (the incarnation of the Word), and God's spontaneity to move us to acknowledge and confess this revelation such that our sin and blindness are overcome (the outpouring of the Holy Spirit). These miracles rest, however, entirely on God's side: "God is not prevented either by His own deity or by our humanity and sinfulness from being our God and having intercourse with us as with His own. On the contrary, He is free for us and in us. That is the central content of the doctrine of Christ and of the doctrine of the Holy Spirit. Christology and Pneumatology are one in being the knowledge and praise of the grace of God. But the grace of God is just His freedom, unhindered either by Himself or by us" (2–3).

In beginning this elucidation of Christology, Barth does not begin with the question of whether the incarnation is possible or coherent. He does not ask whether such a thing could occur in light of our general knowledge of nature and history, nor does he set forth general conditions that must be true for this event to be considered meaningful or possible. In contrast, he begins with the reality of the incarnation as a given, and only asks as to what must be true of God and God's freedom in order to explain how this has in fact occurred. He therefore moves not from questions of possibility to reality, but takes the incarnation as real and only then moves to questions of its possibility (3).

To begin with the possible, he contends, is to place presupposed limits upon what one is able to accept, and this in turn distorts revelation in that it places strictures on what may or may not be believed about it. Both the inherited Enlightenment restrictions on the miraculous and the scientific convictions of historical criticism contained in the nineteenth century's liberal tradition are indirect yet unquestionable targets of his polemic.

Nevertheless, his rejection expands beyond his liberal inheritance: "It may be asserted very definitely that no matter whether a theology claims to be liberal or orthodox, it is not a theology of revelation in so far as it rests openly or secretly upon this reversal, in so far as it asks first what is possible in God's freedom, in order afterwards to investigate God's real freedom" (4). As we have already witnessed, this movement from reality to reflection upon the conditions of its possibility, rather than an approach that moves from general criteria that constrict what is considered possible at all, is a central element of Barth's dogmatic reflection. So also is his corresponding conviction that theological method must follow and be determined by the reality of its subject matter set forth in Holy Scripture, rather than strictly set forth the shape and scope and indeed possibilities of what can be accepted from Holy Scripture (see 8–9).

With Christology one approaches the center of the witness of Scripture: "Jesus Christ is not one element in the New Testament witness alongside of others, but as it were the mathematical point toward which all the elements of New Testament witness are directed" (11). This statement is yet another witness of Barth's christocentric focus, here hermeneutically expressed. Christ stands at the center of Scripture and is the lens through which it is interpreted. At the heart of Christology lies this twofold and dialectical statement: "The Word or Son of God became a Man and was called Jesus of Nazareth; therefore this Man Jesus of Nazareth was God's Word or God's Son" (13). Two things should be noted about this statement at the outset. First, it is in actuality quite rare that the NT speaks in such a straightforward way about Jesus Christ. Just as the Trinity as a doctrine is not explicated in Scripture but is a faithful interpretation of it, so the NT does not provide a detailed description of Christ's divine and human identity and speaks of such things most often only indirectly and only by placing them in subordination to the name and person of Jesus Christ himself (13–15). Yet just as with the doctrine of the Trinity, the "christological dogma" of the incarnation and of the divinity of Christ is a faithful commentary of the biblical text and the truth to which it witnesses (13–14).

The second thing that should be noticed is that the twofold nature of the statement reveals that one might begin christological reflection with the reality that God's eternal Word, or Son, became human, but one might also begin with the acknowledgment that this man Jesus of Nazareth is God's eternal Son. These statements are not harmonized in the NT but stand as correspondent witnesses. Barth finds the first type represented in the Gospel of John, whereas he finds the second represented in the Synoptic Gospels (Matthew, Mark, Luke), and he finds both represented in the writings of Paul (15–16). Even though they take different approaches, the Gospel writers should not be contrasted as historians but each seen as a witness, though each begins from a different side of the twofold description of the eternal Son as this man Jesus (the Gospel of John), and Jesus as God's eternal Son (the Synoptic Gospels). In holding both the divine identity and the human identity of Jesus together in this dialectical tension, and in seeing this dialectical paradox already present in the Gospels, Barth rejects all Docetic and Ebionitic positions that deny Christ's full humanity or divinity, respectively (17–25). As he concludes, "To sum up: that God's Son or Word is the man Jesus of Nazareth is the one Christological thesis of the New Testament; that the man Jesus of Nazareth is God's Son or Word is the other" (23). These statements cannot be synthesized but must be held up as a twofold witness pointing to the reality of Jesus as both the divine Son of God and a fully human person. In the end we are left not with a synthesis of the two statements but with a single name: Jesus Christ (24–25).

Jesus Christ the Objective Possibility of Revelation (§13.2)

Having begun with the reality of the revelation of God in Jesus Christ as witnessed in the biblical canon, Barth turns to the question of what must be true of God and divine freedom for this objective reality of revelation to have occurred, and what conditions must exist to make this revelation intelligible. In short, the fact of the incarnation now requires that an interpretation of this fact be given—the reality requires an elucidation of its possibility (25–26).

What Barth in fact addresses in this section is the identity of God as well as the nature of God's freedom that serves as the prior condition that makes the incarnation possible, as well as real and effective (27). This account, again, is derived not from a general notion of what is possible, but from reflection upon the particular revelation of God as Barth asks what must be true of God for the incarnation to have taken place (27–31). In short: "The possibility of revelation is actually to be read off from its reality in Jesus Christ" (31). Such reflection in turn leads us to a number of conclusions about God.

First, God is not captive to the boundary that separates him, in regard to both his being and holiness, from our created and fallen state. That God can humble himself and enter our world reveals his very glory: "The majesty of God in His condescension to the creature—that is the most general truth always told us by the reality of Jesus Christ" (31). God assumes our nature "without ceasing to be Himself" (32). God remains God even in this condescension and is free to become "identical with a reality different from Himself" (44). Throughout this section Barth will maintain that God is not compelled to do this, but that this condescension is always an act of pure grace and divine freedom, even as it reveals the very nature of God (32–33, 35, 39).

Second, Barth states that the incarnation shows us that while it is proper only to say that the Son, and not the Father or the Holy Spirit, became human, it is also not correct to deny that God "in his entire divinity became man" (33, 44). In this sense, he protects against a conception in which the incarnation is an exception and, crudely put, simply a peripheral element of God's activity and existence only pertaining to the Son. The incarnation rather must be seen as "the common work of the Father, the Son and the Holy Spirit" (33). Here we see a tension between the doctrine of appropriation (in which the incarnation is attributed to the specific person of the Son), and that of God's perichoretic activity, in which the works of the three persons of the Trinity are not divided and are mutually implicated. Here in Christology as earlier in his discussion on the doctrine of the Trinity, Barth attempts to respect both of these doctrines and holds them in a dialectical tension of mutual if paradoxical affirmation.

Third, Barth states that the incarnation reveals to us that God is willing and able to take a form that is recognizable to us and in this identifies with us (35–36, 44). This again is predicated upon God's veiling and unveiling of himself in human form. In language reminiscent of Calvin's that God stoops down to our level to speak to us, Barth writes, "God bends down to us as it were, by assuming this form familiar to us. His love is already announced to us in the fact that even in His veiling—in which He has first to be unveiled as God, to be believed in as God—He yet does not meet us as a stranger" (36–37). Echoes of Calvin and perhaps even of Kierkegaard resonate in this passage.

Fourth, the incarnation shows us that even in this act of condescension God remains true to himself and remains God even in becoming human (37–38, 44). God's immutability is, paradoxically, not sacrificed but demonstrated in the incarnation. The incarnation is not a lessening of God, or even a change in God, but is a revelation of who God truly is. The incarnation and its mystery is that God, without ceasing to be God, became this man, Jesus of Nazareth (37–39). God is truly himself even as he takes on this human form, and the humility shown in this condescension is not contrary to, but rather is a revelation of, God's own nature. In this, the incarnation poses no threat to God's immutability but instead upholds and reveals it, though an immutability perhaps reconceptualized.

Finally, and not unrelated to the third point above, the incarnation shows that God is free not only to be with us but also to be one among us, to become a man, a human person (40, 44). Barth emphasizes here that in taking on flesh God took up our earthy and physical existence (40–44). In this, God's revelation and incarnation are interwoven, for God's revelation requires the means of God's incarnation, even as the incarnation serves the end of revelation. We again see that questions of form and content are deeply interconnected in Barth's christological thinking and that the content of God's revelation cannot be extricated from its form. God's revelation and the incarnation are intricately interconnected and even identified in the canon's witness to Christ. God's revelation means incarnation, just as incarnation means revelation (43). That this could happen has nothing to do with an intrinsic ability or capacity within humanity by which this could occur, but rather speaks to the miraculous work of God, from whose side alone the incarnation becomes a reality and can in turn exist as a possibility (43–44).

The Time of Revelation (§14)

This paragraph is without question one of the most difficult segments of the first volume of the CD. Here Barth takes up the question of God's revelation in Christ not from the perspective of the constitution of Christ's person along the traditional categories of divine and human natures, as he will in the next paragraph (§15), but rather under the rubric of time.

Most often when we think of Christ's appearance in the world, we think of a specified period of time within a larger framework of universal history. The time of Jesus is therefore understood to be roughly 4 BC to AD 30, and this span of time is thought of, even by many with what we might think of as a "high" Christology, as a bounded period of time within a larger general framework of the world's history. This is not how Barth approaches this question.

God's Time and Our Time (§14.1)

Barth commences by asserting that the statement "God reveals Himself" is equivalent to the statement "God has time for us" (45). Just as God cannot be known by beginning with a general concept of "being" and then moving to understand God as a specific instance of this general reality, so, he argues,

God cannot be placed within a general concept of time. God must be known in relation to his own uniqueness and reality, and it is not "being" that defines God, but God who defines his own unique character and "being." In like respect, Barth contends that to understand revelation, we cannot begin with a general conception of time into which we "fit" the period of revelation, but that all of time is defined in relation to this specific time that God has for us in Jesus Christ. In short, the time of the incarnation is "fulfilled time," but it includes within itself the whole of all history. As he writes, we must be aware that "we have no other time than the time God has for us," and "that God has no other time for us than the time of His revelation" (45). Barth's thoughts, so often counterintuitive in his radical commitment to christological particularity, are never so much so as they are here.

In this section Barth surveys complex questions of time by examining in a number of small-print surveys the positions of various historical figures, including those of Augustine, Immanuel Kant, and Martin Heidegger. These (quite technical) discussions must here be left to the side in order to elucidate the main contours of his position for our own purposes. He begins to put this forth by noting that the time of revelation cannot be thought of simply as created time or fallen time (47). Rather, the time of revelation must be thought of as redeemed time, a time that takes account of created time, as well as one that takes up and overcomes our own fallen or "lost time" (47). Perhaps the best way forward is to take up a passage describing this redeemed time:

> But this different time is the new, the third time, which arises and has its place because God reveals Himself, because He is free for us, because He is with us and amongst us, because in short, without ceasing to be what He is, He also becomes what we are. God's revelation is the event of Jesus Christ. We do not understand it as God's revelation, if we do not state unreservedly that it took place in "our" time. But conversely, if we understand it as God's revelation, we have to say that this event had its own time; in this event it happened that whereas we had our own time for ourselves as always, God had time for us, His own time for us—time, in the most positive sense, i.e. present with past and future, fulfilled time with expectation and recollection of its fulfillment, revelation time and the time of the Old Testament and New Testament witness to revelation—but withal, His own time, God's time; and therefore real time. (49)

All of the major themes of the paragraph under discussion can be elucidated from this passage.

First, the time of revelation is a third time over against the other two of created and fallen time. It is hard for us to imagine that not only the natural order but also time itself is affected by the fall of humanity, but for Barth, this is unreservedly true. We have no access to pristine created time once the fall has occurred, and the time with which we are left is fallen time. Christ redeems not only the created order but also time itself (Rom. 8). Just as sin affects all, so Christ redeems all, and this includes time.

Second, while on the surface the time of the incarnation, of Christ's life, death, and resurrection, are set within "our" time, in reality our time, and history itself, are framed and included within Christ's own time. This time is not simply a span of years within a larger timeline (i.e., 4 BC to AD 30); rather, all timelines are taken up and included within Christ's own, for here eternity and time meet. His time is "present with past and future," a "fulfilled time." The time that came "before" this appearance is what Barth designates as the time of "expectation," whereas the time that follows is the time of "recollection" (49). These correspond in turn to the time of the OT (the prophets) and the NT (the apostles), respectively. Both are included in God's larger purpose and plan of salvation for the world.

Barth therefore takes up the question of the incarnation under the rubric of time: to say that "The Word became flesh" is therefore to say that "The Word became time" (50). The incarnation is the Word taking up not only physicality but also temporality, and both point to an inconceivable miracle in which our physicality and temporality, our flesh and our time, are redeemed. This certainly entails that Christ appears "within" our time. But it also entails that as the eternal Word of God, Christ exists not only within but also as the Lord over time. The Word enters time without succumbing to time, sanctifying and lifting it out of its mundane existence for this holy purpose. The incarnation is therefore an eternal, though not timeless, reality (50–51). It is a reality that transcends our experienced time yet takes all of human history into itself. As strange as it may seem to us, it is not so much that our time includes the history of Jesus Christ within it but that the time of Jesus Christ includes all time within itself. The time of Christ cannot be thought of therefore as solely "past" or "future" but rather is ever "present" (see 51–52). This is not a denial of historical succession but is a recognition that all historical moments and events find their ultimate meaning in God's salvation that comes to the world in Christ.

A third important concept that is translated into temporal terms is the now familiar one of veiling and unveiling. Barth translates the christological logic and grammar of divine and human natures into the medium of eternity and time: "The veil of which we must speak in this context is general time, the old time, our time, so far as He assumes it in order to make it—and this is the unveiling—His own time, the new time" (56). But just as there is not a power or capacity in humanity that gives rise to the incarnation, so there is not an intrinsic power or vector of history that produces the appearance of Christ. It is the eternal Word alone that calls this history into existence. Barth's christological logic therefore is consistently upheld: "*Revelation is not a predicate of history, but history is a predicate of revelation*" (58; cf. 58–59).

As we noted, Barth's exposition strains against our well-worn channels of thinking about the incarnation and of time itself. Earlier theological examinations of Christ as both divine and human also point to an inconceivable and inexpressible mystery but at least speak in the traditional language of "natures" with which we may be familiar and from which we can get our bearings. His discussion of Christ here, which speaks in terms not of a dialectical relation of divine and human "natures" but of eternity and time, has no such established tradition by which we might find our footing. Yet the inner logic of both frameworks is in fact the same. Just as Barth refuses to sacrifice Christ's humanity to his divinity (Docetism), or his divinity to his humanity (Ebionitism), so he refuses to sacrifice Christ's transcendent eternity to his immanent historicity, or his historicity to his eternity. In both, it is the divinity of the Word that calls forth and gives existence to Christ's humanity as well as in the second instance to Christ's time on earth. So he can speak of the time that Christ assumes in language that follows the same grammar and is reminiscent of the language of the Word taking on flesh: "In every moment of His temporal existence, and also at every point previous or subsequent to His temporal existence, in which He becomes manifest as true God and true man and finds faith and witness, Jesus Christ is the same. The Word spoken from eternity raises the time into which it is uttered (without dissolving it as time), up into His own eternity as now His own time, and gives it part in the existence of God which is alone real, self-moved, self-dependent, self-sufficient" (52).

The language of *assumption* is helpful here: just as the Word assumed flesh and redeemed and sanctified it without destroying it as flesh (i.e., as a creaturely reality), so also the Word assumed time and redeemed and sanctified it without destroying it as time (i.e., as a creaturely reality). To say that God has redeemed our fallen nature is, for Barth, no different in meaning than saying that God has redeemed our time. Put briefly: "God has real time for us" (53). Just as the incarnation shows us that God in his freedom can cross the boundary between his existence and that of our own (as examined in the prior section), so also the incarnation demonstrates that God can cross the boundary between eternity and time, assuming time without sacrificing his eternity, revealing himself in our flesh, and thus revealing himself in our time. In the assumption of both flesh and time, the taking up of created realities with eternal ramifications is predicated on a decision within eternity. To truly contemplate this section and consider its ramifications is to realize that Barth's radical reformulation of the doctrine of election in the second volume of the *CD* is already prefigured here, for God's assumption of flesh and of time is grounded in a single covenant of grace, a covenant itself grounded in an eternal decision in which God determines from all eternity to "have time for us" (55).[1] Because of this, fallen time is "taken away," though its effects linger, and this not only speaks to a divine patience but also calls us to endurance, watchfulness, and a need for both a hastening and waiting in the meanwhile (see 67–70).

In his discussion of Christ's divinity and humanity under the rubric and through the lens of time rather than nature in this difficult section, Barth is at his most innovative in the first volume of the *CD* and prefigures moves that will be developed in later volumes, even while he sees what he is doing as simply elucidating the view of time and history provided within the Old and New Testaments. Thus there are extensive exegetical investigations of Scripture in the small-print segments throughout this subsection. These small-print investigations are challenging but well worth the effort for the light that they throw upon both the OT and the NT. For those who find this entire discussion of time somewhat esoteric, careful attention to his grounding of this theme in Scripture may merit some reconsideration of this judgment. Especially worth pondering in this regard is his understanding of "the fullness of time," as well as his examinations of expectation and recollection in relation to history and time in both the OT and the NT. These are taken up respectively in the next two subsections.

The Time of Expectation (§14.2)

As the time of God's incarnation in Christ, fulfilled time is correlated with two other kinds of time: that which anticipates the appearance of God's revelation in Christ, and that which follows from it. The first is "the time of expectation." This is, in essence, the time of the OT, "the time of the witness to the expectation of revelation" (70). This time looks forward in hope for a coming redemption that exceeds both the expectations and the possibilities of the nation of Israel. This time is not simply the period before Christ

---

1. With regard to such considerations, Barth's extensive quotation of Wichelhaus should not be overlooked—in it, one sees a position very close to what will become Barth's own as expressed in the doctrine of election in *CD* II/2, one in which there is a single covenant of grace, and where the gospel is to be understood as "the temporal execution of an eternal counsel" (see *CD* I/2, 55).

in general, but is the particular history of Israel in its relation to God, the "pre-time to revelation" (70). It is a time that is both united with the time of fulfillment that is its content and the revelation it attests yet also distinct from the fulfilled time of revelation itself. It cannot be so different as to be thought of as not pertaining to revelation at all, and it cannot be so identified with fulfilled time as to be thought of as identical with the unique revelation of God in Christ (70–71). It is therefore both identified with and distinct from fulfilled time. Yet revelation is not simply "the future" for the time of expectation—insofar as the time of expectation is a genuine witness to the time of fulfillment, it participates in the future revelation and in that sense such revelation is paradoxically already present within it (71).

This fact leads to a highly dialectical relationship between the time of expectation and the time of fulfillment, the time of the OT and that of Christ's appearance. Insofar as the time of expectation uniquely participates in and witnesses to the time of fulfillment, it is a history set apart and distinct from all other general histories that precede the appearance of Jesus Christ. This fact does not entail that the history of Israel, in itself, is revelation, however. As the history of a people among other ancient peoples in the Near East, it, too, lies within common time and can straightforwardly be described in a general narrative of world events. To grasp this idea, we might think of a history of Israel's kingdom recounted in a secular history text that places it as a minor player among Israel's (and Judah's) surrounding Egyptian, Babylonian, and Assyrian neighbors. Yet such a general narration of Israel's identity is not sufficient to capture its true meaning and significance, for what is found (or, more accurately, veiled and unveiled) within this history is the expectation of revelation, and this expectation of revelation *is itself* revelation (71). It breaks into history as God addresses Israel and establishes a covenant with it; it is not an achievement of Israel or the result of its particular religious insight. Once again, revelation is not a predicate of history, but history is taken up as a means of revelation (71). The expectation itself is the result of a divinely given disclosure in God's unique encounter with Israel.

Interestingly, the confirmation of this revelation does not reside in the OT itself. That revelation is found within the OT, Barth states, is established by the revelation that has been revealed in the life, death, and resurrection of Jesus Christ (72). Barth's reading of the OT is profoundly shaped by this christological lens. Rather than distorting the truth of the OT, he insists that this lens makes its perception possible, and a right interpretation of the OT follows from, and can only follow from, its use. Christ is the fulfillment of all of the hopes and dreams and promises of the OT, and it is only by looking in retrospect from the vantage of Christ that we can see that the expectation of the OT points to him as the culmination of its history. In light of such an understanding, we might rightly say that "the hopes and fears of all the years" of Israel and indeed of the unknowing world are met in Christ's birth in the little town of Bethlehem. The rest of this section comprises an examination of Israel's expectation and hope in its OT history (72–80), all fulfilled, Barth argues, in Jesus Christ, the expected one. This entails that the OT and the NT must be read together as a united witness to Jesus Christ, for all of the covenants of the OT point to a single one fulfilled in him (81–84; cf. 93–94, 94–101).

The Time of Recollection (§14.3)

If the time of expectation precedes fulfilled time, then the time of recollection is the period that follows it. This, too, is not a general history that follows the birth and appearance of Jesus, but is a particular history, that of the apostolic witnesses to the life, death, and resurrection of Christ. It is, like the time of expectation, distinct from fulfilled time, but it is nonetheless related to it and participates in it. If the time of expectation is the time of the OT, then the time of recollection is the time of the NT (101).

While it may seem that this time of the NT is more logically and obviously related to revelation than that of the OT, Barth states that this is, in fact, not the case. This is because the relation between the time of fulfillment and the time of recollection cannot simply be placed under the category of cause and effect (102). Barth writes, "That New Testament history, the history of the proclamation, of the Evangelists and apostles, takes its rise in revelation, is no less a miracle than that the Old Testament finds its goal in the same revelation. In both cases there is the possibility of offence" (102). Barth's conception of revelation here in the apostolic witness of the NT is, like the OT, not one that can simply be read off of the surface of history. Instead, the NT, like the OT, can be rightly understood only through faith, for both the OT and the NT writings point beyond themselves, the OT pointing forward, the NT backward, to fulfilled time, the person of Christ, as the incarnation of God, yet a God veiled and hidden even in the act of revelation.

Barth's language of offense draws, of course, both upon the NT language of Jesus ("Blessed is the one who takes no offense at me" [Matt. 11:6; Luke 7:23]) as well as upon Kierkegaard's emphasis that Christ causes offense to modern (and in reality, all) sensibilities in the claim that he is God.[2] In the case of the NT as well as the OT, it is possible to fail to perceive the revelation

---

2. See Søren Kierkegaard, *Practice in Christianity*, ed. and trans. Howard V. Hong and Edna H. Hong (Princeton: Princeton University Press, 1991); see also Kierkegaard, *Philosophical*

that they attest, and to see them not as witnesses that point beyond and away from themselves to Christ, but solely as objects of historical interest in their own right and as descriptions of the religious practices of their various times. This is, however, to miss their true meaning, significance, and purpose. Yet as Barth notes, "If it is otherwise, if the witness finds real hearers, in either case it is due to the power of revelation, it happens by grace" (102).

So in the case of neither the OT nor the NT can their true content be understood by the discernment of a historical—that is, naturally perceptible—causal relationship between a religious personality named Jesus and the contextual setting that gave rise to him (OT) or the religious practice of communities that took their rise from him (NT). Such "naturalization" of revelation is, in fact, a failure to understand revelation at all. For if the OT and NT are simply the records of the past religious experience of ancient peoples, then there is no way to assert that they have abiding, normative value for us—they are simply relics of a people's religious past. And we cannot make an exception for the NT based on our own personal preference for it (102–3). Such is a fundamental misunderstanding of what revelation is: it is not equated with the history of Israel or the church, but the witnesses of those histories point to a content and revelation that speaks through yet transcends them, even as they point to it. They point to God present to us in history, hidden in the veil of the lowly human life of Jesus of Nazareth. Moreover, the living Jesus Christ continues to take up their witness as the means for his own address to us even today. Barth writes, "The New Testament makes no claim at all in favour of the religion documented in it, but it does claim to be heard as witness, as witness to the recollection of a revelation which is just as much beyond the factual condition and content of the New Testament as it was beyond the condition and content of the Old Testament, but with this difference that the completed event of revelation does not lie before but behind the witness to it" (102–3).

And so the perception of the true identity of Jesus Christ as the revelation of God, as God with us, is not a matter of religious genius, nor is it discernible simply on the basis of historical observation, but instead requires faith and the miraculous work of the Holy Spirit. The power that makes such perception possible lies not in the witnesses of the NT themselves but only in the revelation to which they attest: "In other words, even in relation to the New Testament's claim to revelation, we are pointed to Jesus Christ Himself, to the act of lordship in which He gives the Holy Spirit of hearing and obedience

---

Fragments, ed. and trans. Howard V. Hong and Edna H. Hong (Princeton: Princeton University Press, 1985), 93.

to whom He will. The Evangelists and apostles are only servants of His Word; they cannot substitute their word for it. The truth of His revelation is grounded and proved solely by Himself" (103).

Barth spends the rest of this subsection in the numerically numbered points providing a discussion of how the NT speaks to and illuminates God's incarnation in Christ as the fulfillment of OT expectation, a discussion that is a mirror image of that regarding messianic expectation in the OT provided earlier in the last subsection. It is in fact quite helpful and insightful to cross-reference and compare these lists in the subsections on expectation and recollection (cf. 103–6 with 80–84; 106–13 with 84–94; 113–21 with 94–101). Of particular interest is that Barth holds a dialectical position on the resurrection of Christ, seeing it as a real event in time but also as one that transcends time, for the resurrection is not simply a "past" event but is an eternal and thus ever-present one, as well as one that grounds our future hope (116–17).

One final observation should be made before leaving this discussion on the time of revelation. Barth ends this paragraph with a return to a common theme: in order to understand all things aright, we must properly understand Christ and Christ's relationship to the church and to ourselves:

> New Testament faith is constantly characterized by the distinction in unity between Christ and ourselves. It is not a continuation of Christ's faith and still less a kind of prolongation of the existence of Christ Himself, but it is faith in Christ. The forty days and the apostolic age, fulfilled time and the time of recollection, are two different things. There is no word of the apostles and their communities after Pentecost thinking that they were living directly in the eternal presence of God in the days of Easter. Revelation remains revelation and does not become a revealed state. Revelation remains identical with Christ and Christ remains the object of Christian faith, even though He lives in Christians and they in him. (118)

The OT and the NT are therefore witnesses, one in expectation, and one in recollection, but the revelation that they attest is present to each, even as it is distinguished from each as the reality is distinguished from its witnesses. For Barth, the quintessential witness who bridges these times is none other than John the Baptist, the figure who stands between the ages of expectation and recollection (120–21). He belongs to the past age, but he points to the new. It should not be surprising that John the Baptist will hold a unique place of importance throughout Barth's theological work. Finally, these two ages of expectation and recollection (and Barth's subsections that discuss them) are best read as mirror images of each other. He views both the OT and the NT, the time of expectation and the time of recollection, Israel and the church, through the lens of fulfilled time, which is the time God has for us in Jesus Christ, centered in Christ's appearance on the earth, and at the center of this center, the forty days of Easter.

The Mystery of Revelation (§15)

In this paragraph Barth turns to what we might think of as Christology proper, the traditional examination of the person and work of Christ. This paragraph is perhaps easier to follow than the previous one, if for no other reason than that he stays quite close to the doctrinal patterns and thought forms of the greater tradition of the church. In short, the entire section attempts to examine what it means to say that Jesus Christ is "very God and very Man" (122–23).

The Problem of Christology (§15.1)

In examining the person of Jesus Christ, we come to the heart of Barth's entire dogmatic project, for dogmatics as a whole must have a christological center. He begins his discussion by highlighting this truth in a crystalline and pointed way:

> A church dogmatics must, of course, be christologically determined as a whole and in all its parts, as surely as the revealed Word of God, attested by Holy Scripture and proclaimed by the Church is its one and only criterion, and as surely as this revealed Word is identical with Jesus Christ. If dogmatics cannot regard itself and cause itself to be regarded as fundamentally Christology, it has assuredly succumbed to some alien sway and is already on the verge of losing its character as church dogmatics. (123)

While all of dogmatics must be so determined, there nonetheless has to be a special Christology within it, "an express doctrine of the person of Jesus Christ" (123). This is the focus of the entire paragraph, and to remember this allows us to briefly survey the whole. While this special Christology awaits an exhaustive treatment in the doctrine of reconciliation, here Barth provides a remarkably comprehensive account. That he places the Trinity and Christology at the head of his dogmatics is no accident, for he maintains that the failure to do so in the past has allowed dogmatics to fall prey to foreign principles that undermined and replaced, rather than undergirded, Christian truth (124).

The Christology in this subsection draws heavily on scriptural materials as well as the patristic christological formulas. Once again the overarching patterns and principles that we have witnessed above continue to hold: the relation between God and humanity is initiated from the divine side, and the relation cannot be reversed. The Word assumes human flesh in a miraculous way apart from any intrinsic power or capacity in humanity that must be presupposed for this miracle's possibility. Moreover, humanity does not gain any power over God in God's condescension to humanity. Throughout this passage these patterns of the unity of God with humanity in Christ, of the distinction of God and humanity as seen specifically in that drawn between Christ's divine and human natures, and of the irreversible and asymmetrical relationship between them, are all firmly maintained and consistently held (e.g., 125). Barth finds these patterns presciently articulated and held in the patristic era, whereas they were neglected and even undermined in the modern one, which, he charges, abandoned the mystery of the incarnation and exchanged Christ's divine identity for an ethical one, or, in his phrase, a "Christology of moral example" (129). In such modern Christologies, Christ is not the norm by which all else is understood and measured, but instead, a prior sense of the divine in "mind or conscience or feeling" is the standard by which Christ is evaluated and his uniqueness described (130). Barth's criticisms of such a position should not be surprising in light of his consistent rejection of natural theology and all dogmatic programs that begin on foreign soil external to Christology.

A significant part of Barth's exposition is devoted to upholding the patristic christological formulas and criticizing modern departures from them, often executed in lengthy small-print discussions (e.g., 126–31). He, in essence, is narrating the tradition, both upholding and defending its oldest forms against modern critics, but also subjecting such critics themselves to stringent evaluation and holding them to account. What is striking in reading this section is how traditional he is here, and how sympathetic he is to premodern forms of thought, patristic christological reflection, and the creeds (he will be more innovative in the fourth volume of the *CD*). What makes such reflection superior to much modern thought about Christ, he argues, is its awareness of the necessary tension in, and yet firm commitment to, viewing Jesus as both God and human.

The early church was fully aware that there could be errors on either side of resolving this tension (Docetism and Ebionitism). In their firmly held christological convictions, the theologians and councils of the early centuries respected and preserved the dialectical paradox that arises from the NT witness that God is this man Jesus and that this man Jesus is God. Another way to say this is that patristic Christology did not lose sight of the fact that this revelation of God in the incarnation is a mystery (131). The loss of this dialectical tension, and thus the loss of the mystery, was one of the many mistakes of the modern liberal tradition, Barth insists, and why it is inferior to the "primitive Christology" of the early church (132).

Very God and Very Man (§15.2)

The second subsection of this paragraph is an examination of Christ's divinity and humanity. Barth gives significant attention to grasping the meaning of John 1:14—the "Word became flesh" (132). He provides an extended discussion of this phrase, composed of multiple points. First, it is the Word that is the subject and that initiates the action. In this, the incarnation is a divine act, a sovereign act of lordship (134). Second, this action was an act of divine freedom; it was not compelled or simply the result of an evolutionary world process (135). Consistent with earlier statements, he emphasizes that the Word would be the Word apart from this becoming flesh, "just as Father, Son and Holy Spirit would be none the less eternal God, if no world had been created" (135; cf. 136). Third, even in the act of incarnation, the Word remains sovereign and free, and the relation between it and the flesh is an irreversible one, just as that between God and humanity is an irreversible one (136). The Word would be the Word apart from being flesh, but the flesh has no existence at all apart from the Word. The Word therefore does not change in the act of the incarnation, just as the flesh is not divinized or worshiped (136). Fourth, a proper understanding of this statement preserves a proper understanding of Mary, who, because of the incarnation and the hypostatic union of the Word with flesh that she bears, is truly the "Mother of God," but who also as a creature remains a servant and not a lord of heaven (138).

While Barth defends the patristic account of Mary as the "Mother of God" (as Luther and Calvin also held), he emphasizes that this is in truth a statement regarding Christ and derived from the ramifications of his identity, not an exaltation of Mary for her own sake. It is a logical entailment of Jesus being the incarnate divine Word who is born into the world. When this careful and dialectical relationship between Word and flesh is forgotten, it opens the door to an independent focus upon Mary herself, and he has no time for such independent Mariologies: "Mariology is an excrescence, i.e., a diseased construct of theological thought. Excrescences must be excised" (139). He provides an extended discussion of Mariology, including the Roman Catholic doctrines of the immaculate conception, perpetual virginity, and bodily assumption of Mary (139–46). His conclusion is stark. Against the necessity of Mariology for the church, as claimed in some Roman Catholic thought, he affirms the Evangelical conviction that "where Mary is 'venerated,' where this whole doctrine with its corresponding devotions is current, there the Church of Christ is not" (143). Even more strongly: "In the doctrine and worship of Mary there is disclosed the one heresy of the Roman Catholic Church which explains all the rest" (143). It is the quintessential expression of the mutual and reversible relationship in which the creature cooperates with God for the achievement of its own redemption (143). The foundational doctrine lying behind this Mariology is nothing other than the doctrine of the *analogia entis*, the analogy of being, and it is not surprising that Barth brings his discussion around to this topic (144). His rejection of Mariology is a specific application of his rejection of the *analogia entis*, and it is also a rejection of a synergistic account of salvation in which God and humanity cooperate to achieve the world's redemption.

At this point it might be observed that when Barth takes up the question of Christology, which is the heart of his dogmatic project, he does not leave his polemics behind. His extensive disputes with both recent Protestant liberal Christologies and Roman Catholic Mariology demonstrate that the twofold arguments against these two "heresies" are deeply woven into his understanding of his own dogmatic project. If against the first he posits the early church's Christology, against the second he posits the Protestant and Evangelical tradition. Indeed, it is the patristic and Reformation traditions to which he is most loyal and that most shape his own theological and christological thought.

Barth's polemical points follow accordingly. He argues that in the specific relationship between Christ and Mary in Catholicism, which he takes to be a microcosm of Catholicism's understanding of the relation of Christ and church, one finds a flagrant violation of the proper ordering of the Creator and the creature and as a result a sacrifice of "the being of the Church" (see 145–46).[3] A proper and right understanding of the relation of Christ and church is, in truth, an implication of a correct understanding of the person of Christ, and it is this relation of Christ and church that the Evangelical statement of faith sets over against Catholic Marian dogma (see 146). The christological logic of the incarnation that describes the irreversible relation of the Word and the flesh that is assumed in the incarnation in turn governs the relation of Christ and his earthly body, the church, as well as all relations between Christ and his followers. If this is forgotten, then Barth's extensive

---

3. Barth can thus write with regard to Catholicism that "like Mary (and like the pardoned human creature in general) the Church also possesses a relatively independent place and function in the redemptive process" (*CD* I/2, 146).

and lengthy attention to Mariology in a section on the person of Christ can only appear to be arbitrary or misplaced.

Barth moves from this discussion of Christ's divinity and his singular agency that cannot be shared with a human person (i.e., Mary) to a consideration of Christ's humanity and his identification with us. He does this through a sequential list of points as well. His first is that in the incarnation the Word took up all that makes us human, sharing our nature, form, and historicity (147). Here the integrity of the human creature is affirmed. The Word became a real human person as we are. His second point, however, is that we should not understand this to mean that the Word adopted a particular human person for his act of revelation. Instead, the Word assumed flesh understood as "human essence and existence, human kind and nature, humanity" (149). What Barth is driving at in this second point is that the Word did not adopt a person who existed independently before that person's adoption by the Word—in brief, he rejects all forms of adoptionism (adoptionism being, crudely put, that Jesus existed before God chose him to be the Messiah), another early christological heresy rejected by the church along with Docetism and Ebionitism (149). It is the Word that gives reality to the humanity of Christ; the humanity has no existence apart from this miraculous event in which the Word, or Son, assumes it to himself, which is to say that there is no person of Jesus independent of the Word (150).

In making this point, Barth consistently holds and makes reference to the *anhypostasis/enhypostasis* Christology of the early church (see 163, 164). This formula was an important one for him. The first term, *anhypostasis*, designates the negative point that the humanity of Christ has no independent existence apart from its being assumed by the Word. It is an intrinsically antiadoptionist principle, and it is concordant with his constant iteration that humanity has no intrinsic capacity for the work of reconciliation and that this is enacted solely from God's side. The second term, *enhypostasis*, designates the positive point that the human nature assumed is a full and complete one and possesses its own integrity. This is concordant with his efforts (which increased as the CD progressed) to speak of the real and true role of correspondence and of human obedience and agency in response to the initiative of God.[4]

The third point Barth posits is that the Word assumed a humanity that was under the judgment of God—that is, fallen humanity (151). This is another

---

4. For a further discussion of the *anhypostasia/enhypostasia* formula in relation to Barth's theology, see Thomas F. Torrance, *Karl Barth, Biblical and Evangelical Theologian* (Edinburgh: T&T Clark, 1990), 125, 198–201; and Kimlyn J. Bender, *Karl Barth's Christological Ecclesiology* (Burlington, VT: Ashgate, 2005), 4–5, 11–12, 63–65.

of his very controversial positions but one that he is adamant to maintain. In considering his position, we must remember two things: first, Christ's assumption of our fallen state is crucial for his identification with us as we exist as fallen creatures; and second, Christ's assumption of fallen humanity does not mean that he himself succumbed to the effects of the fall and committed any actual sin. Barth's emphasis seems to lie with the first of these. He wants to take with full seriousness the NT pronouncement that Christ "was made sin for us" (2 Cor. 5:21). He is fully aware that with his trajectory on this question he is moving beyond a dominant patristic and later tradition that equated the sinlessness of Jesus not only with the fact that he did not commit actual sin but also with his freedom from being born with a fallen nature inherited from Adam. Nevertheless, Barth is committed to seeing Christ as one who fully identifies with us in our sinful estate, including his assumption not only of our full humanity but also of our fallen humanity. In accordance with this conviction, he insists that "there must be no weakening or obscuring of the saving truth that the nature which God assumed in Christ is identical with our nature as we see it in the light of the fall. If it were otherwise, how could Christ be really like us?" (153). It should not be surprising that this remains a contentious issue for later theology.[5]

Barth's fourth and final point in this discussion of Christ's humanity moves against the grain of the last and asserts that Christ is also very different from us, for in the human life he lived, "what we do is omitted, and what we omit is done" (155). Christ does not sin; with him there are neither sins of omission nor sins of commission. In his earthly ministry he truly lived a sinless life. Even as he fully identifies with us in our humanity, even our fallen humanity, he does not sin but lives a fully obedient life. This obedience consists not in a simplistic conformity to moral platitudes or even principles, but in his perfect acceptance of the judgment and righteousness of God and the acknowledgment of God's true lordship. Christ's obedience is fully understood only by comprehending his full acceptance of his identity and task, the bearing of the wrath of God and the acceptance of its full consequences (157). It was this obedience by Christ that was the means by which God reconciled the world to himself (158).

Following these discussions on the divinity and humanity of Jesus Christ, the final element of this subsection is an examination of the event of the union of these natures, the event of the incarnation itself. Here the emphasis is not

---

5. For a recent sympathetic reading of Barth's position on Christ and original sin that engages his critics, see Darren Sumner, "Fallenness and *Anhypostasis*: A Way Forward in the Debate over Christ's Humanity," *Scottish Journal of Theology* 67, no. 2 (2014): 195–212.

upon "Word" or "flesh" but upon the verb, the action—"became" (159). The questions range around how the Word in this act of becoming can remain the Word without change in taking humanity to himself (159). Barth's emphasis here, as always, is upon the agency and freedom of the Word in this event and the rejection of any sense of reciprocity that would entail a "capacity, power or worthiness" from the human side needed to make this possible (160).

Barth is, in truth, quite traditional on such questions, and his responses follow the basic Chalcedonian governing convictions that hold that, in the union of Christ's person, the divine and human natures coexist without change, confusion, division, or separation. The Word does not change in the union with the flesh, but neither is the product of this union a third thing that is neither fully human nor fully divine (160–62). In addition to affirming patristic christological positions, he addresses the tensions between the later Lutheran and Reformed traditions pertaining to Christology by noting that while the Lutheran tradition placed its emphasis upon the completed unity of the hypostatic union and its ontic character, the Reformed tradition emphasized the event character of the union and the distinction between the natures. It focused not upon the ontic aspect of the union but upon questions of how this event was known, and thus its noetic character (161–62, 163–71).

This distinction between ontic and noetic can be confusing for those not familiar with it. Yet Barth spends some time in sorting out these historic differences between the Lutheran and Reformed traditions, and careful attention to his descriptions can tease out his underlying points. While for the most part he sides with the Reformed against the Lutheran tradition, he is not above putting critical questions to the Reformed position (170). He concludes that it may be that in the end both positions are needed to give a full Evangelical witness to the mystery of the incarnation in all of its breadth and depth. The Lutheran witness provides an emphasis upon the union of the natures and their inseparability, as well as the unity of the person of Jesus Christ. The Reformed witness emphasizes the integrity and the distinction of the natures that remain even in the union and thus the lordship and sovereignty of the Word in this union with humanity. In the end, the mystery of the incarnation perhaps requires both for a full Evangelical witness to that which neither can fully do alone (see 171).

The Miracle of Christmas (§15.3)

In the final subsection of this paragraph Barth examines the miracle of the virgin birth in relation to the mystery of the incarnation (172–202). The attention and focus that he provides to this question could only have struck some of his contemporaries as odd. Many had abandoned the virgin birth as a legend that had infiltrated the biblical text, and his energetic defense of the doctrine sets him off from a number of his contemporaries (he especially engages Emil Brunner's dismissal of the doctrine).

To understand Barth's exposition requires a number of important though easily overlooked distinctions. Fundamentally, he makes an argument that the virgin birth, though not widely attested in the NT, is a proper doctrine not only because of its biblical testimony but also because of the manner in which it complements and comports with the subject matter of the NT. He does not in fact think that the virgin birth lies at the heart of the Christian faith (as the incarnation does), but neither is it simply a myth to be discarded. It points to a deep truth.

Barth designates the incarnation—the Word taking flesh, God present in human form—to be the *mystery* at the heart of Christ's identity, whereas the virgin birth is the *miracle* that serves as a sign of that mystery. The important distinction is that between the *content* or reality of the incarnation (the mystery) and the *form* or instantiation by which that mystery becomes manifest to us (the miracle). The latter is the virgin birth, the *sign* given so that the unique and singular and incomparable identity of this child Jesus as the Son of God might be recognized. The former is the incarnation itself, the *thing signified* by the sign of the virgin birth, the reality or content of what is to be believed and confessed by the church about him. Barth concludes, "The mystery does not rest upon the miracle. The miracle rests upon the mystery. The miracle bears witness to the mystery, and the mystery is attested by the miracle" (202).

Once again, careful attention to Barth's language of form and content is required to gain traction here. Throughout this section he emphasizes that it is not the miracle that makes the mystery, but the mystery that makes the miracle. Put pointedly: "The man Jesus of Nazareth is not the true Son of God because He was conceived by the Holy Spirit and born of the Virgin Mary. On the contrary, because He is the true Son of God and because this is an inconceivable mystery intended to be acknowledged as such, therefore He is conceived by the Holy Spirit and born of the Virgin Mary" (202). If this distinction between mystery and miracle (and thing signified and sign) can be learned, then his larger argument can be grasped (see 184). Yet it must also be noted that he refuses to separate form (virgin birth) and content (incarnation) even as he distinguishes them. Such a separation would not only cast aside the form but also betray the content (179). As he argues, the virgin birth is a guard posted "at the door of the mystery of Christmas" (181).

One of the great challenges that Barth provided in his day and provides to our own is his firm rejection of the willingness of many past and present to dispense with the signs—that is, miracles—of the NT while seeking to hold to the mysteries apart from these signs. He demurs: "Sign and thing signified, the outward and the inward, are, as a rule, strictly distinguished in the Bible, and certainly in other connexions we cannot lay sufficient stress upon the distinction. But they are never separated in such a ('liberal') way that according to preference the one may be easily retained without the other" (179). He is reacting against the Protestant liberal tradition, and he seems to take particular offense at Brunner in this regard, though he could make the same case against Bultmann. The remaining investigation of this subsection is composed of commentary upon the lines of the creed pertaining to Jesus's miraculous birth (see 185–96). Here Barth's renunciation of human cooperation in salvation in any form and his emphasis upon God's sovereign salvific activity are once again reaffirmed, for here in the virgin birth "God does it all Himself" (177).

COMMENTARY

The Doctrine of Christology as a Biblical Question

At the heart of the doctrine of the Trinity is a christological question: Who is Jesus Christ? The early church, in battles that need not be rehearsed here, confessed that the Son was not a creation of, but rather was begotten by, the Father, and therefore the Son shared in the essence and existence of God. As the incarnate Word, Jesus Christ was God's own Son, and this eternal Son was Jesus Christ—two truths that, as Barth realized, are juxtaposed but not harmonized in the NT witness. Further reflection by the early church extended such official conciliar recognition to the Spirit, and the doctrine of the Trinity and the christological and pneumatological convictions of the church were codified in creeds and definitions at such councils as Nicaea (AD 325), Constantinople (AD 381), Ephesus (AD 431), and Chalcedon (AD 451).

It is again helpful, however, to remember that these decisions and the debates surrounding them were not simply philosophical or, more cynically, merely political in nature. They grew out of reflection upon the biblical witness, in which Jesus is announced as the Word of God through whom all things were made and through whom all things exist (John 1:1–3; cf. Eph. 1:3–14; Col. 1:15–17; Heb. 1:2). The NT writers shockingly place God and Jesus in a relation of shared action and identical if parallel honor, as when Paul writes that "for us there is one God, the Father, from whom are all things and for whom we exist, and one Lord, Jesus Christ, through whom are all things and through whom we exist" (1 Cor. 8:6). Jesus Christ is portrayed in the NT as the fulfillment of all of God's promises of old and the ground and hope of the future, the one who is "the Alpha and the Omega, the first and the last, the beginning and the end," another title that Christ shares with God the Father (Rev. 22:13; cf. 1:8). Even in the earliest Gospel, Jesus is portrayed as rebuking the seas in a way that the OT reserved for God himself (see Mark 4:35–41; cf. Ps. 107:23–32), and his walking on the water and calling out to the disciples with the terse identification "It is I" has direct allusions to God's own traverse upon the waters in the OT and declaration of his name as "I AM" (see Mark 6:47–52; cf. Job 9:8; 38:16; Ps. 77:19; Isa. 43:16; for the divine name, see Exod. 3:14).[6]

One of the commendable achievements of the nineteenth-century liberal tradition was an attempt to take the humanity of Jesus with full seriousness. Yet something was lost. Jesus was portrayed as a moral teacher or exemplar, as an apocalyptic yet tragic crucified prophet, or as a religious genius—and there were more portraits than these of what came to be called "the historical Jesus." While some like Schleiermacher brilliantly attempted to retain Jesus's uniqueness, efforts such as his to ground this uniqueness in a perfected human religious feeling, capacity, or inner life all in time had the effect of making Jesus more an object of esteem, imitation, and perhaps even love, but not of worship. This was especially true for those who saw the high claims of the early church as Greek philosophical incursions that distorted Jesus's very human life and attempted to divinize it.[7]

Barth opposed the liberal tradition on a number of fronts, but this question of Christ was a particularly pivotal conflict, for he opposed this entire tradition of beginning with Jesus as a historical figure whose meaning could be exhaustively determined by historical investigation. In his briefest and most pointed volley, he succinctly asserted the most basic theological principle: "There is a way from Christology to anthropology, but there is no way from anthropology to Christology" (*CD* I/1, 131). This meant that Jesus Christ must be understood first as a movement of God to humanity, and only then as a movement of humanity to God. Despite all of Barth's significant

6. For the significance of these passages involving the sea in Mark, consult the discussion of Mark 4 and 6 in James R. Edwards, *The Gospel according to Mark* (Grand Rapids: Eerdmans, 2002); for a rebuttal of a popular recent attempt to see the divine claims for Christ as simply later developments of ecclesial politics, see Kimlyn J. Bender, *Confessing Christ for Church and World: Studies in Modern Theology* (Downers Grove, IL: InterVarsity, 2014), chap. 7.

7. For an accessible history of Christology in the modern period following the Enlightenment, see Alister E. McGrath, *The Making of Modern German Christology, 1750–1990*, 2nd ed. (Eugene, OR: Wipf & Stock, 2005).

development from the Christology of this first volume of the *CD* to the last, he never reversed an order that began with an understanding of Christ as the eternal Son of God who in humility went to a far country (see *CD* IV/1, §59.1) before moving to understand Christ as the Son of Man who lived a human life in full obedience to his Father and returned home in exaltation to him (see *CD* IV/2, §64.2). These two portraits of the Son of God and the Son of Man, the divine and human existence of Christ, are closely juxtaposed in Barth's exposition of Christology, but the irreversible ordering remains important and consistent in all its forms and developments from first to last.[8]

Barth's theology reminds us that every generation within the church must begin with the most basic question asked in the NT: "Who do you say that I am?" (Mark 8:29). That all persons must answer this question (if only implicitly) entails that, in the words of the philosopher William James, this is a "forced option," an unavoidable decision. Barth's own response to this question is to set forth the importance and implications of the church's historic confession that Jesus Christ is Lord, the Son of God and Son of Man attested in Holy Scripture. The incarnation of the Word is the movement of God to the world for the purpose of divine revelation and human salvation. Christology therefore stands at the center of theology because Jesus Christ stands at the heart of God's own identity. The christological doctrines of the church are also, like that of the Trinity, a matter of confessing the truth that has been found in Scripture. Therefore in Christology, worship and truth cannot be separated: *Lex orandi, lex credendi*, "The law of prayer is the law of belief"—that is, as we pray and worship, so we believe and confess. And Jesus was worshiped by the church long before the intricacies of Christology were addressed by the ancient councils at Nicaea and Chalcedon. Yet the theological reflection that they both concluded and initiated must nonetheless follow such worship, for setting forth the reasons for this worship is part of the church's witness. The church is called to confess the content of its worship and belief before the world and in each age, for the question that rings through the ages is Jesus's own: "Who do you say that I am?"

God Makes Time for Us

That God has assumed flesh bestows honor upon the physical creation beyond the original divine declaration of its goodness. The physical world possesses a true dignity not only because it was created by God but also because of the incarnation, the result of God's decision to make this world

---

8. For a comparison of Schleiermacher and Barth on such points, see Bender, *Confessing Christ for Church and World*, chap. 12.

and human flesh itself his residence, an act of divine humility in which "God bends down to us as it were, by assuming this form familiar to us" (36). That God is free to condescend to us in this way, free to humble himself in the Son, may well show how far our conceptions of what is possible for God are removed from what God truly has done in Jesus Christ, and how our own conceptions of power and glory may require revision. That God is exalted and indeed glorified in this divine concealment lived in the veil of a human life lies at the heart of revelation: "The majesty of God in His condescension to the creature—that is the most general truth always told us by the reality of Jesus Christ" (31).

Moreover, not only the incarnation but also the bodily resurrection of Christ grant honor to our own lives of dust. The resurrection fills us with the hope for a redeemed future in which we, too, will be raised to a new embodied life just as Christ was raised in body. In brief, any form of denigration of the physical world or of the body is anathema to Christian faith in light of a God who assumed a body in the Word and who in the Spirit raised that body to new life, an affirmation of God's original declaration that the created world was good.

What must also be said, however, in light of Barth's rich exposition, is that time itself is assumed and thus may be redeemed. Many have watched not only their bodies but also the time of their life shrivel up and approach death and meaninglessness. That Christ assumes time entails that he will redeem not only our fallen mortal bodies but also our fallen finite lives. Barth's theology here points to what may be one of the greatest mysteries of "so great a salvation": God is able not only to bring our dead bodies to life but also to resurrect the time of our lives and that of history itself so that they are taken up into his own, and thus given a final meaning, purpose, and fulfillment. In other words, our hope is that the time of our life might itself be redeemed and not simply wasted and meaningless. And this redemption of time, for Barth, extends beyond the duration of our own personal lives and includes within itself all of human history.

That God assumes time in this way and does so by assuming the particular time of Israel and the church, the time of expectation and the time of recollection, has implications also for how we read the biblical canon. First, it entails that Scripture must be read with Christ as its center, and with Christ as the lens through which all else is understood. Second, it entails that the OT and the NT be read together, despite their very real diversity and the differences between them, as a common witness to a single history, that of Christ, which includes both the time of his expectation and the time of his recollection. Certainly this should not entail superficial readings of Christ into the OT that ignore the integrity of the OT itself. Yet Scripture in both of its Testaments is nonetheless rightly read and understood as a united witness to a single Lord. Revelation thus determines our approach to the canon, even as the canon testifies to this revelation.[9]

QUESTIONS FOR REFLECTION

- What does Barth mean when he states that dogmatics must fundamentally be Christology? Should theology be so centered on Christ (i.e., christocentric)?

- Explain in your own words the following statement: "Revelation is not a predicate of history, but history is a predicate of revelation" (*CD* I/2, 58). How does Barth understand revelation and history and their relationship? How are they distinguished?

- What is objective revelation? What is subjective revelation? In Barth's terms, what does it mean to say that God is "free for us," and how does this differ from God being "free in us"? How does Barth differentiate objective and subjective revelation and these freedoms? Are these helpful distinctions? Why is he more interested in the *objectivity of faith* (i.e., what is believed and confessed) than in the *subjectivity of faith* (i.e., how we believe and confess)?

- What do you make of Barth's claim that Christ was born with a human nature like ours, one in a fallen world—that is, a fallen human nature? Does this entail for Barth that Christ is sinful? What does it mean to say that Christ is without sin (Heb. 4:15)? What does it mean to say that Christ identifies with us, and that he "was made sin for us" (2 Cor. 5:21)?

- In light of the biblical witness, what should Christians say about Mary, the mother of Jesus? Should there be an independent doctrine of Mary (i.e., a Mariology) in dogmatics? Why or why not? Have Protestants ignored Mary in their flight from what they take to be Catholic excesses?

- How does Barth understand the relationship between the mystery of the incarnation and the miracle of the virgin birth? How are they distinguished? How might the relation between mystery and miracle be compared to the distinction of revelation's content and form?

9. For the christological implications for reading Scripture as the canon, see Bender, *Confessing Christ for Church and World*, chap. 6.

- What is the relation for Barth between the incarnation and the virgin birth on one side, and the resurrection and the empty tomb on the other? How does his discussion of both inform our understanding of miracles? Is the virgin birth a necessary doctrine for the church? Why or why not? What are the consequences of relinquishing the church's confession of the virgin birth? Of the bodily resurrection of Christ? What might underlie such rejections?

- What is Barth's understanding of the time of expectation? Of the time of recollection? Of "fulfilled time," or the time of revelation? How does he distinguish between the time of revelation and the time of recollection (see *CD* I/2, 118)?

- What does it mean when Barth says that "God has time for us" (*CD* I/2, 45; also 54, 55, 56)? What impact for the church and its ministry might occur if this is remembered? How might this change how we think of time itself? How might it make us consider how we have and make time for others?

- How should we understand the freedom of God? How is this freedom defined in light of God's revelation? How should divine freedom shape how we understand human freedom in light of this revelation? How might divine freedom challenge popular conceptions of freedom in Western culture?

☩ 8 ☩

The Outpouring
of the Holy Spirit

CD §§16–18

With the third part of chapter 2 of the doctrine of the Word of God, Barth turns from a discussion of Christology and objective revelation to a focus upon pneumatology (i.e., the doctrine of the Holy Spirit) and subjective revelation. Part 3 comprises three paragraphs (§§16–18) that address the topics of the Holy Spirit, revelation and its relationship to religion, and the life of faith of the children of God. In this first volume of the *CD* Barth takes up pneumatology in a provisional way (as he did Christology in part 2), intending for a more dedicated and comprehensive account to be provided in the fifth and final volume of the *CD* on the doctrine of redemption. Because this final volume was in fact never written, his discussion of pneumatology here takes on added significance for this very reason, though it should be noted that he also addresses pneumatological questions in significant ways especially in the fourth volume, on the doctrine of reconciliation.

The Freedom of Man for God (§16)

In §16 Barth provides a pneumatological mirror image of the christological discussion of §13. Where in the latter paragraph he addressed Jesus Christ as the objective reality and possibility of revelation (in that order), he now focuses on the Holy Spirit as the subjective reality and possibility of revelation. This is "the third and last step" in the "development of the concept of revelation as the necessary basis of a Church doctrine of the Word of God" (203). Barth now takes up the *effect* of revelation, just as he earlier discussed its *content* in part 1 on the Trinity and its *act* in part 2 on Christology (*CD* I/1, 296).

Barth's discussion of the Holy Spirit as the subjective reality of revelation examines both the Holy Spirit's work of imparting revelation to humanity and how the believer comes to perceive and appropriate revelation in faith and obedience. In light of all that we have seen, it should not be surprising that his primary emphasis is on the work of the Spirit rather than the faith of the believer. Put more precisely, this relation of the Spirit and the believer is rendered by positing that the faith of the latter is effected only by the unique and singular agency of the former. Barth takes up the subjective reality of divine revelation and human receptivity under this umbrella of "the outpouring of the Holy Spirit" (204). Whereas the focus in Christology is upon the freedom of God to reveal himself, here in pneumatology it is upon the freedom of humanity to receive revelation, though this freedom is consistently presented as divinely established and not an intrinsic human possibility. It is, once again, the freedom of God that is determinative for this exercise of human freedom. As Barth writes, "This freedom of man's can only be a freedom created by God in the act of His revelation and given to man. In the last resort it can only be God's own freedom" (204–5). This truth will shape everything that Barth says in this entire section as he attempts to preserve divine sovereignty and prevenience in revelation while upholding the integrity and real agency of the human person who receives it.

The Holy Spirit and the Subjective Reality of Revelation (§16.1)

If subjective revelation pertains to the freedom of the human person to receive revelation, then the first question to be asked is how this freedom has become real (*not* how it might be possible). Again we see Barth's emphasis that theology must begin not by laying down conditions that determine what is possible to be sought or believed but by looking at the reality of God's own revelation that itself determines what is possible. It is what God has actually done that determines the possible (205). In the second part of the chapter under review on objective revelation (i.e., Christology), this rule entailed that the incarnation of the Word in the person of Jesus Christ determined what could be said about God's event of self-revelation. The reality of the incarnation set forth what was in fact possible for God. In this third part on subjective revelation (i.e., pneumatology), this rule requires that the reality that persons in fact exist who have been converted and addressed by the Holy Spirit must determine what is in fact esteemed possible regarding conversion and the human reception of revelation:

> The existence of men who render faith and obedience to the Word of God; the fact there is such a thing among men as faith and obedience to the Word of God; the entire correspondence on man's side to the divine act of revelation: all this is just as seriously the content of the biblical witness to revelation as is the objective reality of revelation, i.e., Jesus Christ as the incarnate Word of God. Scripture did not attest for us the existence and work, the deeds and words of God in Jesus Christ, and yet leave open the question of the result of it all on the men whom it is supposed to reach. (206)

It is worth appreciating that in the first volume of the *CD* Barth emphasizes both the objective and subjective acts of divine revelation. He does not see God's revelation as fully described by a Christology that sets forth the person and work of Christ, but rather he insists that it also requires a full account of the Holy Spirit's work of making that revelation in Christ real and effective in the conscious life of believers. Both the work of Christ and that of the Holy Spirit are attested in Scripture, and emphasis is placed not only upon revelation in history "there and then," and thus *extra nos* ("outside of us"), but also "here and now" and inside of us. In short, revelation is both the incarnation of the Word in the world and the outpouring of the Holy Spirit in the life of the believer.

For Barth, to set forth this subjective side of revelation is to be faithful to the biblical witness to a revelation that includes both divine hiddenness in the act of divine disclosure and divine impartation in this very act of hiddenness. In other words, revelation is God's unveiling, veiling, and impartation. Or again, Barth's theology is trinitarian, christological, and pneumatological. In this third part of chapter 2 the focus is on the third but always presupposes the prior two. That this third is taken up under the doctrine of the Holy Spirit, rather than under a doctrine of humanity that focuses on an intrinsic capacity or capability that makes faith possible, says much about how Barth understands human faith itself, and it also sets forth and sets apart his own position (following that of the Reformers) from what he takes to be the heretical mismoves of Neo-Protestantism and Roman Catholicism.

The dedication to a relationship between God and humanity in revelation that is both objective and subjective is attested when Barth insists that the doctrine of the Word of God includes an exposition not only of God as

God is in himself but also of God as he exists in relation to us in Christ and the Spirit. This relation with humanity is not extraneous, but is integral, to revelation (207). Yet this relation must be carefully understood and ordered. Barth again sets forth the rules and logic of this ordering in an important opening passage:

> Not God alone, but God and man together constitute the content of the Word of God attested in Scripture. Yet the relation between the two is not an indifferent one. It is not reversible. It is not a relation in which man can be, as it were, the partner and workmate of God. It is not of such a kind as to permit us to intrude ourselves in place of biblical man with our own reflections and meditations upon ourselves, and with the view-points and principles by which we usually make up our minds. God and biblical man confront one another as the Lord confronts the servant, the Creator the creature, the Reconciler the pardoned sinner, the Redeemer the one who never ceases to expect His redemption, the Holy Spirit the Virgin Mary. It is this man who together with God (this God) constitutes the content of the Word of God attested in Scripture. And it is as the witness to this man that Scripture is meant to win our ear, having something to tell us about man in the sight of God and therefore about God's revealedness for us. But in this sense and with this restriction Scripture does in fact have something quite definite to say not only about God but also about man, and with a like seriousness also about man. The Holy Spirit acting upon man is also God. Hence his work upon us is also revelation, and knowledge of him is knowledge of revelation, and therefore rests upon knowledge of the witness to revelation. (207; cf. 235)[1]

To grasp this passage is to grasp the essence of the paragraph under discussion. The grammar, or logic, of this relation of God and humanity is set forth here in a way consonant with what has come before in the first part regarding the immanent and economic Trinity and God's relation to the world, as well as in the second pertaining to the relation of the Word and the flesh of Christ and correspondingly to that of his divine and human natures. But now this logic, which Barth sees as quintessentially and uniquely presented in the event of the incarnation of God in human form, is transposed in the key of the work of the Spirit and the life of the believer. This should not be taken

---

1. Barth later echoes these sentiments in the next subsection: "The fact that man's existence is involved does not mean that we can ascribe to man, or to these particular men, the role of autonomous partners or workmates with God co-operating in the work of revelation. Man's existence is involved only as the humanity of Christ is necessarily involved in the doctrine of the incarnation, or the *virgo Maria* [virgin Mary] in the doctrine of the mystery of the incarnation. We are concerned with the existence of man or of definite men only as an existence posited from God's side, and posited afresh in the act of His revelation" (*CD* I/2, 235).

to imply that such patterns have any abstract or independent status apart from the material, concrete themes under discussion (i.e., God's relation to the world, the Word's relation to the flesh, or the Holy Spirit's relation to the believer's faith and obedience). But the patterns exist, nevertheless, and they hold across the discussions of the *content*, *event*, and *goal* of revelation—and thus in theology (i.e., the doctrine of the Triune God and creation), Christology, and pneumatology.

Such patterns also correspondingly hold in all of Barth's discussions of the church and the believer. Ecclesiology is in fact a derivative doctrine, predicated upon Christology in form and materially falling under the doctrine of the Holy Spirit as the agent who brings the church into existence. The question of the faith of the believer and the doctrines of justification and of sanctification are therefore set within this larger ecclesiological context. Pneumatology follows in Christology's wake, just as ecclesiology is set within pneumatology, and the faith of the individual is set within ecclesiology. The answer to the existence of the church is found in the church's indication of "the mystery of Pentecost" wherein men and women are called and adopted as the children of God (221–22).

The explication of Christian existence therefore proceeds in Barth's thought as the unfolding of nestled and expansive relations and realities—of Christology, of pneumatology, of ecclesiology, and of the individual Christian, and in that order. Here again, we see that his thought is ruled by doctrines that are best thought of not so much as separate pearls on a string but as concentric circles, or even as nested Russian dolls. It is striking that in a section that speaks of the faith of the individual believer, this faith itself is set within larger ecclesiological (and hence communal), pneumatological, christological, and indeed theological (and trinitarian) contexts. While this deep integration of doctrines is one of the strengths of his theology, some critics of it, and of his pneumatology and ecclesiology in particular, have asked whether he provides enough emphasis on the Spirit and the church in themselves, for even in this section on pneumatology it does not take him long to shift back to Christ as the divine subject and agent of action in relation to the church. There are reasons for why he makes these moves, and reasons that go beyond what we can explore here. Nevertheless, his construal of the relation of Christ and Spirit was and remains a contentious aspect of his theology, as is his understanding of the relation of divine and human agency.[2]

---

2. For an overview of recent criticisms of Barth's pneumatology with particular attention to the question of the Spirit and the church, see Kimlyn J. Bender, *Confessing Christ for Church and World: Studies in Modern Theology* (Downers Grove, IL: InterVarsity, 2014), chap. 1.

These relations of divinity and humanity are pointedly expressed when Barth speaks of the mystery of the church and the believer within it. As he writes, the life of the children of God as the life of the church "is divine and human, eternal and temporal, and therefore invisible and visible. It is also human, also temporal, also visible. Always in its entire hiddenness in God it is also a historical reality. How can it be otherwise, seeing it has its origin, its ground, its centre in the incarnation of the Word?" (219). This quotation, of course, needs to be interpreted in light of the logic outlined above. Barth is not asserting that the church *itself* is divine so that the lines between the Creator and the creature are blurred. Far from it. It is divine not intrinsically but rather in the sense that Christ through the Holy Spirit calls it into existence, and thus it is divinely created and sustained.

Nevertheless, it can truly be said that just as Christ was both divine and also human and historical, so likewise the church is both divinely called and a created, concrete, and visible community of faith in history (219). If, in the last christological section, we saw that God has time for us, now we are given time for God. Once again, Christology is analogically translated to pneumatology and its ecclesiological concerns, with the logic of the first holding for the second. With regard to the existence of Christians, Barth can therefore assert, "The problem of their existence as the Church can be perceived with a perspicacity which is proportionate to our constant perception of the problem of the God-manhood of Jesus Christ" (219). And just as the eternal and divine Word took to himself a visible and temporal body in space and time, so also the church, though invisibly called into being by an eternal God, is called into a visible and concrete historical existence. In this way, too, the church truly is the "body of Christ" in a manner that corresponds to Christ's own earthly body and the locus of the believer's awakening to faith and obedience: "In Him and through Him the Church is the wholly concrete area of the subjective reality of revelation" (220). The church thus lives not as an extension of the unique hypostatic union but as a parable to it.

It should be admitted here as well that Barth's construal of the church and the believer was and remains contested. He was often criticized in light of his early theology (such as the *Romans* commentary) for providing no positive description of human faith and action, no constructive account of the church or of the human person and his or her concerns, capacities, and agency. Such appraisals of his early theology are understandable, even if many criticisms of it dealt in distortions of his actual positions. Yet regardless of such estimations, here in the *CD* he intentionally attempts to address such early concerns about a lack of attention to human belief and agency. He does so, however, without setting up an independent anthropology, something he insists would undercut the objectivity of revelation and the singular effective agency of the Holy Spirit.

The idea that God is everything and the human person nothing was never accepted by Barth as a description of his theology, though it was a stereotype that without question took its rise from his early one-sidedness.[3] However, the problem of human integrity and agency cannot be resolved, he insists, by grounding this relation of God and humanity in an examination of human capacities or any other existential element of human life. It must take as its sole starting point the revelation witnessed in Holy Scripture. In no way does he appear so different from the theology of his day, and in many ways from the Christian expressions of our own, as when he states that in this sphere of human faith we have to acknowledge Scripture and it alone as the source of our knowledge not only of Christ but also of the movement of the Spirit and of our understanding of the identity of the human believer. As he starkly exclaims in this regard, "We must submit to our bondage to Scripture" (208). This is as it must be, because Scripture not only illumines our knowledge of God but also provides the true knowledge of ourselves: "Actually Scripture does not abandon us even on this its subjective side. We are not left to our own guess-work or to the findings of a religious anthropology—not even to those of a Christian anthropology, which claims to assert something different from what it has previously been told" (208).

For Barth, when one forgets this and turns away from the Bible to the believing subject, from the Scripture principle to an autonomous anthropology, it is inevitable that theology's focus will turn from the Holy Spirit to humanity and human experience itself as the beginning and end of all religious knowledge. This leads to an abstraction of humanity from its relation to God, which in turn brings about a state in which there are in effect not one but two sources of revelation: Scripture, and the experience of the human person. Once this move is made, Barth argues, it is inevitable that in time the second will usurp the first as the ultimate authority, basis, source, and norm for theological reflection (209). This turn to a revelation within the self is precisely, he contends, what lies at the heart of Protestant liberalism (208–9). Liberalism sees the human person not in the light of revelation as a creature or pardoned sinner but as an autonomous agent defined by constitutive and definitive rational, religious, and moral capacities. Or as he puts this, liberalism is concerned "with man in himself, the man who understands himself because he controls himself" (209). With such moves we are on the

---

3. For Barth's estimations of such characterizations of his theology, see his book *How I Changed My Mind* (Richmond: John Knox, 1966), 48; see also *CD* IV/1, 89–90.

soil of anthropology and natural theology, and Barth has made his thoughts on such things quite clear.

If the first thing to notice in Barth's exposition of subjective revelation is the ordered relation between the Holy Spirit and the faith and life of the believer, then the next thing of specific importance is the radical particularity of that relation. The address of God that establishes this relation is not a general but a specific one, establishing a particular relation between God and a particular people. The relation that exists between God and humanity is therefore not accessible to us through innate reason, feeling, or the conscience but is a relation established by a specific revelation to a specific people—Israel in the OT and the church in the NT—and recounted to us through their testimonies (209–11).

Barth is careful to specify, however, that it is not because persons find themselves in these groups that they receive revelation; rather, they receive revelation because God reveals himself and establishes these groups (210). There is no room for boasting in one's membership in the community of Israel or the church, but only in God. He recounts that there are numerous persons witnessed in the OT and the NT who appear to be genuine recipients of God's revelation even though they do not belong to either Israel or the church (210). Yet this fact itself needs dialectical qualification, for the existence of such exceptional figures further highlights the regular means of God's action of calling persons in and into the context of a community of faith: "The exception, therefore, proves the rule. God Himself and God alone turns man into a recipient of His revelation—but He does so in a definite area, and this area, if we may now combine the Old Testament and the New Testament, is the area of the Church" (210). God will not allow membership in the group to supersede or determine his action in awakening believers to faith and obedience, but this does not entail that the Christian community is an expendable collective subordinated to individual and personal faith. Barth in fact thinks of the community primarily not as a collection of individuals, but as a corporate person.[4]

This observation then leads to a further important point of Barth's understanding of the relation between the Holy Spirit and humanity—namely, that this relation is between the Holy Spirit and the community first and the individual believer second. In other words, this relation is one in which the community and the individual believer exist in their own corresponding

---

4. This corporate anthropology has an impact even upon how Barth's theology is best translated. See Garrett Green's comments in the translator's preface to Karl Barth, *On Religion: The Revelation of God as the Sublimation of Religion*, trans. Garrett Green (New York: T&T Clark, 2006), x.

dialectical yet inextricable relation. As Barth has set forth the vertical irreversible relation between the Holy Spirit and the church as well as the believer, he now sets forth the horizontal dialectical relation of the church and the believer and does so with remarkable precision. All the while, he retains the ordering of the primary vertical relations of God and world, of Christ and church, of Spirit and believer, while presenting a more reciprocal one between the community and the individual that nevertheless prioritizes the church:

> Put pointedly and to be taken *cum grano salis* [with a grain of salt], there exist over against Jesus Christ, not in the first instance believers, and then composed of them, the Church; but first of all the Church and then, through it and in it, believers. While God is as little bound to the Church as to the Synagogue, the recipients of His revelation are. They are what they are because the Church is what it is, and because they are in the Church, not apart from the Church and not outside the Church. And when we say "Church", we do not mean merely the inward and invisible coherence of those whom God in Christ calls His own, but also the outward and visible coherence of those who have heard in time, and have confessed to their hearing, that in Christ they are God's. The reception of revelation occurs within, not without, this twofold coherence. (211; see also 217)

So in addition to explicating the vertical relation of the Spirit and the believer (and of Christ and the church), Barth sets forth the dialectical horizontal relation between the church as a corporate body and the individual Christian within it. This relation is not strictly irreversible but is a reciprocal one. In presenting this relation, he carefully protects against two mistaken viewpoints. In the first, the corporate body is the mediator of grace such that it takes a cooperative and synergistic (i.e., working together) role alongside the divine work of leading persons to faith and obedience. In short, the community for this reason takes absolute precedence over the believer. Barth rejects this viewpoint and any such cooperative understandings of God's action and the church's activity. As he pointedly asserts, "God Himself and God alone turns man into a recipient of His revelation" (210).

Yet Barth also rejects an opposite mistaken viewpoint that sees the church simply as a collection of individuals where a personal relation between God and the individual believer is all that matters and where the church is entirely peripheral to what is fundamental to Christian faith, at best a voluntary society of individuals self-chosen for fellowship. True, the Christian owes his or her faith solely to God and is a recipient of revelation only by divine grace. But the Christian also, he insists, only exists as a believer in the community of faith, and it is the signs of the community that are taken up by God to awaken faith in the believer. There are no Christians who do not exist in the church, which is the "outward and visible coherence of those who have heard in time, and have confessed to their hearing, that in Christ they are God's" (211).

The relation of the Christian community and the Christian individual is therefore a nuanced and dialectical one in Barth's thought. He states that the paucity of references to the church in the NT "shows how naturally existence in Christ and existence in the Church are seen and understood as an actual unity, although the difference between them is as great as that between existence in heaven and existence on earth" (212). This relation of Christ and church and believer is set forth by Barth as a correction to two mistaken ones, and each of them corresponding to a particular tradition that he polemically engages. The first, in which the believer is subordinated to the community and the community made a cooperative partner in the work of divine revelation and salvation with Christ, is his understanding of Roman Catholic ecclesiology. The second, in which the community is subordinated and in the end sacrificed to a religious individualism and immediate relation to Christ, is his understanding of Neo-Protestant ecclesiology.

Barth's understanding of this relation of the church and the believer therefore cannot be fully appreciated apart from its polemical triangulation to the rejected positions of two competing ecclesial and confessional traditions. Moreover, he is fully aware that from the perspective of each of the rival traditions his own may be seen as identical to that of the other rival. And so, while emphasizing the necessity and significance of the church against liberal Protestant views that would see it as secondary or even expendable, he notes that this emphasis may seem to but does not place him in the Catholic ecclesial camp: "This significance of the Church for the subjective reality of revelation is not a Roman Catholic but a biblical and therefore of necessity a universally Christian doctrine" (211).[5] The church is not a human invention but is the product of God's own will and action. Barth's understanding of the relation between the church and the believer, just like that between God and humanity in revelation, must be predicated upon and explicated in the light of the biblical witness. Both relations are ultimately revealed and therefore divinely determined; they are not freely construed.

Subjective revelation is therefore ordered, particular, and communal, as well as dialectical. Barth sets forth the impartation of subjective revelation primarily as he did the prior, objective one—as the clarification, correction,

---

5. He can, however, later add: "We must, of course, make many reservations in face of the Roman Catholic interpretation of the necessity of the Church to salvation. But the necessity itself it would be unwise either to reject or to avoid. Indeed, it is necessarily prescribed for us, when we ask concerning the subjective reality of revelation" (CD I/2, 213).

and exposition of a rightful ordering of divine and human relations as these are made evident in revelation. Where in the christological section this was understood as the ordering of the relation of the divine Word and the human flesh of Christ, here it is the ordering of the relation between the identity and agency of the Holy Spirit and that of the church and human believer. The formal patterns of unity, distinction, and irreversibility continue to hold.[6]

This is particularly true of the move from Christology to pneumatology and ecclesiology. In effect, Barth translates the christological formulas of part 2 now to the pneumatological and ecclesiological categories of part 3, where the central image becomes the church as the body of Christ (220–22). Just as he emphasized the priority of the Word over the flesh of Christ such that the humanity of Christ was entirely dependent upon the agency of the Word for its existence, meaning, and significance, so here he emphasizes that Christ stands over his church, calling it into existence, making it the location for the act of revelation in the present (214–15; see also 216, 220–22; cf. 235). Moreover, in accordance and analogy with the doctrine of the *anhypostasis* in Christology wherein the humanity of Jesus exists only as joined to the Word, the church exists with and only with Christ such that it has no independent existence apart from him or from the Spirit's act of calling it into existence. Yet, because it *does* exist with Christ, and because he has freely joined himself to it as the product, location, and recipient of his revelatory and salvific work, it can be said that *extra ecclesiam nulla salus* (i.e., outside of the church there is no salvation) (216; see also 217, 220). The church therefore serves as the locus and indeed the means of the Spirit's work to awaken persons to faith and obedience. In this, the Holy Spirit's work is a particular work, and not a general revelation within humanity or the world as a whole. It is through the specific preaching of the church and its sacraments, and not through a general immanent religious awareness found in all individuals, that the persons of the world are called by the Holy Spirit to believe the gospel and are converted.

Moreover, while this relation may be effected and sustained through the use of ecclesial signs of preaching and sacrament, it is the agency of Christ and the Spirit through the signs, and not the church's enactment of the signs themselves, that is the true reason for the believer's faith. Barth's understanding of the relation of Christ to the believer, and thus of the Spirit to the believer, is for this reason paradoxically both one that is mediated (by the church) and immediate (directly effected and established by Christ upon

---

6. As Barth states, "There is no time at which it is quite inappropriate to remember that Jesus Christ is the Lord of the Church, and not the Church the Lord of Jesus Christ" (*CD* I/2, 213; cf. 214, 226–27).

the individual believer without intermediary). This paradox leads to the question of how such revelation comes to the human person in this event of subjective revelation.

EXCURSUS: Subjective Revelation and the Divine Use of Signs

The subjective problem of revelation can be succinctly stated in two questions: "(1) How does revelation come from Christ to man? and (2) How, as such, does it come into man?" (222). These questions, Barth posits, cannot simply be answered in relation to Christ but rather require a doctrine of the outpouring of the Holy Spirit. This pneumatological question in turn implies an ecclesiological complement insofar as the Spirit takes up signs within the church for the communication of God's revelation to persons who are called and converted to become believers.

With the introduction of signs, Barth addresses the question of how the revelation that appeared in the person of Jesus Christ now comes to persons in the present. His answer hinges on the fact that just as the incarnation itself was the appropriation of a creaturely reality for God's revelation—namely, the flesh of Christ—so also the Spirit takes up creaturely mediums as the means by which God speaks to us and awakens us to faith and obedience in Christ (223). Again in language that draws upon that used earlier to describe objective revelation, he states that signs serve in the veiling and un- veiling of God, so that "their instrumental function is to veil the objective of revelation under a creaturely reality; and yet to unveil it, i.e., in the actual form of such creaturely reality to bring it close to men, who are themselves also a creaturely reality. They point to revelation" (223).

Here again is the now familiar theme that revelation occurs as God takes up a crea- turely veil for his own unveiling. But whereas the incarnation points to a hypostatic union of God with the creature, a union that is singular, unique, and personal, God himself in human form, now with subjective revelation we see not a personal union but an instrumental appropriation wherein a creaturely medium is enlisted for God's self- communication, serving as a witness that points to the personal and objective revelation of the incarnation. This revelation by means of a sign is itself a miracle, and it is nothing less than a miracle. The signs are what they are—witnesses and the means of God's self- communication—only because the Word of God makes them so. They have no intrinsic capacity to be such in themselves (223–24). They serve in this way as witnesses that point to revelation, and therefore they share in the act of revelation as the *objective side of the subjective reception of faith itself.*

In other words, even though we are here dealing with the subjective side of revelation in part 3 and with the faith of believers, Barth does not leave the objective side of revelation behind. For even revelation's subjective appropriation takes place as God takes up a creaturely medium as a sign external to the believer, and through the use of this sign opens the eyes and heart of the person to perceive the revelation that has appeared in the objective revelation of the incarnation of Jesus Christ. In short, the subjective side of revelation has its own objective element. Appreciating this is central for understanding Barth's theology of the Holy Spirit, for he rejects any form of mysticism and spiritualism that would relinquish this objective side of subjective revelation—that is, any theological position that would forgo the external and ecclesial signs such as Scripture, proclamation, and sacraments and instead commend some type of inner, immanent, and immediate (i.e., not mediated) divine revelation or communion with God within reason, emotion, feeling, or the conscience of an individual person. He finds such moves to immanence at the core of Protestant modernism.

In contrast to such mystical and spiritualistic forms of religion, Barth posits the indispensability of the signs that the Holy Spirit annexes for the conversion and illumination of persons. Moreover, that this is truly an annexation of these creaturely signs for a divine purpose demonstrates that subjective revelation is as much a miracle of God as is the incarnation itself. This subjective counterpart to the objective revelation of the incarnation is every bit as much a work solely of divine grace as is the birth of Jesus Christ. Barth summarizes these themes succinctly in an important concluding passage on signs:

> The activity of the sign is, directly, the activity of God Himself. The manifestation of the sign is God's manifestation, even though it is always a creaturely reality. Again, therefore, it takes place by the omnipotence and yet also the freedom of God's gracious will. God has bound us, but not Himself, to the signs of His revelation. They are testimonies, but they are not limitations to His majesty and glory.
>
> It is because these signs have been given, and by way of them, that men may receive direction and promise from the side of the objective reality of revelation, of the incarnation of the Word. The fact that God's revelation is also a sign-giving is one side, the objective side, as it were, of its subjective reality. We are saying the same thing when we say that this giving of signs is the objective side of the Church as the sphere in which God's revelation is subjectively real. (224; see also 227–28, 231–32)

Barth does in fact stress that God's revelation comes to humanity "both immediately and mediately" (224). That is to say, revelation is immediate in that the creaturely signs have no intrinsic capacity to communicate God or power transferred by God to them—through the event of revelation, God remains the acting and effective Subject. The signs do not possess an intrinsic internal potency or capability to communicate revelation or grace. Yet revelation is nevertheless also mediated, for it "never does come without creaturely mediators or media" (224). He rejects an immediate mysticism in which revelation occurs directly and immanently within the human person apart from external words, sacraments, or signs. Yet he also equally renounces a sacramental and ecclesial form of mediation in which the signs themselves are seen as efficacious by means of their own performance and where God's own agency is seen as not the sole cause but the first in a line of causes imbued with their own intrinsic powers of grace, a view he locates in Roman Catholicism (227–28). In short, while we are bound to the signs, God is not—their efficacy ever relies on him, but his activity never is of necessity bound to them (224, 231–32; cf. 236).

Barth's discussion of signs leads naturally to a discussion of sacraments. In point of fact, he never provided a comprehensive and final discussion of the sacraments of baptism and the Lord's Supper in the CD. He did discuss the first in an unfinished fragment at the end of his dogmatics (CD IV/4), though he never addressed the second in the CD in a dedicated discussion. Regardless, we can see here in his discussion of signs (and earlier, in his discussion of proclamation as preaching and sacrament) how he approaches all such divine actions through created media, at least at this point in his thought. To say that his understanding of the relation of divine agency and the creaturely sign is highly paradoxical and dialectical does not do it justice and remains an understatement. What can be said, again, is that the relation between God and the elected sign is an ordered and irreversible one (see 223–42).

A final observation we might make is that in this entire discussion of subjective revelation, Barth draws no clearly marked distinctions between the work of Christ and of the Spirit in this divine address to the believer. This is because he thinks of the Spirit's work within the believer not as a distinct second revelation but as an element of the one revelation of God. The revelation of the Spirit is not an addendum to the revelation of God in Christ or an independent work from it but is rather the culmination of a completed event with its own integrity. As he puts this point, "Subjective revelation is not the addition of a second revelation to objective revelation" (238). Rather, as he further explains this, "Subjective revelation can consist only in the fact that objective revelation, the one truth which cannot be added to or bypassed, comes to man and is recognised and acknowledged by man. And that is the work of the Holy Spirit" (239; cf. 249).

The Holy Spirit and the Subjective Possibility of Revelation (§16.2)

The prior quotation leads us to consider the next subsection. Having outlined the subjective reality of revelation seen in the establishment of believing men and women joined together in the church, Barth turns to examine the conditions that make this reality possible. This, again, is not a project of putting forth external criteria that must be met for revelation to be thought of as a coherent concept or deemed possible. It is rather a consideration of the actuality of revelation with the purpose of understanding it. This is the case because "the question of understanding cannot precede the question of fact. It must invariably follow it" (243).

Barth now turns from reality and the realm of fact, which is, for him, the realm of exposition and description, to the realm of understanding. He puts forward two questions that frame how such understanding can be sought. First, how is humanity freed to receive God's revelation? And second, what must be true of the Holy Spirit for this to occur (243–44)? Addressing the first question, and following the logic set forth in the section on Christology, he states that the freedom of humanity to receive revelation occurs only because of divine freedom and action, and in this case, the distinctive work of the Holy Spirit. Just as there is no intrinsic capacity in humanity for the incarnation to become a reality, so there is no intrinsic capacity within humanity to receive revelation and achieve conversion (244). As Barth states, "To receive the Holy Spirit means an exposure of our spiritual helplessness, a recognition that we do not possess the Holy Spirit" (244). Here again pneumatology follows the same patterns as Christology, a logic in which there is no possibility for revelation apart from the miraculous work of the Word and the Spirit and no confusion of God and humanity (245).

Barth spends the rest of this subsection unpacking a number of ramifications of this position (246–79). The first is that the outpouring of the Holy Spirit makes it possible for revelation to reach humanity because the Spirit brings the Word of God to human hearing in a definite way and in the particular sphere of the church (246–57). Just as the particular location of objective revelation is the person of Jesus Christ himself, the very incarnation of God, so the particular location of subjective revelation, the place where revelation is heard and encountered by persons today, is the church. The close relation of Christ and church again comes to the fore here: "The Church is the one particular spot which corresponds to the particularity of the incarnation. It is there that revelation is really subjective, for there Jesus Christ the Head has in His own people His body, there the only-begotten Son of God has in them His brethren" (247).

The second implication of the fact of subjective revelation is that it is indeed possible for God's revelation to reach the human person, because the conditions of this possibility are addressed to the human person in the very occurrence of the divine encounter (257–65). The first thing proclaimed by the Word is, however, that the human person is precisely *not* free to receive it, and what the encounter reveals is not human possibility but impossibility (257–58; cf. 262). The human person is shown to be not simply disabled but completely lost in sin with no ability to reach God: "He is not only a sick man but a dead one" (257). There are many things the natural human person can do—achieving communion with God is not one of them. Humanity is lost, and this lostness and complete inability is what is first revealed to the person addressed by the Word. The freedom that allows for the reception of the Word of God is itself a miraculous gift of the Word given by the Spirit of God (259). As Barth writes, "We are to understand, therefore, that for God to be revealed involves the dislodging of man from the estimation of his own freedom, and his enrichment with the freedom of the children of God" (260). Here again, Barth's conception leads to a strong notion of election, and he follows the Reformation emphasis upon the incapacity and bondage of the will.

The third implication of the outpouring of the Holy Spirit in subjective revelation is that while the Word of God remains the master of the relation between God and the human person, the human person is nevertheless not only judged but also shown mercy in this event and is made a participant in this reality in such a way that his or her own identity is not abolished (265–79). Here Barth is presenting the other side of the first two points he has made. Even though this subjective revelation occurs only through God's agency, and even though human freedom itself is a gift of God, the fact also remains that God does not eradicate but establishes and embraces the agency and freedom of the creature in this event. In other words, the human person is not simply a passive object but a willing agent, freed to respond to the divine grace with the full breadth and depth of his or her being. Revelation occurs as the person, in the full consciousness and uniqueness of his or her existence, encounters and fully experiences this divine address. This revelation is not only a judgment on the person's helplessness but also a mercy of empowerment that includes all that he or she is as a human person, the full wealth of his or her existence (266). Subjective revelation is not magical manipulation but personal encounter, for "the possibility given us by the outpouring of the Holy Spirit is the possibility of a direct confrontation of the whole man by God," for in revelation "the whole man is addressed and challenged, judged and pardoned by God" (267).

Throughout this subsection Barth focuses on what the subjective awakening of the creature to faith and obedience entails. While this is a work of the Spirit, to be awakened by the Spirit is nothing less than being confronted by Jesus Christ as the revelation of God, the one who is our Lord, and the one we are to believe and obey in life and in death.

The Revelation of God as the Abolition of Religion (§17)

In §17 Barth faces up to a question that has been swirling below the surface for some time: How does God's revelation in Jesus Christ as a particular, unique, and singular event compare to the general phenomenon of religion as a fundamental aspect of human life and existence? With regard to subjective revelation, he frames this question in terms of how the unique work of the Holy Spirit is to be coordinated with other religious experiences and traditions. In light of the radical particularity we have seen consistently emphasized in his theology, as well as the unique and incomparable reality and significance of the special revelation that has come in Christ, we can perhaps safely assume that he will take a rather critical view of general religious claims. And with some important qualifications, that is what we find.

Here it is important to highlight a difficulty with the English translation of this paragraph. Its title is rendered in translation as "The Revelation of God as the Abolition of Religion," but in truth, the German word here translated as "abolition" (*Aufhebung*) does not have solely negative connotations as the English word "abolition" seems to suggest. It rather implies not only judgment and negation but also an affirmation and indeed renewal.[7] This is indeed the path Barth will take in discussing the relation of revelation and religion.

The Problem of Religion in Theology (§17.1)

The essence of this paragraph hinges on the distinction between revelation and religion as Barth understands them. Revelation is the movement from God to humanity comprising the incarnation of the Word and the outpouring of the Holy Spirit that brings about human knowledge of God and the salvation of the world. This revelation is in turn attested in Holy Scripture and proclaimed by the church. Barth's doctrine of revelation is thus a doctrine of the Word of God in its threefold form.

Barth's contrasting understanding of religion is more complicated in that he can refer to religion in two different senses. Religion in the first sense is defined as humanity's quest for transcendence, a movement from the side

---

7. For a brief discussion of Barth's use of *Aufhebung*, see George Hunsinger, *How to Read Karl Barth: The Shape of His Theology* (Oxford: Oxford University Press, 1991), 98, 193. For a very helpful discussion of the difficulties of translating this term and of Barth's understanding of religion, see Garrett Green, "Translator's Preface" and "Introduction: Barth as Theorist of Religion," in Barth, *On Religion*, vii–xi and 1–29, respectively. This book contains Green's new translation of the paragraph of the *CD* now under discussion and is an improvement on the original translation. For an insightful examination of Barth's understanding of religion in relation to world religions, see Sven Ensminger, *Karl Barth's Theology as a Resource for a Christian Theology of Religions* (London: Bloomsbury, 2014).

of the world to reach some type of divine reality. It presumes and takes for granted what Barth has consistently rejected—namely, that humanity has within it a natural capacity for reaching God through its own efforts or capabilities. In short, religion attributes a possibility to the human person (or humanity corporately) that revelation shows to be an illusion. Revelation, rather, demonstrates that the only relationship between God and humanity is one established from God's side, and it is established precisely through the work of Christ and the Holy Spirit (280).

Religion in the second sense is defined by Barth as the form of human life (including all "competence, experience and activity") that is the concrete and historical response to revelation, or the embodiment of religion in the first sense (280–81). Religion is in this sense a human phenomenon comprising beliefs, practices, and institutions and the historical concrete embodiment of this system of beliefs and practices. In this regard, Christianity as a human phenomenon, which includes such beliefs, practices, and institutions, is *itself* a religion and is open to historical and empirical investigation. Barth fully admits that to speak of revelation as an encounter between God and humanity entails that one must in turn speak of human, visible things such as the church, sacraments, and human experience. And insofar as these latter things are seemingly paralleled in many different religious traditions, this leads to the logical and unavoidable question of whether revelation, which gives rise to Christianity, is not simply one particular instance of a more general class of religious experience and religious phenomena. As he then comments, "From this aspect what we call revelation seems necessarily to be only a particular instance of the universal which is called religion. 'Christianity' or the 'Christian religion' is one predicate for a subject which may have other predicates. It is a species within a genus in which there may be other species" (281). In short, such a viewpoint holds that there are in fact numerous religions, of which Christianity seems to be but one (281).

The question that Barth here raises, interestingly under the subjective rather than objective reality of revelation and thus under the question of pneumatology rather than Christology, is a common one and one that continues to engage contemporary discussion. From the perception of historical observation, it appears that Christianity is but one of many different religions that have appeared in the history of the world, and revelation as the content of the church's teaching might in this regard be classified as but one example of a broader category of religious experience and its manifestation. Such thinking was growing in influence in Barth's early years and had been on the rise throughout the nineteenth century in Europe. Christianity was more and more seen as but one among many different religions. This observation in his day pressed toward a relativistic conclusion, whether positively or negatively stated: positively, that all of the religions were either specific historical and contingent expressions of a much more basic religious awareness of a god or divine reality, or, negatively, that the very existence of different religions undercut the validity of them all, for all were but human inventions that sought and provided for their adherents a sense of existential meaning, transcendence, and hope.

As stated, both of these options were present in the nineteenth century and flowed into Barth's own context early in the following one. The first was present in some positive forms of comparative religion, where Christianity's uniqueness was set aside and all religions embraced as specific examples of a more fundamental and underlying general and universal religious awareness. The latter view was evident especially among the skeptics and critics of religion, of whom Ludwig Feuerbach, Karl Marx, and Sigmund Freud are prominent examples, and this skepticism gave rise to a rejection not only of the unique claims of Christianity but also of all religious traditions.

Interestingly, Barth does not dismiss but in fact embraces much found in these viewpoints. He admits that a general search for transcendence seems to drive much of culture and human life, and that they are determined "by a reverence for something ostensibly more than man, for some Other or wholly Other, for a supreme Relative or even the Absolute" (282). He is fully aware of the wealth of deities in the multiple cultures that history attests and that some form of worship seems to be prevalent throughout all places and times, with numerous religions having their own form of holy texts and scriptures (282). In fact, to understand revelation, one must begin by understanding that God has entered a world in which there seem to be numerous parallels and analogies to it, and this itself hides both the uniqueness and the singularity of God's revelation. Barth writes,

> The revelation of God is actually the presence of God and therefore the hiddenness of God in the world of human religion. By God's revealing of Himself the divine particular is hidden in a human universal, the divine content in a human form, and therefore that which is divinely unique in something which is humanly only singular. Because and in so far as it is God's revelation to man, God Himself, and the outpouring of the Holy Spirit, and therefore the incarnation of the Word, can be seen from this side too, in the hiddenness which is obviously given to it along with its true humanity as a religious phenomenon, as a member of that series, as a particular concept within general observation and experience, as one content of a human form, which can have other contents and in which the divine uniqueness of that content cannot be perceived directly. (282–83)

A number of things need to be unpacked here to understand Barth's position on religion as a human phenomenon. First, he does not deny that, in light of natural observation, the claims of the Christian religion seem to be on par with those of many different religions. Claims about Jesus may supersede those of many other religious figures, but all religions have their own revered persons, whether it be Muhammad, the Buddha, or Moses. Other religions also have their own scriptures, religious practices (including sacraments), and social organizations. They also may have convictions about God, life after death, and the meaning and purpose of human life and the cosmos. Barth sees no reason to deny any of this, and in fact embraces all of these observations. When God becomes incarnate in human life, his revelation is hidden not only in his human form but also among a plethora of human practices and religious claims. And the Christian faith that attests it can itself be considered as a "religion" (283). Barth concedes that, on the level of historical observation, the Christian faith does appear to be but one among a number of religious faiths.

Nevertheless, Barth does not follow this concession to a conclusion of religious relativism, whether one that positively embraces a divine reality underlying all contingent historical manifestations in various religions or one that negatively judges all religions to be but human constructions of meaning and purpose with no transcendent referent. The first he will designate as *mysticism*, the latter as *atheism*, two seemingly opposite positions, but ones that Barth in fact sees as two sides of one religious coin (314–15; cf. 318–25).[8]

Instead, Barth pushes on to concede the widely attested existence and potency of human religious expressions as well as their apparent similarities to Christianity, while also maintaining that the revelation of God that comes in Christ is not on the same plane with such religion of any type and is unparalleled and without comparison, utterly unique and particular in kind and in

---

8. Barth's judgment on mysticism is incisive, but he reserves harsher words for atheism. Nevertheless, his judgment upon both differs little in the end: both turn to the worship of the self and become captive to their own forms of ideology and idolatry. Their ultimate goal is that the human person might be liberated from God and his commands: "Man is finally and ultimately free of God and His law" (CD I/2, 323). But the end result is a hollow victory in which the person is left alone and isolated. In truth, while mysticism and atheism seem to be conservative or radical rejections of religion and its external ritual, Barth contends that neither in the end can really judge religion with a force that shakes it to its core. A real rejection would require a judgment from outside of religion entirely; it would require a revelation: "The real crisis of religion can only break in from outside the magic circle of religion and its place of origin, i.e., from outside man" (324). And this is, Barth asserts, precisely what happens as God's revelation in Jesus Christ breaks into human life and pronounces judgment upon religion for its "unbelief, unrighteousness, and idolatry" (329; cf. 324–25).

substance. He fully admits that one must embrace the religious character of Christianity, for to deny this would be to deny the human aspect of revelation, that God's revelation encounters humanity in its concrete and historical existence, taking on human form as the veil in which the unveiling of revelation occurs.

And yet the key question is not whether revelation comes to expression in the form of human religion. Rather, the primary question is whether revelation judges and provides the criteria for *all* human religion, or whether a general understanding of religion provides the criteria by which revelation itself is judged and evaluated. In short: Does religion serve as the "norm and principle by which to explain the revelation of God," or do we instead "interpret the Christian religion and all other religions by what we are told by God's revelation" (284)? This is the fundamental question. The modern period largely gave the first answer (see 284–91, esp. 285, 288). As Barth continues, "To this common denominator the aims and the programmes of all the more important tendencies of modern theology can be reduced" (291). The correct answer, he insists, can only be the latter, in which revelation is the norm and standard by which all human religion is evaluated and judged. The final answer to religion in this sense, and thus in turn to natural theology, is a robust, unapologetic, and expansive Christology (see 291–92; cf. 295–97).

This answer, perhaps surprisingly, entails not the "abolition" and rejection of religion in every sense, however. While Barth rejects the human search for transcendence as a form of human hubris ending in idolatry (the first sense of religion), revelation does not denigrate the human requirement for a concrete form of belief and practice altogether (the second sense of religion). As he has said earlier, the fact that God encounters humanity requires that we indeed speak of human things. The answer is one of a rightful ordering of these things, not an unqualified rejection of human practice. Revelation and religion, just as God and humanity, must therefore be set in an irreversible and ordered relation, where the first serves as the norm by which the second is judged, evaluated, and redeemed (296, 297). He writes,

> Our basic task is so to order the concepts revelation and religion that the connexion between the two can again be seen as identical with that event between God and man in which God is God, i.e., the Lord and Master of man, who Himself judges and alone justifies and sanctifies, and man is the man of God, i.e., man as he is adopted and received by God in His severity and goodness. It is because we remember and apply the Christological doctrine of the *assumptio carnis* [assumption of the flesh, i.e., the incarnation] that we speak of revelation as the abolition of religion. (297)

That religion is not simply abolished, but rather redeemed, may be one of the most unexpected turns in Barth's discussion of religion, a discussion that is admittedly quite critical. That he predicates this relationship of divine revelation and human religion upon the prior unique one of God and humanity in Jesus Christ should by now not be surprising, for, as he concludes, the christological dogma of the early church is the presupposition of all practical thought, and this pertains to the relation of revelation and religion as well (297).

Religion as Unbelief (§17.2)

Before human religion can be redeemed, however, it must be judged and exposed for what it is—namely, unbelief in God's revelation, an assertion of humanity's freedom and independence over against God (299–301). This leads to Barth's critical evaluation not only of all religions in general but even of Christianity itself. This is another remarkable move in his argument—he is at this point more critical of Christianity than of other "rival" religions. It is, of course, to be expected that his evaluation of Christianity is nevertheless highly dialectical in its articulation.

Christianity thus stands as a paradox. On one side, as a social organization enduring through time comprising convictions and practices, it stands under the condemnation of God in view of its sinfulness. The history of Christianity is rife with tragedy and failure. In this regard, Christianity stands on the same plane as all human religious traditions and thereby falls under a common divine judgment. Yet this is not the end of the story. For on the other side, as the "locus" of revelation, and thus of "true religion," Christianity stands apart from and over against the other religions of the world.

Both of these sides must be taken into account, and Barth throughout this section dialectically relates these two realities of the church: first, its creaturely and historical existence in which it parallels other religions and in its sins mirrors and at times even exceeds them; and second, the manner in which the church, in spite of its failures, nevertheless stands apart from other religions as the locus of revelation and as its witness and herald. The dialectical relationship between the church's horizontal similarity and indeed compatriotism with other religions in human history and sin and its vertical relationship with divine revelation as called into existence by the Holy Spirit to be a witness to the world comprises a fundamental tension throughout this section. Indeed, Barth is adamant that while judgments can be made between Christianity as the "true religion" and other religions, this does not imply an inherent superiority of Christianity or entail that it is the "true religion" due to an intrinsic quality of itself or its members (298). The key words here are "inherent" and "intrinsic." The truth is not something that Christianity innately possesses but something to which it witnesses only by grace. Christianity does not possess a permanent "nature" of truthfulness. It is the "*locus* of true religion" only by divine election and mercy. Here, too, the event character of revelation and of Christianity is evidenced (298).

Once this dialectical relation of Christianity as both fallen and reconciled religion is understood, Barth's following argument can be brought into focus. He turns to an evaluation of religion from the vantage point of revelation, and what he concludes from this is that every human person can be rightfully considered and understood in relation to Jesus Christ, a relationship that determines and defines the identity of each and every individual (297–98). This means that the human person is not an autonomous agent possessing a general religious awareness but rather is the recipient of a relationship to a living God as this has been established through Jesus Christ. In other words, it is not a general religious awareness or feeling but instead a particular relation to the particular person of Jesus Christ that ultimately defines the identity of each and every human person.

Insofar as religion signifies the rejection of this particular relation and its replacement with a permanent human capacity for the transcendent and divine, religion shows itself not as benign but in truth as unbelief in God and God's revelation. But to condemn religion as unbelief is not simply a judgment upon religions other than Christianity; it is a judgment and condemnation of all of humanity and thus falls upon Christianity as well (300). Here we see again an absolute judgment upon all, Christian and non-Christian alike. This absolute judgment frees Christianity from endless arguments as to its own intrinsic superiority to other religions and to every aspect of their cultural, social, and even political histories. Christians need not strive to prove all other religions as wrong or deny any and all truths within them. The absolute judgment upon all religions, including Christianity, entails that relative judgments can be made without the need for denying everything in other religions.

That religion is in fact unbelief is made clear from the standpoint of the revelation attested in Holy Scripture. First, revelation shows that any attempts from humanity's side to know God are ultimately futile, and religion is the quintessence of this kind of attempt to reach the divine on our own (301). In this sense, religion in its first sense is shown to be not complementary to revelation but diametrically opposed to it in its presumption to achieve what revelation shows to be impossible. In rejecting revelation, religion is "the contradiction of revelation, the concentrated expression of human unbelief" (302–3; cf. 314). As Barth concludes, "In religion man bolts and bars himself against revelation by providing a substitute, by taking away in advance the very thing which has to be given by God" (303).

Second, revelation demonstrates the utter unrighteousness and sinfulness of those who are from the standpoint of salvation reconciled to God, and thus displays that they are helpless, damned and lost apart from this divine act that comes through Jesus Christ (307). Religion is in the end an attempt at self-justification and self-sanctification, and this again reveals not a true worship of God but a tragic failure to know and grasp that this is impossible. Revelation, on the other hand, illuminates the reality that our efforts are an affront to God and that our sins have already been taken away by Christ, who has taken upon himself the sins of the world (309).

Careful consideration of these realities shows Barth explicitly rejecting both the cognitive and the moral ability of humanity to know God or to save itself, respectively: the first results in *idolatry* (i.e., pertaining to "a conception of the deity"), the second in *self-righteousness* (i.e., pertaining to "the fulfillment of the law"). Both are forms of unbelief (314–15). The knowledge of God and the salvation of God are possible only through God's own action, and Barth spends significant time examining Scripture in small-print excurses to provide warrant for this claim as well as to argue that the Bible at its heart is not a book about "religion" if such is understood as an authorization for self-deification (idolatry) or self-justification (self-righteousness) (303–7 and 310–14, respectively; see also 315–16). That religion is unbelief in these two forms is again made manifest by the revelation of God in Jesus Christ that shows religion in its true light (314).

True Religion (§17.3)

In taking up the theme of religion now in a third subsection, Barth presupposes the dialectical tension that he has earlier addressed in the prior two. First, as a human phenomenon, and even more as a sinful one, religion is placed under the judgment of God, shown to be a form of unbelief consisting of idolatry and unrighteousness. Both of these noetic (i.e., dealing with knowledge) and moral (i.e., dealing with action) categories are contained within unbelief. Idolatry at its heart hinges upon a false God and knowledge of God, while unrighteousness rests upon a false sense of self-mastery, self-justification, and fulfillment of the divine law. Barth can draw deeply upon his Reformation roots in making these claims, with Calvin's arguments against idolatry and Luther's arguments against works-righteousness providing both resources and context for his arguments against religion.

A second factor is also in play, however. Religion, while judged for its idolatry and unrighteousness, is nevertheless in another respect unavoidable and even necessary. As noted earlier, Barth shifts between different senses of "religion," and he does so here, for religion is now defined not as unbelief but simply as the human aspect of revelation itself in terms of both its medium and its effects. Revelation always comes through the mediation of created realities (i.e., the flesh of Christ, the written words of Scripture, the spoken words and signs of proclamation in preaching and sacrament). In this regard, religion is not intrinsically sinful or heretical. Barth has already stated that to deny this historical and phenomenological element to revelation would be to deny revelation itself, for it comes by means of created realities divinely annexed for God's purposes of gracious self-communication to us. This entails that Christianity, while a religion in the first sense above, and thereby standing in fallen camaraderie with other religions and beside them under God's judgment, is also, as the elect and chosen "locus" of revelation and the witness to its occurrence, the "true religion." In this third subsection ("True Religion") Barth explores this positive side of the dialectic, as in the former one ("Religion as Unbelief") he explored the negative side.

Barth begins this subsection not by contrasting true and false religion but by again distinguishing between revelation and religion. Reiterating the negative judgment upon all religion, he asserts that no religion, including Christianity, is in itself the truth of God. Only revelation can be thought of in such absolute terms: "For as the self-offering and self-manifestation of God, as the work of peace which God Himself has concluded between Himself and man, revelation is the truth beside which there is no other truth, over against which there is only lying and wrong" (325). Here he is drawing a distinction between revelation and religion akin to the distinction between the Creator and the creature, and perhaps even more pointedly, between a holy God and sinful humanity. This distinction between a holy Creator and a sinful creature is now translated into the realm of religion, where divine revelation stands over against sinful religion. In this absolute contrast, *all* religion, as not only a human and social phenomenon but also a fallen one, stands under the judgment of God that revelation brings. In other words, there is no religion that does not need forgiveness and justification, just as there is no good person who does not need forgiveness and justification. Neither religion as a social entity nor the human person as an individual stands before God unblemished and without sin. Both stand in need of justification and forgiveness. In this sense, religion itself cannot be "true" or "righteous" intrinsically—this is an impossibility.

But in this subsection Barth does not focus simply upon the negative side of religion, the side that displays religion as unbelief, as idolatry and self-righteousness. For God's revelation brings with it not only condemnation but also mercy, and as there is mercy for humanity, so there is with it mercy for all human things, and this, astonishingly, includes religion itself. Barth now turns the dialectical wheel to this other side, to the "abolition" (*Aufhebung*) of religion now seen not as its condemnation and rejection but as its redemption and reconstitution. The hope for religion, as for the human person, is that it can be justified and redeemed (326). Both religion and the believer are in need of grace, and such grace is indeed shown to both. This is not an optimistic possibility that we might conjecture; rather, it is the firm conclusion of a reality that has indeed already occurred. Therefore, even though religion stands condemned before the holy light of revelation, it can also be justified and even sanctified by that very revelation. Barth proceeds, "Revelation can adopt religion and mark it off as true religion. And it not only can. How do we come to assert that it can, if it has not already done so? There is a true religion: just as there are justified sinners. If we abide strictly by that analogy—and we are dealing not merely with an analogy, but in a comprehensive sense with the thing itself—we need have no hesitation in saying that the Christian religion is the true religion" (326).

Here we see a number of important themes that bring all that Barth has said into a conclusive whole. The first is the theme that hangs over this entire paragraph: the notion of an "*abolition*" (*Aufhebung*) *of religion*. It should now be clear that this pattern of dialectical judgment and mercy, of condemnation and redemption, lies at the center of all that Barth is attempting to accomplish in his discussion of religion. For as much as he emphasizes the negative judgment upon religion, this itself serves a larger message of redemption. This dialectic of a divine "No" that serves a larger divine "Yes" is a theme that can be found even in his early critical *Romans* commentary, and it is a motif that runs throughout his entire theological corpus from that point forward. His evaluation of religion fits this pattern of divine judgment and grace, for it is but a variation of the larger subject of God's relation to all things in the world—a relation of condemnation and negation set within a larger purpose of justification, reconstitution, grace, and hope. Barth's discussion of religion takes place within his larger understanding of the gospel itself, a message of both judgment and mercy. It is this gospel, as the revelation of God, which illumines religion and allows us to know it as it truly is, to see its terrible condemnation, but also to witness its redemption in true religion.

Barth's discussion of Christianity and other religions also presents a second theme that runs through his entire theological corpus: the tension between *absolute and relative judgments*. Let us consider the first. An absolute judgment is one that relativizes all other judgments and renders them of no consequence. Such judgments follow from a comparison between the Creator and the creature, and specifically, between a holy God and human sinners. Even if some persons are "better" than others in moral character and practice, revelation demonstrates that "all have sinned and fallen short of the glory of God" (Rom. 3:23). In this sense, whatever relative differences may exist between persons, such differences are in the end nullified and of no account. In the light of God's revelation and righteousness, all are idolaters and unrighteous sinners, persons "having no hope and without God in the world" (Eph. 2:12).

From another perspective, however, Barth reserves the possibility for real if relative judgments between members of a class standing equally under an absolute judgment. As but one later example, he can prefer democratic forms of government over totalitarian ones, though again, in absolute terms, neither of these are the kingdom of God and both fall far short of its true perfection. With regard to our topic at hand, we have seen above that while Barth places all religion under divine condemnation, this does not entail for him a denial that there are truths and benefits to be found in various religions or that some display these more than others. Some aspects of them may in fact be embraced as a recognition of "human greatness," and Christians need not renounce all "human values" found within them. He does not think that one has to become an unreflective "Philistine" and embrace a pure form of iconoclasm that rejects outright everything in other religions entirely (300–301). In this sense, relative judgments can be made between good and better things, or between things that are to be rejected and things that can be appreciated and even embraced.

Barth draws upon such distinctions made between absolute and relative judgments in this examination of true religion, though here the judgment hinges not on relative evaluations of good and bad, or good and better, things, but upon the more significant distinction between fallen and redeemed religion. If from the perspective of revelation all religions, including Christianity, are shown to stand under judgment as sinful, he can also state that Christianity, though possessing no intrinsic truthfulness as a religion, is the locus of God's justifying grace and the attestation to that grace. In this respect, and as a witness to revelation, Christianity can be seen as "true religion" (326). Christianity can be seen as such, however, only in faith, and its task is not to assert its intrinsic truth and holiness against the falsity and unrighteousness of other religions, standing in judgment over them, but rather to accept revelation's own judgment upon itself. Barth's entire position might be rightly summarized by the words of Peter that judgment must begin with the household of God (1 Pet. 4:17). He rejects Christian triumphalism of any

kind, and he constantly holds in tension both Christianity's sinful identification with the other religions of the world and its election, justification, and
sanctification to be "true religion"—that is, a true witness to the truth of
God's revelation in Jesus Christ. In its justification and sanctification, it can
in turn provide an obedient correspondence to revelation in its faith and life.
Yet a true knowledge and worship and service of God in Christianity takes
place only as the Holy Spirit makes it so (344–46, 347).

This dependence upon the Spirit should lead Christianity to be perma-
nently and consistently humble, and it has, Barth argues, paid a price when it
has forgotten this and turned from humble witness to triumphal apologetics
(325–38). For once again revelation's superiority to religion, even the Christian
religion, is absolute, and it is put by Barth in a now familiar formula: "The
religion of revelation is indeed bound up with the revelation of God: but the
revelation of God is not bound up with the religion of revelation" (329). By
this point, the logic and grammar of such an asymmetrical statement should
be both familiar to us and readily understood.

Yet having reverted again to the negative side of the equation regarding
religion, Barth can nevertheless turn the dialectical tables once more with the
purpose of arguing that the deeply dialectical reality of Christianity should
not and does not undermine its confidence. However strongly this absolute
judgment upon the Christian religion need be emphasized, this does not entail,
he insists, that the Christian faith is made "weak or uncertain or hesitant,
or that the decision for the truth of the Christian religion is robbed of its
firmness and confidence" (331). Rather, the promise of God gives it a proper
confidence to fulfill its task of witness in the world (331–33).

The third and final theme that we might highlight in Barth's discussion of
Christianity and religion is his understanding of *faith and history*. Barth applies to the history of religion the same form of argumentation that he applies
to all such matters that mirror his distinction of the invisible and the visible
church. From the perspective of human history, as a purely social and cultural
phenomenon, the story of Israel and the church is a story of ambivalence,
of some triumphs but more defeats, of human failings, shortcomings, and
weakness. Yet he points to a history hidden behind this natural and temporal
veil, a history that is known by faith in the relation of God and his people
Israel, of Jesus and his church: "It is a story whose source and meaning and
goal, the fact that the Christian is strong only in his weakness, that he is
really satisfied by grace, can in the strict sense nowhere be perceived directly"
(337). He has no reason to think that this will change in the future, for we
cannot expect that "the history of Christianity will be anything but a history
of the distress which Christianity creates for itself" (338). This recognition,

Barth asserts, lies at the heart of the Reformation discovery and at the root of Protestantism as true religion (343).

Barth closes this subsection in a familiar fashion, with a number of points examining the relationship between Jesus Christ and the Christian religion. He follows the familiar logic of the relationship between Christ and the church in setting these forth, explicating these points under the themes of creation (346–48), election (348–52), justification (352–57), and sanctification (357–61).[9] And while Barth's entire discussion is characteristically marked by a strong dialectical character, he can provide somewhat of a resolution to the paradoxical nature of the Christian religion at the end:

> Therefore the true and essential distinction of the Christian religion from the non-Christian, and with it its character as the religion of truth over against the religions of error, can be demonstrated only in the fact, or event, that taught by Holy Scripture the Church listens to Jesus Christ and no one else as grace and truth, not being slack but always cheerful to proclaim and believe Him, finding its pleasure in giving itself as promised to the service offered to Him, and therefore in being His own confessor and witness in the confession and witness of the Church. In fact, it all amounts to this: that the Church has to be weak in order to be strong. (344)

The Life of the Children of God (§18)

This paragraph extends the concluding discussion of the last one—that is, the sanctification of the Christian religion, the church, and the Christian. Barth now turns to consider the correspondence and the conformity of the Christian community and religion to Christ that result from subjective revelation. He does so by addressing two primary questions: First, what does the life of the children of God look like? And second, what things characterize this life? He now at last addresses the human response to revelation and the

---

9. Indeed, such christological analogies are not superimposed upon Barth's theology here but are explicitly given by Barth himself: "The Christian religion is simply the earthly-historical life of the Church and the children of God. As such we must think of it as an annexe to the human nature of Jesus Christ. And we must remember what we are told concerning His human nature in John 1:14. There never was a man Jesus as such apart from the eternal reality of the Son of God. . . . The human nature of Jesus Christ has no hypostasis of its own, we are told. It has it only in the Logos. The same is true, therefore, of the earthly-historical life of the earthly body of Christ and His members, who are called out of the schematic, bare possibility into the reality by the fact that He, the Head, has taken and gathered them to Himself as the earthly form of His heavenly body" (CD I/2, 348). It is also certain that this relationship between Christ and the Christian religion cannot be reversed (350).

proper form Christian life (and thus Christian religion) takes for those who have been addressed and renewed by the Holy Spirit. Here we see that Barth's ecclesiological convictions are mirrored in ethical ones.

Man as a Doer of the Word (§18.1)

After a brief and very helpful recapitulation of what has already been discussed—the subject, event, and effect of revelation, or the Triune God, the incarnation of the Son, and the outpouring of the Spirit, respectively—Barth turns to an examination of the human subject who has been addressed and converted by the Word of God, "man himself as the recipient of revelation, i.e., believing and perceiving man" (362). Such a person is united both with Christ and with Christ's "body on earth," the church (362–63). Barth's description of the individual Christian is therefore ever bound up with his understanding of the relation this person has to Christ and to the Christian community. It is also helpful to remember that he is thinking of the person primarily in corporate and representative terms rather than solely as a single individual.

Barth unsurprisingly commences with a warning that even here one cannot examine the human person as an independent topic of investigation if such is to mean the person understood apart from revelation and abstracted from his or her relation to Christ and the work of the Spirit. To see the human person in this way is no longer to see him or her as fallen and as also reconciled in Christ. To fail to understand the person simultaneously as a sinner and as justified (to put this in Luther's famous formula: *simul iustus et peccator*, "simultaneously justified and a sinner") is to misunderstand the person entirely. It is to deal with an abstraction and not with the reality of the person's true identity as known in revelation. Barth's anthropology is a thoroughly theological and christological one and is framed entirely in these terms.

The human person is on this account understood not by nature but only by grace, through the lens of faith, and in the light of his or her relation to revelation (362–71). It is also true, however, that if the human person in his or her paradoxical existence as reconciled sinner is to be truly understood, the person must be understood in all of his or her concreteness and complexity (364). Throughout this paragraph Barth tries to balance a firm rejection of an absolute independence of the creature with an affirmation of the creature's integrity expressed in "acts of free determination and decision" (364). Wishing to preserve the divine determination of humanity's identity and existence and also humanity's self-determination and distinct agency, he argues for a noncompetitive account of divine and human freedom. He expresses this paradox in this way when reflecting upon the human person, again marked by an irreversible syntax: "The grace of revelation is not conditioned by his humanity, but his humanity is conditioned by the grace of revelation. God's freedom does not compete with man's freedom. How could it be the freedom of the divine mercy bestowed on man, if it suppressed and dissolved human freedom? It is the grace of revelation that God exercises and maintains His freedom to free man" (365).

Barth is adamant that God's freedom and human freedom are not competitive, and that the first establishes rather than undermines the second (364–67). Yet of ultimate importance for the identity of the human person is not the fact *that* a person believes, but the object of that belief. Barth therefore again displays his emphasis upon the objectivity, rather than subjectivity, of faith: "It is man who believes. This does not justify him. What justifies him is the fact that he believes in Jesus Christ" (366). While the object of belief is what gives faith its efficacy and purpose, Barth nevertheless does attempt to give the Christian and his or her faith their due. He certainly does not intend to treat the human believer as a purely passive object.

With this emphasis upon the human believer as an acting agent, Barth states that the topic that now arises is the one known as "theological ethics, or more practically as the Christian life" (367). God's revelation logically raises the corresponding question of human life and conduct, of how Christians are to live in conformity to what has been revealed and what they are to do in obedience to the command that it includes (367). This paragraph is thus aptly called "The Life of the Children of God," a title, he concedes, that he owes to Adolf von Harnack (367). He adds, however, that it might just as well have been titled "The Life of the Church" (368; cf. 453). He ends this section with a consideration of the *being* and inward nature of the Christian (which he defines under the category of the love of God), and of the *doing* and outward, social nature of the Christian (which he defines in terms of the praise of God) (369–71). These two themes of the love of God and the praise of God will be the subjects of the next two subsections of the paragraph, respectively. All of the Christian life, Barth insists, is composed of love and praise (371).

A few final observations might be made in regard to this paragraph with an eye toward Barth's larger project. The first is that he thinks of the human response to God's revelation and salvation not in terms of cooperation in that work, but in terms of witness and service. In other words, he thinks of the human response in predominantly ethical categories—that is, in terms of how the Christian community and Christian believer live and are to live in light of a divine event of revelation and salvation that is perfect and complete. His understanding of the Christian life in both its corporate and individual aspects, and thus in regard to both the church and the Christian, is portrayed in terms of witness, not of cooperation or of strong understandings of synergistic mediation (i.e., cooperative salvific agency between God and the church or the Christian). The Christian's task (as the church's task) is therefore not to do what God does or to extend Christ's work, but to live a life of thankfulness and obedience in light of a salvation accomplished by God alone, through Christ alone, and that we can receive by faith alone, for it is a matter of grace alone (and that is attested in Scripture alone).

The second observation follows closely upon the first, which is that this ethical life is construed as one that is in "conformity" or correspondence to what has been revealed of God's own being (367). There is an analogical reflection in the created human life of the church and the individual believer of God's own life as this has been revealed in his action of self-disclosure and salvation in Christ. As Barth elsewhere writes, "What the community owes to the world, and each individual within it, is basically that in its life, and in the lives of all its members, there should be attempted an imitation and representation of the love with which God loved the world" (*CD* III/4, 502).

The third observation then follows upon the second, which is that Barth thinks of the ethical agent who lives this life of correspondence firstly as a corporate agent and only secondly as an individual one. The agent of ethical action is the Christian community and only secondarily the individual Christian. For Barth, ethics is social ethics before it is personal ethics, for the believer exists always within the context of the Christian community, a judgment that comports with his earlier reflections upon the relation of the church and the individual believer. As he notes, the "life of the children of God is simply the life of the Church of God" (453; cf. 368). The description of the Christian life is therefore a description of the Christian community before it is a description of the Christian believer.

A fourth thing revealed in this paragraph about Barth's larger program is that, just as the believer's faith and activity must be understood within the larger framework of God's revelation and salvation, so also ethics must be understood and included within the larger framework of dogmatics. As he writes, "Human self-determination, and therefore the life of the children of God, is posited under the predominant determination of revelation" (368). Just as he rejects a consideration of the human person abstracted from revelation, or an independent anthropology abstracted from the larger context of Christology and pneumatology, so also he rejects an independent ethics abstracted from the more fundamental context of dogmatics (see 371). In short: he includes theological ethics as a subset of dogmatics and does not treat it as an autonomous discipline.

In making these moves, Barth was going against the grain of much of the eighteenth and nineteenth centuries, when many treated ethical concerns al-

most entirely apart from theological ones, or, in other cases, reduced the latter to the former, dissolving dogmatics into ethics. To treat ethics in such an
independent way always entailed that its starting point was not revelation but
rather some capacity or experience of the human person or some other cultural or social reality. In contrast to such an anthropological grounding, Barth
insisted, Christian ethics must be *theological* ethics, and to be theological,
ethics must begin with revelation and therefore must be framed and included
within dogmatics and shaped by christological convictions. Learning this les-
son here will help in reading all of the ethical sections in the other volumes of
the *CD*. Barth always framed ethical questions by setting them within rich and
developed descriptions of theological realities. Or, in perhaps more familiar
terms, he always discussed the imperative (i.e., how we are to live and what
we are to do) in light of the indicative (i.e., the reality of who God is and what
God has in fact done in Christ). In this, too, Barth swam against the dominant
currents of the modern period.

The Love of God (§18.2)

"The Christian life begins with love" (371). So begins this second of three
subsections in §18, and it, like the next and final one, can be dealt with quite
briefly. Barth in this subsection addresses the Christian life as one of love
for God and neighbor, echoing the two great commandments of Jesus, with
the emphasis in this section falling upon the first commandment. Love is
the most basic and essential element of all Christian action, and it is what
marks all human life and action as Christian: "Wherever the Christian life
in commission or omission is good before God, the good thing about it is
love" (372). But just like faith, love itself is not self-generated; the fact that
we can love God and others follows from the reality that God first loves us,
that we are loved. God's love for us precedes and makes possible our love for
God and for others. In this way, our love, like our faith, is a gift of God, and
not the result of any natural love found in us (372–73). The relation between
this divine love and our own is irreversible, for the former is the basis and
ground upon which the latter rests (400). Here too, however, Barth wants to
take with full seriousness the fact that it is humans who love, and therefore
that love is also a "creaturely reality" and not simply a divine one (373–74).
He again delicately balances the realities of divine and human agencies as
they are ordered according to a christological logic:

> We cannot therefore say that it [the creaturely reality] is the product of a trans-
> formation of the creaturely into divine reality, nor can we say that in it the divine

reality has taken the place of the creaturely. In strict analogy with the incarnation of the Word in Jesus Christ, what takes place in man by the revelation of
God is this: his humanity is not impaired, but in the Word of God heard and
believed by him he finds the Lord, indeed in the strict and proper sense he finds
the subject of his humanity, for on his behalf Jesus Christ stands and rightly
stands in His humanity at the right hand of the Father. For that very reason all
that he can do is in his humanity to seek God in this Jesus Christ, and therefore
to love Him. When the children of God love, they are the earthly members
of His body, longing for their heavenly Head. The earthly members—that is
why their loving, grounded as it is in the love of God, is not transmuted into a
heavenly or divine loving. (373–74)

God's love for us precedes, establishes, and gives meaning to our love for
God, but it is also true that our love for God has its own purpose, value,
integrity, and reality as a rightly given response to that prior divine love. The
only explanation that can be given for this love of believers for God, however,
returns us again to the answers of faith, and then behind faith to its object,
to Jesus Christ (374–75). That Christ calls and converts persons to love him
and to love God is "the miracle of the Holy Spirit and therefore the founding
of love in man" (375). The radical particularity of this divine activity must
be reflected in our definition of love: it is not that we begin with a general
conception of love and then apply this to revelation in order to understand
God, but rather we begin with divine revelation and this in turn defines what
love is. As Barth writes, "To know what love is, we have first to ask concerning the unique love of God for us" (376). Our love, then, must be a reflection
of this very specific form of love. We do not understand this divine love by
beginning with a general conception of love derived simply from observation
of human practices and relationships. We begin, rather, with attendance to
how God has loved us in Christ. And as we know this love, we in turn love,
and live in conformity to this divine love in our human created existence. God
himself creates this "similarity between Him and us" (396; see 395–96). Barth
continues, "What He is for us in His sphere as God, Creator, and Reconciler,
we can be for Him in our sphere as sinful creatures. We can therefore love.
And in loving we can participate in His perfection" (396).

When this divine love is kept in view, and when Scripture is the basis for
our knowledge, then we see that love "has nothing to do with mere sentiment,
opinion or feeling. On the contrary, it consists in a definite being, relationship and action" (377). God is love in himself, and his love for us flows from
his being, in freedom and without compulsion, for God is love even before
and apart from his love for the world and its reconciliation (377, 379). The

concrete form of this love is Jesus Christ himself, and there is no divine love apart from him (378). In short: "Therefore when we try to describe to ourselves the love of God, we can only express and proclaim the name of Jesus Christ" (379).

Barth now further elucidates our response to this love of God (380). What should our answer to this great love be? The answer is that we should be obedient to and fulfill the two great commandments of Jesus: we are to love the Lord our God with all of our heart, soul, mind, and strength; and we are to love our neighbor as ourselves (381). Barth spends some time looking at these passages in their biblical contexts (381–401). His conclusion is that to love God is to seek and obey God (389–91). One thing that he rejects, however, is a positive estimation of self-love, disagreeing with Augustine on this matter (387–88; cf. 450–53). He does not think that Jesus's command that we are to love our neighbor as ourselves is a commendation of our love for ourselves: "Our self-love can never be anything right or holy and acceptable to God" (388). Instead, as he later writes, "When I love my neighbour, I confess that my self-love is not a good thing, that it is not love at all. I begin to love at all only when I love my neighbour" (450). Love is truly love, then, only if it has an object outside and beyond the self: "Love must always have an opposite, an object. It is only an illusion that we can be an object of love to ourselves" (388; cf. 450–53). So while Jesus's command simply and realistically acknowledges that we have this love for self, true love is that which has its proper object first of all in God, and then in turn in our neighbor.

The Praise of God (§18.3)

Whereas in the last subsection the emphasis fell upon the first great commandment, the love we are called to have for God, the emphasis in Barth's final subsection of this paragraph falls upon the second great commandment, the love we are called to demonstrate toward our neighbor. He places this discussion under the heading of the praise of God and adds that "no praise of God is serious, or can be taken seriously" that does not include within it full responsibility to this command (401–2).

Barth spends much of the following discussion attempting to explicate the relation between the first and the second great commandments, love of God and love of neighbor (402–11). He provides three alternative ways of understanding their relation, finding some value in each, but ultimately rejecting them all as inadequate. The first way is to see the commandments as two equal and parallel commands. His conclusion is that the commandments cannot be rightly understood this way, for the first takes precedence over the second.

As there is but one God, so there is but one absolute love (402). The love of God stands on a different plane from the love of neighbor.

Neither, however, are they identical with each other such that they can be merged into a higher synthesis whereby love of neighbor is the same as and equated with love for God (402, 403–6). This second alternative is also one that Barth finds wanting. The commandments cannot be identified because the recipients of the love commanded in each cannot be identified. It would be actually blasphemous, he contends, to say that the neighbor is God, and Scripture does not allow this (403, 406). Therefore, love of God cannot be collapsed into love of neighbor, for God cannot be equated with the neighbor. Such a collapse is but another sign of the confusion of God and humanity and of the replacement of theology with anthropology. God alone is to be praised and is the recipient of a unique love, just as God alone is holy. A human person can be loved, but only with the recognition of the person as sinful and under divine judgment. Any attempt to see God straightforwardly in the neighbor such that they are equated would amount to another form of natural theology, an attempt to know God and his commandments "based directly upon creation apart from revelation" (405).

The third position that Barth rejects is one that would seem to be a natural one to embrace in light of the rejection of the second—namely, to see the first commandment as the only absolute command and to consider the second as a separate derivative and subordinate one (402, 406–8). While sympathetic to this answer and upholding its superiority to the prior two, he nevertheless does not adopt it. The commandment to love the neighbor stands, like the first commandment, as a direct, rather than derived and secondary, imperative. It, too, is a form of praise for God (though not for humanity). The praise of God of this second commandment is neither relative nor secondary.

Barth finds the resolution and meaning of the tension between the two great commandments in the eschatological nature of Christian life in which the church lives now between the resurrection and the ascension of Jesus Christ (408). The commandments to love God and neighbor are two equally divine commands, but ones of a different order, the first superior and eternal, the second subordinate and temporal, if nevertheless absolute in this temporal sphere. As Barth can say, the "two times and worlds are not symmetrical" (410). The first commandment points to a love that exists for One beyond time, a love commanded of the creature qua creature in relation to an eternal Creator. The second points to a love that is given to the neighbor for the sake of temporal existence, for the creature in relation to other creatures within this world as it now exists and in this time between Christ's first and second appearances. Love of neighbor is given for the sake of the love of God, for "the commandment of love to the neighbour is enclosed by that of love to God" (411). Yet the objects of these loves are not confused and are ever differentiated.

The rest of this subsection is concerned with specifying what such love of neighbor entails (411–14) as well as stipulating who the neighbor to be loved is (414–30) and what form such love should take (430–50). Barth's discussion throughout this subsection hinges again on a pattern of explication in which the love of the neighbor is given its own identity, form, content, and purpose, but where it is framed within the larger commandment to love God, and in which these commandments are, however intimately connected, never confused such that the recipients of love are confused. The church, as the creature of God, is to attend to these commands to love and to obey them. In its own way, and in its own "simple sphere," the church is to "let our walk and activity be the walk and activity of those who are thankful," and this thankfulness to God is the form of love that in turn overflows in a second form of love for our neighbor (413).

It is striking, however, that when Barth turns to consider the identity of the neighbor to be loved, he identifies our neighbor not as the person in need of our compassion, but rather as the one who shows compassion to us, thus following Jesus's parable of the merciful Samaritan (416–19). He places the argument of the neighbor in the language of benefaction and defines the neighbor as our benefactor. This leads to a natural question: Am I ever called to love my neighbor not only as the benefactor of mercy shown to me but also as one to whom I am to extend mercy, as the recipient of my compassion? In brief: Am I not also called to be a benefactor? Barth concedes that the answer to this question is, of course, an affirmative one. But he adds two very important caveats. The first is that the commandment to love my neighbor as someone in need cannot be thought of as a law, as if mercy followed only from obligation. To view it this way is, in effect, to view the other person simply as an obligation for my action, as primarily the presentation of a "task" for me to fulfill. And the reason why love of neighbor cannot be thought of this way is found in the second caveat: even before I assist my neighbor, I have received from him or her, and therefore my neighbor is already my benefactor before I am his or hers. Barth explains, "And his benefaction to us as a suffering fellow-creature in need of help consists in the fact that even in his misery he shows us the true humanity of Jesus Christ, that humanity which was not triumphant but submissive, not healthy and strong, but characterized by the bearing of our sins, which was therefore flesh of our flesh—the flesh abandoned to punishment, suffering and death" (428).

This is a remarkable passage. It shows that in the face of the weak, the sick, and the poor, I am confronted with the form and re-presentation of the human life of Christ, the Word who assumed the form of a servant who was weak, poor, and smitten. This misery of my neighbor may not be so readily apparent; Barth notes that it may in fact be hidden behind a veil of health and strength (428). Yet however this need of my neighbor is presented to me, what I first receive from this person in need is a confrontation with Christ's humanity, for "it is in this actual misery of his that there consists his actual similarity to the crucified Christ" (429). Therefore, "in recognizing my neighbour in my fellow-man, I am actually placed before Christ" (429). The neighbor in need stands before me as a representative of Jesus Christ, and he or she does so whether or not the person is aware of this fact (429). And in this sense, I receive before I give, for this person, in showing Christ to me, is my benefactor before he or she is the recipient of my compassion.

In defining the neighbor as not simply an object of my compassion but as a subject who shows Christ to me, Barth guards against an objectification of those in need. In brief: he will not allow human relations to be thought of as interactions between good Samaritans and helpless neighbors, or benefactors and recipients. In the light of the love of God, *all* are recipients first. And secondly, even in the event of one's confrontation with another in need, the one who is called to show compassion is first a recipient of the neighbor in need who "has already been of benefit to us" in presenting Christ to us (428). In this construal, both the one in need and the one who confronts that need are given dignity in the light of a gospel that reveals the true state of each: both persons are neighbors whom God can use to help the other, for both persons are in radical need, though this need may take different forms. Here again relative distinctions of giver and recipient are placed under the aegis of a larger absolute need of both in light of God's beneficence to all, as well as of a larger form of beneficence that both can serve. A few pages later Barth can summarize this way of thinking:

> To accept my neighbour necessarily means to accept his service. As we have seen, if I really recognize him as my neighbour, he serves me by showing me in his own person my sin and misery, and in that way the condescension of God and the humanity of Jesus Christ the Crucified. We had to lay all the emphasis upon the fact that this is the actual content of my meeting with the neighbour as such. Of course, Jesus Christ is always concealed in the neighbour. The neighbour is not a second revelation of Jesus Christ side by side with the first. When he meets me, the neighbour is not in any sense a second Christ. He is only my neighbour. And it is only as such and in this difference from Christ, only as a sign instituted by Christ, that we can speak of his solidarity and identity with Christ. (434–35)

Barth thinks of the neighbor therefore as a kind of witness, even as a sign. He writes, "Whether willingly and wittingly or not, in showing it, my neighbour acquires for me a sacramental significance" (436). The question of law and obligation I might have toward a neighbor in need can then only follow upon the service and benefit I have received from my neighbor: "In relation to our neighbour, then, the road does not lead, as we are often told, from Law to Gospel—there is no road that way—but from Gospel to Law" (437–38). To receive the grace of God, which is to receive the love of God, results in love and grace shown to our neighbor in need. And because this love of God is nothing other than the love shown us in Christ, so our love extended to the neighbor takes this form of showing Christ to him or her: "To love the neighbour, therefore, is plainly and simply to be to him a witness of Jesus Christ. That the duty of love is the duty of witness results from the fact that I am summoned by my encounter with the neighbour to expect to find in him a brother of Jesus Christ and therefore my own brother" (440; see also 441–50).

The recognition that our service to our neighbor as a witness ultimately depends on God leads us finally to prayer. Prayer is nothing less than the subjective act of the church in correspondence to the church's proclamation and sacraments in the objective sphere. We might say that for Barth, prayer is the most human of all human acts, that which is most proper and most fitting for those who have received God's love and grace: "Praying, asking of God, can consist only in receiving what God has already prepared for us, before and apart from our stretching out our hands for it. It is in this praise of God that the children of God live, who love God, because He first loved them" (454).

COMMENTARY

The Relation of Jesus Christ, the Holy Spirit, and Other Spirits

As earlier witnessed, Barth's rejection of any attempt to ground theological reflection in human subjectivity was mirrored in his renunciation of an independent doctrine of the Spirit separated from the revelation of God in Jesus Christ. Yet whether Barth has given pneumatology its due is a question that has continued to haunt his theology. Barth's position on these matters can, of course, be questioned and pressed. Some will wonder whether he has given adequate weight to the Holy Spirit's unique work to guide the church and individual believers. Others will question whether he has given sufficient attention to the agency of the church or of the human person and whether his emphasis upon objectivity in salvation leaves little place for the Spirit's work and for human reception and sanctification. How such questions are answered reveals in turn whether one thinks of Barth's understanding of the Holy Spirit as deficient, or whether one assesses it as simply based upon different fundamental convictions. For instance, Barth understood the revelatory and salvific work of Christ as perfect and finished, and for this reason, the Spirit's work could not be thought of as an augmentation to this work, but rather had to be understood as a culmination of it. The Spirit's work certainly could not be seen as independent of Christ's own. As Barth stated, heresies of the third article arise when the "Holy Spirit has ceased to be the Spirit of Jesus Christ" (257).

This understanding did not detract from the Spirit's work, in his estimation, but entailed that the Word and Spirit could not be separated in even the slightest way, and this was the case in matters of salvation as well as revelation. Claims for a new salvific work of the Spirit could, if not carefully qualified, undermine the perfection and completed nature of Christ's work. Similarly, claims of a new revelatory work of the Spirit that stood apart from but claimed the same authority as the Word could, in his own experience, be a claim for a justification for personal or cultural or political programs that opposed the gospel. His opposition to the theology of the German Christians sympathetic to Nazi ideology stood as a witness to this danger. But he did not believe that this episode was a singular occurrence or challenge in the church's history. It simply brought the underlying problem of natural theology to the fore and pressed it upon the church (CD II/1, 172–78).

The questions Barth raises are of utmost importance, for the church can never see the revelation that the Spirit brings as something that undermines God's revelation in his Word. This was one of the greatest convictions of the Reformation and one that continues to challenge the church today. But it is a conviction that long predates the Reformation itself: "Beloved, do not believe every spirit, but test the spirits to see whether they are from God" (1 John 4:1). This testing is a perennial task set before the church, for the temptation to get caught up in and baptize worldly spirits on any side of the cultural or political spectrum remains constant. Albert Speer, Adolf Hitler's famous architect, got caught up in such spirits in Nazi Germany. Years after its fall and his own imprisonment, he spoke a prophetic word back over his life, ensconced in a short caption under a photograph of an earlier time when he stood beside Hitler poring over plans for a new Berlin. That caption was as brief as it was poignant: "One seldom recognizes the devil when he is putting his hand on your shoulder." It is in those times that the Word must be heard against our inclinations most of all. Yet it is the self-delusion that tempts us in those times that makes a constant attention to the Word all the more necessary, especially because our betrayals may come in more understated ways and during more ordinary times, and perhaps in the guise of much more benign devils.

Revelation and Religion, Christianity and World Religions

One of the pressing questions standing before the church is the relation of Christianity to other world religions. Barth's position is, as we have seen, quite complex. From the perspective of an absolute judgment, he rejects all religions as attempts at human transcendence, and all are thus equally opposed by God's revelation. In this sense, all religions fall under the absolute judgment of God upon idolatry, as well as upon the oppressive force that religion can be.

In another respect, however, he does not believe that Christianity must unquestionably reject every element of other religions, nor does he think that Christianity should be concerned with defending its own intrinsic superiority to other religions. Rather, Christianity itself must accept God's judgment upon its own failings, and one of the striking aspects of Barth's writing on human religion is his insistence that revelation stands in judgment not only over the world religions but also over Christianity itself. Yet he does, in the end, provide a place for true religion as Christianity witnesses not to its own intrinsic superiority but to the unique revelation of God in Christ. He therefore ultimately rejects two positions: (1) a Christian triumphalism that stands in judgment of other religions and rejects everything about them on principle; and (2) a religious pluralism that sees all religions as equally valid and Christ as simply one manifestation of divine presence (or as a religious genius or exemplar of moral excellence).

Barth's challenge to contemporary Christians may be precisely in rejecting these two alternatives as a false choice. For him, the answer to the problem of Christian triumphalism could never be capitulation of the church's confession of the lordship of Christ, in essence a rejection of the scandal of particularity and the uniqueness and divinity of Jesus Christ as the revelation of God. To give up on this claim would be for the church to lose its heart and commission, its very reason for existence. The scandal cannot be renounced, but rather must be embraced and confessed. Yet to proclaim Jesus Christ as "the way, and the truth, and the life" who alone reveals the Father (John 14:6) and as the Lamb of God "who takes away the sin of the world" (John 1:29) is not a claim for the superiority of the church, nor is it a claim that the church possesses this truth, for witnessing to the truth is not the same as possessing it. It is, rather, the proclamation that God has judged all persons and things and found them wanting, and that includes Christian triumphalism and the hubris and failures of Christianity as a religion with its own idolatrous and self-righteous episodes and perennial self-justification. But it also means that, as the church proclaims not itself but Jesus Christ as Lord (2 Cor. 4:5), it can be taken up by God to serve as true religion in the world and has indeed been established and commissioned as such.

The church's humility is thus rightly expressed not in the renunciation but in the firm confession of the scandal of the gospel and a true understanding of it. Any church that gives up on the scandal, and thereby the worship and confession of the Lord Jesus Christ, and does so due to a fear of the offense it may give, might be reminded that if it silences its evangelical witness to Christ, then it will be replaced by another, for even if all became silent, "the very stones would cry out" (Luke 19:40 RSV).

Love of God and Love of Neighbor as the Basis of Theological Ethics

While Barth places his emphasis upon the divine prerogative and providence that precede all human action, he does not exclude or denigrate human agency and action. God's work of salvation and revelation in Jesus Christ calls forth from the human person both faith and obedience in light of this divine work. This commitment to address human faith and action is seen in the very structure of the dogmatics, for Barth insists that dogmatics must incorporate ethics within itself. In the first volume, such later sections on theological ethics are prefigured in his investigations of divine and human freedom as well as his discussion of the Christian life as one marked by the love and praise of God.

For Barth, all questions of what persons are to be and do can be understood only if such persons themselves are considered in the light of their relation to Jesus Christ and what he has done on their behalf, as well as in the context of the Christian community in which they find themselves. He challenges many modern conceptions of ethics in stressing that the life of the Christian community takes precedence and provides the context for the individual Christian and his or her life. He also insists that theological ethics is predicated on a divine command that does not undermine but rather establishes the freedom of the person, and he rejects modern conceptions of individual autonomy predicated upon an individual's unassisted reason. In short: he rejects modernity's individualism and its conception of the autonomous ethical agent, and he also prioritizes what we might term communal ethics (i.e., social ethics) over personal ethics (though the latter are taken up into the former) and the life of the Christian community over that of the individual, while never simply subsuming the individual into the community.

Barth therefore presents a challenge to a culture that still defines ethical reflection largely in terms of the autonomous individual who makes decisions. In contrast, he considers the most important decision not to be the one that we make, but the one that has been made by God to be God for us. In turn, it is the church, and then the individual believer, that is marked by a life that corresponds to that divine decision and to the divine life that has taken human form in Jesus Christ. The life of the church and the life of the believer are set against this backdrop and determined by this divine action, yet determined, Barth wants to insist, in a way that does not abrogate but rather establishes human freedom and sets it upon solid ground for discipleship and obedience.

This Christian life is one marked by the love and praise of God. This love that we have for God is a response to that which God has first shown us. Barth provides a needed corrective to the common practice of beginning with an abstract concept of love and then applying it to God. Rather, it is God's own action that defines what love is and what in turn the church is to be and do in order to be loving. In this light, perhaps nowhere does the gospel cut against the grain of current culture as deeply as with its concept of love. This divine love is predicated not on feeling, emotion, or sentimentality, but upon concrete action, the divine self-giving in Jesus Christ: "In this is love, not that we loved God but that he loved us and sent his Son to be the atoning sacrifice for our sins" (1 John 4:10; cf. Rom. 5:8). God's love is based in a free decision to love the world, but it is sustained by a divine faithfulness to his covenantal promise. This faithful love in turn illuminates how tepid, ephemeral, fickle, and fragile human love truly can be.

If the church were to take this divine faithfulness to heart, it might realize that the greatest gift it has received is from a God who has kept his promises and fulfilled them all in sending his Son to the world, for "in him every one of God's promises is a 'Yes'" (2 Cor. 1:20). The church might do well to ponder that it never is so close to reflecting the love of God as when it remains faithful in fulfilling its entrusted commission to announce this divine love and faithfulness to a world of broken promises and dreams. Such divine faithfulness is also reflected in Christian lives of faithfulness to decisions and promises implicitly or explicitly made. Such faithfulness would revolutionize friendships, marriages, families, and the life of the Christian community itself. God cares about more than such personal promises, of course. But he does not care about less, and the biblical witness attests that God seems to have a particular concern for those who are most dependent upon the faithfulness and promises of others—such as the alien, the widow, the orphan, and children, who bear the brunt and are most helpless in the face of broken promises.

God's freedom therefore sets the parameters for human freedom even as it establishes such creaturely freedom. Moreover, while God's faithfulness cannot be perfectly replicated in the human sphere, it is nevertheless the pattern for what the Christian life is to be. This passage bears repeating: "What the community owes to the world, and each individual within it, is basically that in its life, and in the lives of all its members, there should be attempted an imitation and representation of the love with which God loved the world" (CD III/4, 502). This love is nothing if not the faithfulness of a promise kept.

QUESTIONS FOR REFLECTION

- How should we understand the work of Christ and the work of the Holy Spirit? With such matters in mind, explain in your own words the following quotation from Barth: "Where the Holy Spirit is sundered from Christ, sooner or later He is always transmuted into quite a different spirit, the spirit of the religious man, and finally the human spirit in general" (251).

- In what way can one say that the church is a divine institution? What might this mean? What does it not mean?

- How should we understand the work of the church in relation to the work of Christ and the Spirit? What are we to make of Barth's favored concept of witness as designating the specific task of the church and the Christian? How does he distinguish discipleship from imitation in relation to a believer's following Christ (see 276–78)?

- How should the relation between the church and the individual Christian be understood? Does the church take priority over the individual believer? Or is the opposite the case? How does Barth understand their relationship?

- What did Barth find so appealing about Luther's hymns, which were, in his estimation, "completely lacking in all lyrical quality, i.e., in all emphasis upon the emotion of the subject" (see 253)? Why does he consider it a compliment when he says of Luther's hymns that in them "we never find either God's child or God's Church preoccupied with themselves, but always turning to the recognition and praise of God and His acts, with the greatest concentration upon the second article as understood in all its biblical simplicity" (253)?

- In what ways is the Holy Spirit confused with human emotion or experience today? How is this done on different ends of the theological spectrum?
- How might Barth's theology speak to current worship practices, including matters of liturgy and music?
- How might Barth's discussion of world religions contribute to a Christian understanding of them? In what ways is the distinction of absolute and relative judgments beneficial for this understanding?
- How does Barth undermine a dualism and contrast of benefactors (those who help others) and beneficiaries (those who receive help)? How does he think of the neighbor in both senses? How is Christ present to me both in benefactors (when I receive help from a neighbor) and in beneficiaries (those neighbors whom I help)? How does Barth present a challenge to those who would objectify the poor or deny their dignity? In what does their dignity lie, as he understands this?

Holy Scripture

CD §§19–21

Chapter 3 of Barth's doctrine of the Word of God is dedicated to a discussion of Holy Scripture. This third chapter of the *CD* contains three paragraphs (§§19–21) that examine the nature, authority, and freedom of Scripture and its relation to the church. This chapter moves along the progression of Barth's earlier outline of the threefold form of the Word of God, as the expansive investigation of revelation as the first form of the Word of God in the prior chapters now is followed with an extensive exposition of Holy Scripture as the second form of the Word of God in this one. Barth's doctrine of Scripture as the Word of God provides one of the most significant theological discussions of the Bible in the twentieth century, but it has not been read without controversy.

The Word of God for the Church (§19)

In the first of these three paragraphs Barth sets his discussion of Scripture within the larger field of God's act of revelation and situates it between God's personal presence in Jesus Christ on one side and the church that receives God's address in the present on the other. His understanding of Scripture is, as should be expected by now, a highly dialectical one. He takes with full seriousness the divine origin and efficacy of Scripture as the written form of the Word of God through which God addresses and, in Calvin's terms, rules his church. He also, however, fully embraces the ramifications of Scripture's human origin and authorship, as well as the complicated history of the Bible's composition, redaction, collection, and canonization.

Scripture as a Witness to Divine Revelation (§19.1)

Barth starts this paragraph by returning to the very beginning of his dogmatics, reiterating that its theme "is the question of the Word of God in the proclamation of the Christian Church, or, concretely, the question of the agreement of this proclamation with Holy Scripture as the Word of God" (457). Here we should notice the implicit threefold nature of what he is addressing: first, the Word of God, which is both identical with, yet also distinguished from, proclamation and Scripture; second, proclamation, which is tested for and by its agreement with Holy Scripture; and third, Holy Scripture itself, which, like proclamation, is identified with the Word of God and yet can be distinguished from it. This Word of God is, as he has explained earlier, God's revelation in Jesus Christ, and more expansively, Jesus Christ as the Word of God incarnate who speaks to the church through Scripture and proclamation. We are confronted again with his famous understanding of the threefold form of the Word of God in Christ, Scripture, and proclamation. The particular form that he examines in this paragraph is Holy Scripture, and in it he provides his most developed and systematic thought on the Bible.

It is impossible to say how many readings of Barth's understanding of Scripture falter here at the very outset. Those who see Scripture as a record of an ancient people's religious experience or as mythological stories will chafe against his firm insistence that Scripture is the Word of God that rules the church with the authority of Christ himself—an unquestionably "high" and authoritative view of Scripture. For other readers, and specifically for those who see Scripture primarily in divine terms and straightforwardly equate the Bible with God's revelation, his language of Scripture as a "witness to divine revelation" and full acceptance of its complex human origination will cause concern that he has a "low" view of Scripture. Set against both a view that sees Scripture as simply a human record of past experience, and an alternative view that sees Scripture as an inspired, timeless, and perhaps inerrant text of direct divine revelation (and *direct* is the crucial word here), Barth's view of Scripture, in all of its dialectical complexity, may appear hopelessly muddled. The purpose at hand must be to understand his view, and thus to unmuddle it, not to pronounce a definitive judgment upon it.

What must first be acknowledged is that Barth considers Scripture to be the Word of God in its participation in the entire divine act of God's self-revelation through Christ and the Spirit, yet he also appreciates its distinction from the Word of God in its first form, which is the incarnation of the Word in Jesus Christ. It is helpful here to remember that we are dealing with an analogy to the Trinity in Barth's estimation. The Word of God is one reality, but one in a threefold form. God's Word is one divine revelation, but God's Word comes to us in a threefold way, as revealed, written, and proclaimed. And as he has already explained, the latter two are *indirectly* God's Word insofar as they are witnesses to God's personal presence in the Word incarnate in Jesus Christ. In view of the preeminence of God's personal revelation in Christ, Scripture and proclamation are the Word of God in a participatory if derivative sense because they witness to him. As Barth puts this point, "It is because God has revealed Himself, and as He has done so, that there is a Word of God, and therefore Holy Scripture and proclamation as the Word of God, and therefore a relation and correspondence between the two, and therefore the possibility and necessity of this question of their agreement" (457).

In light of this description, it is understandable that Barth places Scripture under the category of *sign*, but as the sign that is the norm and source of all other signs, for in a real sense it participates in even as it is distinguished from that which it signifies. As a sign that stands over and in distinction from other signs, "it acquires in the Church . . . the dignity and validity of the Word of God" (457; cf. 459). As the normative witness to God's revelation in Christ, Scripture is the source and the norm for the church's proclamation and for all that the church confesses and teaches: "For that reason, at every decisive point we took our answer to the question of revelation from the Bible. And the Bible has given us the answer. It has attested to us the lordship of the Triune God in the incarnate Word by the Holy Spirit" (457). In other words, Scripture attests the *content* (the Triune God), the *event* (the incarnation of the Word), and the *goal* (the outpouring of the Spirit) of revelation. Scripture thus serves as the means by which we know God, but it does so because it finds its place within the revelatory act of God itself, a movement that comes from God through Christ and through the Spirit. Scripture, as the testimony of the prophets and apostles, stands as the divinely appointed witness, the sign, by which God's revelation is known in the present, and it thus stands within God's own divine act of self-communication, God's movement to us.

Scripture on this account is understood neither as the religious musings of an ancient people nor as a divinely dictated book of propositions. Certainly Barth recognizes that such religious reflections and propositional content can be found in its pages. But its primary identity as *Scripture* is that it is a witness to God's revelation. As he stated in an earlier essay on Scripture, "It is precisely not the right human thoughts about God that form the content of the Bible, but rather the right thoughts of God about humans" (*WGT*, 25). Scripture stands between revelation and the church's proclamation, and thus between Christ and the church. It is the site of God's revelation to us in the present, and as such, it is the Word that the church hears that becomes the source and norm for its own proclamation, the "superior authority confronting the proclamation of the Church" (457). The absolute authority of Christ that the church acknowledges and confesses is concretely expressed in the obedience it gives to Scripture, the testimony and vehicle of Christ's own address.

Scripture therefore stands as an authority above and over against the religious experience of the individual or the collective group, and above and over against the church's own confession and dogmas. Correspondingly, the authority of Scripture as articulated in the Scripture principle is the hallmark of the Reformation and of Evangelical dogmatics that follows in its spirit. Barth again sets such a position over against the rival traditions of Neo-Protestantism (and its precursors in Reformation-era "fanatics" and spiritualists) and Roman Catholicism throughout this paragraph, especially in significant historical small-print sections (for instance, see 459–60).[1] Insofar as the church has an authority in its confession and teaching (and Barth does not deny this ecclesial authority but will embrace and discuss it in the following two paragraphs), it has this only because "Scripture has already told us what we are asking about when we ask about God's revelation" (462).

A further noteworthy aspect of Barth's reflection upon the authority of Scripture is that this authority cannot be established through arguments that we might give for why it should be so. The authority of Scripture is not argued, but rather is acknowledged, by the church. Only God's own Word, as heard in Scripture, can establish Scripture's authoritative standing. As he writes, "It is only by revelation that revelation can be spoken in the Bible and that it can be heard as the real substance of the Bible. If it is to be witness at all, and to be apprehended as such, the biblical witness must itself be attested by what it attests" (469). Scripture is, therefore, self-authenticating—or perhaps better yet, divinely authenticated by the God who speaks through it and whose lordship is expressed through it (458; cf. 460–61, 462). If the Bible required an apologetic demonstration for its authority to be acknowledged, then its authority would rest upon human argument, not upon divine testimony. Scripture is

---

1. Barth maintains that "if the Church dared simply to abandon the sign of the Bible dominating its worship and instruction, it would be the end of Protestantism. For in so doing it would cease to protest—the only protest which concerns it" (*CD* I/2, 460).

therefore confessed to be what it is as an act of obedience that acknowledges the divine Word that comes to us through it (461).

This confession of Scripture's uniqueness and particularity entails also a particular confession of how it is to be read. Scripture must be read, and is only rightly read, in light of its own subject matter, and not by the approach of a more general hermeneutical method brought to the text and imposed upon it (470–71).[2] Barth insists that a general rule for interpreting texts must not be brought to this text but must be learned from this text itself (466; also 468–72).[3] Scripture is for this reason not only self-authenticating but also self-interpreting, a conviction he will explore further in the following paragraphs.

Barth's discussion of Scripture is an attempt to give a comprehensive account of the Bible that takes up all relevant themes: "its nature as sign, its relation to the thing which it signifies, its normative and critical character in relation to the Church's proclamation, its limiting and determinative significance for the life of the Church both as a whole and in each of its members" (458). The fact that the Bible is a sign in relation to a thing signified entails that his discussion cannot be anything but dialectical, for the relation of sign and thing signified intrinsically raises questions of identity and difference, as does the fact that he thinks of Scripture in terms of its relation both to divine revelation on one side and to the created realities of words and texts and human authors on the other. This dialectical tension of identity and difference, and in turn the theme of indirect identity, is encapsulated in the statement that Scripture is a *witness* to revelation. This entails first that the Bible is distinguished from revelation, for "a witness is not absolutely identical with that to which it witnesses" (463). In brief, the Bible is not God; it is not divine.

Barth fully acknowledges the Bible as a human document. Yet, through this human testimony, God himself speaks, and his Word comes to us not in spite of but through and by means of this testimony: "In the Bible we meet with human words written in human speech, and in these words, and therefore by means of them, we hear of the lordship of the triune God" (463). Moreover, insofar as this witness is the very means by which this revelation comes to us,

2. As Barth will later write, "The universal rule of interpretation is that a text can be read and understood and expounded only with reference to and in the light of its theme" (*CD* I/2, 493). Insofar as this is so, we see here a confluence of Barth's special and general hermeneutics, for this rule, learned from Scripture and its particular content, can then be more generally applied to all reading.

3. Barth writes, "Biblical hermeneutics must be guarded against the totalitarian claim of a general hermeneutics. It is a special hermeneutics only because hermeneutics generally has been mortally sick for so long that it has not let the special problem of biblical hermeneutics force its attention upon its own problem. For the sake of better general hermeneutics it must therefore dare to be this special hermeneutics" (*CD* I/2, 472).

it participates in revelation itself. He distinguishes the Bible from revelation but paradoxically identifies them as well, something often overlooked by critics of his doctrine of Scripture:

> But the concept of witness, especially when we bear clearly in mind its limiting sense, has still something very positive to say. In this limitation the Bible is not distinguished from revelation. It is simply revelation as it comes to us, mediating and therefore accommodating itself to us—to us who are not ourselves prophets and apostles, and therefore not the immediate and direct recipients of the one revelation, witnesses of the resurrection of Jesus Christ. Yet it is for us revelation by means of the words of the prophets and apostles written in the Bible, in which they are still alive for us as the immediate and direct recipients of revelation, and by which they speak to us. A real witness is not identical with that to which it witnesses, but it sets it before us. Again this corresponds with the facts on which the truth of the whole proposition is founded. If we have really listened to the biblical words in all their humanity, if we have accepted them as witness, we have obviously not only heard of the lordship of the triune God, but by this means it has become for us an actual presence and event. If we want to think of the Bible as a real witness of divine revelation, then clearly we have to keep two things constantly before us and give them their due weight: the limitation and the positive element, its distinctiveness from revelation, in so far as it is only a human word about it, and its unity with it, in so far as revelation is the basis, object and content of this word. (463)

This passage is quoted at length because if it is understood, one is well on the way toward making sense of Barth's doctrine of Scripture, for it is a worthy summary of his entire discussion. Here again we are confronted with a dialectical pattern of exposition that speaks of both differentiation and identity, of a contrast between direct identity and indirect identity, and of a mystery in which revelation is an event of divine activity through a human form, a kind of unveiling by means of veiling and further impartation. These themes can be examined in turn.

First, and as already noted, Barth's understanding of Scripture reveals both a distinction of the Bible from revelation and an identity with it. Readers who find such dialectical statements problematic or, worse, hopelessly confused and confusing may at this point be helped by observing that his line of argumentation follows prior trinitarian and christological patterns that speak of God as both one and three and of Christ as both divine and human, both Word and flesh. His description of Scripture strongly echoes his earlier discussions of the Trinity that began with the observation that revelation demarcates Jesus from his Father yet also attests their identity. Moreover, we see here in his doctrine of Scripture christological forms of depiction and argument that are analogical to those appearing in his discussion of the first form of the Word of God where Christ is depicted as both divine and human. When these correspondences and parallel forms of explication and argument are appreciated, one can begin to grasp the analogical richness and logical character of Barth's doctrine of Scripture, even if some may not find his conceptual and dialectical descriptions convincing on all counts.

This understanding of distinction and unity in understanding the Bible as both God's Word and human words leads, second, to an appreciation of the difference between direct identity and indirect identity. The first form of the Word of God, as the personal presence of the eternal Son in Jesus Christ, is directly identified with God, yet even this personal Word of God comes hidden in human flesh. In contrast, Scripture is entirely human, a witness to the incarnation of God but not the incarnation itself, nor a second hypostatic union. Nevertheless, Scripture stands in analogy to the incarnation insofar as in the movement of God to humans it, too, exists by means of God's annexation of creaturely means for divine self-communication. It is the divinely appointed witness that attests God's Word in Jesus Christ and the means by and through which Christ continues to speak to his church. Moreover, because it is the product of a divine act of the election, calling, empowerment, and inspiration of these human witnesses, Scripture can be rightly called the Word of God, though as a witness to revelation it is indirectly, not directly, so. This dialectical idea of indirect identity is crucial for understanding Barth's doctrine of Scripture as the second form of God's Word (and proclamation as the third form of God's Word), but it is one of the most difficult of his concepts to grasp.

Third, because Scripture is God's Word hidden and revealed through human words, Scripture is a mystery that is rightly understood only by faith (as the Trinity and the incarnation themselves are mysteries). Unlike many who have extolled the natural qualities of Scripture, whether its aesthetic beauty, moral insight, or self-evident wisdom, Barth states that on its surface, Scripture is a work that is marked (perhaps especially in its OT books, but not only there) by ambivalent stories, moral ambiguity, and questionable claims. In his view, Scripture, like the suffering servant in the book of Isaiah, is not proved by a readily apparent beauty or majesty (Isa. 53:2). Barth does not argue for the Bible's identity as God's Word based on its visible qualities at all but fully accepts that the books of the Bible are "jars of clay" in which the treasure of revelation is hidden. This treasure is revealed only by the miraculous work of the Spirit that allows us to perceive it by faith. It is God's Word in humble human form.

Barth's claim that this form is not only human but also fallible has been one of his most controversial ideas, yet he is adamant that the Bible's humanity must be fully embraced with all its implications, for "there is no point in ignoring the writtenness of Holy Writ for the sake of its holiness, its humanity for the sake of its divinity. We must not ignore it any more than we do the humanity of Jesus Christ Himself" (463). The written nature of Scripture is thus not peripheral but rather is essential to its nature as normative witness, a sign that it is a historical text that takes its rise in a specific place and time, and thus a sign of its particularity and contingency. Scripture therefore must be understood historically, though it is more than historical, for it points to a God who stands over history (see 464, 466–67). For this reason, the interpretation of Scripture must also go beyond a historical and critical description of the past religious thoughts of ancient writers; it must address the content of Scripture, God's own self-revelation that these writers, as witnesses who point away from themselves, attest.

Fourth, Scripture is God's Word not because the text possesses "divinity" as a permanent possession or intrinsic quality, but because it is the site of the divine event of revelation that occurs ever anew as God chooses to speak through it and becomes present to its hearers. Scripture becomes the Word of God as God miraculously speaks through it afresh in an event of divine announcement in which the hearers are confronted with the presence and voice of God himself. This event is not under human control but is a matter of divine decision and freedom (527; see 527–37). Because Scripture is the witness to the original personal divine presence and address in Jesus Christ and is in turn the site and means by which this event of revelation in the past becomes an event of revelation for us in the present, it is rightly called the Word of God. This does not mean, however, that our faith *makes* the Bible the Word of God. While this has been a charge often leveled against Barth, it drastically misreads him. It is not our faith that makes the Bible the Word of God; rather, it is the will and the work of God that make it so, though the Word of God does demand our faith (534). Scripture is not the Word, however, because of our faith. As Barth writes, "Scripture is recognized as the Word of God by the fact that it *is* the Word of God" (537). As one interpreter of Barth's view of Scripture has put this, Scripture has its "being in becoming," which is to say, it becomes the Word of God because it is already the Word of God, and is so apart from any experience or faith on our part.[4] Barth's

---

4. Bruce McCormack, "The Being of Holy Scripture Is in Becoming: Karl Barth in Conversation with American Evangelical Criticism," in *Evangelicals and Scripture: Tradition, Authority and Hermeneutics*, ed. Vincent Bacote, Laura C. Miguélez, and Dennis L. Okholm (Downers

understanding of Scripture cannot be fully understood apart from an understanding of this actualism that marks it.

Finally, revelation is mediated and immediate, and the Bible follows in this pattern. All revelation is mediated in that it comes to us through God's act of taking up a created medium for the purpose of addressing us (the Word of God comes to us through the flesh assumed by the Son in the incarnation, through the written text of Scripture, and through the spoken words of proclamation and the signs of the sacraments). Barth rejects any notion of an immediate revelation that attempts to bypass this act of veiling and unveiling, and he esteems such to be a spiritualism that sacrifices all objectivity. But there is another sense in which he insists that revelation is in fact immediate, and that is because it is Christ himself, apart from the need of mediators, who speaks through Scripture and the proclamation of the church. Christ is the only agent of revelation in the same sense that he alone is the agent of salvation. He requires no mediator to make him present but as Lord speaks in freedom to his church through Holy Scripture. It is only in this way, in which Christ takes up the witness of Scripture as the means of his announcement and presence in the church, that we can speak rightly of revelation as mediated to us. For those who are not prophets and apostles, Christ's words come to us through the words of the biblical witnesses, who are the "immediate and direct recipients of the one revelation" (463). In this time of Christ's ascended lordship, revelation is mediated by Scripture as Christ speaks through it, and thus believers today, unlike the prophets and apostles of old, are indirect recipients of revelation in that Christ comes to us not in his earthly personal presence but through the witness of Scripture by the Spirit.

Scripture as the Word of God (§19.2)

In the next subsection Barth continues this examination of what it means to say that Scripture is the Word of God. As a witness to the Word of God incarnate, Scripture is differentiated from revelation and is "a human expression of God's revelation" (473). Yet what is heard in the witness is more than simply a human word—what is heard is revelation itself and "therefore the very Word of God" (473). This dialectical relationship between human witness and divine Word is the topic that he now seeks to clarify further. He does so in an examination of points numbered sequentially discussing themes that he will explore in more detail in the following two paragraphs on the authority and freedom of the Word of God (§§20–21).

Grove, IL: InterVarsity, 2004), 55–75. As he writes, "Where and when the Bible *becomes* the Word of God, it is only becoming what it already is" (66).

The first theme is that the Word is heard in specific texts acknowledged and confessed by the church as Holy Scripture (473–81). Here Barth raises the question of the canon of Scripture—that is, that the Bible exists as a specific collection of texts that are acknowledged as the place where God's Word is heard and that in turn serve as the source and norm for all that the church confesses, teaches, and proclaims. He insists that the authority of these texts is not constituted by a church decision, for their authority and status as Holy Scripture are better understood as discovered and acknowledged than as decided and authorized by the church. As he pointedly contends, "In no sense of the concept could or can the Church give the Canon to itself" (473). The canon stands over the church and must be received and confirmed by it rather than understood as the product of the church's own will and decision (473). He is, of course, fully aware of the long and complicated history of the canon's composition, formation, and reception, however, and discusses this history in extensive small-print sections (see 473–74, 476–78). But in spite of this messy human history, and perhaps better stated, through it, the biblical witnesses are nevertheless rightly understood as imposed upon the church rather than simply decided to be authoritative by the church's own will. This confirmation of the canon is, correspondingly, not simply a matter of a past church decision but requires continual confirmation by the church in the present (see 474–75). One of the interesting implications of Barth's understanding of the canon is that as only God can establish it, so also God alone can close it (481). Just as Barth distinguishes the divine Word and human words of Scripture, so he also distinguishes between the divine and human judgments that determine the constituency and scope of the canon.

The second theme that Barth introduces follows from the first. If the first dealt with the nature of the canon and its form and contents, this second pertains to the constitution of the canon as including both the OT and the NT and therefore takes up the question of its unity (481–85). He reintroduces the themes of expectation and recollection from his discussion of the time of revelation (§14) and now applies them to the topic of the canon. In this light, the OT is the witness of expectation, whereas the NT is the witness of recollection, with both together comprising the canon as a united witness of God's revelation in history centered upon Jesus Christ. Against calls in his day for the revision of the canon, and specifically for a replacement or abandonment of the OT (influenced by contemporary forms of anti-Semitism in Germany), Barth firmly holds that such calls must be unhesitatingly and firmly rejected (see 488–90). The unity of the Testaments, regardless of their differences (or the differences of the writers and books within them), lies in the unity of their object: both the OT and the NT are testimonies that witness to God's revelation in Christ, the first in anticipation, the second in remembrance (482). As he can later state, "the Christ of the New Testament is the Christ of the Old Testament, the Christ of Israel. The man who will not accept this merely shows that in fact he has already substituted another Christ for the Christ of the New Testament" (488–89).[5]

The third theme that Barth discusses is the particularity of the canon: it is in these books and not others that the Word of God comes to us. Here we see the question of the particularity of revelation and the scandal of the gospel extended from Christology to Scripture, the particularity of God's Word in the particular person of Jesus Christ translated into the question of the second form of the Word of God, that of Holy Scripture as canon (485–92). The uniqueness and contingency of Scripture are a reflection of "the uniqueness and contingency of the revelation attested in it" (485). The uniqueness of Scripture is due to the uniqueness of what it attests—the God who raised up Jesus Christ from the dead by the power of the Holy Spirit, and it is Christ's resurrection that stands at the center of Scripture (485–86).

Barth's understanding of the canon is therefore entirely christological and trinitarian in form and content, and the particularity of the canon is preeminently predicated upon the particularity of the person of Jesus Christ as God's revelation and secondarily predicated upon the particularity of the divinely appointed prophets and apostles who testified to the expectation and appearance of this revelation in Christ (486; cf. 490–92). All future witnesses to Christ are thus dependent upon these first witnesses, who are not only first in time but also first in status, and as such whose testimonies provide the source, norm, and standard for all future witnesses. To hear and receive Christ is to hear and receive these witnesses, who are rightly understood as witnesses rather than as "geniuses" or "moral heroes" (491).[6] They are what they are only by the divine commission they are given to attest the unique revelation they have seen and heard, and their existence is nothing less than "the existence of Jesus Christ for us and for all men" (486; also 487, 490).

---

5. Barth is particularly vigilant on this point because of the contemporary situation in which he is writing, one marked, in Germany, by a rising anti-Semitism and calls for a renunciation of the OT itself. He spends some attention on the question of the OT and Judaism as a witness to revelation, and his own discussions are not without difficulty (see CD I/2, 510–12). He equally opposes an independent treatment of the OT apart from the NT. Such an abstraction of the OT from the NT also fails to reckon with the true identity of the OT as a witness to Jesus Christ (489–90).

6. Barth's understanding of the prophets and apostles as witnesses draws heavily upon Kierkegaard's distinction between an apostle and a genius. See Søren Kierkegaard, *The Book on Adler*, ed. and trans. Howard V. Hong and Edna H. Hong (Princeton: Princeton University Press, 1998), 173–88.

The fourth theme that Barth introduces is that of an indirect identity and unity of the form and content of the canon in Holy Scripture (492–95). This once again is his highly dialectical understanding of the unity of and distinction between revelation and its witness, of the divine Word and human words. As he insists, the "distinction of form and content must not involve any separation" (492). While revelation and the witness to revelation can and must be distinguished, one cannot have revelation apart from this witness (492; cf. 500–501). Against all manner of historical-critical readings that attempt to get behind the texts to a truth that allows us in the end to relativize them, he asserts that form and content, while in an important sense distinguishable, are nevertheless inseparable. God's revelation cannot be abstracted from these witnesses and thereby from the canon itself (492–95). This is what it means to speak of the indirect *identity* of revelation and the Bible. The history of historical criticism is in truth a history that sundered form and content in that it sought not the revelation that came *through* these texts but rather a truth that lay *behind* them (492–95).

The fifth theme that Barth discusses is the uniqueness of the canon in light of other written texts, a return, he concedes, to the third theme above. The prophets and apostles, and therefore the writings they bequeath to us as Holy Scripture, are set apart for a particular role and dignity (495–502). Here the particularity of the canon outlined in the third theme above now flows into a discussion of the canon's uniqueness. He stresses that, just like with the prophets and the apostles, the unique authority and dignity of these texts that comprise Holy Scripture do not rest on an intrinsic quality of excellence that sets them apart from others. Other texts may have more aesthetic beauty and, he concedes, may even provide more personal edification than some of the biblical books (495–96). If such qualities were in fact what constituted such texts as Scripture, the canon might indeed be expanded. But it is their nature as authoritative witnesses to revelation, not an implicit profundity or beauty, that makes them such. And as such witnesses, they are unique and stand apart from all other texts and literature, even apart from all later witnesses to Christ (496–97).

Barth is fully aware, however, that as the product of a human and historical process Scripture may be seen as a relative rather than absolute norm. In other words, the question might reasonably be asked whether God alone possesses an absolute authority to which Scripture itself must be subject. For how can so much be attributed to Scripture when it is written in the words of human persons and arises out of history? He, of course, does not deny that the authority of God stands above that of all human things, nor does he deny that Scripture is the product of human witnesses and therefore would seem to fall under this judgment. Yet he holds that Scripture possesses a unique divine authority because its ultimate origin lies in God, even if its proximate origin lies with the human authors who composed it. Scripture stands dialectically between God and humanity, the place where God's unique authority is in fact revealed to us: "The answer is that there is indeed only one single absolute fundamental and indestructible priority, and that is the priority of God as Creator over the totality of His creatures and each of them without exception. Yet how strange it is that we learn of this very priority (in the serious sense, in all the compass and power of the concept) only through the Bible, and only through the Bible as it is read and understood and expounded as witness of revelation and therefore as itself the Word of God" (497–98).

Barth consequently rejects a simple opposition of absolute authority (God) and relative authority (the creature) with regard to Scripture. Such a binary decision cannot take full account of the truly paradoxical identity and mystery of Scripture. He insists that even the terms "absolute" and "relative" must be understood in light of revelation, and not used as presuppositions by which we make sense of revelation: "According to the Bible, the in itself unthinkable co-existence of absolute and relative is made possible by the fact that it does not speak of the absolute but of the goodness and patience of the Creator of all things revealed to us in Jesus Christ, nor does it speak of the relative, but of the creatures of this Creator" (498). Scripture therefore stands in an analogous relation to the covenant of God with humanity that is incarnate in Jesus Christ. The Bible is the witness to the Word of God, and, as it participates in the mediation of this Word, may itself be called the Word of God.

Absolute and relative paradoxically coexist not only in Christology but also here in Holy Scripture (499). This, Barth is adamant, is not the divinization of human beings—there is no direct identity of the witness of these persons with the divine Word that comes to us. But there is an indirect identity. And just as even in the person of Christ the humanity is not divinized yet is inextricably united to the Word, so also here, the Word of God comes to us in the words of human persons that, without ceasing to be human, are now taken up for the purpose of divine self-communication through an act, an event, of divine decision and election (499–500). In this sense "Scripture, too, stands in that indirect identity of human existence with God Himself." And so Barth can conclude regarding such christological observations: "It [Scripture] too can and must—not as though it were Jesus Christ, but in the same serious sense as Jesus Christ—be called the Word of God: the Word of God in the sign of the word of man, if we are going to put it accurately" (500; cf. 501–2).

The sixth and final theme in this series is closely related to the prior ones, and particularly to the question of the relation of Scripture as a witness to the Word of God that is indirectly identical to the Word. Here, Barth takes up the question not so much of the relation but of the divine act and event that confirm and attest Scripture to be this Word of God (502–26). In other words, he asserts that Scripture's status as the Word of God is not so much due to a state of possessing a divine quality but rather is due to a divinely determined event. Here once again we are faced with the actualism, or event character, of his understanding of revelation. The recognition of Scripture as the Word of God is therefore dependent upon a divine act and the reception of faith, rather than being the result of an appeal to an enduring quality of the text that makes it so (see 530). To make Scripture's status dependent upon and defined by such a quality would, he insists, mean that Scripture's authority rests upon an intrinsic capacity of the text itself rather than upon the act of the God that speaks through this text and in so doing authenticates it.

Barth's understanding of Scripture as the Word of God, and of inspiration, is thus a dynamic rather than static one. The recognition of the Bible as the Word is itself a miracle and work of the Spirit perceived by faith. The Bible is not a magical divine book of oracles but rather is a *sign*, a witness to God's revelation of himself in Christ through the Spirit (see 506–12). As Barth can write, with allusions to patterns now quite familiar,

> That the Bible is the Word of God cannot mean that with other attributes the Bible has the attribute of being the Word of God. To say that would be to violate the Word of God which is God Himself—to violate the freedom and the sovereignty of God. God is not an attribute of something else, even if this something else is the Bible. God is the Subject, God is Lord. He is Lord even over the Bible and in the Bible. The statement that the Bible is the Word of God cannot therefore say that the Word of God is tied to the Bible. On the contrary, what it must say is that the Bible is tied to the Word of God. (513; cf. 530)

In other words, Christ does not exist for the sake of the Bible, but the Bible exists for the sake of Christ. The Bible's uniqueness is therefore grounded not upon an intrinsic quality of its text but upon the use God makes of it. Barth sees his position here as nothing other than a faithful extension of the Reformation tradition (see 514–26). It was the post-Reformation period, in contrast, that saw the collapse of the Word of God into the text and a direct identification of them such that the Bible became a "codex of axioms." And in view of this, Barth's judgments are stern: "The Bible was now grounded upon itself apart from the mystery of Christ and the Holy Ghost. It became a 'paper Pope,' and unlike the living Pope in Rome it was wholly given up into the hands of its interpreters. It was no longer a free and spiritual force, but an instrument of human power" (525).

In this doctrine of Scripture that arose from Protestant scholasticism, things were claimed of the Bible that in light of an examination of its actual composition and history could not be sustained. Such claims could also not be squared with what Scripture says about itself and its own origin and tradition (526). The result was a host of problems, not least of which were untenable claims for the Bible's strict inerrancy and Docetic views of its nature and composition, as well as a growing skepticism of the Bible itself in light of the findings of historical criticism that affirmed its very human character.

EXCURSUS: The Bible and Fallibility

Perhaps Barth's most controversial statement about Scripture is that the biblical witnesses, as human persons, "speak as fallible, erring men like ourselves" (507). Here he turns to the humanity of the witnesses, and he extends this even to the point of acknowledging not only the full humanity but also the fallibility of their words if considered on their own terms, rather than as witnesses to revelation. Their word "can be subjected to all kinds of immanent criticism, not only in respect of its philosophical, historical and ethical content, but even of its religious and theological" (507; cf. 509). It can even give us offense at times. His conclusion is stark: "Only the miracle of faith and the Word can genuinely and seriously prevent us from taking offence at the Bible" (507).

An evaluation of Barth's claims must await the commentary below, but here it might be simply noted that he attempts to take the findings of historical criticism, and of the humanity of the text, with full seriousness. He affirms both its "human imperfection" and "divine perfection" simultaneously (508). He is fully aware that the accounts of Scripture are historically conditioned and have historical parallels, and he also observes that in their bewildering diversity they provide no systematic cohesiveness or easy harmonization. Moreover, he certainly does not think that the Bible provides us with an exhaustive and complete account of all truths; but neither does he think that our own age does so. He does not think Scripture, as a witness written by specific persons in a specific place and time, was ever intended to provide such a comprehensive account of all things, and his historical outlook prevents him from thinking that this is even possible (see 508–12). Nevertheless, his willing admittance of "error" in Scripture has remained one of his most controversial qualities and has been strongly criticized in some quarters.

It must be admitted that Barth does not shy away from such criticisms but meets them head-on. With regard to the Bible, he insists that we take the humanity and even frailty and fallibility of its witnesses with full seriousness, for they were persons as we are. He balances the divine freedom that calls Scripture into existence with the human freedom that entails that these witnesses write as human persons with all of their limitations. Taking this miraculous nature of Scripture and its humanity to its full conclusion, he states that "every time we turn the Word of God into an infallible biblical word of man or the biblical word of man into an infallible Word of God we resist that which we ought never to resist, i.e. the truth of the miracle that here fallible men speak the Word of God in fallible human words—and we therefore resist the sovereignty of grace, in which God Himself became man in Christ, to glorify Himself in His humanity" (529). To deny the humanity and fallibility of the witnesses, he avers, is to deny the miracle of Scripture—that God's Word comes to us through the words of finite and fallen persons (529).

Authority in the Church (§20)

This paragraph turns from an exposition of the nature of Scripture to an examination of the relation between the authority of Scripture and the authority of the church. Necessary for understanding this section is a grasp of the distinction between direct and indirect authority, between absolute versus relative authority, and between formal versus material authority.

Barth begins this paragraph by drawing certain trinitarian and christological parallels to how Scripture and the church's confession are related (538). Once again we see in his presentation the generative results of the deep connections between the doctrine of the Trinity and the doctrine of revelation as he has outlined them. He reminds his readers how the one revelation of the Triune God is further divided into the doctrine of the incarnation (objective revelation, i.e., Christology) and the outpouring of the Holy Spirit (subjective revelation, i.e., pneumatology). This division in revelation is the basis and in turn the pattern for an analogous and corresponding further distinction between revelation itself and its attestation and mediation in Holy Scripture, as well as both an objective element and a subjective element with regard to Scripture (538–39). In other words, revelation is the movement of God in the incarnation of the Word (or Son) and the outpouring of the Holy Spirit, and this triune movement of divine revelation is attested and announced by the objective Word in Holy Scripture and the subjective work of the Holy Spirit within us that allows us to receive it and to be transformed by it. Both revelation itself in its triune form, and its attestation in Scripture (and later in proclamation), are a divine work (538–40). Scripture as the second form of the Word of God follows the trinitarian and christological patterns of the first form of the Word of God, which, in its full sense, is the revelation of God in the incarnation of the Son and the outpouring of the Spirit (Trinity), and, in its strict and narrow sense, is the incarnation of the Word in flesh (Christology). Correspondingly, Scripture is the second form of the Word, through which God speaks by the power of the Spirit (trinitarian pattern), and, in its strict and narrow sense, is the Word of God spoken through human words (christological pattern).

The division of the objective and the subjective in revelation into the incarnation of the Word and the outpouring of the Spirit is therefore reflected in a correspondent division between the objective Word in Scripture and the subjective work of the Spirit in us. Barth states that we must distinguish between "that which enlightens and those who are enlightened, between something objective and something subjective, between the eternal aspect and the internal, or, to put it concretely, between the possibility of God for man and the possibility of man for God" (539). It is necessary to make such a twofold distinction with regard to Scripture, he insists, so that we can understand how Scripture serves as the witness to revelation that presents a truth to us outside of ourselves yet is also confirmed within us. This distinction therefore repeats "on a lower level the division into the doctrine of the incarnation of the Word and that of the outpouring of the Holy Spirit" in the doctrine of revelation and, behind that, of the Son and Spirit within the Trinity (539).

This division of objective and subjective elements with regard to Scripture parallels earlier discussions of God's revelation as a work that comes to us from outside ourselves as well as a work of the Spirit within us. It is, however, not so simple as this. For now Barth translates this division between objective and subjective elements in regard to Scripture into a division between authority (objective) and freedom (subjective) in the church, and these are the corresponding themes of this and the following paragraph, respectively (539). Further complicating matters, having made this objective and subjective distinction between authority and freedom, he in turn divides each of these themes of authority and freedom into *two further subdistinctions*, so that both authority (objective) and freedom (subjective) have their own corresponding objective and subjective elements: first, with regard to authority, there is both the authority of Scripture within and over the church (objective) and the church's own circumscribed authority that is established by this prior authority of Scripture and is obedient to it (subjective); and second, with regard to freedom, there is both the freedom of Scripture in the church (objective) and the delimited freedom of the church itself that is grounded in this prior freedom of Scripture and made possible by it (subjective).

This division of authority (the "external determination") and freedom (the "internal determination"), as with the distinction between Scripture's objective attestation and witness to revelation and its subjective confirmation and empowerment by the Spirit, shapes all that will be said in this and the next paragraph of the *CD*. It also—and this should not be missed—is the reflection of the christological and ecclesiological patterns that we have seen before in regard to the relation of Christ and the church. In this paragraph, the relation is that of Scripture (Christ's voice in the present [see 539]) over tradition (including all of the church's confession, dogma, and teaching). The relation of Scripture and tradition is thus analogical to the relation between Christ and the church, and its logical order follows from the question of how Christ's lordship is expressed not only in but also over the church in the present. In both relations, the first term stands in an irreversible and asymmetrical relation to the second, and the second is called into existence and established by the first. In sum, the second form of the Word of God in Holy Scripture with its objective and subjective elements is a direct if analogical reflection of the division within revelation of the incarnation of the Word and the outpouring of the Spirit (see 539–40). And the relation of Scripture and tradition (i.e., ecclesial decisions, confessions, and teachers) is a translation into a new key of the relation of Christ and the church, answering the question of how Christ speaks to his church during the time of his ascension and exercises authority over it, and how the church in turn is to respond. In short, Barth presents the doctrine of Scripture as much in christological and ecclesiological terms as in epistemological ones, and truly, it is these christological and ecclesiological patterns that give context to the others.

If authority and freedom are the themes set forth to describe the unique reality that is Holy Scripture, they are also secondarily the themes that then set forth the character and qualities of the church's confessions and doctrines (i.e., its authority) as well as its practice of biblical interpretation (i.e., its freedom). The authority and freedom of Scripture in turn establish, even as they qualify and circumscribe, the authority and freedom of the church (539). As Barth succinctly puts this, "Holy Scripture is the ground and limit of the Church, but for that very reason it constitutes it. Having authority and freedom in the Church, it lends that authority and freedom to the Church" (539). The rest of this paragraph is an attempt to specify the nature of the authority that Scripture and the church, respectively, possess, as the following paragraph will do so with the question of their freedom.

The Authority of the Word (§20.1)

Barth here sets forth the unique nature of the authority of Scripture exercised in the church, an authority that stands over and takes precedence over all authorities. It possesses this not simply because of its chronological placement as the oldest of church traditions, its texts being the oldest accounts we have of Israel and Christ. That it is the oldest is, of course, true, and its antiquity does provide a particular kind of rationale for Scripture's unique status and authority. But if it were distinguished from other authorities solely on the basis of its chronological priority and placement at the head of a list, Scripture would still stand on the same plane as others—it would simply be the oldest of a long line of traditions extending through time, and its authority would remain "mediate, relative and formal" (540).

Barth turns to define each of these three very important adjectives, and understanding them is crucial for understanding his entire discussion of authority. To say that an authority is *mediate* (elsewhere, he uses the term "indirect") is to say that it is "temporal, historical and human," and as such, it is always open to further correction and augmentation in light of other similar authorities or further knowledge that might be gained in the future. To say that an authority is *relative* is to say that it can at best only represent divine authority and provide a qualified and limited authority. It therefore must appeal to a higher absolute authority that takes precedence over it and can in turn correct it. To say that an authority is *formal* is to say that it stands on the same level as other authorities, as a form of witness, but not as the ground and basis of all witnesses themselves (541). In one sense, as the oldest historical record, Scripture does have a unique standing in relation to other witnesses as one older than they and thus closer to the time of revelation. And in this sense, its authority might be thought of as mediate, relative, and formal. Yet if Scripture were only this, Barth argues, it could never demand our absolute obedience. An appeal could always be made to divine authority itself as immediate (rather than mediate), absolute (rather than relative), and material (rather than formal). In this, divine authority would be distinguished from the authority of Scripture (as discussed above). Furthermore, if Scripture's authority were such a mediate, relative, and formal one, appeal could always be made to some other mediate authority in opposition to Scripture.

To make either of these moves, however, would require that the church already knew what divine revelation is, and such knowledge would then serve as the criterion and norm by which other authorities were judged, including Holy Scripture, and how they might be adjudicated when conflicts arise between them. In short, the church would then possess a knowledge and corresponding authority that would stand above all other authorities and appeals made to them. Possessing knowledge of divine revelation *in itself*, the church would therefore serve as the norm by which all other forms of knowledge and authorities were judged, and this would include Scripture.

Barth presses his argument onward: "If this were the case, the Church would itself actually be a direct, absolute, material authority. It would always, in fact, be the Church which instituted this authority and necessarily recognized itself in it. Its obedience to this authority would, in fact, be the fulfillment of its own striving and volition. It would then be quite impossible to find in it obedience and not self-regulation, to see in the authority accepted in the Church an authority over the Church and for the Church" (542).

This is precisely what Barth states must be opposed. For what stands at the center of this discussion of Scripture and the church is nothing less than the relation of Christ and the church. And for the church to judge and determine the veracity of the revelation that appears in Holy Scripture would be to reverse the irreversible relation between Christ and the church, for Scripture, as the authoritative witness to Christ, is the voice of Christ not only in but also over the church. The church is, rather, obedient to Christ, and this obedience is concretely demonstrated and instantiated in its obedience to Holy Scripture. As Barth continues, "To a relationship of obedience two partners are necessary. They have a definite unity but they are no less definitely distinct in this unity. They stand in a definite and irreversible order, united, but distinct" (542). In brief, the voice of Christ that the church hears in Holy Scripture is one it must obey, not one it is to authorize or authenticate. The church does not test the veracity of Scripture against its own internal criterion and norm of truth that it possesses within itself. If such were the case, this criterion and norm would stand over Scripture. Rather, the church is itself tested by the criterion of the canon of Scripture.

Here it is crucial to understand that what Barth is doing is translating the logic of the first form of the Word of God to the second. Earlier, we saw that the ordered relation that Barth finds in Christology between the divinity and humanity of Christ in the unique and singular hypostatic union was analogically predicated of the relation that he finds between the divine Word and human words that together exist as Holy Scripture. That analogous pattern regarding Scripture was evident in the prior paragraph on Scripture itself. Now, in his discussion of authority, he is applying the christological logic that governs the relation of Christ and the church to the relation of Scripture and the church and their respective authorities. The irreversible and ordered relation between Christ and his church is here reflected in the relation between Scripture and the church's tradition, confessions, and dogma. To understand the nature and order of the first relation of Christ and church, which Barth set forth at the very beginning of the *CD* in his discussion of "the being of the Church," is to understand the shape and order of the second, for Scripture serves as the living voice of Christ in and over his church.

For Barth, during the time of the ascension Christ exercises his lordship in and over the church through Scripture. The supremacy of Christ over his church is thus reflected in the supremacy of Scripture over all church authorities. The pattern of Scripture and church tradition is, like the earlier relation, one of unity and distinction, as well as of an irreversible order wherein Scripture stands not only within but also over the church, just as Christ stands over it as Lord and master. Just as Christ calls the church into existence, so also Scripture calls forth a confession from the church that hears the Word that is spoken through it. The authority of Christ expressed in Scripture therefore establishes a real, if relative and circumscribed, authority in the church. Yet Christ and the church stand ever on different planes. There are "two partners," but they are not the same: "One of them, and only one commands. The other has to submit to this command—just to submit" (542). And just as we have no direct access to God apart from the mediation of Jesus Christ, so we have no direct access to God or to Christ apart from the mediation of Scripture.

Scripture therefore stands in a singular place, again with analogical reverberations to the incarnation's own uniqueness. In one sense, it stands, as a human book, on the side of humanity. But as the authoritative witness to Jesus Christ and the means by which Christ's voice is heard in the present, Scripture stands on the side of Christ's direct, absolute, and material authority. This status of Scripture is predicated on the unique status of the authors of Scripture. They have lived in the time of revelation and belong to it, and as such, they have received revelation directly, whereas we today receive it indirectly, through their testimonies in Scripture (543–44). The prophets and apostles are what they are because of the obedience they have given to revelation as its witnesses. Barth can even (surprisingly) say that it is this obedience that makes them prophets and apostles and why they have the Holy Spirit and are commissioned to be Christ's witnesses to the church and to the world (543).

In contrast to Scripture and to the prophets and apostles whose testimony constitutes it, the church receives revelation indirectly through their testimony, and it is what it is only as it "repeats this relationship of obedience" (543). The church cannot, however, exactly replicate it, for the prophets and apostles exist as authorized and authoritative witnesses to revelation in a way that no later witnesses in the church can. This is why, in turn, their witness forms the canon that judges and serves as the norm for all later witnesses. As Barth writes, "A revelation which the Church can recognize and evaluate on the basis of its own possession of revelation and from an independent view of revelation, even if it is called the revelation of God or Christ or the Holy Spirit, is not as such the revelation on which the Church of Jesus Christ is founded" (543). Moreover, any church that ascribes such immediate (direct), absolute, and material authority to itself is not the church of Jesus Christ, for to exist under the authority of Christ is to exist under the authority of Holy Scripture, which participates in Christ's own direct, absolute, and material authority. And just as the church does not exist as an extension of the incarnation, neither do the church's dogma and tradition exist as an extension of the authority of Holy Scripture. Holy Scripture, like Christ himself, exists as an absolute authority that stands over all that comes after in the church. The church can therefore appeal to no higher authority than that of Scripture.

Barth's dialectical thought on Scripture and its relation to both Christ and the church and its confession is crisply summarized when he states,

> It is therefore true that Holy Scripture is the Word of God for the Church, that it is Jesus Christ for us, as He Himself was for the prophets and apostles during the forty days. The result is that in their witness the Church itself has to do personally with its Lord. Therefore in the *per se* mediate, relative and formal quantity of Scripture, in which their witness is presented to us, it has to do with the self-subsistent and self-maintaining direct and absolute and material authority, with its own existence, nature and basis. Consequently the Church cannot evade Scripture. It cannot try to appeal past it directly to God, to Christ or to the Holy Spirit. It cannot assess and adjudge Scripture from a view of revelation gained apart from Scripture and not related to it. . . . Scripture confronts it commandingly as Holy Scripture, and it receives revelation from it in an encounter which is just as concrete and concretely ordered as that which according to Scripture originally took place between the Lord and His witnesses. It obeys Holy Scripture. (544)

This discussion of Scripture is really, at its heart and once again, a discussion of Christ and the church. While the written testimony of Scripture is from one perspective an account produced by human persons and thus stands on the side of the church, it also exists in a unique relation to Christ. A church that does not recognize this unique relation of Scripture to Christ will see revelation as "only a memory" and will lose a sense of its absolute uniqueness. Such a church will think of itself not as possessing an indirect, mediate, relative, and formal authority that stands under Christ's own, but will instead understand its authority as identical with the direct, absolute, and material authority of revelation itself. Thus, the chasm that exists between revelation and the church, a chasm bridged only through Scripture, will give way to an unbroken line of continuity and continuous development. Christ's voice will be subsumed into the church's own, as his history is extended into the history of the church. In time, the church will think of itself as an elongation of the original revelation, in effect, an extension of the incarnation (545). This is, in the end, nothing less than a confusion of revelation and the church such that the dialectical relation and differentiation between them is lost, amounting to "a pantheistic identification of Church and revelation" (545). The end result is the sublimation of Christ into the church that is concretely expressed in the sublimation of Scripture into tradition, so that the distinctions of Christ and Scripture and church are sacrificed and abandoned (see 549; cf. 551, 553, 563). In short: the relation of Christ and church becomes a reversible one of two symmetrical partners, and in the end the distinction between them cannot be sustained, nor can they be differentiated. When this occurs, Christ becomes an implicate and predicate of the church, rather than the church being derived from the lordship of Christ. Barth sharply concludes, "Inevitably it will become a Church which rules itself under the pretext of obedience to revelation" (545).

This loss of the distinction of Christ and the church, exemplified in the loss of the unique authority of Scripture over the church and its dogma, life, and experience, is precisely, Barth believes, what has occurred in Neo-Protestantism and Roman Catholicism, and he spends much time contrasting the Scripture principle of the Protestant tradition from the guiding convictions of these other traditions (544–72). The Evangelical understanding of this distinction, which he puts forth in opposition to these other two, is one in which Scripture mediates between Christ and the church such that Christ cannot be subsumed into the church and the distinction between them lost. In such an understanding of Christ, Scripture, and church, absolute and material authority can be ascribed only to Holy Scripture and not to the church itself (see 546). This is because Scripture precedes the church not only in time but also in order and status, for the testimony of the prophets and apostles founds the church and is not produced by it (see 552). Moreover, Scripture is the testimony by which the Word of God, Christ himself, is heard again and ever anew in the church. Barth concludes,

> The Word of God in the revelation of it attested in Holy Scripture is not limited to its own time, the time of Jesus Christ and its Old and New Testament witnesses. In the sphere of the Church of Jesus Christ it is present at all times, and by its mouth it wills to be and will be present at all times. This is the Evangelical confession of faith. In this confession of the vitality and therefore of the presence of the Word of God as already actualized and to be actualized again and again there is included the Church's confession of itself, i.e., of its institution and preservation by the Word of God for the authority entrusted to it and the mission enjoined upon it. (573)

So even as Barth upholds the absolute distinction between Scripture and tradition, as he does between Christ and the church, this distinction does not empty the church's teaching of all authority but rather establishes it. As placed under the Word of God, listening for the voice of God in Holy Scripture, the church must teach and confess what it has heard there, and as it does so, it does possess a real, though circumscribed and qualified, authority. For this reason, the "Evangelical confession of the Word of God includes a confession of the authority of the Church" (574). Yet this authority ever stands under a greater one, for the church is not left alone to its own authority but possesses it only as it is granted by the living Lord. The church speaks only because it has first listened and heard the Word in Holy Scripture, and the church can only respond to a voice greater than its own. It has no authority other than this limited one of response, never one of its own intrinsic rule. Here we see that Barth's idea of "the church alone with itself" returns in his notion of "self-government," a term that he rejects as describing the church's rightful polity (575; see 575–85). Self-government, rather, describes the two alternatives of Roman Catholicism and Neo-Protestantism, as he writes of each, respectively:

> In the one case the final decision rests with the teaching office of the Church which comprises both Scripture and tradition and expounds them with unchallenged authority, identifying itself with revelation. In the other it rests with the less tangible but no less infallible authority of the self-consciousness and historical consciousness of man. But either way it rests with the Church which then has to obey it. And to the extent that this is the case, the Church knows no higher authority than its own. (575)

The irony, Barth contends, is that in claiming absolute authority for itself, the church in fact loses its own legitimate authority. "The Church is no longer the Church where it does not know a higher authority than its own, or an obedience other than that of self-government," for the church cannot be both obedient to Christ and self-governed (575–76). In contrast to the latter, the obedient church recognizes its Lord and "a real authority which transcends its own authority" (576). It should not surprise us that he ends his discussion on the authority of Scripture with a return to a discussion of a right understanding of Christ and the church, for Scripture itself is set within this larger context and relationship. The question of Scripture is, at its heart, a christological question, and Scripture is the specific answer to the question of how Christ exercises his lordship over the church during the time of his ascension. It is an answer governed by the particular order of the relation of Christ and his church, a relation of "irremovable distinction" governed by a distinctive christological logic (576; cf. 577). As Barth explains, the church is related to Christ

> as the human nature which He assumed is related to His divinity. It looks up to Him, as He is present to it, and it partakes of His Holy Spirit, as the earthly body looks up to its heavenly Head. He and He alone, with the Father and the Holy Spirit, can have divine glory and authority in the Church. But He does have it. The Church would not exist without Him, just as the creature would not exist without the Creator. It is the same relation as that of the Creator and creature which exists between Him and His Church. In His distinctness from it He is one with it; and in its distinctness from Him it is one with Him. The relation between Jesus and His Church is, therefore, an irreversible relation. (576)

There is thus a permanent and irrevocable distinction not only between Christ and the church as that of the Lord and his servants, but also between the authorities that they possess. They are not partners on the same plane, nor are their respective authorities the same. The authority of Christ is direct (immediate), absolute, and material—it is the authority of God himself. In contrast, the authority of the church is indirect (mediate), relative, and formal—an authority befitting the creature. Scripture mediates between this absolute authority of God and the authority of the creature, as it correspondingly stands between Christ and the church and mediates their relation. As Barth writes, "There is, therefore, no direct connexion of the Church with Jesus Christ and no direct life by His Spirit" (580). The relation of Christ and his church is, rather, mediated by the testimonies of the prophets and the apostles as their testimonies are taken up by Christ anew to address the church in the present. The church cannot have Christ apart from this testimony in Scripture, for the church "can distinguish between seeing Jesus Christ" and "hearing His prophets and apostles and reading their Scripture, and yet it cannot separate these things, it cannot try to have the one without the other" (583). Barth's discussion of the authority of Scripture thus brings us back around to the Scripture principle (581).

Authority under the Word (§20.2)

> All that we have still to say about the authority of the Church itself can be understood in the light of the commandment in Exodus 20:12: "Honour thy father and thy mother." (585)

In the prior subsection Barth emphasized the singular authority of Scripture, for it is "the authority of Jesus Christ in His Church" (585). Now he considers the authority of the church itself, one that is always dependent upon Christ and Scripture and subordinate to them. He begins by noting that the church can be understood as possessing authority akin to the way that parents possess authority due to the fifth commandment of the Decalogue, which requires that they be honored. Such authority is real and divinely established by the commandment, but he notes that it must be subjected to the greater absolute authority of God expressed in the first of the Ten Commandments. These two commandments—to worship only God and to honor parents— cannot be in ultimate contradiction since both are divinely given, even if they do appear on the surface to raise the difficulty that they seemingly stand in conflict with each other. Yet just as parents are granted an authority that does not overturn that of God but exists in subordination to it, so also the church has a genuine authority that does not contradict the authority of Jesus Christ but is established by it (586). This is its mediate, formal, and relative authority that is a "reflection" and "sign" of the divine authority of Christ exercised in Scripture (see 586–87).

The prior subsection was concerned with the vertical relation of Christ and his church, concretely expressed in the relation of Scripture and the church's confession and tradition. In contrast, the current subsection is concerned with horizontal relationships. One question that Barth raises, but does not extensively explore here, is the relation between the authority of the church and the authority of the family and of the state. Much more attention is given, rather, to the relation of the church and the individual believer that exists within it, and he again places them in a dialectical relation, one where, while dissent is possible, the regular order is that the conviction of individuals is a gift received from and shaped by the conviction and teaching of the church. For this reason, the church rightly calls for the affirmation of its confession from its individual members. This is so because the Word of God is heard first not by individuals apart from the church, but by the church and individuals within it (588). In this the church's confession holds an indirect, material, and relative superiority to the individual's own confession. To honor this superiority of the church's confession as a reflection of Christ's lordship is to honor Christ himself. This is not to overlook the fact that the church is a church of sinners. But it is to recognize, Barth writes, that as I have been forgiven, so have others in the church, and their confession is something I should hear and receive with reverence before I make my own (588–90).

Throughout this section Barth is outlining and circumscribing the church's authority in terms of two relations. In regard to the first vertical relation, the church's authority stands under the authority of Christ concretely exercised in the written witness of the prophets and apostles appointed to testify to him—that is, Holy Scripture. In regard to a second horizontal relation, the church's authority is relative, though real and prior, to the individual and that person's confession. Even though the church remains on the side of creation and even of the fall, and even though it may need to be corrected at times, its correction comes from those who are within it and who attend to the Word of God. The church, as a reflection and sign of divine authority, and as a witness to the witness of Scripture, possesses a real authority that must guide, inform, and even govern the confession of the individual. Christ is present where two or three are gathered, and insofar as this is so, the individual must reckon with the confession of the church, not as the words of God, but as a witness to the Word that the church has previously heard in Holy Scripture. The church's confession must therefore be taken with supreme seriousness, and to depart from it, even when necessary, is a grave and weighty thing (592–93; cf. 596).

The authority of the church takes concrete shape in the life of the community, though the forms in which it is exercised cannot be precisely delimited or exhaustively specified, for this authority is continually expressed through time in new ways. Nevertheless, Barth points to three instances where church authority has been expressed and exercised with enduring effect. The first of these is the ecclesial decision to specify the contents of the canon of Scripture: "We assume that between the Church now and here and the Church then and elsewhere there exists a unity of confession in respect of the compass of Holy Scripture, the so-called biblical Canon" (597). Though he addressed it earlier, he states that it is here that the canon must receive a formal discussion, because "the fixing of the Canon is the basic act of Church confession and therefore the basic establishment of Church authority" (597; cf. 598, 602). While the final decision to close the canon is one that only the Holy Spirit can make, we as members of the church must begin ever again with the church's decision and confession of these books as Holy Scripture. It is to them that we go expecting to hear the Word of God (598–99). A change of the canon would for this reason require a recognition by the universal church that such a change was needed—and he has no expectation that this will ever come to pass.

The second form of church authority that Barth sets forth is the recognition of teachers of the church—that is, "specific expositors and preachers of the Bible" (603). Interestingly, he does not identify the quintessential teachers of the church with the early church fathers, though he does recognize their importance. It is rather Luther and Calvin, he proffers, who are the paradigmatic teachers of the church, for they called it back to the Word of God and brought about its reformation (605–6, 609). In his discussion of the church's authority expressed in past teachers and tradition, Barth rejects not only certain strong notions of Catholic traditionalism, where the dogmas and fathers of the church stand on the same plane as Scripture as a second source of revelation, but also a biblicism in which it is believed that Scripture can be rightly read without any reference to those who have gone before us in faith (607). He is particularly fearful that those who claim to read the Bible apart from all other voices in the church, including its past teachers, in the end do not make the Bible preeminent over their thought but instead make their own subjective thought preeminent over the Bible. He comments on such biblicism: "In actual fact, there has never been a Biblicist who for all his grandiloquent appeal directly to Scripture against the fathers and tradition has proved himself so independent of the spirit and philosophy of his age and especially of his favourite religious ideas that in his teaching he has really allowed the Bible and the Bible alone to speak reliably by means or in spite of his anti-traditionalism" (609; see also 728).

In contrast to such biblicism, the Evangelical Scripture principle of the Reformers was not a repudiation of all tradition but was a rejection of antitraditionalism itself (609). In their rejection of both a traditionalism that held tradition to be on the same plane as Scripture, and a biblicism that renounced tradition altogether, and in light of their unique achievement of calling the church back to the Word of God, Barth states that Luther and Calvin continue to hold an unrivaled place in the identity of the Evangelical church (611). In order to evaluate if later teachers might serve the church in the same way, he stipulates a number of criteria that might be used to test whether such persons qualify (613–16).

The third and final ecclesial authority that Barth names is that of the confessions of the church that serve as "specific declarations of a common faith" (620). Confessions serve as guiding commentaries to Scripture that, while not infallible, provide guidance and direction for the church's exposition of the Bible within a definite ecclesiastical understanding (620; cf. 649–50). They are not an extension of revelation but rather a response to it (621). Like church teachers, church confessions stand under Scripture, and they have authority only insofar as they do not claim such for themselves but instead serve as a declaration of what the church has heard there. Confessions make this declaration in and for a particular place and time and in engagement with the spirit of the times (621). In Barth's construal, the confession is to Scripture as the church is to Christ.

Barth is quite frank in his acknowledgment that confessions are limited both in their scope and in what they can accomplish—they address a particular time and place, they address a particular problem and never can provide a timeless, universal account of the faith, and they inevitably appear too late, only after error has appeared in the church. In language both vivid and somewhat alarming, he writes that a confession "is only an attempt to cover the well when some children at least have been drowned and the great wasting of the Church has already taken place" (633). That this is the case reveals that the confession is "a document of human and therefore limited insight" (633). Nevertheless, such "spatial, temporal and material limitations" do not entail that the confession has no authority (634). Insofar as it speaks faithfully in the light of Scripture to its time, it serves as a commentary and teacher of Holy Scripture for the church and an articulation of the truth that has been heard within it. It is a particular form of human obedience to the Word of God even in its creaturely fallenness, and it is, in the end, the Word alone that can justify and validate it. To be guided by the confessions is to take them as our ecclesial parents. They thus deserve to be honored as we honor our own parents—namely, to be always respected, always revered, always consulted, but not slavishly imitated or inflexibly followed—for our obedience is to the Word of God and not to the confessions themselves (see 651).

Barth ends this subsection, as he has so many others, by elucidating this topic in light of the framework of the relation of Christ and the church and distinguishing the Evangelical understanding of this relation from the Roman Catholic and Neo-Protestant alternatives to it. He concludes,

> As a Church authority the authority of the confession, too, cannot be absolute, but only a relative one. The infallible and therefore final and unalterable confession is the praise which the Church as the body eternally united to its Head will offer to its Lord in this its own eternal consummation; it is thus an eschatological concept, to which no present actualization corresponds, to which every reality of Church confession, everything we now know as dogma old or new, can only approximate. What we know as dogma is in principle fallible and is therefore neither final nor unalterable. (657)

All confessions are therefore open to future revision. And this revision can result only from a fresh hearing of the Word of God (658–60).

Freedom in the Church (§21)

In this paragraph Barth turns from the theme of authority to that of freedom. His discussion parallels that of authority insofar as in the first subsection he begins by addressing the Word and its direct, absolute, and material freedom while moving in the next subsection to examine the indirect, relative, and formal freedom that the church possesses under the Word. This paragraph therefore follows the prior one very closely in form and structure even if the content has now shifted from the objective reality of Scripture (authority) to its subjective reality (freedom) outlined earlier (see 661). Yet as noted above, each of these topics has a corresponding objective and subjective element within it: the authority of the Word (objective) versus the church's authority under the Word (subjective), and the freedom of the Word (objective) versus the church's freedom under the Word (subjective).

The Freedom of the Word (§21.1)

The church must be understood in terms not only of the authority it stands under and exercises but also of the freedom it has received and in which it then lives. It is composed of members who are not only hearers of the Word but also doers of it (661). Freedom therefore pertains particularly to the life lived by the church. Here again Barth attempts to designate a form of human obedience that follows from, and does not precede, the divine act of revelation and salvation that establishes the church and the individual believer. Yet he also seeks to stipulate the character of this obedience in such a way that it is not portrayed as extrinsic to the human person or as denying and nullifying real human freedom. He attempts to designate the real, irreversible relation between the activity of God and the actions of human persons that preserves the integrity and self-determination of the latter. In sum: this section provides a description of the subjective human response to divine prevenient action with particular application to the question of Scripture—namely, how freedom is established by, rather than abrogated by, authority. As he states, divine authority is not tyranny and does not annihilate human response, but rather is "the power of an appeal, command and blessing which not only recognizes human response but creates it" (661). Authority and freedom are thus not antithetical but coexist in a mutual correspondence: true authority engenders and fosters true freedom, and true freedom recognizes and obeys true authority (see 661–63; cf. 665–66).

In arguing for a complementarity of authority and freedom, Barth is contending against an Enlightenment tradition (stemming from Kant and others) that saw them to be in fundamental conflict. For such modern thought, obedience to any external authority, whether of thought or practice, can only be a betrayal of the individual's autonomy and freedom. Such authorities (whether Scripture, church, or any tradition) had to be set aside and replaced with an appeal to the self's own reason, for absolute obedience to an external authority sacrificed the autonomy and freedom of the individual. Barth rejects such a view, and his understanding of freedom is more Pauline than Kantian: true freedom is obedience to a true authority, because this authority is God's alone, and God does not undermine human freedom but rather makes such freedom real and possible. So while he acknowledges that there is a rightful fear of the misuse of human authority, such fears regarding God's authority are misplaced, for divine authority is not that of a tyrant. Obedience to God is not the end of freedom but is its foundation. He explains,

> The man mastered and compelled is precisely the man whom God loves, who is therefore set upon his own feet and made truly responsible. To recognize and respect authority as a member of the Church means to love God in return and therefore to be willing and prepared to assume responsibility—real co-operative responsibility. The Christian is not a stone that is pushed, or a ball that is made to roll. The Christian is the man who through the Word and love of God has been made alive, the real man, able to love God in return, standing erect just because he has been humbled, humbling himself because he has been raised up. (662)

Here again the patterns of a divine prevenience and providence that do not nullify but establish human freedom are all on display in their dialectical form, and this theme of the mystery of God's authority that does not undermine but gives rise to human freedom shapes the entire first subsection. Barth differentiates this theological and dialectical relation of authority and freedom from other current political and philosophical understandings of authoritarianism and liberalism (see 663–66).

In light of revelation, it is therefore necessary to speak of both divine authority and human freedom, and God's Word is rightly understood only when both the authority that it possesses in itself and the free obedience that we in turn render to it are appreciated (666). Authority and freedom stand in an analogical relationship to objective and subjective revelation, and in turn to the Son and the Spirit: "As the Son can be revealed only by the Spirit, and in the Spirit only the Son is revealed, so authority must necessarily be interpreted by freedom, and freedom by authority" (666). Both authority and freedom are "predicates of God's Word," and they exist and are understood only in light of the Word and in relation to each other (666). Barth is also adamant that one cannot simply allocate them to different traditions, as if Protestantism stood for "freedom" over against a Catholic understanding of "authority," or as if the Reformation stood for "authority" against Neo-Protestant conceptions of "freedom" (see 666–69). It is the rightful understanding, relation, and ordering of authority and freedom, not a choice between them, that distinguishes the Reformation position from that of Catholicism and Neo-Protestantism. At this point, it should be evident that Barth's theology is preoccupied not with choosing between alternative realities (divine or human, Christ or church, Spirit or structure, event or institution, Scripture or tradition) but with the proper ordering of these realities such that God is rightfully worshiped as Lord and the creature rightly established in a proper and fitting form of obedience. The freedom of the Word of God gives rise to the freedom of the church, a freedom under the Word (669).

The freedom of God and the freedom of humanity, and specifically, the freedom of Christ and the freedom of the church, are mediated by Scripture. Barth again takes up the question of the relation of Christ and the church through an examination of the mediation of the prophets and apostles whose testimony becomes Holy Scripture (669–70; cf. 673–74). But whereas in the preceding paragraph he examined the relation of Scripture's authority to church authority, he now focuses upon Scripture's freedom in relation to church freedom. Nevertheless, the discussion follows very similar lines. Just as Scripture shares in the direct, absolute, and material authority of Christ, so also it shares in his direct, absolute, and material freedom (670). The prophets and apostles exhibit not only a divine call but also, in their persons, a real obedience expressed in choice and decision as they stand in an asymmetrical relation to the Lord who has called and confronted them. In short: just as Christ chose the disciples, so also, in a corresponding way, they chose him (670). The freedom of his call is met with their subsequent free response.

It must be added, however, that the relation between Christ and the apostles is a unique one and as such cannot be replicated or extended in the history of the church. Though the church must offer a corresponding free obedience, the unique relation of Christ and the apostles entails that the authority and the freedom they possess is of a singular and exclusive kind. Barth ever maintains the irreversibility not only of the relationship of Christ and the apostles but also of that between Christ with the apostles on one side and the church on the other. He is resolute in preserving the deep chasm that separates Christ and the apostles, but also the chasm between Christ with the apostles on one side over against the history and tradition of the church on the other. It is Scripture, as the testimony of the apostles, that in truth is the bridge that crosses the chasm (see 671–73).

Coming to the end of his discussion of the freedom of the Word, Barth provides a numbered list of qualities of this freedom (see 673–95). These points introduce motifs that we have already witnessed and that are now given particular shape under the theme of the freedom of Scripture. As we might well expect, he ends with an articulation of the relation between Christ and the church now under the aegis of freedom. In this relation, the believer (and the church) is "certainly responsible, but not autonomous" (693). He returns, yet again, to the language of Christ as the head and the church as his body, with believers as members within it (693). The freedom of the Word of God as found in Holy Scripture is the means by which this body is governed by its heavenly head: "To say that Jesus Christ rules the Church is equivalent to saying that Holy Scripture rules the Church" (693; cf. 693–94). It is in this second form of the Word of God that Christ is present to and rules his church between the ascension and his second coming, and rather than undermining Christ's immediate relation to his church, Scripture in fact establishes this immediacy (694). The proper response and concrete expression of hope by the church, and its proper form of thankfulness for this governance, is prayer (695). "Because it is the decisive activity prayer must take precedence even of exegesis, and in no circumstances must it be suspended" (695; cf. 453–54, discussed earlier).

Freedom under the Word (§21.2)

In the last paragraph we saw that though Scripture has a unique and un-paralleled authority, this authority gives rise to a real, if relative, author-ity for the church in its canonical decisions, the teachings of its prominent biblical expositors, and its confessions. Here Barth makes a similar move in addressing the freedom that the church possesses under the freedom of the Word of God. His language and argumentation by now should be familiar. While circumscribed and qualified by the freedom and power of the Word that establishes it, the church nevertheless is granted by that Word a freedom and power that is proper to it, for divine freedom does not destroy but rather establishes human freedom (696, 710). That such human freedom might exist is the end and goal of God's exercise of divine freedom on our behalf. The specific freedom of the church is in effect the acceptance of a responsibility to interpret the Word of God as Holy Scripture (696). This freedom of the church and of its members is not an intrinsic capacity or possession but rather is a gift of God's free revelation. This truth explains why the proper response on the part of the human in light of divine authority and freedom is prayer, for the church and the Christian undertake biblical interpretation from the vantage not of autonomy but of dependence upon God (697–98). For this reason the church can serve the Word of God in a way that eschews either "self-confidence" or "self-despair," and such service is the purpose and goal of its freedom (see 701–5).

It should not be surprising that Barth carefully qualifies this freedom as a freedom under the Word. It is not, as many have argued, a freedom of conscience for its own sake, as if the conscience were an inviolable faculty that justified all belief and behavior. Such subjectivism, in which the inner thoughts of the individual are ultimately more authoritative than the Word itself, is rejected. Just as the authority of the church must be subjected to the authority of the Word, so also the freedom of the church must be so subjected. This subjection concretely entails that the conscience of individual members within it must be disciplined first by Scripture. It entails, secondly, that the individual is required to listen respectfully to others in the church "notwithstanding their individual responsibility" for biblical interpretation (697). The original basis, limitation, and determination of human freedom in the church is the freedom of the Word of God, whereas in a secondary manner, this ecclesial freedom is also qualified by the prioritization given to the corporate body in interpretation over a sovereign and singular appeal to the individual's conscience (697).

Throughout this subsection we see again the balance between the church and the believer. On the one hand, the individual cannot be abstracted from the larger context of the church and exists only within it. Yet, on the other hand, Barth does not allow the individual to be subsumed into the community such that the uniqueness, agency, and decision of the individual become unimportant. While the Word of God comes to the individual only as a member of the body of Christ, it nevertheless comes to the individual and is heard by the individual as a unique agent. As Barth puts this, "Only as the Word which comes to me can I hear it as the Word which comes to the Church and therefore to others too" (703). Here his dialectical understanding of the relation of church and believer continues to hold true, and he rejects both a radical individualism and a sacrifice of the individual and his or her agency to the community.

Barth turns in the final pages of this subsection to expound upon the meaning of this freedom to interpret the Word in a numbered series of implications, a now familiar formula. The first element of this freedom is that the interpretation of the Word of God in Holy Scripture is the responsibility of every single believer, for it is "not the concern of a special office but of the whole Church" (714; see 711–15). The second implication of this freedom is that the exegesis undertaken by the church and its members must freely subordinate all "human concepts, ideas and convictions to the witness of revelation supplied to us in Scripture" (715; see 715–22). In the final three points of his numbered list he presents three elements of biblical interpretation that comprise its practice, three movements in the reading of Scripture.

The third implication of the freedom given to the church, and the first of this list of biblical interpretive practices, is that scriptural interpretation begins with observation, the explanation (*explicatio*) and presentation of the content of Scripture and its illumination. This is the first step of exegesis, and it includes the most important element of "literary-historical investigation" (723; see 722–27). But exegesis can never be straightforward historical study, for what is to be heard and considered is not simply what the prophets and apostles themselves said, but what was said to them before they themselves spoke, the "object" that they attest and to which they serve as witnesses. The interpreter's task is therefore to "reproduce and copy the theme whose image is reflected in the picture of the prophetic-apostolic words and controls those words" (723–24). Fidelity to the object that their words attest is the beginning of all biblical exegesis (725).

The fourth point in Barth's numbered list and the second moment in biblical interpretation is reflection (*meditatio*), which he takes to signify the discernment of the truth of what is found in the explication of Scripture, a second interpretive act in terms not of time but of type, and one between the acts of explication and application (727–36). Interpretation entails not only an observation of what is in Scripture and an explication of what it says but also a discernment of the truth of its content. It also requires an awareness of the philosophical convictions that lurk in our own background as we attempt to understand and articulate this truth (730).[7] Here an objective understanding moves on to become a subjective one, one in which we not only observe but also interpret and make sense of the text, hearing not only its ancient meaning but also its claim upon our own lives. This movement to determine the meaning of the message for us is, he contends, an unavoidable step from the first one of explication.

The final element of biblical interpretation, following upon explication and reflection (and the fifth point discussed in Barth's numbered sequence on the implications of freedom) is appropriation, or application (*applicatio*) (736–40). Proper interpretation must move from the explication of the text, to reflection and discernment of its truth, and then proceed to its application and assimilation in Christian life and practice, which is its ultimate goal. All three of these movements (*explicatio, meditatio, applicatio*) are integral to the interpretation of Scripture, and the exclusion of any results in a failure of interpretation as a whole (736). Exposition that does not in the end lead

---

7. One cannot help but think that Barth has Rudolf Bultmann in mind throughout this section, agreeing with Bultmann on the question that philosophy is unavoidable and that there is no interpretation without presuppositions, but he is more circumspect than Bultmann as to philosophy's ultimate usefulness and normativity. Perhaps nowhere is this as apparent as when Barth writes, "As exponents of Scripture, we should not allow any understanding of reality to impose itself as the normal presupposition for the understanding of the reality of the Word of God" (*CD* I/2, 733).

to application is not true exposition (736). It therefore follows that Barth fully rejects strong distinctions of "theory" and "practice." It also once again demonstrates why dogmatics must presuppose and incorporate exegesis as well as include ethics within itself. This final movement of interpretation in assimilation is not to be understood, however, as a kind of pragmatism by which we "use" Scripture for certain practical ends. We do not make use of Scripture; rather, it makes use of us, for it is the subject, not the object, in our reading (738).

COMMENTARY

Rethinking Biblical Infallibility and Fallibility

For some, a significant difficulty with Barth's doctrine of Scripture is his acceptance of biblical fallibility. He writes, "If God was not ashamed of the fallibility of all the human words of the Bible, of their historical and scientific inaccuracies, their theological contradictions, the uncertainty of their tradition, and, above all, their Judaism, but adopted and made use of these expressions in all their fallibility, we do not need to be ashamed when He wills to renew it to us in all its fallibility as witness, and it is mere self-will and disobedience to try to find some infallible elements in the Bible" (531). Such words require both explanation and perhaps, for some, resistance.

To begin, certainly some things can be conceded. First, Barth has a high view of Scripture that he sets against all other earthly and ecclesial authorities. Someone who did not have such a view would not say the things about Scripture that he has said, nor would such a person have the over fifteen thousand references to Scripture that he has in the CD. No modern theologian has so extensively engaged the Bible on so many fronts, and few have set it so firmly over the church and the individual conscience. It is, for Barth, the voice of Christ for us today. Second, it should be admitted on all sides that the authors of Scripture were fallible at least in their own lives as presented in Scripture itself. It is simply true that much of the Psalter is attributed to a man who was both an adulterer and a murderer (David), that his son, though the author of wisdom, could act in foolish ways with great cost not only to himself but also to his people (Solomon), and that the two greatest apostles, Peter and Paul, are portrayed as, respectively, a cowardly blasphemer (Matt. 26:74) and an accomplice to the murder of the first Christian martyr and a persecutor of Christ and his church (Acts 7:58; 9:1–2). Indeed, these great apostles did not always agree with each other (see Gal. 2:11). Such examples could be multiplied, but this should be enough to put to rest a view of the authors of Scripture as morally infallible in their lives and purely exemplary as persons. Barth was not the first to notice these things, of course. Yet his attention to such matters highlights God's use of fallible persons, and for Barth, this was not an embarrassment to Christianity but a testimony to the graciousness and power of God. Scripture is a witness composed by divinely appointed yet frail and fallible witnesses, not moral heroes or religious geniuses (491; cf. *CD* I/1, 112–13). This should lead us not to despair but to hope, for if this was true for others in the past, God may make use of us in our fallibility in the present.

Much more difficult, however, is Barth's attribution of fallibility to the text of Scripture itself. Here, too, perhaps some things might be noted that do not eliminate this tension but may help qualify and contextualize it. First, his statements on Scripture must be seen in their entire context in the canon of his work. For although he may have spoken of errors in Scripture, one is hard pressed to find an actual instance of him calling attention to one. He is much more concerned with the exegesis of biblical texts than with drawing attention to modern historical or scientific difficulties with such texts.[8] Second, he takes the humanity of the text with full seriousness, as well as the challenges it presents with respect to certain factual and scientific claims. In this regard, his position might be better described as postcritical rather than precritical. He was fully aware of the results of biblical criticism and the discrepancies between the biblical cosmological view of the world and our own, as well as the difficult historical questions raised by critical study of the Bible. For instance, the biblical picture took the sun as moving in the sky whereas our modern view places the earth as moving around a stationary sun, yet Barth did not think that such matters deserved any sustained attention or consternation. Moreover, the Gospel writers recount the stories of Jesus with a relative indifference to strict chronological ordering of events or the precision of modern historiography, as is readily apparent when they are compared one with another, and numerical and other discrepancies are not difficult to find. Barth was simply not concerned with harmonizing differences between the

---

8. Mark Galli writes, "The paradox is that, when it comes to using the Bible, Barth seems to treat the Bible as if it were inerrant! That's hyperbole, to be sure, and a phrase Barth would decidedly reject. But when he exposits the Bible, he does so as if it is completely trustworthy and authoritative. He never dismisses a passage as being in error. He has no interest in undermining the authority of the Bible—in fact, it is Barth who rescued the Bible from the relativistic Scripture reading of nineteenth-century liberalism." *Karl Barth: An Introductory Biography for Evangelicals* (Grand Rapids: Eerdmans, 2017), 114.

Gospels or other narrative accounts or resolving such scientific and histori-cal issues. He saw biblical tensions as things best left standing as pointing to a deeper mystery, rather than as problems that required a synthesizing of positions or a reduction of them (for examples of this, see *CD* I/1, 179–81).[9]

In short: Barth simply accepted that the ancient worldview was not our own and that the biblical writers were not attempting to write according to the standards of modern historiography. He had little time for attempts to reconcile such matters through scientific or historical harmonization. And although he did not think of the creation accounts as myth, and thought such "myth" language not only inappropriate but also misleading, neither did he think of these accounts as strictly historical records in the modern sense (for who was there to see such things?), and he preferred the term "saga" to describe them. Regardless of one's view of Scripture, almost all Christians have made peace with the fact that the earth is moving around the sun, and they are not troubled by the fact that Scripture can state that God has set "the earth on its foundations; it can never be moved" (Ps. 104:5 NIV).

Yet more problematic, perhaps, is Barth's acceptance that the biblical writ-ers could succumb to theological errors. Here, too, my comments must be brief, and I can only offer some observations. Perhaps we might begin by recognizing that assertions of the Bible's inerrancy and plenary inspiration do not get us very far in the actual understanding of how Scripture is to be interpreted and read, and really get us no further than Barth's own claims of its fallibility. For even though Barth conceded human fallibility, his emphasis upon Scripture's absolute authority, his actual exegesis of texts, and his refusal to specify any errors in actuality entail that his claims of fallibility must be set within the larger context of these claims and exegetical practice. Moreover, on the opposite side, claims for inerrancy still require that we specify what does and what does not count as an error (and this has been more difficult to do than one might expect in actual practice).

Indeed, Barth's position of scriptural authority with a concession of fal-libilism and a position of scriptural authority with a qualified inerrancy may not actually look different in practice when applied to an actual text. Perhaps one example will suffice. In the light of Christ's command to love our en-emies (Matt. 5:44; Luke 6:27, 35), the psalmist's cry for vengeance against Babylon and the joy that comes for anyone "who seizes [Babylon's] infants and dashes them against the rocks" (Ps. 137:8–9 NIV) might be received by Barth and his critics with the same shock. We could imagine that Barth may

---

9. See the discussion of this text and its examples in the introduction to *Thy Word Is Truth: Barth on Scripture*, ed. George Hunsinger (Grand Rapids: Eerdmans: 2012), xv–xix.

judge this joyful infanticide, in the light of Christ, to be a theological error of the psalmist. His critics may not do likewise, but in practice, their response and interpretation of this text may be the same as Barth's—that is, such imprecatory words to dash infants against rocks cannot be seen as the direct expression of the will of God and cannot be considered a divine command for the church to follow. These words certainly cannot be appealed to in a simplistic way as God's Word for us as if this means we should see them as an appropriate example for imitation.

Such a view becomes clear when we remember that Christ can both appeal to the OT as the Word of God and also challenge its individual claims, evident with his indifference to its food laws (Mark 7:18–23; cf. Lev. 11; Deut. 14). But with specific regard to the example given here, he could also take the retaliatory commands of the OT and leave them behind, and indeed overturn them with his own authority. So while Christ can say that God's Word cannot be broken (John 10:35), he can also speak as if his own commands supersede OT ones, and that the latter can no longer bind us in the same way as his own (cf. Exod. 21:23–24 with Matt. 5:38–39). In doing so, he set such commands aside. Whether or not the psalmist's imprecatory words of joy at the destruction of babies were theologically fallible or not, the end result is the same: such words do not set forth the path Christians are to follow.[10] Here Barth may appear more honest than those who emphasize plenary inspiration in a flat way, and more realistic in his understanding of the biblical canon, when he states, "Holy Scripture has always been defined in the Church with varying degrees of emphasis on the constituent parts," for the church "does not in fact and practice treat all parts of the Bible alike" (478). If there is any remaining challenge to this assertion, we might in reply simply ask how many sermons have been preached on the Gospels, and how many on the mildew laws of Leviticus (Lev. 14:33–57).

We might conclude that a doctrine of Scripture, whether conceding errors of some kind in the Bible (which themselves would need to be defined) or insisting upon inerrancy (which must also be defined), does not put to an end the most pressing questions of Scripture's interpretation, but may in the end ironically leave them as before. Yet Barth's fallibilism may be challenged, and the issue has been put in a helpful way by Katherine Sonderegger, who, when considering Barth's account of fallibilism, and in agreement with it,

---

10. It is a failure to see both sides of this distinction—Christ's direct appeal to the OT as divine Word and his challenge to specific OT instruction—that mars Mark Thompson's generally good discussion of such issues. See Thompson, "Witness to the Word: On Barth's Doctrine of Scripture," in *Engaging with Barth: Contemporary Evangelical Critiques*, ed. David Gibson and Daniel Strange (New York: T&T Clark, 2008), 196.

nevertheless incisively concludes, "Do we not need, then, a 'reliabilism' to accompany a strong doctrine of fallibilism, so that the particular shape and detail of a scriptural text can reliably guide the theologian in constructing doctrine, and the believer in constructing a Christian life?"[11] Such questions are pressing and remain.

In the end, the church is rightly challenged to remember that it must stand under and live with Scripture, as Barth insists: "When the Church has suffered seriously, i.e., not from without but inwardly and essentially, it is never because it has lived too much but too little under the Word of Scripture" (502). Perhaps Barth and his critics can in the end fully agree on that which is central and cannot be sacrificed: "Under the Word, which means Holy Scripture, the Church must and can live, whereas beyond or beside the Word it can only die" (585). This is so because in the end the Word rules all: "The whole truth is that in spite of all appearances to the contrary, Holy Scripture has more power than all the rest of the world together" (678).

QUESTIONS FOR REFLECTION

- How is the particularity of God's revelation in Jesus Christ (the scandal of the gospel) reflected in the particularity of the biblical canon?
- How should we think of the following?

  The canon as open or closed
  The unity of the OT and the NT
  The authority and the freedom of Scripture
  Scripture's infallibility and fallibility

- Why is the age of Scripture an inadequate means of expressing its authority?

11. Katherine Sonderegger, "The Doctrine of Inspiration and the Reliability of Scripture," in *Thy Word Is Truth: Barth on Scripture*, ed. George Hunsinger (Grand Rapids: Eerdmans: 2012), 23. She sees Barth as becoming more mindful of this matter as the *CD* progressed. Henri Blocher provides a yet more critical evaluation of Barth's position when he states, "If the fallible human witness of the writers only becomes the Word of God when and where *visum est Deo* (it please God), a 'happening' that ever eludes our grasp, Scripture as a permanent resource, as a corpus that can be objectively exegeted, is 'too human' to be a reliable guide in theology" (Blocher, "Karl Barth's Christocentric Method," in Gibson and Strange, *Engaging with Barth*, 51). Blocher's essay is perhaps best read in tandem with Sonderegger's and that of McCormack mentioned above ("The Being of Holy Scripture").

- Does the church give the canon its authority? Does it give the canon to itself? Why or why not?

- How does Scripture stand in relation to other church tradition? Why does Barth reject both any traditionalism that equates Scripture and church dogma, and any biblicism that renounces any place for tradition at all?

- What is the role of confessions of faith (see 650–51)? In what way are they to be understood? What is their relation to Scripture? To the faith of an individual believer?

- What is the role of historical-critical study of the Bible for the life of the church? Is it necessary, and if so, why? Is the interpretation of the Bible solely a matter of historical study? Why or why not?

- Why does Barth hold that prayer must exist as the beginning of all scriptural study and hearing (see 698)?

- What persons in the history of the church (besides Luther and Calvin) meet Barth's criteria for being a church father (or mother)?

- What is the place for personal narratives of faith (see 709)? Why does Barth seem particularly critical of these? Is there a place for testimonies in the life of the church?

- What is Barth trying to communicate in the following passage, and what are his central points and concerns?

> Is there a worse threat to freedom itself than the establishment of man as his own lord and lawgiver? Who can exercise a worse tyranny over us than the god in our own breast? And what further tyrannies does not this first and decisive one drag in its train? It is inevitable that the man who claims to be directly in communion with God, and free from all concrete forms of authority, will all the more certainly be delivered over to the powers of nature and history, to the spirit of the age and of contemporary movements, to the demons of his situation and environment. (668)

- What does Barth mean when he states that where there is no genuine authority, there is no genuine freedom (668)?

- What does it mean to say that the rule of Christ through Holy Scripture is the proper form of government in the church (see 693–94)? Why does Barth reject "self-government" as a proper description of a church's polity?

- What does Barth mean when he states, "Those who are silent in deference to scriptural learning, the congregation which is passive in matters of biblical exegesis, is committed already to secret rebellion" (715)?
- What are the strengths and weaknesses of Barth's designation of the creation accounts as *saga*? Why does he reject the category of myth for these accounts? Why does he not think of them as straightforward historical or scientific description?

✦ 10 ✦

Church Proclamation
and Dogmatics Revisited

CD §§22–24

Having addressed revelation in the second chapter of the *CD* and Holy Scripture in the third, Barth now turns in the fourth to proclamation as the final form of the Word of God. In this sense, after hundreds of pages, he thus returns full circle to themes introduced at the beginning of the *CD*. Chapter 4 in turn brings the first volume of the *CD* to a close.

The Mission of the Church (§22)

In chapter 4 of Barth's doctrine of the Word of God he examines the proclamation of the church, the third form of the Word of God. Like the prior chapter on Scripture, this chapter comprises three paragraphs (§§22–24). Here we find a discussion not only of the nature of the Word of God but also of dogmatics as a function of the hearing and teaching church.

This final chapter on church proclamation must be seen against two backgrounds in order to appreciate its setting and purpose. First, as an examination of the final form of the Word of God, this chapter (chapter 4) follows those of Scripture (the second form of the Word of God; chapter 3) and revelation (the first form of the Word of God; chapter 2). Barth's rich and extensive discussion of the revealed Word of God (i.e., revelation) in chapter 2 comprised extended discussions of three aspects of revelation itself: its trinitarian nature (part 1, the Trinity), its objectivity in the incarnation of the Word (part 2, Christology), and its subjectivity in the outpouring of the Holy Spirit (part 3, pneumatology). His discussion continued by examining the second form of the Word of God, Holy Scripture, in chapter 3. Now, in chapter 4, he takes up the third and final form of the Word of God: the proclamation of the church. The manner in which proclamation serves as a witness to revelation parallels and echoes many of the themes earlier considered in examining Scripture itself as a witness to revelation, though also with important differences. In this regard, this final chapter, on proclamation, follows in the logical order of Barth's exposition of the one Word of God in its threefold form as revealed, written, and proclaimed. It therefore brings to an end an extended discussion of what Barth outlined in §4 above.

There is another background against which to see this final chapter, however. Insofar as Barth takes up the question of proclamation as human speech as well as the task of dogmatics as that of the hearing and speaking church, he is bringing the first volume to a close by returning to the themes addressed at the very beginning of the *CD*. His discussion in these final three paragraphs (§§22–24) will revisit subjects found in the first two (§§1–2) as well as the seventh (§7), but is especially a recapitulation of the themes of the third (§3). Indeed, before diving into the first paragraph of this final chapter (§22), we may find it helpful to read and compare the thesis statement of this paragraph with that of the third (§3) and notice their similarities. In effect, Barth is bringing the first volume to an end by returning to where he began—with an examination of proclamation as the speech of the church and dogmatics as the practice of the church's examination of that speech. As he begins this section, he explicitly draws attention to this recapitulation: "We have reached the final and really critical point in the doctrine of the Word of God, that which is both its starting-point and its end: the Word of God as the preaching of the Church" (743).

The Word of God and the Word of Man in Christian Preaching (§22.1)

This first paragraph begins with the mystery of God's Word in the human words of preaching as the theme of dogmatics (743). As the mystery of Scripture was set forth as the divine Word that comes to the church through the human testimony of the prophets and apostles, so now Barth takes up the mystery of proclamation in which the contemporary pronouncement of God's Word comes through the human words of the preacher. Preaching now is the third site of God's event of revelation, following God's personal revelation in Jesus Christ and in the written text of Scripture, and preachers take their place as the human witnesses to revelation in this third form of God's Word. As persons in the church proclaim the Word of God that has been heard in Scripture, these persons "who as such are identical neither with Jesus Christ nor with the prophets and apostles, become indirectly and by faith . . . the bearers and speakers of the Word of God as it becomes a word spoken by them in the form of their human word" (744).

With this quotation, we see that Barth's account of proclamation is characterized by a logical order and familiar dialectical patterns of unity and distinction. Such patterns are also evident in the manner in which the church's preaching stands under Scripture and in turn under the revelation that comes in Christ, yet how it also exists in unity with them such that the one Word of God, Jesus Christ, speaks to the church in proclamation as he does in Holy Scripture. Just as Christ's own voice comes to us through Holy Scripture, so it also comes through the proclamation of the church. Yet here too there are necessary differences, for just as Scripture is identified as the Word of God yet is distinguished from the revealed Word, so also proclamation is the Word yet also distinguished and placed under the Word revealed and the written Word of Holy Scripture. As Barth writes, "The Church exists as the earthly body of the heavenly Lord and as the community built upon the foundation of the apostles and prophets; and the connexion between these two things is not torn by the subordination of the first witnesses to Him of whom they bear witness, nor again by the subordination of those who receive this witness to those from whom they receive it" (744).

Barth's understanding of the Word of God in this threefold form is therefore one of both equity and subordination, for both the written and the proclaimed Word of God stand as witnesses to the proper and personal form of the Word in Jesus Christ, and the proclaimed Word itself stands under the written testimony of Scripture. This hierarchical ordering is in fact the movement of Christ to his church and the "connecting link" between them, yet it also "consists in the one Word of God, which in these three different forms, in none of them less than in the others, in none of them diminished and weakened, but in all three remaining the selfsame Word, constitutes the life and the foundation of the Church" (745). Proclamation itself is therefore rightfully identified as the Word of God, for "in the preaching of the Church as well we have to do with the Word of God in an undiminished meaning of the term and therefore with God Himself" (745). God's revelation comes through this threefold form. This is at the heart of the trinitarian analogy, though Barth is more ready to allow for a qualified subordination of the second and third forms of the Word to the first in the doctrine of revelation than in the doctrine of the Trinity, where he renounces subordination entirely.

Moreover, in each form, God's Word comes by taking up a created medium for divine communication, in which the Word of God takes precedence and is demarcated from, yet is freely joined indivisibly with, this created medium. This union is absolutely and singularly unique in the incarnation, where God and humanity are joined in the person of Jesus Christ. But it is incontrovertible that Scripture as a witness to Christ and proclamation as a witness to Scripture exist for Barth in an analogous manner to Christ in that they, too, are the sites of an event in which the divine Word takes up human words for the purpose of divine revelation. This unity-in-distinction of divine Word and human words is a readily apparent christological analogy found in Barth's expositions of Scripture and proclamation. By now, these trinitarian and christological patterns should be recognizable and familiar.

So with these patterns in view, we can make good sense of Barth's central affirmation that guides this first subsection on Christian preaching and serves as its theme: "Therefore, to state the problem, we must begin with the affirmation that, by the grace of revelation and its witness, God commits Himself with His eternal Word to the preaching of the Christian Church in such a way that this preaching is not merely a proclamation of human ideas and convictions, but, like the existence of Jesus Christ Himself, like the testimony of the prophets and apostles on which it is founded and by which it lives, it is God's own proclamation" (745–46).

Barth does not think that this affirmation can be argued or independently verified based on external criteria of adjudication, but must simply be recognized by the church. The church does not argue, but confesses, that God has spoken through the church's proclamation. It is a matter not of apologetics but of acknowledgment. Only the Holy Spirit can confirm that God has so spoken, and, as with Scripture, the ultimate foundation for the church's claim that proclamation is the Word of God is the internal testimony of the Holy Spirit. Here again in proclamation we see the conjoining of an objective external Word that comes to the church and the subjective internal work of the Holy Spirit that confirms this truth and makes possible its reception and acceptance. There is in proclamation, as in revelation and Scripture, both an objectivity and subjectivity, both an external Word that confronts us, and an internal work of the Spirit that enables our perception, understanding, and reception of the Word and that effects our conversion.

Barth therefore has a very high view of preaching, for it is the vehicle of God's own proclamation to the church in the present, the living voice of Christ to his earthly body. In the act of proclamation the preacher stands "in indirect identity with Jesus Christ and the biblical witnesses" and as such "certainly does not need any forgiveness of sins, just as certainly as he does need it in so far as he is the one who discharges this commission in his own words" (747). These quotations reveal that Barth's view of proclamation, as of Scripture, is highly dialectical. One can perhaps discern three different types of dialectic at work in his discussion of proclamation in this paragraph.

One type of dialectic is that of the divine Word that comes through human words. This divine-human dialectic has been witnessed earlier in the discussion of the incarnation and of Scripture, and is now seen in the third form of the Word of God, proclamation itself. It is of course related to Barth's dialectic of veiling and unveiling, just as it is also marked by patterns of unity, differentiation, and asymmetry. In short: God in his Word takes up such human words and employs them for his own self-communication. There is nothing, however, in the human words themselves that makes them capable or sufficient for this use; that they are so used is a miracle of God's grace.

A second type of dialectic is that of sanctification and sin. While this does not pertain directly to the first form of the Word of God, Jesus Christ, we saw even there that while Christ commits no actual sin, Barth holds that the Word assumed a fallen human nature. We see this dialectic also at work in his discussion of Scripture, where Scripture is the Word of God but also is the fallible words of human persons. The same kind of dialectic holds true here as well. Insofar as proclamation is the commissioned preaching of God's Word, it has no need of repentance or confession (747). It is, quite simply, God's Word proclaimed. But insofar as preaching comes in the words of a fallen human creature, it is open to correction, and the church rightly examines and tests it. This is precisely why dogmatics, as the testing of the church's speech according to its standard in Holy Scripture, is necessary. Of course, these two forms of dialectic are not unrelated, for Barth thinks of humanity in its current state as fallen. Therefore the created and fallen nature of humanity, as well as the proper ordering of divine and human agency, can be witnessed when Barth writes, "It is only from the belief that the Church's proclamation is really divine that the recognition of the hopelessness of its humanity follows, and therefore the recognition that in its humanity it can live only by its divinity, that is, by the grace of the Word of God given to the Church" (752).

A third and final type of dialectic is that of God's judgment and mercy, both of which are pronounced in God's proclamation. Here we see again that Barth preserves the tension of God's "No" and God's "Yes," yet with the former always serving the larger purpose of the latter, so that asymmetry is evident here as well. Proclamation is therefore a word of both condemnation and grace, and these are united in the one divine Word that is proclaimed to the church. Yet they are also distinct messages that do not exist in a dualistic complementarity; rather, the former serves the purpose of the latter. So Barth can state that the proclamation of the Word of God is such that "God exposes man as a sinner even as He is gracious to him" and "opposes man as He receives him" (754). The preacher, as a human speaking of God, falls under this divine judgment as does the church, but this condemnation is not the last word, for, even though the sinfulness and frailty of the preacher and the church must constantly be kept in view, they cannot overthrow the larger and more determinative fact that the church is the body of Christ and that Christ is its head. The church is for this reason not only the object of God's judgment but also, even more importantly, the recipient of his promise and grace. And because of this, the church is commissioned to speak boldly and can do so (754–55). The church's proper preparation for such speech must first be prayer and then "serious and honest work" in attending to Scripture (755).

The preaching of the church is therefore to be done with confidence, though again, only God can ultimately confirm that proclamation is his Word (748–49). If there is a new element in this section from Barth's prior discussions of proclamation, it is the emphasis that is now placed upon the resurrection as that which constitutes the grace given to the church and that which empowers its speech, so that Barth asserts that "Jesus Christ in the power of His resurrection is present wherever men really speak really of God" (752; cf. 749, 756). What is impossible for human persons to accomplish, Christ has already accomplished.[1] The reality of revelation again takes precedence over questions of its possibility, and that it has occurred is a miraculous act of divine grace. It is not at all due to an intrinsic power or capacity of the human words themselves, or of the person of the preacher himself or herself (749, 752–53, 756).

Yet if this means that the human speaker is left with no room for boasting, Barth insists that it also leaves the speaker with no room for laziness or indifference (756). The commission to speak is rightly taken up when we acknowledge that we have no ability to speak God's Word, but that we are commanded to speak nonetheless, trusting that God will speak through our speech, for "God alone can speak about God" (756). So while human frailty and human sin must be ever acknowledged, and such must in turn qualify and chasten human pride, they cannot become a justification for timidity, for such things "can never become arguments against the positive truth that the members of the Church in all their humanity are invited to share in God's own

---

1. That it is impossible for humans to speak of God, and yet that the church is obligated to do so, are long-standing convictions for Barth. See *WGT*, 171–98.

work of proclaiming His Word" (757). Barth can therefore conclude, "The Church looks to Jesus Christ. It allows him to be its own life, and therefore its consolation. It does not cling to its own humanity—either in arrogance or diffidence—but to the task imposed upon it in its humanity. And as it does so, it can confess, but with a final certainty, that as it speaks about God in human words, it proclaims God's own Word" (757).

Pure Doctrine as the Problem of Dogmatics (§22.2)

In this subsection Barth focuses on Christian proclamation as a human activity. While preaching is the vehicle for God's speech, it is nevertheless also a human practice that can be performed well or badly (758–59). Because this is the case, the church has warrant, and is in fact required, to test its speech, and this critical examination is done formally by the discipline of dogmatics. With this discussion of the church's speech and dogmatics, we return to the topics of the very first pages of the *CD*.

This human task of proclamation is the most weighty one laid upon the church in Barth's view, and he states that the proper form of obedience to this divine command is composed of decisions where "the only will of man is to co-operate in the realization of God's work as He Himself has determined it down to its details and form" (760). Such is a rare positive reference by Barth to divine and human cooperation, a term that he generally rejects. It is therefore not unexpected that he immediately qualifies this obedience as one that recognizes that God alone makes this service of preaching ultimately effective. Nevertheless, the church has its proper obedience to render, and it does so by speaking of God with a conscientious concern for truthful speech. He concludes, "The comprehensive term to denote the content of the service of God as understood in this way is that of pure doctrine" (761). Pure doctrine is, he succinctly states, the problem of Christian preaching (761).

Barth distinguishes doctrine from theory, for theory implies a reciprocal relationship of knowing and activity between the knower and the thing known (761–62). Doctrine, by contrast, implies the superiority of the object known to the knower who is now a recipient, rather than an effective agent, in this act of knowing. In short: doctrine pertains to "an object transcending the scope of human observation and thought," though it is not an inert object but rather a Subject that is known in the revelation of the Word of God (761). Doctrine is therefore the attentive and responsible presentation of the truth that has been heard in Scripture and the church's proclamation, and this truth is nothing less than God's personal address to us. Yet doctrine is the church's response to revelation and not revelation itself, for it is not God's own speech and "not in itself the same thing as what God does when He speaks His Word" (762). Rather, doctrine is teaching, instruction, and edification: "It is this function which Christian preaching has to perform" (763).

Once again we see a highly dialectical type of construal. On one side, Barth is adamant that revelation, as God's address to the church, is something that God alone can do. And yet he is equally adamant that the preacher must speak. The preacher's own speaking is not directly the Word of God, but only indirectly so, as God's address comes through this human pronouncement. We are back to the themes of indirect versus direct identity and of revelation as an act of veiling and unveiling, as Barth's description of preaching upholds both the unity of divine and human speech and the distinction between them. Preaching is defined as an exposition of Scripture with the ultimate purpose not simply of teaching its objective material, but of pointing beyond it to the God who stands behind it and speaks through it, even though this divine speech cannot be effected from our side. This leads to high paradox and dialectical mystery, as when Barth cryptically writes,

> The aim of all the indirectness with which the Church in its own proper author-
> ity and freedom grasps and expounds the Word is the directness of revelation
> which becomes real, and the directness of faith which becomes alive, at the point
> where God in His authority and freedom has Himself spoken and is Himself
> heard. It can only aim at this end; but it can do so and must do so, in so far as
> it is the indirectness of the Church which is itself rooted in faith—the Church
> which knows itself to be called in faith to service, but to service in the strict
> sense of the term. (763–64)

The problem of preaching is therefore not that of making God speak—that is a human impossibility. Rather, the problem is that of attending to the human act—to speak in such a way that the church is faithful to what it has heard and witnessed in Holy Scripture. This is the problem of "pure doctrine" (764). The church's speech is to be a reflection of and witness to God's Word; negatively, it is to remove all things that might hinder such a hearing, all "possible notes of false idolatry and human exaltation" (764). This act of reflective witness and critical removal is in fact never perfectly executed. All human speech fails perfectly to perform such a duty, and there is a strikingly strong notion of both sin and eschatology at work in Barth's understanding of "pure doctrine." He insists that even the best effort we can offer requires God's mercy, and that "we do well to remember that even the best and sincerest accomplishment of the Church in this respect is, in fact, in need of God's grace" (765).

Throughout this second subsection Barth is consumed with delineating, once again, the dialectical relationship of identity and differentiation between the divine Word, which God alone can speak, and the human word, which both serves the divine Word and seeks to be in correspondence to it. All of the christological patterns we have seen previously of unity, differentiation, and irreversibility, as well as divine prevenience and the purely gracious character of this event, are seen here in Barth's discussion of church preaching. These patterns, so well attested in his discussion of the incarnation and Scripture, now take specific yet familiar shape in his discussion of proclamation.

All of the tensions of divine action and human action that we have previously witnessed are also evident here. On the one hand, Barth wants to insist that if true proclamation occurs, then this is only because God himself can make this so. This could, it might reasonably be asked, call into question whether human activity is required at all. Barth is not unaware of this discomfiting conclusion some may draw. Yet, on the other hand, while he wants to acknowledge and preserve God's sovereignty and lordship in this act of revelation, he also wants to acknowledge and preserve a real and true place for the integrity, validity, and, if properly understood, necessity of human obedience and correspondent striving for a proper form of speech. Though revelation only occurs by God's action, this does not dispel the fact that the church is charged with the task of pure doctrine and a concern for it. He is fully aware that God can speak, should God so choose, through very imperfect and flawed human speech (765–66). Yet he insists that this in no way exonerates us for our failures, nor does it abrogate the command that the church pay attention to its speech and strive for its truth. All of these paradoxical thoughts are on display when he states,

> The grace of the Word of God is not magic. It is promised to the Church that is required and ready to serve it. If it makes strong what men make weak, good what men make evil, pure what men make impure, that does not mean that it does everything where men do simply nothing, where men perhaps do not stand under this requirement and in this readiness. When we have done all that was required of us, we must add that we are unprofitable servants. But if we infer from this that we might equally well allow ourselves to be idle servants, we are not trusting in the grace of the Word of God. (765–66)

As always, Barth is preoccupied with questions of the relation of divine and human agency and action. He wants to preserve the priority of the first, while not undermining the integrity of the second. For this reason, while the ultimate efficacy of proclamation is solely due to a divine miracle, this in no way relegates the question of the church's faithfulness and obedience to matters of indifference (see 767). We might say that the critical examination of the church's speech is therefore a requirement for its penultimate efficacy. The testing of this speech for the purpose of achieving pure doctrine brings Barth back to the task of dogmatics, a topic introduced at the very beginning of volume 1. We need only highlight a few themes that remain, since much of this material is prefigured in those earlier discussions.

First, Barth here expands upon his discussion in the last paragraph on biblical interpretation and its three movements of observation (*explicatio*), reflection (*meditatio*), and assimilation (*applicatio*), now making these not only three moments in interpretation but also three subdisciplines within the task of theology itself. The first is the task of biblical theology, the second the task of dogmatic theology, and the third the task of practical theology (see 766). These three aspects of biblical interpretation serve the ultimate purpose of enabling and equipping Christian proclamation. While all are necessary, Barth gives a qualified preeminence to dogmatics, for whereas exegesis is concerned with the foundation of preaching, and practical theology with its form, it is dogmatics that is concerned with its content and therefore concerns itself with whether preaching is in agreement with "the revelation attested in Scripture" (766). This primacy of dogmatics as a kind of first among equals rests upon the fact that the content of the church's proclamation is determined there, so that "the question of the Church's ministry is decided in dogmatics" (767). He continues, "Bad dogmatics—bad theology—bad preaching. And, conversely: good dogmatics—good theology—good preaching" (767). The church must therefore be "concerned and zealous about the purity of its doctrine" (767).

Dogmatics is the church's "most essential task," and it is one that Barth insists is not relegated only to individual professors but rather is laid upon the entire church, without excepting even a single one of its members (768). Dogmatics must undertake this task with no cynicism or skepticism but must always proceed in the confidence that "God's Word has never left itself without a witness in the Church, and will never do so" (775). The proper attitude of the dogmatic undertaking is therefore a dialectical balance of confidence with criticism, criticism with confidence. If there is a proper commencement to this task of dogmatics, it is prayer (776). Its task as a search for the purity of doctrine can be briefly stated, for it concerns "a question whether the words, the phrases, the sequences of thought, the logical construction of Christian preaching have or have not the quality of serving the Word of God and becoming transparent to it" (777). Its subject matter "consists essentially in the totality of what it hears from the Church—the contemporary Church—as its human speech about God" (778). While its subject matter is therefore defined as the church's speech, it must also be remembered that, as discussed in chapter 2 above, the subject matter is ultimately God's revelation that stands as the referent to this speech.

Second, Barth emphasizes that pure dogma is not a static deposit of theological propositions (768). It is not a timeless body of knowledge, but an event in which the Word is spoken by the power of the Holy Spirit, and this miracle must occur ever anew (see 768). As with Scripture, Barth refuses to think of doctrine as a timeless collection of propositional content that can perfectly and comprehensively capture God's truth. His great fear is that, when this is done (and he thinks it was done by Protestant orthodoxy in the seventeenth century), the Bible and doctrine are understood as possessions of the church that the church controls such that the authority and freedom of God in his Word are lost (768). In contrast, he states, "Pure doctrine as the fulfillment of the promise given to Church proclamation is an event. It is the event of the grace of the Word of God and of the obedience of faith created by this grace" (768).

The very fact that the Holy Spirit must be invoked to speak anew undermines any view that thinks of doctrine, or Scripture, as a static book of truth. Barth thinks of doctrine in terms of a divine speech-act, and he thinks of it eschatologically. There is not, in this life, any perfect and complete description of Christian doctrine. The church never achieves as much. It can only, and must ever, strive after it. This is its endless task: "Whatever stimulates, maintains and guides this activity is good dogmatics; whatever checks it, lulling the Church into a comfortable sleep, is certainly bad dogmatics, even when the texts it reproduces or itself originates are in themselves excellent" (769). Here again we see the distinction that Barth makes between the act of confessing and the products of such an act in the confessions themselves. The first is always a requirement for the church, and the second, while possessing a relative authority, are ever in need of review and must also be open to revision and augmentation in light of a fresh hearing of God's Word in Scripture. Barth's view of confessing and confessions is thus an instance of his actualism.

Finally, Barth briefly notes that there must be both a standard (the "objective possibility" of the church's proclamation) by which the church's speech is tested and a method by which this criterion is rightly used and applied (the "subjective possibility" of the church's proclamation) (781–82). As in the prior chapter on Scripture, this one on proclamation begins with an introductory paragraph on the nature of proclamation and dogmatics (§22), which is then followed by a paragraph discussing the objectivity of proclamation and the

formal task of dogmatics with its dogmatic norm (§23), which is in turn followed by one discussing the subjectivity of proclamation and the material
task of dogmatics with its dogmatic method (§24). Yet whereas in the chapter
on Scripture Barth examines the questions of authority and freedom, here
on proclamation he examines the questions of the hearing church and its
dogmatic norm, and the teaching church and its dogmatic method. He gives
a helpful summary of such parallels between the second, third, and fourth
chapters in a concluding small-print section (781–82).

Dogmatics as Ethics (§22.3)

Before moving to these discussions of the norm and method of dogmatics,
Barth concludes this paragraph with a brief subsection on the question of how
dogmatics includes ethics within itself. He has already addressed much of the
material found here, and his present answer runs along the same lines as that
given earlier (see §18 and the discussion of this paragraph above). He states
that Christian ethics, like Christian dogmatics, is derived from God's revelation
in Christ and is not based upon a general anthropology or natural theology. It
therefore must be included within dogmatics and not set forth as an independent discipline. Whenever ethics has been set forth in such an autonomous
way, he contends, it has sought to "reverse the roles" and subsume dogmatics
into itself with the result that dogmatics becomes an "ethical system." And
since all general ethical systems are based in general anthropology, the end
result is that theology becomes simply "applied anthropology" (782–83; cf.
790). Consequently, its norm ceases to be the Word of God and instead becomes a general theory of the good, and the Word of God is retained only as
it serves as an illustration and historical medium for this more determinative,
foundational, and abstract idea that is known apart from revelation (783).

Barth's position is that ethics must be included in dogmatics, and for the
simple reason that a knowledge of the good is in truth a knowledge of sanctification, and this is something that is only revealed to us in Christ. There
can be no general ethics for the same reason that there can be no natural
theology. That which is good (ethics), as well as that which is true (theology),
is something that is only revealed to us, and ethics therefore must be Christian
ethics, and Christian ethics must be set forth within Christian dogmatics. In
this conviction, Barth believes that he is following the trajectory of the Reformers: "The ethics of Luther and Calvin is to be sought and found in their
dogmatics and not elsewhere" (783).

Throughout this subsection Barth examines the history of the separation
of dogmatics and ethics, and he gives evidence of his rejection of the division

of theory and practice once more. This subsection also demonstrates that he understands humanity and its action (like its faith) only as they are framed by and folded into the larger context of God's work that gives them meaning and purpose. In short, he has no interest in a "holy man" abstracted from a holy God and as a topic unto itself (790).[2] Yet this talk of a holy God must nevertheless take up the question of God's relation to the Christian as a human person and the life that he or she is to live. When dogmatics is cut off from such ethical concerns, Barth avers, it is no wonder that it appears to be "aloof from life and of doubtful value" (787). Dogmatics therefore requires ethics even as ethics requires dogmatics, for as he writes, "Dogmatics itself is ethics; and ethics is also dogmatics" (793). Yet these are not parallel, for dogmatics must take priority because the question of God precedes, even as it includes, the question of human action (see 794). So while in principle there is nothing preventing a separation of dogmatics and ethics for the sake of exposition, this separation must not be a principled one, and ethics must find its ultimate home under the canopy of dogmatics (see 794–95).

In addition to the ordering of dogmatics and ethics, another theme that is addressed here is the nature of human action. Barth does not think that we can consider humanity apart from its activity, for these are deeply entwined: "The ethical question, i.e., the question concerning right conduct, is the existential problem of man. As we will, we are; and what we do, we are. It is not as if man first exists and then acts. He exists in that he acts" (793). Here Barth's concern to take human action seriously displays an actualism wherein the human person is defined by his or her decisions and actions, as well as displaying an affinity to existentialism's concern that actual existence precedes questions of essence. Yet Barth is equally adamant that human existence is not the theme of dogmatics. While dogmatics takes this question of human action into itself, it is not exhausted by it. Nor is human existence a "given" that theology in turn has to answer and address (and hence Barth's actualism cannot be straightforwardly equated with existentialism). It is not culture or the human situation, but the Word of God, that provides not only the answer but also the question of human existence (793). In stark contrast to other existential theologians such as Paul Tillich, Barth writes,

> The Word of God is not the Word of God unless it precedes this question of man's existence, unless it is its origin even before it becomes its answer. And theology has ill understood its task unless it regards this question as one which

2. Barth finds a similar danger in allowing dogmatics to be rolled into church history, for there, too, the subject matter ceases to be God in his revelation and is instead the Christian person as a historical personality (CD I/2, 791).

is not first answered in the Word of God but already grounded in it, the question which in the first instance is put by the Word of God itself. It is only in this way that it can approach it as a genuine and urgent question. Therefore the theme of dogmatics is always the Word of God and nothing else. (793)

Dogmatics as a Function of the Hearing Church (§23)

Barth opens this paragraph by dismissing a common division in some forms of Catholic theology between the teaching church as composed of hierarchical clerics that instruct and the hearing church as composed of the laity that listen. He not only rejects an absolute distinction between these but also reverses their order insofar as a distinction remains. In other words, there is only one church (Barth always rejected strong clergy/laity distinctions), and it hears and listens to the Word of God before it teaches. In this paragraph he takes up the dogmatic task as one of listening to the Word of God as the norm for the church. The overarching theme is that the church must listen to the Word of God before it attempts to proclaim it, and that every single member of the church is both a hearer and a teacher of the Word of God (797–98).

The Formal Task of Dogmatics (§23.1)

In this paragraph Barth comes full circle to where he began the CD—with an examination of dogmatics as the testing of the human word of proclamation (798). Because we have encountered this general topic before, this paragraph can be examined quite briefly. To begin, he recounts that because church proclamation is a Word that comes from outside the self (like Scripture and Christ), dogmatics is an examination not of an immanent revelation within the self but of a revelation that comes from without. For this reason, the church is not left alone in conversation with itself but is confronted by an external Word from God (see 799). The task of dogmatics, as the initial task of the church, is to listen to this Word. This act of reverent attention is the first and formal task of dogmatics and of the church itself and that which precedes all reflection, judgment, and speech.

This shapes how proclamation is conducted. The most important acknowledgment is that God himself speaks in preaching, and therefore human speech does not effect this divine speaking but serves it. The church begins by acknowledging that with regard to church preaching, "God Himself speaks for Himself" (800). Dogmatics is the investigation of how the church is to speak in light of the fact that God himself speaks in preaching (800–801; cf. 821–22). That God has spoken in the past presents the church with the promise that

God will speak to the church in the present: "It is because the Word of God is Jesus Christ, and Jesus Christ is for all time attested in Holy Scripture, that the promise that God Himself will speak in the proclamation of the Church is recognizable and meaningful" (801–2). Here again we see that dogmatics, as reflection on the proclamation of the church, is a reflection upon the Word of God in all of its fullness, as proclamation, Scripture, and Jesus Christ. Church proclamation is rightly understood in relation to these other two forms, and rightly understood as God's address to the church today: "That Church proclamation is the Word of God means that God speaks as much for Himself in Church proclamation as He has spoken, speaks and will speak for Himself in Jesus Christ and in the prophets and apostles as witnesses to Jesus Christ. Therefore the formal task of dogmatics in regard to Church proclamation consists in confronting it with its own law in all its transcendence, in reminding it that it is the Word of God because Jesus Christ and He alone speaks in the prophetic and apostolic witness" (802).

In brief, the task of dogmatics is "a call to the teaching Church to hear, that is, to listen to Jesus Christ as attested in Holy Scripture" (802; cf. 812). The church's only remedy against the maladies that plague its proclamation is to "seize the weapon of continually listening" (804; cf. 812). Barth is aware that in its critical task of challenging the church's speech dogmatics may come into some tension with the church. But this tension can be alleviated if it is always remembered that, in the end, dogmatics serves the church and stands in solidarity with it and shares its own concerns (805–6). For its part, the church must also recognize the danger of straying from the Word and falling into heresy and therefore acknowledge the necessity of the dogmatic task (807). The church must recognize its need for dogmatics just as dogmatics must always remember that it is a servant, and not a lord, of the church.

Barth spends some time addressing the dangers that can befall the proclamation of the church. The first of these is a focus upon beauty as its own end. The truth proclaimed by the church must have an intrinsic beauty, but this beauty cannot be its goal—its purpose cannot be simply a matter of "dilettante contemplation and enjoyment" (808). As he states, "If instead of calling to decision it becomes an object of contemplation, it ceases to be the truth" (808). He thereby draws attention in this section to the dangers not only of heresy and idolatry but also of aestheticism—a love of beauty for its own sake that divorces proclamation from its necessary call for decision.

The opposite danger of this aestheticism is a kind of "false moralistic earnestness" that focuses upon human action as that which determines the efficacy of proclamation and the church's ministry. Barth's words here are as pointed in our day as in his when he states that in this moralism the church goes about serving the Word of God "as though it is a matter of the organization and running of a business" (808). In contrast to aestheticism, this moralism does acknowledge the necessity of a decision, but decision is relegated to the realm of human agency, "as though man has to make the Word of God powerful by the weight of his own will, as though it lies in man's hands to compel decisions about it" (808). Dogmatics must finally eschew both aestheticism and moralism and fulfill its task of calling the church to listen to Christ in the Word, and do so with a reminder to the church that the church can err, but more importantly still, with a cheerful reminder of the divine promise that assures the church that, apart from any merit of its own, "it is in good hands and therefore on the right road," for the church "can and will hear the Word of God afresh" (808–10).

The Dogmatic Norm (§23.2)

That proclamation has a norm, and that dogmatics in turn does as well, is crucial for Barth. This Word that appears in Christ and is attested in Scripture is the transcendent norm against which all church proclamation is judged. This focus upon the transcendence of the Word that comes from outside the church, upon the communication of this Word through the human witnesses of Scripture, and upon the nonidentity of this Word with the human words themselves are all themes that we have already examined (813–14). Dogmatics is the discipline of the church that holds the church and its proclamation to the light of this norm in order to assess the purity of its doctrine, though it can only follow, and not produce, this Word (814–15).

Barth's definition of the norm of dogmatics is familiar if we have come this far. The norm is nothing other than "the revelation attested in Holy Scripture as God's Word" (815). He here is taking up the question of objectivity in the realm of dogmatics and its formal character—that is, its character as having a norm. In light of this, he offers a numerical list of the differing modes ("heteronomous forms") that this one singular obedience to the one true authority ("theonomy") takes in dogmatics as expressed in its norm (816).

The first is that dogmatics must have a "biblical character" (816–22). Dogmatics must follow a particular path of thought and reflection in light of Scripture's object and subject matter. The end result is that dogmatics, like the authors of Scripture, must serve as a witness to the Word of God. Second, dogmatics must have a confessional attitude (822–39). This entails that dogmatics listen not only to Scripture but also to the "voice of the teachers and doctrinal decisions" that have shaped the contemporary church (822, 828–29). In this act of listening, dogmatics must also take a particular stance, even as it argues its position before the entire church catholic (see 824–30). This straightforward defense of confessional exclusivity that attempts to be simultaneously ecumenically inclusive and representative of a catholic universality is one of the most striking aspects of Barth's dogmatic enterprise. The third and final formal characteristic of dogmatics and its obedience is its necessary willingness to listen to the contemporary teaching church, what he calls a church attitude (839–43). It must listen for the Word of God in the proclamation of the present and with regard to the contemporary situation in which the church finds itself, entering into the labor and struggles of the church today. A church attitude requires not only a particular positive path of attention but also some specific things that must be rejected by dogmatics, of which Barth mentions four: an attempt to speak in a timeless way (841); a love of form that places beauty rather than theology's object at the center (841–42); a nostalgia that begins not with the church of today but with the church of the past (842); and the opposite error, which is attention to the spirits of the age that ignores the church's past entirely (843). These are thus four things that dogmatics must reject, respectively: the temptations of timelessness, aestheticism, romanticism, and secularism. Opposed to them are the forms of obedience displayed in a biblical character, a confessional attitude, and a church attitude.

Dogmatics as a Function of the Teaching Church (§24)

In the last paragraph Barth presented dogmatics as a function of the hearing church and focused upon the external Word that comes to us and the formal task of dogmatics as one of calling the church to hear that Word as the norm of its proclamation. In this paragraph he takes up dogmatics as a function of the teaching church, one that has heard the Word and now proclaims what it has heard to the world. The material task of dogmatics is to summon the church to teach the Word, and dogmatics follows a particular and exemplary path in light of what it has heard.

The Material Task of Dogmatics (§24.1)

Jesus stated that those who are blessed are not only those who hear but also those who do what he has said, and Barth echoes this injunction in the realm of dogmatics when he insists that the task of the church is not only to hear but also to teach the Word of God. Dogmatics assists the church in this task (844). If the first, formal task of dogmatics is a critical one, testing the church's speech in light of its norm, then this material task is a positive and constructive one, teaching the Word of God as the content of dogmatics and of church proclamation (844).

Whereas in the paragraphs on Scripture Barth focused on the questions of authority (objectivity) and freedom (subjectivity) of the Word of God, here in discussing proclamation and dogmatics he is focused upon the questions of the formal task of dogmatics (i.e., a critical one in light of a norm) versus the material task of dogmatics (i.e., a constructive task in light of content to be taught). Dogmatics must have these two tasks because the church itself must be both a hearing church (objectivity) and a teaching church (subjectivity) (844). It is important to remember, he insists, that the norm and the content of the church's proclamation are indirectly identical: "In both cases we are speaking of the Word of God in the revelation attested in Scripture, where norm and object are one and yet different, just as Law and Gospel are one and yet different" (844). Therefore dogmatics must serve both the hearing and teaching church by calling it to attend to this norm and, in turn, proclaim and teach this content.

Barth seems to hold that no true hearing can in fact end with hearing; it must result in proclamation and teaching (845). Yet he is also particularly concerned about the temptation for the church to hear the Word and yet stave off the demand to preach what it has heard. Succumbing to such temptation is to fail to understand the purpose of hearing. As he insists, the task of witness and proclamation is not secondary to the hearing of the Word, but is its end and goal, for the Word of God "is given to man that he may go out into all the world and preach the Gospel to every creature" (846). Barth's judgment on the failure to fulfill this commission is harsh: "Even if the Church itself tries to be only a hearing Church, an audience entertained but finally not involved, it ceases as such to be the Church" (846). True hearing must therefore result in the church's proclamation and teaching: "The notion and obligation of pure doctrine laid upon the Church does not imply only that the purity of doctrine should be tested and restored by renewed hearing of the Word of God, but also when this happens it involves a new attempt to teach it" (846).

So if the formal dogmatic task is a critical one that guards against heresy, the material dogmatic task is a positive one that must guard against indolence. As Barth writes, "False teaching is forbidden by the norm, but silence is forbidden by the object" (849). Both dangers are to be avoided, for the church must be neither a "heretical Church" nor a "dead Church" (850). So while the critical task must continue, the church cannot use the unfinished and never-ending nature of this duty and its lack of purity of doctrine as excuses to push off its constructive work of proclamation and confession. The concern for purity is ongoing, but this can never be used as an excuse for indifference regarding the church's call to proclaim the gospel and to teach what it has heard (see 849–50). Whereas Jesus Christ is the norm that must be heard above all other voices such that heresy is averted, now dogmatics calls the church not only to hear but also to proclaim Christ to the world, for he is not only the norm of its hearing but also the content of its proclamation, "the specific theme or object to which the teaching Church is dedicated" (848; cf. 856). He is both norm and content, for it is his living presence, mediated by Scripture, and alive within the church, that governs the church as well as empowers and compels the church to proclaim him (849). This is the church's true purpose, as Barth writes: "For it is an honour and a joy, an inner necessity and a gracious privilege to serve and therefore to teach the Word of God. Indeed, it is the whole meaning of the Church's existence" (852–53).

The Dogmatic Method (§24.2)

Having discussed the dogmatic norm in the second subsection of the last paragraph, Barth in this subsection examines the dogmatic method, "the procedure which dogmatics must adopt if it is successfully to handle its material task, i.e., the unfolding and presentation of the content of the Word of God" (853). This constructive task of dogmatics is not superior to the church's preaching but stands with it and exists in its service (853). Moreover, it does not replicate the unique task of preaching but seeks to provide an exemplification of this move from hearing to teaching as it presents church doctrine (854–55).

Barth spends some time both demarcating dogmatics from preaching as well as articulating the proper work of dogmatics. The purpose of dogmatics is in the end neither to provide the final judgment upon the church in its speech nor to revive the church in its teaching. This critical and reviving function can only, in the end, be achieved by the Word of God and its singular power (854). The task of dogmatics is rather a modest one: to test the church's speech in light of this Word as norm and to serve the church's teaching of this Word as content (see 854). In this, dogmatics provides its own modest witness to the Word of God in correspondence to the singular ones of Scripture and the church's proclamation (855). Dogmatic thinking is therefore both captive to its object and lives in the freedom that this object gives (855–56). In line with his thought throughout this first volume of the CD, Barth emphasizes that it is the content and object that provides dogmatics with its method and its way (856). The dogmatic task as he construes it, as a twofold one composed of critical (formal) and constructive (material) elements, is, respectively, a task marked by a dialectic of captivity and freedom, of norm and object, and of law and gospel. Such language appears throughout this subsection in making these dialectical distinctions.

The question of the relation of God's absolute sovereignty and human freedom makes another appearance in this subsection, but now under the three themes of theonomy (sovereignty), heteronomy (the human forms of obedience), and autonomy (human freedom and decision). Precedence is again given to theonomy: "Both the autonomy and heteronomy of dogmatics describe as from below, and from the point of view of man himself, what from above and from the point of view of God is to be described as theonomy" (857). In other words, it is the divine reality and activity that precedes and frames human existence and agency, and this is as true in dogmatics as it is in any relation of God with humanity and of Christ with the church. As Barth will later write, "What we have to remember is that the autonomy of dogmatic thinking and speaking cannot be a primary but only a secondary autonomy" (884). This entails that human autonomy is always circumscribed and qualified by divine sovereignty.

This allows for the distinction of theonomy on one side, and human heteronomy and autonomy on the other. From the standpoint of the norm that governs it, dogmatic obedience is described in terms of heteronomy, whereas from the standpoint of the freedom exercised in its method, as autonomy (857). In effect, heteronomy describes the stance of obedience that dogmatics takes as it orients itself to the absolute authority of God. This obedience is concretely embodied in the biblical, confessional, and church attitudes that dogmatics adopts in light of and in obedience to the norm of the Word of God (858). Barth discussed such heteronomy in the last paragraph. Autonomy, in contrast, is the free decision of dogmatics to obey that it freely offers, what we might see again as the heart of the subjective obedience and decision that the church renders. If heteronomy in this chapter echoes the discussions of authority in the chapter on Scripture, then autonomy in this chapter echoes the discussions of freedom in that former chapter. We see again a parallel of objective and subjective elements in each chapter and in each paragraph. Barth thus explicates the dialectical relation of heteronomy and autonomy as he did earlier in outlining that of authority and freedom.

In doing so, Barth again gives precedence to heteronomy over autonomy but argues at the same time for the necessity and integrity of the latter. Dogmatics cannot simply be conformity to an external law and the external adoption of required attitudes or stances (i.e., heteronomy), but it must rather embrace its object and its task with a wholehearted and genuine free decision, self-determination, and obedience (i.e., autonomy) (858). This kind of freedom is not, however, an arbitrary choice but is a conformity to the theonomy of

God. As such, it is not simply an external compliance to an external norm, but is a true existential decision of faith and obedience resulting from a real and living encounter with a living Lord.

For Barth, the answer to objections to heteronomy, of obedience to external norms, is not to posit a radical and unfettered freedom of the self, but rather an encounter with a living God who awakens us to faith and obedience within the deepest existence of our being. Barth simply will not accept Enlightenment rejections of heteronomy in favor of autonomy but instead places both of these under theonomy. This passage on theonomy, heteronomy, and autonomy is quite difficult and requires slow and patient reading, but it is crucial for understanding his conception of the relationship of divine and human activity and agency, now addressed in dogmatics, but also applicable to his reflection on ethics. It is, in truth, an advancement from his earlier discussions of agency in both nuance and detail.

In this final section of the final paragraph of this chapter Barth is thus involved yet again in the deepest of discussions of human subjectivity and freedom, and this setting deep in the chapters is precisely where he regularly places such discussions (see esp. §6.3–4; §18; §21.2). He understands human obedience as properly given to God (theonomy), and therefore to an external authority (heteronomy), but he also stresses that this obedience must be one that we freely and authentically choose (autonomy). On the surface, these things may seem to be hopelessly in contradiction. Yet he rejects the conflict of heteronomy and autonomy precisely because he thinks that God does not enslave us but gives us true freedom. The obedience that dogmatics renders is therefore that which comes from our own free and authentic decision (see 857–60). Obedience is not to an external law, though it does originate, paradoxically, in response to an external Word. Yet this Word comes to us in our innermost selves and transforms us as a gracious gift of the Holy Spirit, and therefore this obedience is a matter of autonomy, not heteronomy (859). For this reason, the dogmatic method that is followed can only be predicated on an internally given free decision and offered to others for their adoption, but not commanded of them (860). As Barth explains, "Basically, then, the decision in relation to dogmatic method is a free choice from within and a free offer from without" (860). Yet in the end, human obedience is second to divine freedom and sovereignty, such that dogmatic work is made effective only by divine action (see 884).

This freedom is complemented by the fact that dogmatics cannot be bound to a scheme of presentation or method wherein the content of the Word of God is presented in a system. If this were the case, then the system itself would dictate the exposition and become the content of dogmatics (see 861–69). If the particular danger of the hearing church is heresy, and that of the teaching church indolence, the danger of dogmatics seems to be that of systematization, wherein the Word of God is exchanged for an overarching schema (see 883–84). Moreover, Barth opposes a doctrinal reductionism that demarcates between what is fundamental and what is peripheral based upon a principle or central doctrine or dogma. Such a principle also replaces the Word of God as the content of dogmatics with what it posits as a conception of the Word of God. Neither system nor principle can stand in for the Word of God, which must remain at the center of dogmatics, a center that is not under our control but rather is something that controls us (866, 868). As Barth concludes, "In the last resort we may say that dogmatic method consists simply in this: that the work and activity of God in His Word are honoured and feared and loved (literally) above all things" (867).

Just as dogmatics cannot be systematic, so neither can it be comprehensive—as the Word is free, so the Word is inexhaustible. For this reason, Barth rejects a comprehensive schema in favor of one that simply takes up themes found in revelation in a way similar to many past dogmatic and theological presentations (see 869–70). When all is said and done, dogmatics must follow revelation, and therefore it must be at its heart and in essence Christology. But it must include within itself not only the atonement and work of Christ in reconciliation but also the divine work of creation and redemption (872–73, 883). So while reconciliation is the epistemological key to the whole, it is important to note that Barth does not simply collapse creation and redemption into reconciliation. Neither, however, does he collapse reconciliation and redemption into creation, as if they were the completion of creation (874). God and humanity can be rightly understood only in light of reconciliation—that is, in the light of Jesus Christ and his atonement, incarnation, death, and resurrection (875). The same is true of redemption, which also can be understood only in light of reconciliation but cannot be collapsed into it (875–77). So while creation, reconciliation, and redemption at their heart are one, they must be treated in distinction from one another as well, for they are not reducible to one another, just as the Creator, Mediator, and Redeemer, as the Father, Son, and Spirit, cannot be collapsed into one another (877–79).

When this irreducible threefold division of creation, reconciliation, and redemption is understood, as well as the fact that God cannot be collapsed into these works, then Barth's remaining dogmatics are open before us. This first volume on the Word of God is followed by volumes on the doctrine of God (II), the doctrine of creation (III), and the doctrine of reconciliation (IV). The fifth and final volume, the doctrine of redemption (V), was never written.

Barth spends the final pages of this first one articulating the reasoning for this content and ordering of dogmatics (879–884).

COMMENTARY

Preaching and the Temptations of Aestheticism and Moralism

When Martin Luther thought of the Word of God, he did not simply think of it in relation to Scripture. His primary referent for it was the verbal proclamation of the gospel. He famously defined it in relation to preaching in *The Freedom of a Christian*: "The Word is the gospel of God concerning his Son, who was made flesh, suffered, rose from the dead, and was glorified through the Spirit who sanctifies. To preach Christ means to feed the soul, make it righteous, set it free, and save it, provided it believes the preaching."[3] For Barth, too, preaching was of preeminent importance. Yet his understanding of it, with its affinities to Luther, differed significantly from two other conceptions that have marked the modern period. While these are types, and therefore rarely exist in pure form, such a typology may have some comparative benefit when used to contrast differing understandings of preaching with Barth's definition of proclamation.

One type of preaching is predicated on an understanding of the gospel as transference of either experience or doctrine. In the first form, preaching is the communication of the religious feeling or fervor of the speaker, a religious experience given speech. In the second form, preaching is a kind of teaching, a transmission of information about God achieved through biblical and doctrinal instruction. In both, preaching is first and foremost a matter of communication, the transmission of either religious experience or theological truth, each thought of as standing in a long line of historical mediation from the time of Christ to today. The first focuses upon the historical communication of piety, whereas the second emphasizes the historical transmission of doctrine. But in both, it is the preacher (and the church) who is the determinative communicative agent, regardless of the great differences between these forms of preaching. Both forms of preaching are understood in terms of the transmission of an experience or of doctrine that is transferred to the hearers by which they are awakened or illumined. More ambiguous is what role God plays in such transmission.

---

3. Martin Luther, *The Freedom of a Christian*, in *Luther's Works*, vol. 31, ed. Jaroslav Pelikan and Helmut T. Lehmann (Philadelphia: Fortress, 1957), 346.

A second type of preaching is predicated on an understanding of the gospel in ethical terms. Here preaching is moral exhortation, and it, too, can be found in two forms. In the first, preaching is the call for personal moral transformation, a call to personal holiness and a changed life. In the second, it is a call for social ethical action, a call to shared efforts for justice and for a changed society and redeemed (or overthrown) systemic structures. Here, too, it is the preacher who is the exhortative agent, regardless of how different these forms of preaching may be. Both are in the end imperative calls for a changed life, whether personal or corporate. Again, more ambiguous is what role God plays in such moral exhortation. In each of these understandings of preaching, whether thought of as communicative or exhortative, proclamation might occur simply through the activity and gifts of a talented preacher. Such a preacher, in possession of native gifts and wisdom, can instruct, exhort, inspire, and even entertain us. In Barth's understanding of proclamation, by contrast, if God does not speak, the instruction, exhortation, and edification in the sermon blows away as sand slipping through our fingers, leaving us with empty hands and having a conversation with ourselves.

For this reason, Barth's understanding of preaching does not map easily onto such forms of preaching. For if one thing sets him apart from all such homiletical conceptions, it is his firm conviction that proclamation is ultimately an event in which God himself encounters his people, in which Christ announces his presence to his bride, in which the Spirit confronts the fellowship of hearers with a word of conviction and consolation—in short, one in which God is the determinative agent of proclamation and whose action is defined and clear, and in which the ambiguity in preaching pertains to specifying what role preachers themselves play. The primary agent of proclamation is therefore not the preacher, but rather the God who is preached and indeed speaks. And preaching is therefore not definitively understood to be the expression of personal or corporate piety and religious feeling, or the teaching of doctrinal content, or the exhortative call to personal or social transformation (even though preaching may include all of these). Preaching is first and foremost an event in which the crucified and risen Lord makes himself present to the church. It is an event in which Christ speaks a word of judgment and grace upon the preacher and the congregation and in which his lordship confronts us anew by the power of the Spirit. Here, too, the event character of revelation and the actualism that characterizes it mark all that Barth says about preaching. As with Scripture, it is not what the church does as it preaches, but what God does, that is truly determinative and effective.

When this truth is understood, Barth's injunctions regarding preaching are made intelligible. The particular temptations to which it might succumb also come into view. Such temptations belong, for Barth, to dogmatics, but they apply directly to the preaching that theology serves. Here we can speak of two that he directly identifies and that are relevant to our own time. The first is a love of the beauty of an elegant delivery for its own sake, the pleasure taken in an exquisite form that may well overshadow the content. This is the temptation of *aestheticism*, a celebration of the imagination that at its worst tends toward its veneration and neglects the first task proper to all preaching, the hard and rugged attention that must be given to set forth the subject matter of the gospel. Today this aestheticism often takes the form of a love for the ironic observation, for the clever witticism, for the dry turn of phrase that demonstrates a kind of detached superiority, often embodied in a minimalist refinement or accompanied with maximum self-revelation. It can be evidenced, however differently, in an ostentatious display of literary sources and of one's own worldly sophistication, or in a homespun self-deprecation, or in a revelry in the ambiguities of a dark world in which all cats are gray and all judgments complicated or suspended.

Certainly sermons might display beauty, and no form is ruled out of bounds from the start.[4] But aestheticism can become a danger not only for its tendency to value form over content, and therein for the correspondent danger it introduces to smuggle in a new content altogether, but also for its distaste for and avoidance of the one thing that preaching must drive toward at the end without compromise: the call that opposes all detachment and that exhorts a decision (808). Preaching announces Christ, and the message of the gospel calls into question not only the wisdom of the world but also its conceptions of what is beautiful (1 Cor. 1:18). This message includes with it a call to a faith and obedience that stands under the shadow of a cross that lacks all aesthetic appeal. Yet the church that preaches cannot be silent here. Barth's words bear repeating: "Even if the Church itself tries to be only a hearing Church, an audience entertained but finally not involved, it ceases as such to be the Church" (846).

A different temptation falls along other lines and may afflict those who escape the first one. This is the temptation of moralism, at its best posing a prophetic challenge, but one that, when torn from the finished work of Christ and all that work accomplished and signifies, ends up with a cheap grace that exonerates a congregation that revels in the condemnation pronounced on "ungodly" pagans, but that has no awareness of its own sins or need for forgiveness. It may, alternatively, result in a graceless exhortation that browbeats

---

4. Barth certainly did not reject beauty as such, though he was wary of its dangers in relation to theology. See his discussion in *CD* II/1, 651–52.

a congregation that despairs in its own failures, the quiet acquiescence of a helpless people in a condemnation deserved. In both of these forms of moralism the gospel is nothing but imperative, an activism that focuses upon the maxim "God helps those that help themselves," and in the end elides even the beginning of that maxim so that it effectively trusts only the help that the church gives itself and the world. This is a view in which all that happens—the effectiveness of the sermon, and all that follows from it in the church's life—is a matter determined by the energy and exertion of the human will. At its worst, it places the salvation of the world in the hands of the church, with the kingdom's realization, whether in a person or in society, hanging in the balance of human effort and success.

Such "moral earnestness," in Barth's words, sees preaching and the Christian life solely in the category of human will and activity. It matters not whether this is a personal or social earnestness, nor from what side of the theological spectrum such views originate. In the end, the church is the determinative agent of change, even as it overlooks the truth of the gospel of Christ, whose acknowledgment must include at the very least "the truth that absolutely nothing can be done in our own strength" (808). In such preaching, it is indeed true that ethics swallows up dogmatics, and that the indicative of the gospel (that which God has done in Christ) is set aside for the imperative of the personally or socially urgent (that which we ourselves must do). Such preaching in time grows tiresome, not least because it either provides cheap and insincere exoneration or, more typically, places a burden upon others that no one can bear. This confusion of proper and improper burdens does not respect the great distinction between the Lord who has borne all things for our salvation and those who are called to bear the burden of witness to that fact. This is a burden for those who are weary and heavy-laden and who need rest, even as others may rightly at times require prophetic confrontation (Matt. 11:29–30). But the discernment of what needs to be spoken in any given moment is a matter of great pastoral wisdom—and ultimately a matter of divine conviction.

If preaching is to be kept from such aestheticism and moralism, it must remember always that Christ himself through the power of the Spirit makes proclamation effective. Preaching must set him forth before his people. Christ is more beautiful than our rhetorical forms or clever phrases, and the reality of what he has accomplished, truly understood, is a greater call to faith and, yes, obedience than any heavy-handed tactics of moral earnestness can accomplish. There is a place for all of these things—for religious fervor, for solid doctrinal teaching, for personal exhortation, for corporate challenge, even for beauty—if they are always subjected to and disciplined by the gospel. But that is the key.

When they take on their own life, when they overshadow the message of the cross, then the personality of the pastor takes up a larger role than is merited. A cult of personality may come in its wake, and this has plagued the numerous tributaries of the church. Preachers, as all Christians, are called not to be forceful and remarkable personalities but to be witnesses who point away from themselves to Christ. Perhaps a sermon can be rightly prepared and framed if in the pastor's study the words "He must increase, but I must decrease" are kept ever in mind (John 3:30). The sermon's effectiveness, however, ultimately lies beyond the work done in the study. When this is remembered, it should engender in the pastor great humility, but also full confidence.

The Relation of the Church and the Theological Academy

The theological academy and the church often seem to be on diverging courses, or even parallel tracks. Here Barth never lost his pastoral instincts, even if his mature labors took place in academic appointments. For him, dogmatics (and formal theology generally) served the church. Neither academy nor church has fared well when the reciprocal relationship between them has been neglected from either side. He was well aware of the temptation to theoretical pursuits in the academy that left the church far behind. He was also aware that when ecclesial practice of any kind (whether preaching, liturgy, instruction, or service) was cut off from formal and critical theological examination, the church was prone to move forward with little reflection in a mindless form of habit or a triumphalism blind to its shortcomings. Yet in the end, he subjugated the task of dogmatics to proclamation and the church, rather than the church to the academy. He could starkly underline not only the provisional nature of theological work but also its final purpose: "All the conclusions of dogmatics must be intended, accepted and understood as fluid material for further work. None of the results of dogmatics—really none at all—can be important. The only important thing is the activity of the Church, denoted by the results so far attained, in its striving for purity of doctrine" (769).

These are words of critical exhortation that perhaps should be offered to the churches today. A failure of catechesis (instruction) is everywhere evident. Persons who have been raised within the church or converted to it often lack a basic knowledge of Scripture and its overarching narrative. They often have never learned to think reflectively upon the content that Scripture proclaims or upon the demands of the discipleship that it enjoins. They often exhibit a staggering blindness with regard to the temptations on the right and the left that press against the church and pose a constant threat to it in an offer to exchange the gospel for a political platform. Such things are all true.

Yet Barth had hope for the church precisely because he never placed his hope in the church itself.[5] His hope lay elsewhere. This kept him both from a theological superiority marked by a haughty gaze from one who viewed the church from the academy's towers, and from a despair that abandoned the church altogether. In contrast, he insisted that theological work stands within the church and shares its joys, sorrows, and commission. And it is this conviction, he maintained, that allowed dogmatics to do its proper work, work that, in reality, may be presently done "more seriously and fruitfully in the unassuming Bible class of an unknown country parson than in the most exact academic discussion imaginable." There was no room for dogmatic boasting here: "School dogmatics should not try to regard itself as better dogmatics, only as a necessary second form of dogmatics" (CD I/1, 279).

Barth's exhortation is therefore properly given not to the church but to his own humble practice of dogmatics. All who serve as teachers for the church, located in the academy, might do well to consider his words, which are, of course, an implicit challenge to those in the church as much as they are an explicit and direct challenge to those who serve the church in the academy: "Dogmatics can give this summons with so much the more authority and emphasis the more it realizes its own solidarity with the teaching Church. It must not speak and think in the manner of a timeless Church discipline, but with full participation in the energies and hopes, the cares and struggles of the Church of its own age" (805).

QUESTIONS FOR REFLECTION

- How should preaching be understood? Why does the church preach? How does Barth challenge common conceptions and practices of preaching? How does he challenge a cult of personality with regard to pastors?
- Does bad theology lead to bad preaching? Does good theology lead to good preaching? Why or why not? What should be the relationship between theology and preaching? Between the church and the theological academy (seminary or divinity school)?
- Is the preaching and teaching of the Word of God "the whole meaning of the Church's existence" (852–53)? Why or why not?

5. By this point, it should be clear that this conviction was at the very center of what he understood to be the Evangelical (i.e., Protestant) witness.

- What is the place of prayer in relation to preaching? Why does Barth think that prayer is so important for preaching and for dogmatics?
- Is heresy still a category that is appropriate to use today? What makes something "heretical"? Can some views be properly deemed heretical? By what standards is this decided? Who is authorized to decide this? Why is heresy a necessary category if we are to have a conception of truth? Why does Barth consider a church that is silent to be as threatening as a heretical one?
- Is indolence (laziness) a danger to preaching? In what way? How does indolence make itself present in the life of the pastor? In the members of the church at large who listen to preaching?
- Consider what it means for preaching and teaching to exhibit the following:

  A "biblical character"
  A "confessional attitude"
  A "church attitude"

  What might such things look like for preaching? For church instruction of youth and adults? For formal theological education (including dogmatics)?
- Consider and reflect upon what Barth means when he speaks of the following and why he says that dogmatics (and preaching) must reject them.

  Timelessness
  Aestheticism
  Romanticism
  Secularism

  Do you agree with Barth's estimation of each of these? Why or why not?
- Must theology be practiced from within a specific tradition of the church (i.e., Roman Catholic, Eastern Orthodox, Lutheran, Reformed, Baptist)? Why or why not?

Conclusion and Commencement

If you have made it this far, much of the *CD* lies behind you, but much more lies ahead. I hope you will continue.

It should perhaps be clear by now why some have found Barth so compelling, but it may become even more apparent as you read on. For if Barth's theology is about anything, it is about the grandeur of the gospel—a gospel that began in eternity as God chose to be God for us, a gospel that proclaims that God created the world as the context for his covenant with us and made the world itself the object of his love (John 3:16), a gospel that declares that this loving God took flesh and lived among us, establishing a fellowship with us and a freedom for us, a freedom that the world cannot give. It is the gospel of Jesus Christ who is "the being of the Church" and its very Lord and life, and the Lord and life of all. If anything, Barth's description of the gospel grew ever more grand and vibrant in the ensuing volumes of the *CD*.

Barth was once asked, during a trip to America late in his life, if he could summarize his theology in a single sentence, having written thousands upon thousands of pages of theological exposition. He answered, "Jesus loves me, this I know, for the Bible tells me so." This simple statement, one readily grasped by a child, consumed Barth for his entire life and led to ever-new avenues of exploration, reflection, wonder, and mystery. It could be argued that the *CD* in its entirety is a commentary on John 3:16 written over thirty years and thousands of pages, and one that was never finished. That the final chapter was never written should perhaps not surprise us. For the very gospel that can be grasped by a child is also one that could ever amaze an old man who had spent his life seeking "to grasp how wide and long and high and

deep is the love of Christ, and to know this love that surpasses knowledge"
(Eph. 3:18–19 NIV).

Barth may not be considered by some to belong to the upper echelons
of theologians and thought unworthy to take his place among the likes of
Luther and Calvin, though time is perhaps a better judge than we about
such things. Regardless, it is not difficult to argue that Barth was the most
important and influential Protestant theologian of the twentieth century.
He shared with Luther and Calvin a singular focus upon Christ, the gospel,
and Scripture. For Barth, theology was, in short, about God, a God who
was free and above all our ways and thoughts. Yet Barth in time came to
realize that this God did not exclude, but welcomed and established, a life
with us. This was the secret, he learned, of the humanity of God, a God
who not only took on flesh but also did this so that all flesh might live in
fellowship with him. In this joyful announcement of Emmanuel, "God with
us," Barth stands in a line that stretches back to the Reformers and all the
way to the apostles.

Barth also shared, however, in the fallen humanity of those before. He was
a person of not only staggering achievements but also real failings, and there
is no reason or warrant to paper over or defend them. But just as we neither
exonerate nor dismiss Luther as a teacher because of his shameful late statements regarding the Jews, nor commend the execution of Servetus in which
Calvin played his part even as we listen to Calvin's wisdom, so Barth's failures
should neither be lightly dismissed nor made the ground for a definitive final
dismissal of his work.

At the end of the day, the church long past wisely decided that we are not
to be sacramental Donatists, but neither are we to be doctrinal ones. For just
as the sacraments have their enduring meaning and efficacy not due to the
impeccable character of those who administer them but because of the God
who honors them, so the doctrinal teaching of the church's sons and daugh-
ters must be judged on its own merit as tested against Scripture's witness,
even as their sins are in no way overlooked, rationalized, or excused. In this
respect, time will reveal whether Barth's witness in the CD has outlasted his
own personal failings and continues to instruct the church. For in the end, all
cathedrals of enduring stone are built by persons of clay. The cathedrals outlive
them and take on a significance beyond the personal lives of their builders.
Such structures must also be judged by standards that cannot be limited to
those applied to the character of the builders themselves. And so it is here
too. Barth's cathedral continues to draw and edify its steady stream of visi-
tors, if only because it raises our eyes, once again, to mysteries far above its
walls. Many continue to find it so. Whether it will continue to be a place of

instruction and edification for the church, or will in time fall into neglect and ruin, is something only the future can disclose. Barth himself rested content in the fact that the ultimate judgment of his work lay not with his impatient contemporaries or even with the future, but rested with the One who resided beyond time itself and yet who entered it for our forgiveness (1 Tim. 1:15–17).

Appendix

What follows are three reading plans: one for reading volume 1 of the CD in one year, one for reading the entire CD in one year, and one for reading the entire CD over a five-year period. All are based upon a five-day reading week. The pages of the CD are roughly divided into thirds, which are designated with a, b, and c. A page and letter is occasionally duplicated if a section begins close to the beginning or end of a page.

Church Dogmatics Volume 1 (I/1–I/2) in One Year

		Day 1	Day 2	Day 3	Day 4	Day 5	Total Pages	§
I/1	Week 1	3–7b	7c–11b	11c–17a	17b–21a	21b–24	24	1
	Week 2	25–31b	31c–36a	36b–40a	40b–44	47–51a	27	2, 3
	Week 3	51b–55a	55b–61a	61b–65a	65b–71b	71c–75b	24	3
	Week 4	75c–80a	80b–87	88–92b	92c–99a	99b–104a	29	3, 4
	Week 5	104b–109a	109b–111a	111b–115a	115b–120b	120c–124	20	4
	Week 6	125–132b	132c–136b	136c–139a	139b–143a	143b–149b	25	5
	Week 7	149c–156b	156c–162a	162b–165a	165b–168b	168c–174a	25	5
	Week 8	174b–181b	181c–186	187–190b	190c–198a	198b–201	27	5, 6
	Week 9	202–208b	208c–214a	214b–218a	218b–223b	223c–227b	26	6
	Week 10	227c–230a	230b–236a	236b–244a	244b–247	248–252a	25	6, 7
	Week 11	252b–255a	255b–259a	259b–266a	266b–269b	269c–275a	23	7
	Week 12	275b–279	280–287b	287c–292	295–300a	300b–304a	29	7, 8
	Week 13	304b–308a	308b–311b	311c–315a	315b–320b	320c–324b	20	8
	Week 14	324c–329a	329b–333b	333c–339a	339b–344a	344b–347	23	8
	Week 15	348–353b	353c–358b	358c–362b	362c–368b	368c–375b	28	9

		Day 1	Day 2	Day 3	Day 4	Day 5	Total Pages	§
	Week 16	375c–378a	378b–383	384–390a	390b–394a	394b–398	23	9, 10
	Week 17	399–406a	406b–410b	410c–414a	414b–420b	420c–427b	29	10, 11
	Week 18	427c–431a	431b–437	438–441b	441c–447	448–452b	25	11, 12
	Week 19	452c–457a	457b–462a	462b–466b	466c–473b	473c–479a	27	12
I/2	Week 20	479b–483a	483b–489	1–7a	7b–13a	13b–17a	27	12, 13
	Week 21	17b–23b	23c–25a	25b–29b	29c–35b	35c–39b	22	13
	Week 22	39c–44	45–49a	49b–54b	54c–59a	59b–63b	24	13, 14
	Week 23	63c–66b	66c–70a	70b–72a	72b–80a	80b–84b	21	14
	Week 24	84c–89a	89b–94a	94b–101a	101b–106b	106c–113a	29	14
	Week 25	113b–121	122–125b	125c–132a	132b–136a	136b–139b	26	14, 15
	Week 26	139c–146	147–151a	151b–155a	155b–159a	159b–165a	26	15
	Week 27	165b–171	172–176a	176b–181b	181c–184a	184b–188a	23	15
	Week 28	188b–196a	196b–202	203–213a	213b–220b	220c–223a	35	15, 16
	Week 29	223b–227a	227b–232a	232b–235b	235c–239a	239b–242b	19	16
	Week 30	242c–246a	246b–249b	249c–257a	257b–260b	260c–265b	23	16
	Week 31	265c–269b	269c–272b	272c–279	280–284b	284c–291a	26	16
	Week 32	291b–297b	297c–301a	301b–307b	307c–310a	310b–314a	23	17
	Week 33	314b–318b	318c–325b	325c–331a	331b–337a	337b–344a	30	17
	Week 34	344b–348a	348b–352a	352b–357b	357c–361	362–367a	23	17
	Week 35	367b–371b	371c–377a	377b–380b	380c–386b	386c–394b	27	17, 18
	Week 36	394c–401a	401b–404a	404b–408a	408b–411a	411b–414b	20	18
	Week 37	414c–423	424–430a	430b–434b	434c–440a	440b–444a	30	18
	Week 38	444b–450a	450b–454	457–461a	461b–466a	466b–472	28	18, 19
	Week 39	473–478b	478c–481a	481b–485a	485b–492a	492b–497a	25	19
	Week 40	497b–502a	502b–506a	506b–512a	512b–519b	519c–526	29	19
	Week 41	527–532a	532b–537	538–541b	541c–546b	546c–551b	25	19, 20
	Week 42	551c–554a	554b–559a	559b–564a	564b–572	573–576b	25	20
	Week 43	576c–580	581–585a	585b–587	588–597a	597b–603a	27	20
	Week 44	603b–609a	609b–612b	612c–616a	616b–620a	620b–625b	22	20
	Week 45	625c–631a	631b–637a	637b–642a	642b–647a	647b–651b	30	20
	Week 46	651c–655a	655b–660	661–669a	669b–674b	674c–685b	34	20, 21
	Week 47	685c–695a	695b–699a	699b–707b	707c–710a	710b–715a	30	21
	Week 48	715b–722a	722b–727a	727b–731b	731c–740	743–750a	35	21, 22
	Week 49	750b–758a	758b–763a	763b–766a	766b–772b	772c–777b	27	22
	Week 50	777c–782a	782b–790a	790b–796	797–804a	804b–812b	35	22, 23
	Week 51	812c–822a	822b–830	831–839b	839c–843	844–848a	36	23, 24
	Week 52	848b–853a	853b–861a	861b–868a	868b–875b	875c–884	36	24

Church Dogmatics (I/1–IV/4) in One Year

		Day 1	Day 2	Day 3	Day 4	Day 5	Total Pages	§
I/1	Week 1	3–36a	36b–71b	71b–87	88–124	125–143a	143	1, 2, 3, 4, 5
	Week 2	143b–186	187–227b	227c–247	248–292	295–333b	190	5, 6, 7, 8
	Week 3	333c–347	348–383	384–414a	414b–447	448–489	156	8, 9, 10, 11, 12
I/2	Week 4	1–25a	25b–44	45–70a	70b–121	122–146	146	13, 14, 15
	Week 5	147–171	172–202	203–242b	242c–279	280–297b	151	15, 16, 17
	Week 6	297c–325a	325b–361	362–401a	401b–430a	430b–454	157	17, 18
	Week 7	457–472	473–512a	512b–537	538–572	573–585a	131	19, 20
	Week 8	585b–609a	609b–637a	637b–660	661–695a	695b–740	155	20, 21
	Week 9	743–774a	774b–796	797–843	844–884	Catch up	144	22, 23, 24
II/1	Week 10	3–31a	31b–62	63–97b	97c–128a	128b–162b	162	25, 26
	Week 11	162c–178	179–204a	204b–254	257–272b	272c–297a	135	26, 27, 28
	Week 12	297b–321	322–350	351–406a	406b–439	Catch up	142	28, 29, 30
	Week 13	440–461a	461b–490a	490b–522a	522b–563b	563c–586	147	31
II/2	Week 14	587–607	608–645b	645c–677	3–34b	34c–76a	167	31, 32
	Week 15	76b–93	94–145a	145b–175a	175b–194	195–233a	157	32, 33, 34
	Week 16	233b–259b	259c–305	306–340b	340c–363a	363b–388a	155	34, 35
	Week 17	388b–409	410–449b	449c–475b	475c–506	509–542	154	35, 36
	Week 18	543–583b	583c–613a	613b–630	631–661b	661c–683a	141	36, 37, 38
III/1	Week 19	683b–708b	708c–732	733–763	764–781	3–41	139	38, 39, 40
	Week 20	42–71b	71c–94b	94c–133a	133b–156a	156b–191a	149	41
	Week 21	191b–228a	228c–253a	253b–288a	288b–317b	317c–329	138	41
III/2	Week 22	330–365	366–388b	388c–414	3–29b	29c–54	139	42, 43
	Week 23	55–90a	90b–132a	132b–149a	149b–175b	175c–202	148	43, 44
	Week 24	203–222a	222b–250a	250b–285a	285b–324	325–366a	164	45, 46
	Week 25	366b–394a	394b–436	437–455a	455b–485a	485b–511a	145	46, 47
III/3	Week 26	511b–540	541–572a	572b–607a	607b–640	3–33b	162	47, 48
	Week 27	33c–57	58–90a	90b–119a	119b–154b	154c–185b	152	48, 49
	Week 28	185c–211a	211b–238	239–288	289–312a	312b–334a	149	49, 50
	Week 29	334b–349a	349b–380b	380c–401b	401c–418a	418b–450a	116	50, 51
III/4	Week 30	450b–476	477–511a	511b–531	3–31	32–72	133	51, 52, 53
	Week 31	73–115	116–148	149–183a	183b–213a	213b–240a	170	53, 54
	Week 32	240b–285a	285b–323	324–352a	352b–376a	376b–397a	157	54, 55
	Week 33	397b–428b	428c–470a	470b–502a	502b–527b	527c–564	167	55
IV/1	Week 34	565–594	595–618a	618b–647a	647b–685	3–21	142	56, 57
	Week 35	22–54b	54b–78	79–122a	122b–154	157–184a	163	57, 58, 59

		Day 1	Day 2	Day 3	Day 4	Day 5	Total Pages	§
	Week 36	184b–210	211–240a	240b–283a	283b–313a	313b–332b	148	59
	Week 37	332c–357	358–387a	387b–413b	413c–445b	445c–478a	146	59, 60
	Week 38	478b–513	514–544a	544b–568a	568b–608b	608c–642	164	60, 61
IV/2	Week 39	643–668a	668b–701b	701c–739a	740–779	3–31a	164	62, 63
	Week 40	31b–69a	69b–104a	104b–131a	131b–156b	156c–192b	161	64
	Week 41	192c–224a	224b–264b	264c–292a	292b–322a	322b–348a	156	64
	Week 42	348b–377	378–403a	403b–432b	432c–464a	464b–498	150	64, 65
	Week 43	499–533a	533b–553a	553b–584a	584b–613	614–641a	143	66, 67
	Week 44	641b–676a	676b–698b	698c–726	727–751a	751b–783a	142	67, 68
IV/3.1	Week 45	783b–811b	811c–840	3–38a	38b–70a	70b–99a	152	68, 69
	Week 46	99b–135b	135c–165a	165b–196a	196b–230b	230c–274b	175	69
	Week 47	274c–303a	303b–333a	333b–367	368–388b	388c–418a	144	69, 70
IV/3.2	Week 48	418b–434a	434b–478	481–520b	520c–554b	554c–576	158	71
	Week 49	577–599a	599b–614b	614c–647b	647c–680	681–701a	125	71, 72
	Week 50	701b–728b	728c–762a	762b–795b	795c–830a	830b–854a	153	72
IV/4	Week 51	854b–878	879–901	902–942	3–31a	31b–67a	155	72, 73, Fragments
	Week 52	67b–100b	100c–127a	127b–162a	162b–189b	189c–213	146	Fragments

Church Dogmatics (I/1–IV/4) in Five Years

		Day 1	Day 2	Day 3	Day 4	Day 5	Total Pages	§
I/1	Week 1	3–11b	11c–17a	17b–24	25–31b	31c–36a	36	1, 2
	Week 2	36b–44	47–53b	53c–61b	61c–67b	67c–71b	35	2, 3
	Week 3	71c–77a	77b–81b	81c–87	88–99a	99b–106	35	3, 4
	Week 4	107–111a	111b–120b	120c–124	125–132b	132c–136b	30	4, 5
	Week 5	136c–143a	143b–148b	148c–156b	156c–162a	162b–165a	29	5
	Week 6	165b–174a	174b–181b	181c–186	187–190b	190c–198a	33	5, 6
	Week 7	198b–204b	204c–209b	209c–214a	214b–223b	223c–227b	29	6
	Week 8	227c–237c	237c–244b	244b–247	248–254b	254c–261b	34	6, 7
	Week 9	261c–266b	266c–275a	275b–283a	283b–292	Catch up	31	7
	Week 10	295–304a	304b–308b	308c–313	314–320b	320c–324b	32	8
	Week 11	324c–329b	329c–333b	333c–339a	339b–347	348–353b	29	8, 9
	Week 12	353c–358b	358c–362b	362c–368b	368c–375b	375c–383	30	9
	Week 13	384–390a	390b–398	Catch up	399–406a	406b–409b	26	10, 11
	Week 14	409c–414a	414b–420b	420c–427b	427c–437	438–447	38	11
	Week 15	Catch up	448–453a	453b–457a	457b–466b	466c–473b	27	12

		Day 1	Day 2	Day 3	Day 4	Day 5	Total Pages	§
I/2	Week 16	473c–487b	487b–489	Catch up	1–7a	7b–10a	26	12, 13
	Week 17	10b–13b	13b–17a	17b–25b	25c–29b	29c–35b	25	13
	Week 18	35c–39c	39c–44	45–50a	50b–54c	54c–58b	23	13, 14
	Week 19	58c–66b	66c–70a	70b–78b	78c–84c	84c–94a	36	14
	Week 20	Catch up	94b–101b	101c–106b	106c–113b	113c–121	27	14
	Week 21	122–125b	125c–132a	132b–138a	138b–146	Catch up	25	15
	Week 22	147–151a	151b–159a	159b–162a	162b–167b	167c–171	25	15
	Week 23	172–176b	176c–184b	184c–196a	196b–202	Catch up	31	15
	Week 24	203–206b	206c–213a	213b–220b	220c–223a	223b–232a	30	16
	Week 25	232b–242b	242c–246b	246c–257a	257b–265b	Catch up	33	16
	Week 26	265c–270a	270b–279	280–283b	Catch up	Catch up	18	16
	Week 27	283c–291a	291b–297b	297c–301a	301b–307b	307c–314a	31	17
	Week 28	314b–318b	318c–325b	325c–331a	331b–339a	Catch up	25	17
	Week 29	339b–344a	344b–352b	352c–357b	357c–361	362–368a	29	17, 18
	Week 30	368b–371b	371c–377a	377b–380b	380c–389b	389c–401b	33	18
	Week 31	401c–407b	407c–414b	414c–423	424–430a	430b–441a	40	18
	Week 32	Catch up	441b–450a	450b–454	457–460b	460c–466a	25	18, 19
	Week 33	466b–472	473–481a	481b–485a	485b–492a	492b–495a	29	19
	Week 34	495b–502a	502b–508a	508b–512a	512b–519b	519c–526	31	19
	Week 35	527–530a	530b–537	538–541b	541c–544b	544c–550a	24	19, 20
	Week 36	550b–554a	554b–559a	559b–564b	564c–572	573–578a	28	20
	Week 37	578b–585a	585b–590	591–596b	596c–603a	603b–609b	31	20
	Week 38	609b–615b	615b–620a	620b–629a	629b–637a	637b–641a	32	20
	Week 39	641b–644b	644c–648b	648c–654a	654b–660	Catch up	19	20
	Week 40	661–666a	666b–672a	672b–679a	679b–685a	685b–690b	30	21
	Week 41	690c–695a	695b–702	703–709b	709c–715a	715b–722b	32	21
	Week 42	722c–727a	727b–736a	736b–740	Catch up	743–750a	28	21
	Week 43	750b–758a	758b–763a	763b–768b	768c–775a	775b–782a	32	21, 22
	Week 44	Catch up	782b–787b	787c–792a	792b–796	797–804a	22	22, 23
	Week 45	804b–812b	812c–816b	816b–822b	822b–828b	828c–833a	29	23
	Week 46	833b–839b	839c–843	844–853a	853b–861a	861b–866a	33	23, 24
	Week 47	866b–870b	870c–877a	877b–884	Catch up	Catch up	18	24
II/1	Week 48	3–9b	9c–16a	16b–21a	21b–31a	31b–36a	33	25
	Week 49	36b–43a	43b–51a	51b–57a	57b–62	63–68a	32	25, 26
	Week 50	68b–73b	73c–79a	79b–84	85–88a	88b–97c	29	26
	Week 51	97c–105a	105b–112a	112b–117a	117b–123b	123c–128a	31	26
	Week 52	128b–136b	136c–142a	142b–147a	147b–154b	154c–162b	34	26

		Day 1	Day 2	Day 3	Day 4	Day 5	Total Pages	§
	Week 53	162c–168b	168c–172b	172c–178	179–186a	186b–193a	31	26, 27
	Week 54	193b–199a	199b–204a	204b–211a	211b–219	220–223	30	27
	Week 55	224–231b	231c–236	237–243b	243c–249a	249b–254	31	27
	Week 56	257–262b	262c–268a	268b–272b	272c–283b	283c–287b	33	28
	Week 57	287c–297b	Catch up	297c–304a	304b–313a	313b–321	34	28
	Week 58	322–330b	330c–337b	337c–341b	341c–350	351–353a	32	29, 30
	Week 59	353b–358a	358b–363b	363c–368a	368b–375b	375c–381a	28	30
	Week 60	381b–386a	386b–393b	393c–398b	398c–406a	406b–411b	30	30
	Week 61	411c–416b	416c–422a	422b–427a	427b–432a	432b–439	28	30
	Week 62	440–450a	450b–454a	454b–461a	461b–464a	464b–470a	31	31
	Week 63	470b–477b	477c–483a	483b–490a	490b–494b	494c–499a	29	31
	Week 64	499b–506b	506c–512b	512c–518a	518b–522a	522b–528b	29	31
	Week 65	528c–532a	532b–538a	538b–542b	542c–549a	549b–558b	30	31
	Week 66	558c–563b	563c–569	570–575a	575b–579a	579b–586	28	31
	Week 67	587–597a	597b–601b	601c–607	608–615a	615a–623a	37	31
	Week 68	623a–629b	629c–634a	634b–640b	640c–645b	645c–653b	30	31
	Week 69	653c–659b	659c–666b	666c–677	Catch up	Catch up	24	31
II/2	Week 70	3–11b	11c–18b	18c–24a	24b–30a	30b–34b	34	32
	Week 71	34c–38a	38b–44b	44c–51b	51c–58b	58c–62a	28	32
	Week 72	62b–67a	67b–72a	72b–76b	76c–84a	84b–93	31	32
	Week 73	94–99b	99c–106a	106b–110a	110b–115a	115b–120	27	33
	Week 74	121–127a	127b–133a	133b–138a	138b–145a	145b–155a	35	33
	Week 75	155b–161a	161b–168b	168c–175a	175b–181a	181b–186b	31	33
	Week 76	186c–194	Catch up	195–201	202–205a	205b–213b	27	33, 34
	Week 77	213c–219b	219c–223b	223c–228a	228b–233a	233b–240b	27	34
	Week 78	240c–247b	247c–252a	252b–259b	259c–267b	267c–273b	33	34
	Week 79	273c–278b	278c–284b	284c–290a	290b–296a	296b–300a	27	34
	Week 80	300b–305	306–313a	313b–320	321–326a	326b–333b	33	34, 35
	Week 81	333c–340b	340c–347b	347c–354b	354c–358b	358c–363a	30	35
	Week 82	363b–366b	366c–372a	372b–377b	377c–384a	384b–389b	26	35
	Week 83	389c–393a	393b–398b	398c–403a	403b–409b	410–419b	30	35
	Week 84	419c–426b	426c–431b	431c–435b	435c–442b	442c–449b	30	35
	Week 85	449c–458b	458c–463b	463c–467b	467c–475b	475c–480b	31	35
	Week 86	480c–488a	488b–494a	494b–501a	501b–506	Catch up	26	35
	Week 87	509–515b	515c–520a	520b–528a	528b–535a	535b–542	36	36
	Week 88	543–551	552–559b	559c–565	566–571a	571b–577a	35	36, 37
	Week 89	577b–583b	583c–588a	588b–597a	597b–602a	602b–608a	31	37

		Day 1	Day 2	Day 3	Day 4	Day 5	Total Pages	§
	Week 90	608b–613a	613b–620b	620c–623b	623c–630	Catch up	22	37
	Week 91	631–636a	636b–641a	641b–649a	649b–653a	653b–661b	31	38
	Week 92	661c–669a	669b–675b	675c–683b	683–688b	688c–693b	32	38
	Week 93	693b–700b	700c–708b	708c–716a	716b–726b	726c–732	39	38
	Week 94	Catch up	733–741	741–748b	748c–754a	754b–763	31	39
III/1	Week 95	764–768b	768c–772b	772c–781	3–10	11–17b	34	39, 40
	Week 96	17c–22a	22b–28b	28c–34b	34c–41	42–49a	32	40, 41
	Week 97	49b–56a	56b–61a	61b–65a	65b–72a	72b–80b	31	41
	Week 98	80c–87a	87b–94b	94c–102b	102c–110a	110b–117a	37	41
	Week 99	117b–124b	124c–130a	130b–133a	133b–141b	141c–147a	30	41
	Week 100	147b–152a	152b–156a	156b–161b	161c–168a	168b–176b	29	41
	Week 101	176c–181a	181b–187a	187b–191a	191b–197a	197b–202a	26	41
	Week 102	202b–206	207–213a	213b–219b	219c–228b	Catch up	26	41
	Week 103	228c–235b	235c–243a	243b–249a	249b–255b	255c–262b	27	41
	Week 104	262c–269a	269b–276b	276c–281b	282c–288a	288b–297a	28	41
	Week 105	297b–306	307–317b	317c–324a	324b–329	330–340a	34	41, 42
	Week 106	340b–344b	344c–350b	350c–357	358–365	366–375a	31	42
	Week 107	375b–383a	383b–388b	388c–396a	396b–405	406–414	31	42
III/2	Week 108	3–11a	11b–19a	19b–27b	27c–36b	36c–42a	42	43
	Week 109	42b–46	47–54	55–62a	62b–68a	68b–71b	29	43, 44
	Week 110	71c–79b	79c–90a	90b–96b	96c–102b	102c–109a	38	44
	Week 111	109b–115a	115b–122b	122c–128b	128c–132a	132b–139b	30	44
	Week 112	139c–147a	147b–157a	157b–164a	164b–172b	172c–175b	36	44
	Week 113	175c–186b	186c–192b	192c–202	Catch up	203–210a	35	44, 45
	Week 114	210b–217a	217b–222a	222b–229a	229b–236b	236c–242b	32	45
	Week 115	242c–250a	250b–260a	260b–265a	265b–274a	274b–285a	43	45
	Week 116	Catch up	285b–291a	291b–296a	296b–301a	301b–308	23	45
	Week 117	309–316a	316b–324	325–331b	331c–340a	340b–344a	36	45, 46
	Week 118	344b–347a	347b–354b	354c–358b	358c–366b	366c–374a	30	46
	Week 119	374b–379	380–383b	383c–390a	390b–394a	394b–399a	25	46
	Week 120	399b–406a	406b–409a	409b–418a	418b–424a	424b–428a	29	46
	Week 121	428b–436	437–441b	441c–447b	447c–454a	454b–459a	31	46, 47
	Week 122	459b–463b	463c–466b	466c–474a	474b–478a	478b–485a	26	47
	Week 123	485b–490b	490c–497a	497b–502a	502b–511b	Catch up	26	47
	Week 124	511c–515b	515c–520b	520c–525a	525b–532b	532c–540	29	47
	Week 125	541–546b	546c–553b	553c–558a	558b–566a	566b–572a	32	47
	Week 126	572b–576b	576c–581a	581b–587a	587b–593b	593c–598b	26	47

		Day 1	Day 2	Day 3	Day 4	Day 5	Total Pages	§
	Week 127	598c–602b	602c–607a	607b–610b	610c–616a	616b–620a	22	47
	Week 128	620b–625a	625b–630a	630b–633b	633c–640	Catch up	20	47
III/3	Week 129	3–8a	8a–14a	14b–18b	18c–26b	26c–33b	33	48
	Week 130	33c–38b	38c–43a	43b–50b	50c–57	58–61a	28	48, 49
	Week 131	61b–67b	67c–73b	73c–78a	78b–84b	84c–90b	29	49
	Week 132	90c–94b	94c–100a	100b–107a	107b–112b	112c–117a	27	49
	Week 133	117b–120b	120c–124b	124c–131b	131c–134b	134c–139a	22	49
	Week 134	139b–146a	146b–154b	154c–159b	159c–164a	164b–169a	30	49
	Week 135	169b–175a	175b–183a	183b–186b	186c–193b	193c–198b	29	49
	Week 136	198c–204a	204b–210a	210b–217a	217b–226a	226b–234b	36	49
	Week 137	234c–238	239–242a	242b–246b	246c–253b	253c–257a	23	49
	Week 138	257b–265b	265c–268b	268c–274b	274c–280a	280b–288	31	49
	Week 139	289–295b	295c–302a	302b–306b	306c–312b	312c–316a	28	50
	Week 140	316b–320a	320b–326a	326b–334a	334b–338b	338c–343a	27	50
	Week 141	343b–349a	349b–353b	353c–360b	360c–368	Catch up	25	50
	Week 142	369–373b	373c–378b	378c–385a	385b–390b	390c–397a	28	51
	Week 143	397b–401b	401c–404b	404c–410a	410b–418b	418c–422b	25	51
	Week 144	422c–428a	428b–433a	433b–441b	441c–447a	447b–450a	28	51
	Week 145	450b–454a	454b–459b	459c–463b	463c–469a	469b–476	26	51
	Week 146	477–483b	483c–486b	486c–493a	493b–499b	499c–505b	29	51
	Week 147	505c–511a	511b–515a	515b–519a	519b–527a	527b–531	26	51
III/4	Week 148	3–8a	8b–15a	15b–19b	19c–23a	23b–31	31	52
	Week 149	32–35b	35c–39a	39b–46	47–53b	53c–57b	26	52, 53
	Week 150	57c–62b	62c–66b	66c–72	73–77a	77b–82b	25	53
	Week 151	82c–86	86–91a	91b–97a	97b–102a	102b–110a	28	53
	Week 152	110b–115	116–121b	121c–129a	129b–134a	134b–139b	29	53, 54
	Week 153	139c–148	149–152a	152b–156b	156c–163a	163b–166	27	54
	Week 154	167–172a	172b–176a	176b–183b	183c–187b	187c–195a	29	54
	Week 155	195b–199a	199b–203b	203c–207a	207b–213b	213c–224a	29	54
	Week 156	224b–229b	229c–236b	236c–240a	240b–245a	245b–250a	26	54
	Week 157	250b–255a	255b–261a	261b–264b	264c–269a	269b–275a	25	54
	Week 158	275b–279a	279b–285b	285c–289b	289c–294b	294c–298a	23	54
	Week 159	298b–305b	305c–312a	312b–317b	317c–323	324–333b	35	55
	Week 160	333b–338a	338b–344b	344c–348a	348b–352b	352c–356a	23	55
	Week 161	356b–360a	360b–363b	363c–367a	367b–376a	376b–382b	26	55
	Week 162	382c–387b	387c–391	392–397a	397b–404b	404c–411a	29	55
	Week 163	411b–416a	416b–422b	422c–427b	427c–432a	432b–436b	25	55

		Day 1	Day 2	Day 3	Day 4	Day 5	Total Pages	§
	Week 164	436c–441b	441c–446a	446b–450a	450b–456a	456b–461	25	55
	Week 165	462–470a	470b–477b	477c–483b	483c–488a	488b–493b	29	55
	Week 166	493c–502a	502b–505	506–513a	513b–521a	521b–527a	34	55
	Week 167	527b–534b	534c–545b	545c–550a	550b–555a	555b–559b	32	55
	Week 168	559c–564	565–568	569–574b	574c–580a	580b–585a	25	55, 56
	Week 169	585b–594	595–600a	600b–607a	607b–618a	618b–623a	38	56
	Week 170	623b–630a	630b–633a	633b–637a	637b–647a	Catch up	24	56
	Week 171	647b–650b	650c–656a	656b–662b	662c–668b	668c–678a	31	56
IV/1	Week 172	678b–685	3–6a	6b–12a	12b–21	22–26a	33	57
	Week 173	26b–34b	34c–39a	39b–44b	44c–50a	50b–54b	28	57
	Week 174	54c–58a	58b–66	67–70a	70b–78	79–84a	30	57, 58
	Week 175	84b–88b	88c–92a	92b–95	96–102a	102b–109b	25	58
	Week 176	109c–115a	115b–122a	122b–128b	128c–135a	135b–142a	33	58
	Week 177	142b–150a	150b–154	157–161a	161b–167b	167c–173a	31	58, 59
	Week 178	173b–179a	179b–183a	183b–188a	188b–192a	192b–197a	24	59
	Week 179	197b–204b	204c–210	211–216a	216b–224a	224b–228b	31	59
	Week 180	228c–235b	235c–240a	240b–244a	244b–256a	256b–259a	31	59
	Week 181	259b–267a	267b–273a	273b–283a	Catch up	283b–287	28	59
	Week 182	288–296b	296c–304b	304c–309b	309c–313a	313b–318a	31	59
	Week 183	318b–322a	322b–329a	329b–333b	333c–342a	342b–347b	29	59
	Week 184	347c–357	358–362a	362b–368b	368c–374b	374c–380b	33	59, 60
	Week 185	380c–387a	387b–391b	391c–397b	397c–403a	403b–407a	27	60
	Week 186	407b–413b	413c–418a	418b–423b	423c–427b	427c–432a	25	60
	Week 187	432b–437b	437c–445b	445c–453b	453c–458a	458b–467	35	60
	Week 188	468–473a	473b–478a	478b–484a	484b–489a	489b–492a	25	60
	Week 189	492b–501a	501b–508b	508c–513	514–520a	520b–528b	36	60, 61
	Week 190	528c–532a	532b–536a	536b–542a	542b–549b	549c–553b	25	61
	Week 191	553c–559a	559b–564a	564b–568a	568b–577a	577b–581a	28	61
	Week 192	581b–591a	591b–595a	595b–599a	599b–605a	605b–608b	27	61
	Week 193	608c–614b	614c–621b	621c–626b	626c–635a	635b–642	34	61
	Week 194	643–646b	646c–650b	650c–656b	656c–662b	662c–668a	26	62
	Week 195	668b–674b	674c–679a	679b–685a	685b–693a	693b–701b	33	62
	Week 196	701c–707b	707c–712b	712c–718a	718b–725a	725b–732b	31	62
	Week 197	732c–739	740–744b	744c–749a	749b–753a	753b–757a	25	62, 63
IV/2	Week 198	757b–761b	761c–769a	769b–779	Catch up	3–11a	33	63, 64
	Week 199	11b–20b	20c–25a	25b–31a	31b–36b	36c–40a	29	64
	Week 200	40b–44a	44b–50a	50b–60a	60b–69a	69b–72b	32	64

	Day 1	Day 2	Day 3	Day 4	Day 5	Total Pages	§
Week 201	72c–83	84–90a	90b–98b	98c–104a	104b–109b	37	64
Week 202	109c–116b	116c–123b	123c–128a	128b–135a	135b–140a	31	64
Week 203	140b–145	146–154b	154c–156b	156c–163a	163b–166b	26	64
Week 204	166c–171b	171c–180a	180b–187b	187c–192b	192c–198b	32	64
Week 205	198c–205b	205c–209a	209b–215a	215b–219b	219c–226a	32	64
Week 206	226b–232b	232c–238a	238b–242a	242b–247b	247c–258a	32	64
Week 207	258b–264b	264c–268a	268b–274a	274b–280b	280c–284a	26	64
Week 208	284b–289	290–296b	296c–303a	303b–310b	310c–315b	31	64
Week 209	315c–322a	322b–330b	330c–336a	336b–340a	340b–348a	33	64
Week 210	348b–353a	353b–359b	359c–362a	362b–367a	367b–372a	24	64
Week 211	372b–377	378–384a	384b–388a	388b–397a	397b–403a	31	64, 65
Week 212	403b–409b	409b–414a	414b–420a	420b–424b	424c–432b	29	65
Week 213	432c–440b	440c–445b	445c–452a	452b–458a	458b–467b	35	65
Week 214	467c–475a	475b–478b	478c–483a	483b–490a	490b–498	31	65
Week 215	499–505a	505b–511a	511b–518a	518b–522b	522c–533a	35	66
Week 216	533b–536a	536b–542	543–546b	546c–553b	553c–556b	23	66
Week 217	556c–563a	563b–570b	570c–577b	577c–587b	587c–591b	35	66
Week 218	591c–598b	598c–602a	602b–607a	607b–613	614–618b	27	66
Week 219	618c–627a	627b–635a	635b–641a	641b–645a	645b–651a	33	66, 67
Week 220	651b–660b	660c–665b	665c–672a	672b–676b	676b–680a	29	67
Week 221	680b–689b	689c–695a	695b–706a	706b–710b	710c–719a	29	67
Week 222	719b–726	Catch up	727–733a	733b–740a	740b–746a	27	67, 68
Week 223	746b–751b	751c–756b	756c–766b	766c–771a	771b–776a	30	68
Week 224	776b–783a	783b–789b	789c–793a	793b–798b	798c–802a	27	68
Week 225	802b–809a	809b–817a	817b–824b	824c–828a	828b–835b	33	68
IV/3.1 Week 226	835c–840	3–11a	11b–18b	18c–26a	26b–32	37	68, 69
Week 227	33–38b	38c–43a	43b–49a	49b–52b	52c–60b	28	69
Week 228	60c–66a	66b–70a	70b–75	76–86a	86b–90b	30	69
Week 229	90c–95b	95c–99b	99c–103b	103c–113a	113b–118a	28	69
Week 230	118b–123b	123c–130a	130b–135b	135c–141a	141b–150	32	69
Week 231	151–154b	154b–160a	160b–165a	165b–171b	171c–180a	30	69
Week 232	180b–187b	187c–191a	191b–196a	196b–202b	202c–211a	31	69
Week 233	211b–220	221–225a	225b–231a	231b–237a	237b–242a	31	69
Week 234	242b–246b	246c–250	251–255a	255b–261b	261c–268b	28	69
Week 235	268c–274b	274c–281a	281b–289b	289c–293a	293b–296b	28	69
Week 236	296c–301a	301b–308a	308b–313b	313c–316b	316c–322	26	69
Week 237	323–330a	330b–335b	335c–340a	340b–350b	350c–356b	34	69

		Day 1	Day 2	Day 3	Day 4	Day 5	Total Pages	§
	Week 238	356c–362a	362b–367	368–374a	374b–380a	380b–388b	32	69, 70
	Week 239	388c–397	397–408a	408b–413a	413b–417a	417b–421b	33	70
	Week 240	421c–429b	429c–434a	434b–440a	440b–446a	446b–451b	30	70
IV/3.2	Week 241	451c–461b	461c–468b	468c–474a	474b–478	481–486a	35	70, 71
	Week 242	486b–492b	492c–497a	497b–502b	502c–508a	508b–514b	28	71
	Week 243	514c–520b	520c–526a	526b–532b	532c–538b	538c–547a	33	71
	Week 244	547b–554b	554c–561a	561b–564b	564c–571a	571b–576	29	71
	Week 245	577–583a	583b–589b	589c–599a	599b–603b	603c–614b	38	71
	Week 246	614c–619b	619c–625	626–633	634–640a	640b–647b	33	71
	Week 247	647c–654	655–660b	660c–664a	664b–673a	673b–680	33	71
	Week 248	681–688a	688b–693a	693b–701a	701b–710b	710c–715a	35	72
	Week 249	715b–721b	721c–726a	726b–734a	734b–742b	742c–751a	36	72
	Week 250	751b–754a	754b–762a	762b–769a	769b–772b	772c–776b	25	72
	Week 251	776c–780a	780b–790a	790b–795b	795c–801b	801c–812a	36	72
	Week 252	812b–816	817–823a	823b–830a	830b–838a	838b–843b	31	72
	Week 253	843c–850a	850b–854a	854b–859a	859b–864a	864b–874a	31	72
	Week 254	874b–882b	882c–889b	889c–898b	898c–901	902–909b	35	72, 73
	Week 255	909b–920a	920b–928a	928b–934a	934b–942	3–10a	43	73, Fragments
IV/4	Week 256	10b–17a	17b–26b	26c–31b	31c–40	41–50a	40	Fragments
	Week 257	50b–58b	58c–68b	68c–75b	75c–82b	82c–90a	40	Fragments
	Week 258	90b–100b	100c–107a	107b–111b	111c–120a	120b–127a	37	Fragments
	Week 259	127b–134a	134b–141a	141b–152b	152c–162a	162b–171b	44	Fragments
	Week 260	171c–179a	179b–189b	189c–195a	195b–201b	201c–213	42	Fragments

Index of Scripture

Index of Names

Adam, 152
Allen, Diogenes, 52
Aquinas, Thomas. *See* Thomas Aquinas
Aristotle, 88
Arius, 118
Augustine, 59, 91n8, 112–14, 139, 195

Bainton, Roland H., 96n12
Balaam, 45
Bender, Kimlyn J., 17n5, 45n4, 57n1, 91n8, 151n4, 156n6, 157n6, 159n9, 165n2
Blocher, Henri, 246n11
Brunner, Emil, 26, 47, 91n8, 154–55
Buckley, Michael J., 130n10
Buddha, 180
Bultmann, Rudolf, 18n6, 29, 76, 89, 89n6, 155, 241n7
Burnett, Richard, xviiin3
Busch, Eberhard, xxiin8

Calvin, John, 30, 68, 104, 137, 149, 184, 208, 233–34, 247, 260, 280
Come, Arnold, xviiin2, xxin6
Currie, Thomas C., 67n3
Cyrus, 45

Dempsey, Michael T., 107n4
Descartes, René, 27, 61, 88

Edwards, James R., 156n6
Emerson, Ralph Waldo, 96–97, 97n13
Ensminger, Sven, 177n7

Feuerbach, Ludwig, 76, 179
Frei, Hans, 6nn3–4
Freud, Sigmund, 76, 179

Galli, Mark, 72n6, 243n8
Gogarten, Friedrich, 76, 89
Green, Garrett, 168n4, 177n7
Guretzki, David, 19n7, 57n1

Harnack, Adolf von, 28, 29, 36, 191
Hegel, Georg W. F., 27
Heidegger, Martin, 139
Herrmann, Wilhelm, 18n6, 28–29, 36, 61, 76, 88
Hitler, Adolf, 34, 61, 200
Hunsinger, George, xixn4, 9n5, 20n8, 45n4, 57n1, 78n2, 89n7, 101nn1–2, 106n3, 177n7

James, William, 157
Jeremiah, 60
Jesus Christ. *See* Jesus Christ in the index of subjects
John the Baptist, 146

Kant, Immanuel, 27, 61, 88, 139, 236
Karlstadt, Andreas, 96
Kierkegaard, Søren, 29, 66, 70, 76, 82, 137, 144, 144n2, 217n6

Lewis, C. S., 97, 97n14
Long, Stephen D., 11n6

Index of Subjects